Listening to Shin Buddhism

Eastern Buddhist Voices

Series Editor: Michael Pye
Shin Buddhist Comprehensive Research Institute
Ōtani University, Kyōto, Japan

Volume 1
Beyond Meditation: Expressions of Japanese Shin Buddhist Spirituality

Volume 2
Listening to Shin Buddhism: Starting Points of Modern Dialogue

Volume 3
Interactions with Japanese Buddhism: Explorations and Viewpoints in Twentieth Century Kyoto

Volume 4
Tile and Bamboo: On Temple Paths in Japan with Beatrice Lane Suzuki

Volume 5
Tracing the Sources: An Anthology of Translations from The Eastern Buddhist

Listening to Shin Buddhism
Starting Points of Modern Dialogue

edited by
Michael Pye

with the assistance of
The Eastern Buddhist Society

Eastern Buddhist Voices 2

SHEFFIELD OAKVILLE

Published by Equinox Publishing Ltd.

UK: Office 415, The Workstation, 15 Paternoster Row, Sheffield S1 2BX
USA: ISD, 70 Enterprise Drive, Bristol, CT 06010
www.equinoxpub.com

First published 2012

© Michael Pye 2012

All rights reserved. No part of this publication may be reproduced or transmitted in any form or by any means, electronic or mechanical, including photocopying, recording or any information storage or retrieval system, without prior permission in writing from the publishers.

British Library Cataloguing-in-Publication Data

A catalogue record for this book is available from the British Library.

ISBN 978-1-908049-16-2 (hardback)
ISBN 978-1-908049-17-9 (paperback)

Library of Congress Cataloging-in-Publication Data

Listening to Shin Buddhism : starting points of modern dialogue / edited by Michael Pye.
  p. cm. — (Eastern Buddhist voices ; 2)
Includes bibliographical references and index.
Papers selected from the journal Eastern Buddhist.
ISBN 978-1-908049-16-2 (hb) — ISBN 978-1-908049-17-9 (pb)
1. Shin (Sect)—Relations. I. Pye, Michael. II. Eastern Buddhist.

BQ8716.L57 2011
294.3'35--dc23
                               2011021719

Typeset by Queenston Publishing, Hamilton, Ontario, Canada

Printed and bound in Great Britain and the USA

東本願寺

Higashi Honganji

Cover illustration

Shin Buddhist devotees streaming into the head temple of the Shinshū Ōtani-ha denomination in the 1950's. (By courtesy of the temple, Higashi Honganji, Kyōto.)

Contents

List of Illustrations	xi
Preface with Acknowledgements	xiii
Conventions on Names, Titles and Scripts	xv
General Introduction	1

Part I Early Interactions

The Buddhist Doctrine of Vicarious Suffering (1927)	15
Kaneko, Daiei	
Mahāyāna Buddhism and Japanese Culture (1931)	27
Yamabe, Shūgaku	
The Idea and the Man (a response to Yamabe Shūgaku) (1932)	33
C.A.F. Rhys Davids	
A Rejoinder to Mrs. Rhys Davids' Comment (1932)	36
Yamabe, Shūgaku	
Editorial from 1934	39
Anonymous	
Editorial from 1949	41
Anonymous	

Part II Two Presenters of Shin Buddhism

Shin Religion as I Believe it (1951)	47
Kaneko, Daiei	
The Meaning of Salvation in the Doctrine of Pure Land Buddhism (1965)	61
Kaneko, Daiei	

Contents

Goodness and Naturalness (1951)   75
Kanamatsu, Kenryō

Part III Three Western Responses to Shin Buddhism

The Concept of Grace in Paul, Shinran and Luther (1976)   87
Buri, Fritz

Nembutsu as Remembrance (1977)   107
Pallis, Marco

Shinran's Way in the Modern World (1978)   123
Bloom, Alfred

Part IV Broadening Perspectives for Shin Buddhism

Freedom and Necessity in Shinran's Concept of Karma (1986)   139
Ueda, Yoshifumi

The concept of the Pure Land in the Teaching of Nāgārjuna (1966)   161
Yamaguchi, Susumu

The Mahāyāna Structure of Shinran's Thought (1984)   173
Ueda, Yoshifumi

Shinran and Contemporary Thought (1980)   213
Takeuchi, Yoshinori

Part V A Dialogue of Shin Buddhism and Zen Buddhism

Shinran's World: A Dialogue of Shin Buddhism and Zen Buddhism (1961: published in three parts in 1985, 1986 and 1988)   233

Nishitani, Keiji (moderator) with Suzuki Daisetsu, Kaneko Daiei and Soga Ryōjin

Synoptic List of Text Titles   277
Character List for Historical Persons   287
Full Details of Original Publication   291
A Note on *The Eastern Buddhist*   293
General Index   295

List of Illustrations

Frontispiece:

Aerial photograph of the head temple of the Shinshū Ōtani-ha denomination, Higashi Honganji, Kyōto. (Courtesy Higashi Honganji) — vi

Participants in the Dialogue, Part V — 234

  Nishitani Keiji, upper left
    Photograph by courtesy of Higashi Honganji

  Suzuki Daisetsu, top right
    Photograph by courtesy of Matsugaoka Bunko Foundation

  Kaneko Daiei, lower left
    Photograph by courtesy of Higashi Honganji

  Soga Ryōjin, lower right
    Photograph by courtesy of Higashi Honganji

Preface with Acknowledgements

In the twentieth century *The Eastern Buddhist* not only shared in pioneering presentations of Buddhism to the west but invited interaction with non-Japanese authors. This interactive process was interrupted by the tragedies of war, and it was some time before they could be set in motion again. Nevertheless the contributions collected here illustrate that earlier efforts were not in vain, and they illustrate how the pattern of intercultural and interreligious communication came to be resumed in the post-war period. This was a time when dialogue between Buddhist and Christian thought began to take off in earnest. In a world and at a time when religious traditions can increasingly be shared, may this process continue.

This book, the second of a series, is the result of cooperative work between the editor and the staff of *The Eastern Buddhist* whose offices are housed within Ōtani University in Kyōto. Indirectly it was also supported in various ways by the head temple of the Shinshū Ōtani-ha branch of Shin Buddhism, the Higashi Honganji 東本願寺, also in Kyōto. In addition, the work of the editor was facilitated by being able to do research at the Shin Buddhist Comprehensive Research Institute, housed in the library building of Ōtani University. To each of these institutions, my gratitude is hereby most warmly expressed.

It was particularly pleasant to enjoy the professional support of staff members of the Eastern Buddhist Society: Dr. Nitta Tomomichi (Secretary-general of the EBS and Acting Editor of *The Eastern Buddhist*) and Dr. Miyako Mao.[1] Their varied and impressive expertise in the languages and texts of Buddhism led to the resolution of many an editorial problem, while they also carried the main burden of the necessary institutional liaisons. Advice on Chinese derivations and transcriptions was kindly given by Peiying Lin, currently a researcher at the School of Oriental and African Studies in London. Important clues for editorial orientation were given by Professors Mark Blum and James Dobbins, both well-known specialists in Shin Buddhist studies and resident in Kyōto during the current academic year. Overall guidance and advice was given by Professor Inoue Takami and Professor Yasutomi Shin'ya of Ōtani Uni-

---

1. All Japanese names are given in the Japanese order, family name first, except where otherwise indicated.

Preface with Acknowledgements

versity. Both are members of the Editorial Board of *The Eastern Buddhist*, with Yasutomi Shin'ya currently being Chief Editor. The editor would like to thank all of these colleagues for their enthusiasm and persistent interest, tempered with patience.

Naturally, responsibility for editorial decisions relating to the re-use of materials from the journal lies not with *The Eastern Buddhist* as such but with the editor of this volume. For his own part, the work has been the start of a renewed learning process in the field of Shin Buddhism and its wider context in Mahāyāna Buddhism. This is a religious tradition which to the casual observer may seem to be quite simple, and in a significant way, like Zen Buddhism, it is indeed very simple. At the same time the exploration of Shin Buddhism leads into profundities and subtleties which for some may be quite unexpected.

Michael Pye
Kyōto 2012

Conventions on Names, Titles and Scripts

In principle, all words from Asian languages are shown in italics with diacritical marks as appropriate. The exceptions are as follows:

Buddha	i.e. for "the Buddha" or in names of buddhas
buddha/s	i.e. for any Buddha or buddhas in the plural
Bodhisattva	i.e. in names of bodhisattvas
bodhisattva/s	i.e. for any bodhisattva or bodhisattvas in the plural
Dharma	i.e. meaning the Teaching of the Buddha
dharma/s	i.e. meaning elements or factors of existence
karma	
Nembutsu	capitalized and with an "m" if the author so used it, otherwise *nenbutsu*
nirvana	when so used in a general context by an author, otherwise *nirvāṇa*
Nirvana	may also be shown capitalised, if the author so used it
Samgha	only when capitalized in English as a proper noun for the Buddhist order, otherwise *saṃgha*

The same exceptions apply for Pāli forms: bodhisatta/s, Dhamma, dhamma/s, kamma, nibbana, Nibbana, Sangha.

In the first half of the twentieth century it was still quite common, in English, to capitalize all kinds of words deemed to be important, and this practice was imitated by non-native users with varying degrees of enthusiasm. Here, however, capital letters have usually been edited out in accordance with current style. When they remain, the intention is to maintain the flavour of the original publications.

Policy on the presentation of personal names, the titles of Buddhist works and the scripts used to represent them been guided by three considerations. First, we have tried to be fair to the authors, seeking to maintain the flavour of their writing while not encumbering them with correctable errors. Second, we have sought to be of service to readers, who may be coming to these writings for the first time. Third, while alternatives provided by authors were in many cases helpful, this also led to considerable unevenness; in this regard we have aimed for greater consistency throughout the volume.

Transliteration systems used here follow modern standards, i.e. by using the *pīnyīn* system for Chinese, and Sanskrit transliteration with diacritical marks as used by Indologists today. This is good practice for Buddhist Studies in general. For Japanese, the Hepburn system is used with slight modifications. The main modifications are the consistent use of "n" instead of the phonetically closer "m" in words such as *nenbutsu* (except when Nembutsu is maintained because of the flavour of the period) and, with some reluctance, the use of an apostrophe to separate potentially confused syllables when the letter "n" is followed by a vowel (e.g. *den'e*). While there is wide-ranging agreement over the Hepburn system there is no completely authoritative guide to its modifications.[1]

Some use is made of spaces and hyphens, although they do not occur in the original languages. Thus endings in Japanese such as -*shū* (meaning denomination) are shown with a hyphen. Endings of Chinese text names such as *jīng* (*sūtra*) and *lùn* (treatise) are shown separated, but not in Japanese where they have become fully integrated. In general, the tendency to break everything up into its components has been resisted. Shinran's famous work *Kyōgyōshinshō* is therefore shown as a single unit and not as *Kyō Gyō Shin Shō*. Many of these things could be handled differently and are in the end a question more of "feel" than of ineluctable rules.

Chinese characters as used in Japan (*kanji*, or Sino-Japanese characters) follow the typological reform undertaken in the postwar years except in some historical China-related contexts. Alternatives may also be shown.

There are many variations in the titles of texts, and in order to avoid constant repetition of alternatives, these have been collated into one single reference list entitled Synoptic List of Text Titles. Further details of editorial policy on the titles of Buddhist works will also be found there.

Japanese Buddhists typically use canonical texts, many of which are presumed to have come originally from India, in their Chinese form. In the first half of the twentieth century, broadly speaking, Sanskrit originals of such Chinese texts were still being identified for the first time, while in some cases it was being ascertained that no Sanskrit origi-

---

1. The two main modifications are based on a complete contradiction. The first (n for m) seeks to move away from pronunciation in favour of consistency with the Japanese phonetic syllabary, the *kana* system. The second does precisely the opposite in introducing a feature which bears no reference to the *kana* system. Western style guides (*The Chicago Manual of Style* etc.) are helpless when confronted by the fact that various government ministries in Japan specify different rules. Moreover the Japanese Foreign Office permits even wider deviations in the writing of Japanese names which bear no relation to the Hepburn system in any of its forms. To add to the confusion, the terms "revised" and "modified" have been used inconsistently by various would-be authorities.

nal could be found at all. There are two reasons why there may be no Sanskrit original for a Chinese Buddhist text. First, it may have been irretrievably lost. It must be admitted that this can never finally be determined, as the very recent discovery of a Sanskrit manuscript of *The Teaching of Vimalakīrti* has shown. Second, however, it may never have existed in Sanskrit to begin with, even though it was named as "a *sūtra*" of the Buddha or was ascribed to a famous Indian Buddhist writer. Reluctance to recognize this led to the invention and use of Sanskrit titles which seemed to create an aura of authenticity, even though this misled students and other readers. In a number of cases the *non*-existence of a Sanskrit original has now become clear for very good reasons of language and content. Important examples of this are the *Sūtra on the Visualisation of Amitābha* (観無量寿経 *Guān wúliàngshòu jīng*, Japanese: *Kanmuryōjukyō*), which is one of the three basic *sūtras* of Pure land Buddhism, and *The Awakening of Faith in the Mahāyāna* (大乗起信論 *Dà shèng qǐxìn lùn*,[2] Japanese: *Daijōkishinron*), a popular text in East Asia which was piously ascribed to Aśvaghoṣa.

To some extent it is the notion of "authenticity" and the very respect in which Sanskrit is held which has led to unnecessary difficulties. As a matter of historical fact there are many *sūtras* in Sanskrit itself which are piously ascribed to the Buddha but which do not in fact go back directly to him at all. Therefore, the mere fact that a *sūtra* developed or was composed in Chinese does not of itself make it less "authentic" than one which first appeared in Sanskrit (which in any case was not the Buddha's own personal language). In the pages of *The Eastern Buddhist*, while the assumptions of traditional piety continue to be evident to some extent, we also find a clear respect for the findings of modern scholarship. This is itself part of the voice of modern Buddhism.

---

2. Or *Dàchéng qǐxìn lùn*.

Introduction

The papers presented here, drawn from the journal *The Eastern Buddhist*, illustrate the increasing emergence of Shin Buddhism as a dialogue partner of major significance in the wider world. This process had already begun in the 1920s and 1930s, as was documented in the first volume of this series, *Beyond Meditation, Expressions of Japanese Shin Buddhist Spirituality*, but it was inevitably checked by the Second World War, during which *The Eastern Buddhist* did not appear. It is not surprising that when publication of the journal was resumed in 1949, new authors began to emerge, and the need to present Shin Buddhism to a western readership was felt all the more keenly. However the renaissance was somewhat hesitant, for various reasons.

After the national defeat, quite apart from coping with physical devastation, economic hardship, demographic disruptions through casualties and so on, all major institutions in Japan had to go through a process of social and political readjustment. In many minds the war was viewed as "a mistake" but in some cases a serious consideration of responsibility for the suffering caused to others also took place. While countless followers of Shin Buddhism had simply been drawn into line with nationalist ideology, largely with the support of the leadership, there was now a new task of reorientation and indeed repentance. While Shintō institutions inevitably made rather heavy weather of this at first, since Shintō had to be disestablished from state patronage, it is fair to say that among Buddhist denominations it was not long before the major denominations of Shin Buddhism began to lead the way. Indeed, the continuing programs for the education of the rank and file of believers in matters of war responsibility, peace education, and the campaign against various forms of social and racial discrimination, are noteworthy and admirable.[1]

While this process of mass re-education was as yet only just beginning, *The Eastern Buddhist* and the circles which supported it were simply not able to engage in renewed and uninterrupted publication. The Editorial of May 1949 reflects this situation, and is reproduced below. Two very slim issues appeared in 1949 and 1951, and after a gap of six years two more appeared in 1957 and 1958. It was not until after a further signifi-

---

1. For a valuable recent study see Ugo Dessì, *Ethics and Society in Contemporary Shin Buddhism*, Berlin (LIT-Verlag) 2007.

cant break that the *New Series* of *The Eastern Buddhist* was launched, in 1965, to be continued with more or less regularity down to the present day. While Suzuki Daisetsu and interactions with Zen Buddhism were immediately prominent in the new series, Suzuki himself died in 1966. This loss was keenly felt both within and without Japan, and as a result the pages of *The Eastern Buddhist* in 1967 were completely taken up with reminiscences and memorials by Japanese and foreign admirers. It was not until 1969 that something approaching normal publication was again resumed, though at first with one issue only.

We therefore find four breaks in the publication of *The Eastern Buddhist*, one for the duration of the war and its immediate aftermath, two following each of the first hesitant attempts to reopen publication in the 1950s, and another significant hiatus taking account of the death of Suzuki Daisetsu, who had been both a founding editor and a leading light. In fact there were two other sad circumstances which influenced the fortunes of *The Eastern Buddhist* during this period in general. First we may recall that Beatrice Lane Suzuki died in 1939, and this undoubtedly inhibited the English language editing of the journal, in spite of her husband's undoubted personal linguistic prowess. Second, a young colleague who was a particularly close personal friend of the Suzukis, Yokogawa Kenshō 横川顕正, died not long afterwards in 1940 aged only thirty-six. Yokogawa had been teaching at Ōtani University throughout the 1930s and had been a source of great encouragement. His article "Shin Buddhism as the religion of hearing," published in the journal in 1939 (and reprinted in *Beyond Meditation*) is only a fragment of what he had to offer in terms of psychological support and intellectual stimulation. These two chronologically close losses undoubtedly affected the viability of the journal quite significantly, which failed to appear in 1940 and 1941 even before the full impact of wartime conditions was felt.

It is perhaps not surprising that the first post-war volumes of the Old Series, which appeared in 1957 and 1958, were mainly concerned with preeminently textual studies in the older traditions of Mahāyāna Buddhism which, though valuable in themselves, are not closely relevant to our present interest. The only exception was a fictitious dialogue entitled "A Discussion between One and Zero," composed by Nanrei Sōhaku Kobori, published in two parts in 1957 (Vol VIII 3), but since this was not very tightly organized it is not reproduced here. It is possible that the emphasis on textual studies at this time reflects a degree of uncertainty, or a temporary loss of self-confidence in questions of presentation at a more ideological level.

In view of this fragmented history, it is our task here to discern the wider picture which links the pre-war and post-war periods, and in which the presentation of Shin Buddhism was essayed and wider reactions harvested. It is possible to see some continuity, in a good sense, between the pre-war and post-war periods, and it is also possible to see that the process of making Shin Buddhism known as a dialogue partner in global terms, though interrupted, was continued right through into later decades of the twentieth century. That is what is being introduced here.

With this in mind, the present volume begins with a brief flashback. One of the names which appears in both pre-war and post-war times, together with Suzuki Daisetsu himself, is the influential Shin Buddhist writer Kaneko Daiei 金子大栄 (1881–1976).[2] We begin here with an article by him entitled "The Buddhist Doctrine of Vicarious Suffering", which is an obvious attempt to address the possible comparison of "vicarious suffering" in the traditions of Buddhism and Christianity. This is already intended as an interactive study. It is followed by an exchange between Yamabe Shūgaku 山辺習学 (1882–1944), writing rather generally on "Mahāyāna Buddhism and Japanese Culture" and C.A.F. Rhys Davids, a well-known British exponent of the Pāli or Theravāda tradition of Buddhism. The latter's writing is marked not only by a decided loyalty to what she presumed to be the oldest traditions of Buddhism, but also by extremely high-flown, not to say adventurous language typical of some enthusiastic religious writing of her period. Yet by her literary devices she was trying to make a serious point about the status of conceptualized doctrine in Buddhism, to which Yamabe was quite able to respond. We see in the contributions of these two Japanese writers, Kaneko and Yamabe, both the opening of Shin Buddhist thinking to the wider tradition of Buddhist thought and, in their responsive formulations, their acceptance of the impact of perceived foreign expectations.

It seems clear that the editors of *The Eastern Buddhist* were by this time quite aware of the various ways in which Buddhism was coming to be perceived in Europe, in the wake of ever more studies of the Indian source materials. The strength of what has been referred to as the "Anglo-German school," to which Mrs. C.A.F. Rhys Davids and in particular her husband T.W. Rhys Davids belonged, was evident. The assumption was widespread that it was the Pāli scriptures of Theravāda Buddhism which represented the early and authentic teaching of the Buddha, while the later developments and indeed the vagaries of "northern Buddhism" or "Great Vehicle" with its apparently extravagant pantheon of buddhas and bodhisattvas,[3] was regarded as religiously regressive. Against this

---

2. His personal name has also been variously transcribed as Taiye, Taie and Daie.
3. It is notable that Alice Getty's *The Gods of Northern Buddhism: Their History, Iconography and Progressive Evolution through the Northern Buddhist Countries*, first published in 1914 (Oxford), was reissued in 1928 and widely regarded as an authoritative reference work during the period under consideration here.

trend, the rather different interests of the so-called Russian school" and the "Franco-Belgian school" had yet to make themselves fully apparent.[4] In this context it was not easy for Japanese Buddhists, so far from the sources in India, and apparently so far down the road in the historical and cultural development of the Buddhist tradition, to assert that their "Buddhism" was authentic and spiritually profound. An unsigned "Editorial" printed in the closing pages of *The Eastern Buddhist* of July 1934 contains the complaint:

> I also read in a European journal that a certain Japanese priest in Berlin had said that he was obliged to go to Germany in order to learn pure Buddhism as Buddhism was degenerated in Japan. I cannot understand what he could have been doing or where he could have been staying in Japan, to have made such a statement, unless he was referring to strict Hīnayāna Buddhism.[5]

Here we see that the common Japanese wish to learn from abroad at any cost was being regarded as almost treacherous in sharing such critical assumptions. And how additionally galling it must have been for many to see China, the great but at that time despised neighbour, as a possible candidate for a modern Buddhist revival, rather than Japan! Such an assumption is robustly rebutted by the Editorial, and because of the affinity of the underlying ideas we therefore include it in full immediately after the exchange between Yamabe and Rhys Davids.

As we pick up the story after the ending of global hostilities, it seems appropriate to take some account of the way in which these devastating events are themselves reflected in the content of the journal. The previously mentioned Editorial of May 1949 provides the link. Though unsigned, this Editorial bears all the marks of Suzuki Daisetsu's authorship, and the fact that he published an article on "Buddhism and Education" in the same issue is significant.[6] In this piece, originally a talk, Suzuki does not mince his words and distinguishes sharply between the character of Shintō and of Buddhism. He distances himself from Shintō by the use of the phrase "Japanese Shinto militarists"[7] (p.41) but also regards a militaristic propensity as being fundamentally characteristic of Shintō, as when he writes:

---

4. These "schools" were first so perceived by Constantin Régamey in *Buddhistische Philosophie*, Bern (A. Francke Verlag) 1950 and further analyzed in the present writer's "Comparative hermeneutics in religion" in Michael Pye and Robert Morgan (eds.) *The Cardinal Meaning. Essays in Comparative Hermeneutics: Buddhism and Christianity*, The Hague (Mouton) 1973.
5. Vol. 6, no. 3, p.317.
6. "Buddhism and Education" in *The Eastern Buddhist* 8, no. 1, pp.36–45.
7. "Buddhism and Education," p.41.

Introduction

> For it is in the very nature of Shinto that it cannot alienate itself from the insularistic idea of self-importance which inevitably leads to an imperialistic assertion of its sovereignty over all the neighbouring nations. (p.39)

And as to Buddhism:

> But Buddhism does not subscribe to the idea of a transcendental God who rules the world from above, for the Buddha lives among us and with us and at the same time above us. He thinks of us as his friends, as his associates, as his children whose welfare and misfortune affect him in a most human way; Buddhists will not wage war, they are pacifists, even defeatists, as I myself am. (p.39)

So, as the reader may well ask, how did it come about that so many Buddhists in Japan supported the wars? Suzuki seems to have had two explanations for this. In this immediate context he is able to blame the Shintoists:

> That they have turned soldier and fought on the battle-fields is due to the most high-handed measures taken up by the militaristic government. This Buddhist attitude of passivity towards things of this earth has been a great virtue and at the same time an inexcusable weakness. (39)

While it became possible to blame Shintoists after the war, the question of whether and how "Buddhism" might have been used to prevent it happening can certainly be posed. Here the underlying views of Buddhism are presented as being of educational value in this respect, but many years before we find an article by Suzuki entitled "Why do we fight?" (1921), in which he had not thought quite so far. This article was a reflection on the First World War, and he answers his own question as follows:

> Why do we fight? Because each ego wants to predominate over others ... National pride in its narrow and arrogant form, and racial prejudice against people not of the same colour, and imperialistic militarism never satiated but always ready for self-aggrandisement, –these are the vices that nowadays set up one nation against another.[8]

One detects a certain resignation about the inevitability of wars, even though conferences were being held in order to avoid them, and this sense of resignation or passivity is still found at some points in the article by Kaneko Daiei, "Shin Religion as I believe it," also published not so long after the war (1951) and reproduced below. The question is whether the Buddhist analysis of these matters comes to rest in a pessimistic view

---
8. "Why do we fight?" *The Eastern Buddhist*, 1, no 4, pp.270–281.

of humankind, as some have supposed. Or is there also some well-spring of new perceptions which is able actively to transform humanity in a manner which goes beyond individual piety? On balance, while showing some sadness, Kaneko's article stakes out a ground for the latter. In an incidental manner, similar questions arise in the article entitled "Goodness and Naturalness" by Kanamatsu Kenryō 金松賢諒 (1915–1986), who refers in several places to "the good soldier" or "the brave soldier" without any critical reflection on the relation of such "good soldiers" to authoritarian regimes. However, the articles in question are included for other reasons, and it would lead too far afield to discuss in full the complex relationships between Buddhist thought and nationalist ideology in Japan, which have been the subject of attention in recent years.

Following Kaneko's article "Shin Buddhism as I believe it," we look ahead to his further article on "The Meaning of Salvation in the Doctrine of Pure Land Buddhism," which appeared in 1965. Thus by bringing altogether three articles by Kaneko, we introduce in this volume a respected "voice" of Shin Buddhism which, bridging the tragic war years, sought to engage international attention in long-term continuity.

The year 1951 also saw the appearance of Kanamatsu's "Goodness and Naturalness," already mentioned briefly above. Kanamatsu had published an English-language booklet on a similar subject shortly before, entitled *Amitabha: The Life of Naturalness* (1949). These two publications were followed in turn by his influential writing entitled quite simply *Naturalness* (1956) which, published in California by The White Path Society, evidently struck a significant chord in the American reception of Buddhism. The Shin Buddhist community in the United States had been stabilizing itself in the post-war period, and consisted of second and third generation Japanese together with a growing number of converts from the wider population. The acculturation of Shin Buddhism was proceeding in various ways, for example by the use of buildings with wooden pews for seating and of terms such as "bishop," borrowed from Christianity. The point of such innovations was to make Shin Buddhist temples seem just like any other "church," and thus acceptable in American society. At the level of ideas and teachings, the idea of salvation by faith was in one sense an easy one to convey, though the faith was directed towards a different name, namely Amida Buddha. At the same time it was not a particularly compelling or attractive idea in any special way. Many Californians wanted their unexpectedly inherited or adopted religion to be somehow different. They would have preferred it to be an alternative to what they perceived Christianity to be. This goes some way to explaining the resonance of Kanamatsu's *Naturalness*, as the definitive version of his book was more dramatically entitled. In fact he continued to present the central concepts of Shin Buddhism, but by accentuating "naturalness" he spoke to an alternative, non-transcendentalist expectation which was gaining ground among the alternative spiritualities which were becoming popular at the time in North America.

In fact the concept of "naturalness" which Kanamatsu was putting forward was an extremely Buddhist one, and consistent with the teachings of Shin Buddhism in particular. The basic concept is that of *jinen* 自然 which can be understood as part of the same Mahāyāna discourse as better known terms such as *tathatā* (suchness) or Suzuki Daisetsu's *sono mama* ("just as they are", cf. the Dialogue which concludes this volume). However in Shin Buddhism the point is emphasized that this suchness, the ultimate reality, of itself comes to fill the mind of the believer, without being dependent on any human "calculation" or effort. Kanamatsu's second book was successful to the extent that it drew the attention of readers back in Japan, and it was therefore eventually translated into Japanese, or so to speak, back into Japanese, under the title of *Jinen*, i.e. naturalness in the sense just explained.[9]

It is interesting to compare the two versions of what is in effect the same book. In the main, *Naturalness* is an expanded and occasionally revised version of *Amitabha: The Life of Naturalness*. One has the feeling that some note had been taken of readers' reactions and also that the author was going all out to build on an apparently good reception. It is all the more interesting to note the rare passages which were later omitted. A chapter entitled "The Saviour and the Revealer" (Chapter III) was renamed "The Revealer and the Saviour," for reasons which can only be guessed at. It is possible that Kanamatsu wanted to play down the word "Saviour." However that may be, he also significantly expanded the opening section, but omitted the following "purple passage" with which Chapter III of the older book had begun:

> In the first chapter we have seen the merging of the finite *I am* in the Infinite *I am* or the self-identity of Me and Thee. In the losing of his egoistic self and in the permeation into others through union with the Universal, Shakyamuni realized the wholeness of his existence. This Universal Being who is manifesting himself in the activities of the Universe always works in the innermost heart of man as the *innate love*. Man attains *eternal life* when the breach between the finite and the Infinite fills with love and overflows. Infinite is the distance that lies between truth and untruth, between death and deathlessness. Yet this measureless gulf is bridged in a moment when the Self-revealing One reveals himself in the serene depths of the heart—in the spirit. There the miracle happens, for there is the meeting ground of the finite and

---

9. Kyōto 1988, translated by Bandō Shōjun 坂東性純.

the Infinite.[10]

This passage is remarkable for its liberal use of phrases drawn from the vocabulary of the more sentimental versions of western religion (one hesitates to say Christianity) current at the time, right down to the use of capital letters and italics for particular words. In the last analysis it remains unclear what metaphysics is presupposed here, even though the discourse is claimed for Śākyamuni and thus somehow for Buddhism. There is another section where the concept of karma is being introduced, and following the assertion that we are hedged in by the fetters of causation (*inga*) the following, rather telling sentences were omitted:

> Try as we will, we cannot alter the revolution of the stars and the paths of orbs and seasons. Indeed, to come down from great things to small, we cannot make our friends do what we would have them do. We cannot force our brothers and sisters to fashion themselves to our tastes, nor guide our parents, wives and children to conform in all things to our ways. Nay, it does not suffice for us to be sincere, nor to have good intentions. How much suffering we may cause to others without wishing it, or knowing it! We can do just as much harm through not knowing as through unkindness. ... Though all of us want peace, war breaks out against our will. Though each of us has no mind to injure others, it may not be impossible for him to kill a hundred or a thousand men in case of war.[11]

Presumably the topic of guiding one's family members was Confucian by derivation and, in the aftermath of the nationalist ideology constructed out of Shintoist and Confucianist elements, came to be regarded as not appropriate for an international presentation. Similarly, the doctrine of karma could be seen here to explain warfare to such a degree as to more or less justify it, even if only by default. It was presumably for such reasons that these paragraphs were quietly dropped during the revision. The proactive re-writing of the book, on the other hand, displays a remarkable enthusiasm for communication, and it is not surprising that it became quite influential. The article reproduced here illustrates the matrix of Kanamatsu's ideas in a usefully brief span.

In the present volume the basic positions of Shin Buddhism itself, as presented by Shin Buddhist writers, are followed by some reactions from western writers. These authors were all looking at Shin Buddhism in a comparative perspective, from western starting points. While the Swiss theologian Fritz Buri (1907–1995) maintained a clear Christian position

---

10. Kanamatsu, Kenryō: *Amitābha. The Life of Naturalness*, Kyōto 1949 (Ōtani Publishing, Higashi Honganji, Kyōto), 33. Ed. The form Shakyamuni (=Śākyamuni) has been left in the quotation to keep the flavour of the original.
11. *The Life of Naturalness*, 56–57.

Introduction

in his exploration of Shin Buddhist concepts, Alfred Bloom (1926–), who was formed in the American Baptist tradition, adopted the Shin Buddhist tradition as his own. Buri's contribution apparently represents the first substantial comparative study of the concept of grace in the two religions. Indeed in its reflectiveness, it is an example of "comparative hermeneutics".[12] For example he explains how the structure of thought focused on salvation by grace gives rise to similar problems in other fields, such as ethics. While Buri takes significant steps in seeking to understand Shin Buddhism, perhaps not always achieving quite accurate perceptions of the relations between the teaching of Shinran and "Amida Buddhism" in general, he also resists some of the images of Christianity which seem to have been current among Japanese Buddhists (such as Suzuki Daisetsu) at the time. It may be noted that not all Christian writers necessarily expound a monolithic understanding of their tradition, for there is a complexity of positions to be found, just as there is within the Buddhist family. Buri's essay undoubtedly formed a valuable jumping off point for later dialogical interactions.

The second western author whom we include here is the Briton Marco Pallis (1895–1989).[13] This author was widely known in the general field of what has been called the "perennial philosophy", a way of thinking which presupposes an inner unity of all religions and sees their value in the promotion of an inner, spiritualised mysticism. Pallis' main reference point for the traditions of Asia lay in Tibet, for he was also a keen mountaineer and a general writer on various associated subjects. The Tibetan connection seems to have matched the contemporary Japanese interest in Tibetan and Central Asian Buddhism as a field of study relevant for understanding the manifold development of Mahāyāna Buddhism in general. While Pallis had a relatively slight relationship to Shin Buddhism, he showed considerable acumen in the way in which he appraised and commented on the practice of the *nenbutsu*.

Alfred Bloom, for his part, seems to have "understood" Shin Buddhism so well that he became a convert and actively supported the promotion of his new faith over many years, eventually being ordained in his sixties in the Jodo Shinshu Hongwanji-ha (i.e. the denomination based on Nishi Honganji).[14] He is particularly well known for his influential early mono-

---

12. Cf. note 4 above.
13. Information about Pallis is mainly available from sources reflecting the point of view of sympathisers of the "perennial philosophy", e.g. <http://www.worldwisdom.com/public/authors/Marco-Pallis.aspx>.
14. The transcription Hongwanji is officially preferred by the denominational authorities. In earlier times both of the leading denominations used this transcription, which is now out of date. Vowel lengthening for Jōdo Shinshū is usually not shown in this name.

graph *Shinran's Gospel of Pure Grace* (University of Arizona Press, 1965) which became a standard teaching resource on the subject for students world-wide. His other written contributions are extremely numerous and have appeared in various quarters such as later issues of *The Eastern Buddhist* and in *The Pure Land*, the journal of the International Association of Shin Buddhist Studies. Like the work mentioned above, the title of which interestingly includes the word "Gospel," the article included here illustrates an early phase in Bloom's personal interaction with Shin Buddhism.

In their different ways, these three non-Japanese writers all contributed to the drawing out of the Shin Buddhist voice in the wider world. It is for this reason that they were hosted at the time in the pages of *The Eastern Buddhist.* In retrospect, it is extremely interesting to be reminded of the very varied range of interested parties in "the west", which at that time, just as now, certainly did not present a monolithic unity of consciousness or a common mode of reception or reaction as regards Shin Buddhism. It makes it difficult to see any real value in a construction such as "the western mind", which is sometimes used as a foil for presenting Zen Buddhism, for example by Suzuki Daisetsu, or "the eastern mind", as by many an author.

Care should also be taken over the use of the term "comparative religion." This has often been used in the sense of a search for some kind of hidden, mysterious or transcendental unity of religions, as in the "perennial" school linked to names such as René Guénon, Frithjof Schuon or Ananda Coomaraswamy. But as we see in the contribution by Fritz Buri, the act of comparison can also be used as a basis for interactive dialogue between two traditions which continue to be regarded as theologically distinct. Quite apart from religiously motivated, or religiously grounded writing, it is important to realize that the act of comparison (which includes both comparing and contrasting) is an essential part of the academic study of religions in general. This has become increasingly clear in recent decades, as this discipline has freed itself from the apron-strings of religious bodies, and from religious agendas of various kinds. From this point of view the three articles included here are definitely period pieces. They therefore have a signal value in illustrating options which were once determinative and which have echoed through various later developments, but which at the same time, as options, require to be placed in a stricter academic context today.

Returning to Japanese authors, and following the impact of Kanamatsu Kenryō, we look ahead to contributions by Shin Buddhist authors who were fully cognizant of the wider discussions and debates which were beginning to take place in post-war Kyōto. Specifically, we introduce here leading articles by Ueda Yoshifumi 上田義文 (1904–1993), Yamaguchi

Susumu 山口益 (1895–1976) and Takeuchi Yoshinori 武内義範 (1913–2002). These articles serve as significant introductions to the thought of Shin Buddhism's founder, Shinran Shōnin 親鸞聖人 (1173–1262), first in its own terms (Ueda 1986), then in relation to the underlying structures of Mahāyāna Buddhism (Yamaguchi 1966 and Ueda, in two parts, 1984) and third in relation to contemporary western and Christian thought (Takeuchi 1980). The chronological sequence of these more or less contemporaneous articles has been abandoned to give a more logical flow for new readers, but it should be remembered that these related areas of thought were all current simultaneously in the minds of the authors of the time.

Ueda Yoshifumi studied at Tokyo University's department of Indian and Buddhist Studies, gaining his doctorate in 1948 and becoming professor at Nagoya University until 1986, after which he became the principal of Chikushi Jogakuen Tanki Daigaku 筑紫女学園短期大学, a junior college for women. He represents a voice from the Nishi Honganji denomination of Shin Buddhism, though not an official one. Indeed his extremely insightful writings make no easy reading for those who would protect doctrinal positions against any tendencies to de-literalise them. A similar profundity is implied in Yamaguchi Susumu's article on the concept of the Pure Land in the teaching of Nāgārjuna. Here we learn that Shin Buddhist conceptions, despite what for some may be their apparent simplicity, bear an intimate relationship to the notion of emptiness (*śūnyatā*) which characterizes all Mahāyāna teaching.

Takeuchi published a book entitled *Shinran to Gendai* 親鸞と現代 (i.e. "Shinran and Modernity" or "Shinran Today"),[15] of which the article published here constitutes the second chapter. In the preface the author writes:

> Through the reflection on the awakening and deepening of his faith in the encounter with Hōnen, Shinran's religious life shaped a logic with a depth all its own. In this book I explain, through Shinran's works, this logic of Faith-Joy, and discuss the relations between Shinran's thought, the problem of secularization in contemporary civilization whereby person to person relationships are being lost, and the existential philosophies and theologies which try to face these problems.[16]

As the reader will find, Takeuchi sees these ideas and problems as structurally similar to those of modern western thought and Christian theology as found in the works of writers such as Arnold Toynbee and

---

15. Tokyo (Chūōkōronsha) 1974. The title was translated as "Shinran Today" in a footnote to the article as published in *The Eastern Buddhist*.
16. This quotation is from the footnote to the title in the original publication of the essay.

Michael Pye

Harvey Cox, Paul Tillich, Dietrich Bonhoeffer, John Robinson and Rudolf Bultmann, Martin Heidegger and Gabriel Marcel. The discussion of the standpoints of these varied religious thinkers, which interlocked at many points, is not only exemplary in itself but was admirably translated by Jan van Bragt (1928–2007), a Catholic missionary known for a lifetime of study of Buddhist-Christian relations.

Finally, we re-compact this period in the presentation of Shin Buddhism by taking a step backwards in time to take note of the interaction with Zen Buddhism. This area is explored in a robust dialogue between Suzuki Daisetsu, Kaneko Daiei, Soga Ryōjin 曽我量深 (1875–1971) and Nishitani Keiji 西谷啓治 (1900–1990), all resident in Kyōto at that time. Though not published until 1985, 1986 and 1988, in three parts, the meetings between these Buddhist thinkers had of course taken place shortly before Suzuki died in 1966. The participants are all major figures in the philosophically religious explorations of Buddhism in the wider context of modern thought. Soga Ryōjin was one of the leading intellectuals of the Shin Buddhist tradition in his day. Nishitani Keiji is well known as a representative figure of the "Kyōto School," a loose designation for that influential stream of intellectual consciousness which spanned religious denominations and universities alike in the city of Kyōto. Both Soga Ryōjin and Nishitani Keiji will figure more fully in a subsequent volume.

The present volume concentrates on the forward-looking presentation of the Shin Buddhist tradition in the twentieth century, covering a broad time-span. At the same time, while "listening" to it, we learn that this Shin tradition is itself at home in the broad tradition of Mahāyāna Buddhism, to which Zen thought also belongs. The latter may be more visible in the perception of many westerners, and yet the deepening dialogue of the twentieth century and its heirs has gradually come to recognize their complex interrelations.

Part I

Early Interactions

The Buddhist Doctrine of Vicarious Suffering

Kaneko Daiei

1

By "vicarious suffering" is meant that the Bodhisattva wishes himself to suffer on behalf of sentient beings in order to save them. This idea of "vicarious suffering" is expressed in many canonical books, and the following quotation is from the *Avataṃsaka-sūtra*, the Chapter on Pariṇāmana:[1]

> The Bodhisattva thinks thus: all sentient beings commit innumerable evil deeds, on account of which they suffer innumerable sufferings, do not see the Tathāgata, do not hear of the Good Law, do not recognize the pure samgha. As they are loaded with innumerable evil deeds and their karma, they are bound to suffer infinite pains. Therefore, I will stay for them in the evil paths and suffer their sufferings so that they may enjoy emancipation. I will never abandon them because of my incapacity of bearing all these "vicarious sufferings" which may cause my retrogression or fear or negligence. Because it is my desire to bear all sentient beings on my shoulders and to save them from such ills as birth, old age, sickness, and death, and to release them all from false philosophy, ignorance, and evils...

But in Buddhism the Bodhisattva seems to denote the historical Buddha Śākyamuni himself as he was intent on the attainment of Enlightenment. Bodhisattva literally means a being who aspires for Enlightenment, and the notion of Enlightenment is generally made to imply the salvation of sentient beings. Therefore, originally, Bodhisattva was the name given to Śākyamuni while he was still in his disciplinary stage before he became the Great Teacher of the world. But the life of Śākyamuni while still in his disciplinary stage was not confined to this life only, but

---

1. Text drawn from the Chinese translation by Śikṣānandha. Ed. Pariṇāma is more usual.

meant the many lives in the past which he spent practising all the virtues in order to save sentient beings. Hence the origination of the *Jātaka* tales. In the *Jātaka* tales we see many instances where he suffered for the sake of all sentient beings—not only human beings but all creatures endowed with life; thus he came to be saviour of the world as well as its teacher.

But in Mahāyāna Buddhism the name Bodhisattva is not confined to Śākyamuni in his disciplinary stage, but is given to anyone who is a true seeker of the Dharma, that is, who disciplines himself with the desire to benefit not only himself but others. Bodhisattva-ship must then be considered as consisting in the spirit of vicarious suffering. Now let us ask how we can take this vicarious suffering for the principle of Bodhisattva-ship.

If pain is everywhere caused by an external cause, vicarious suffering may be to a certain extent possible, as we see in the story of Prince Zenpuku 善伏 who suffered punishment in the place of the real culprit.[2] The rich can taste the distress of the poor by giving up all their property. To give a part of one's skin or blood to others who need them for some medical purposes may be said to be a case of vicarious suffering.

But these things are practised in some extreme cases not commonly met with in our ordinary life, and it is naturally impossible to practise this kind of thing for all our fellow beings. Vicarious suffering will be altogether impossible (it seems to me) when pain is produced entirely by an interior cause: the pain of old age, the pain of an incurable disease, –who could suffer this for the actual sufferer? This impossibility will become all the graver when pain comes from the inmost recesses of conscience which grieves not over the consequence of evil deeds but over the fact of their being committed at all; that is to say, the more inward the seat of pain, the more impossible its vicarious suffering will be.

Even when this vicarious suffering is confined to the person of Śākyamuni who is said to have gone through a life of sacrifice, the problem remains unsolved as long as we are on the plane of common sense. One may say this is a matter of religious faith. If so, how can we have this justified in our religious experience?

2

To inquire into this problem I will take as the basis of my study the noted commentary on the *Kegon* (*Avataṃsaka-sūtra*) by Genju 賢首[3] and also that by Chōkan 澄観,[4] in which various opinions are enumerated con-

---

2. Śikṣānanda's translation of the *Avataṃsaka-sūtra*, Chapter on "Entrance into the Dharmadhātu."
3. Ed. Genju 賢首, i.e. Fǎzàng 法蔵 (643–712).
4. Ed. Chéngguān 澄観 (737–787).

cerning the doctrine of vicarious suffering. In these enumerations no particular interpretations of the doctrine are offered, but they are rich in suggestion.

According to Genju and Chōkan, vicarious suffering is desired by the Bodhisattva. In Maitreya's treatise on Yogācāra philosophy we read: the Bodhisattva with his excellent wisdom and deeds accumulates the pabulum necessary for his Enlightenment and has no other thoughts but pity and sympathy with all suffering beings. He vows to be in the evil paths in order to save suffering beings therein; fixing his abode in these evil paths he stays there and attains Enlightenment. He vows again to bear on himself the outcome of all the evil deeds committed by them in order to save them from sufferings. He wishes to atone for their evil karma. The idea is through this vow not to let all suffering beings be actual sufferers of their own evil karma, but to let them enjoy only the result of their good karma. The Bodhisattva has destroyed all the seeds of passions and gone beyond all the evil paths. According to this, it is evident that to suffer pain for others is the vow of the Bodhisattva.

Genju and Chōkan seem to regard the vow as a fact of experience actually gone through by the Bodhisattva himself, and they are inclined to understand Maitreya in a somewhat superficial manner. But as we know that the doctrine advanced in the treatise on Yogācāra is representative of the views held by the Indian Buddhist philosopher, due respect is to be paid to it, and I wish to elucidate first of all what is meant by the vow (*praṇidhāna*). We already know in the *Avataṃsaka-sūtra* that vicarious suffering is vowed by the Bodhisattva: what is this vow, generally speaking? What does it mean to save all sentient beings through this vow? When this question is made clear, we may perhaps understand what is really meant by vicarious suffering.

The term Bodhisattva means the one who seeks Enlightenment. Enlightenment is the ideal of Bodhisattvahood and the original reason of his being. Therefore, the vow of the Bodhisattva is to realize the original reason of himself, that is, unfold the Buddha-nature in himself. But how does he realize it with the consciousness that it is for his own benefit? As long as we are conscious of the fact that anything is done for the sake of self, in whatever sense this may be understood, there is no way for us to escape the bondage of this self. In order to realize the Original Self it is necessary to deny the notion that it is for one's self. What takes place in our consciousness in the denial of self is none other than the notion that it is for all suffering beings. The realization of the Original Self may thus be possible only when the narrower self is given up and replaced by the notion of all sentient beings. Accordingly, the vow to save all suffering beings means truly to attain Enlightenment.

The idea advanced in the treatise on this interpretation will grow clearer, when we know that the original reason of Selfhood is Enlightenment which is the awakening of the transcendental self, while what it actually experiences in this world of senses constitutes this world of suffering beings. Therefore, the salvation of all suffering beings must come from the eternal vow of the Bodhisattva, and this vow is expressed in his deep feeling towards all sentient beings for whom he desires to suffer vicariously. This is truly the vow of the Bodhisattva, and that it shows no retrogression in its intensity is the very condition of its fulfillment. Therefore, the Bodhisattva entertaining the vow destroys as the first thing all the seeds of passions in himself and goes beyond all the evil paths; it is not thus quite fair to consider his vow a merely idealistic vow which is fine in sentiment but in fact utterly ineffective because suffering beings actually suffer. For as long as the Bodhisattva, through his vow, personally expresses all the sufferings in this world of the senses, he is, in the most realistic sense of the word, vicariously suffering for all sentient beings.

This is evident from those passages in the *Avataṃsaka-sūtra*, to which reference has already been made. In them the reasons are enumerated why the Bodhisattva desires to be the saviour of all beings, and from them we also learn that his heart of deep compassion never shows retrogression in the face of every possible harm and enmity. His large heart is there likened to the sun that does not refuse to shine because of the presence of the blind; the *sūtra* then goes on to speak about the Bodhisattva's desire to suffer for others, and his irrevocable determination that "Even when I am all alone in this resolution I will not falter." According to these statements in the *sūtra*, it appears that from the desire for Enlightenment there issues the vow to save all beings; while the latter are not actually and perceptibly benefitted by the ardent desire of the Bodhisattva to save them, the Bodhisattva never ceases to wish eternally for the benefit of all sentient beings; this is due to the fact that Enlightenment is essentially and ultimately for all beings and not for oneself. Therefore, in spite of the fact that beings to be saved are immeasurable in number, the Bodhisattva, ever intent on saving his fellow-beings, perfects, inwardly in himself, through his vow and virtue, his own being. In other words, while always suffering for others the Bodhisattva realizes his Original Self.

Thus we are able to understand the meaning of the truth constantly reiterated in the *sūtra*, that the Bodhisattva, while all the time desiring to save all beings infinite in number, fulfills his vow and attains his Buddhahood even before all suffering beings are actually saved. This appears to our commonsense view quite self-contradictory. When, however, the Bodhisattva realizes the eternal nature of his vow, he realizes at the same time that Enlightenment is the ultimate end of the vow as well as its own reason; hence the fulfillment of the vow means none other than penetratingly understanding the inmost meaning of the vow itself.

3

Even when vicarious suffering is regarded as the essential intent of the vow of the Bodhisattva, is it possible from the practical point of view for him to say that he vicariously suffers for others if the latter are not thereby benefitted in any demonstrable manner? That is to say, the idea of vicarious suffering must have two factors: the consciousness of suffering in the one who vicariously suffers and the acknowledgment of the fact by the one whose suffering is vicariously suffered by the former. It goes without saying that the fact of vicarious suffering has nothing to do with its acknowledgment on the part of the vicariously suffered; but there must be some meaning in deeds of vicarious suffering, which is to be acknowledged by the vicariously suffered in their inmost hearts.

As long as the vow of vicarious suffering leads to deeds, the latter are as a matter of fact to be recognized by those whose suffering is vicariously suffered. A deed, however great and far-reaching it may be in its influence on society, is not to be considered representative if the motive, that is, the vow is not real and sincere; on the contrary, a deed may not be one of great outward consequence, but if the motive is true and sincere it is the one that is to be thanked for by all people. Therefore, every true and sincere deed must be recognized as containing in itself something representative, and through this medium we find our way of salvation for ourselves. So we read in Chōkan's Commentary:

> When the Bodhisattva disciplines himself in asceticism in order to seek the Dharma for the benefit of all beings, this we have called 'vicarious.' This practice later becomes an ever-excellent guidance for all beings, as they strive after. Enlightenment, and in this sense also the Bodhisattva may be said to 'vicariously suffer' for others. When we read the lives of self-sacrificing Buddhists who perseveringly sought after the path in the face of every possible hardship, we unfailingly feel that their heroic deeds were meant for us, and that but for their efforts how little should we know now of the meaning of our own lives?

Vicarious sufferers are not necessarily limited to such personalities as are known as saintly or worthy. When our spiritual eye opens we shall be able to discover those worthy sufferers everywhere; they are not to be limited to a few historical figures. The question will then turn on the presence of the spiritual eye which detects our vicarious sufferers. The detection is possible only when our spiritual eye partakes of the same nature as that which constitutes the fundamental spirit of the vicarious sufferer himself. And as we can conceive this perceiving eye as a reflection of the pure spirit of the vicarious sufferer we may conclude that to recognize the virtue of the vicarious sufferer is, in itself, due to the action of this virtue. Then what is the deed of vicarious suffering?

4

As long as deeds issue from the vow, what is the most essential is naturally the vow itself and not deeds. But it is also important to investigate the several forms which the deeds assume. We see a sort of answer to the question in the Commentaries on the *Avataṃsaka-sūtra* by Genju and Chōkan.

One of the forms assumed by deeds of vicarious suffering is sympathetic cooperation. This means "living in the same way." Now to save others, one is naturally expected to surpass them in wisdom and virtue, for it is a good swimmer that, can save the drowning. But the saver, in order to save the drowning, must throw himself into the rapids and fight with the waves. Therefore, an excellent saviour of mankind must have within himself a world which is not of this world, though in his outward life living the life of a mortal being which does not differ from that which is lived by his fellow-creatures. By thus transcending the world the saviour has in himself something not bound by pleasure and pain, but by thus conforming himself to the world he is capable of suffering pleasure and pain. If this apparent contradiction is not permitted, it will be impossible for the vicarious sufferer to save others. Then, in what sense is this "transcending and conforming" possible?

To transcend the world means inwardly to abandon all passion, that is, to be delivered from all desires and thoughts, whereas to conform to the world means to have various passions and not to be delivered from desires and thoughts. Thus to conform while transcending means not to abandon passions unnaturally, and to transcend while conforming means in no time to be controlled by passions. Hence the doctrine of "intentional retention of passions." It means that the Bodhisattva retains passions and does not purposely annihilate them in order to conform to the ordinary life of the world. The vow of salvation which has the *bodhi* as its basis is infinite, and as our actual life evolves with nothing to hinder its course, passions are stirred without a moment's stoppage. But from the *bodhi* which is the foundation of humanity issues wisdom whereby all these passions and worldly turmoils are kept under control. Therefore, passions are absorbed in the *bodhi* just as they are and digested therein making the latter ever richer. We read in Asanga's *Mahāyānasaṃgraha* (from the Chinese translation):

> All passions have already been subjugated:
> As poison by itself loses its own poisonous nature,

So ignorance is exhausted by its very ignorance;
And the Buddha attains his all-knowledge.
All confused thoughts become factors of Enlightenment,
And Birth-and-Death (*saṃsāra*) turns into Nirvana;
The Buddha who accomplishes the great skilful means of salvation (*upāya*),
He is indeed beyond comprehension.

This doctrine of "intentional retention of passions" may sound strange when we understand it as meaning that when one is left to oneself no passions arise but they are needed for the benefit of others; for this is a sort of self-justification. If the doctrine is understood in this way—that is while morality based on utilitarian principles is not good, the total absence of practical consideration may cause the motive of doing anything good to wither away, and for this reason the Bodhisattva retains all his passions—if the doctrine is to be understood thus it will greatly lose in its spiritual signification. The essence of the doctrine, as I take it, lies in the ultimate control of passions by means of wisdom. Desires and passions are, so to speak, raw materials of life which are purified by wisdom. No one can exterminate his desires and passions. The wise will not be led astray by them, keeping them always under control. They will thereby enrich the content of their experiences. As long as they have desires and passions they will have to suffer sufferings inherent to life. When sufferings are purified by wisdom they not only become their own spiritual possession but are offerings to all humankind. Those to whom we pay our homage as the spiritual representatives of all sentient beings were not exempt from bitter experiences of life, but in them all the sufferings and tribulations were purified through true wisdom.

Genju and Chōkan recite the following cases as deeds of vicarious suffering, which are however quite problematical. The first one may be termed "intentional commitment of evils." The Bodhisattva purposely commits crimes in order to attain a certain object, and the consequence of it is that he is made to suffer; in other words, he commits an evil deed to fulfil his vow of salvation preparing himself for its bitter retribution. If this is morally permissible, it comes to this that evil deeds are morally justified for the realization of a lofty enhanced ideal as long as one is ready to suffer penalty as the outcome of his evil deed.

Shunchō, a devotee of the *Saddharmapuṇḍarīka*, is said to have been often in prison on the charge of slight crimes, the idea being to approach the jail-birds and save them from spiritual suffering. It is reported that an Indian Buddhist philosopher justified murder for the love of the murdered. And in this case the Bodhisattva would go to hell in a most exalted state of mind. He maintains that such deeds are to be recognized as those of the Bodhisattva inasmuch as a victim of his purposeful crime is thereby relieved of his own suffering due to his past karma.

If such substitution is possible and is acknowledged as Bodhisattva-like morality, we have here an adequate example of vicarious suffering. But we feel that the problem is highly pregnant of grave consequences. We can say that, strictly considered, the deliberate commitment of evil deeds is an impossibility. True morality is to be regulated according to ideas which are universally acceptable and cannot be specified by any definitely itemized clauses of morality. For this reason, unwritten laws of morality are variously applicable according to time and situation. Or the specified items of morality may be idealized so as to mean that the killing of the body is compatible with the saving of the soul. Therefore, if the Bodhisattva is really awakened to the true ideals of humanity, whatever deeds he commits cannot be designated as evil. Consequently, in whatever way the Bodhisattva may act, no retribution can ever be his lot just as a good physician never suffers pain on account of the operation he may perform on his patient.

But the question is more concrete and realistic. What should the Bodhisattva do if the view which he conceives to be true is unfortunately against common sense and the tradition of his time? In point of fact, such disagreements are a matter of rather common occurrence. In this case the Bodhisattva, as the representative of his time and society, must hold himself also responsible for evils of his own time. But this is the negative phase of his moral consciousness, though it is of more significance than is ordinarily imagined, requiring more serious consideration. Still he is required to make some positive assertion that may seem on the surface to contradict the so-called common-sense view of things as well as the tradition of his time. And in this case he is naturally expected to suffer all the bitter consequences of his deeds; for were they not crucified by their contemporaries—they who rendered great real services to humanity?

As is seen here, what is considered an evil deed is not necessarily evil in the moral consciousness of the Bodhisattva himself, being only so when judged by the moral standard of the time. However to judge the conduct of the Bodhisattva, we must resort to the absolute standard of morality and not take it only in its accidental relations to the views cherished by his contemporaries. Behind his positive conduct we can thus see his self-sacrificing spirit with which he is willing to bear on himself all the ills of his time.

The last form of vicarious suffering we may mention is the self-sacrificing deeds of the Bodhisattva, by which he is himself willing to offer his own life, for the execution of anything that is needful for humanity, regardless of personal hardships and dangers. The welfare and progress of society owes a great deal to the conduct of the masses whose merits are usually unrecorded in all history. If the farmer entirely gives up his profession what should become of us? All kinds of labourers form the foundation of society. However magnificent a mansion may be, it cannot retain its splendour if no drudges are available for keeping the establishment in good and clean and sanitary conditions. The smooth working and orderliness of social life will at once be put out of gear if every woman wants to be a lady and every man to be a gentleman of leisure. We know that the stage is not set up for the sake of a curtain-raiser and a utility-man, but without them we cannot have any sort of play. For that very reason, however, there are very few persons who are willing to be curtain-raisers or general utility-men. Therefore, those who perform such parts may regarded as placed on the sacrificial altar when they are evaluated from the general economy of the stage. Fully recognizing the importance of such parts and yet not unconscious of public frigidity, the Bodhisattva offers himself to perform all the ignominious functions in the orderly evolution of the great drama which is known as human life. The original vow of Kṣitigarbha and the universal manifestation of Avalokiteśvara exemplify in the most familiar manner cases of vicarious suffering.

We all know that hidden conduct is the basis of any successful achievement. In all departments of human activity anything worth reputation is preceded by many hard experiences. Social morality is sustained by silent workers who go their own way without demanding wealth or fame as reward. There is no enterprise that does not require perseverance and silent suffering on the part of the workers. Therefore, generally speaking, no work can be accomplished without the spirit of self-sacrifice. Further, when one realizes that the basis of any undertaking is laid in self-sacrificial conduct, the worker must be free from the consciousness that he is doing self-sacrificing work.

5

By the foregoing explanation we have come to understand some of the forms of vicarious suffering; showing that importance is to be attached more to the motive or vow (*praṇidhāna*) which is the basis of conduct, than to conduct itself. That is to say, men of vicarious suffering to whom we feel greatly indebted, realize the vow in their conduct. From this point of view, whatever conduct it may be, as far as it issues from a true sincere vow, it must be regarded as a form of vicarious suffering. While human conduct in general may be regarded in the light of vicarious suffering, it does not follow that the general mass of people are all Bodhisattvas of that order. Very few of them are worthy of our respect and reverence as self-sacrificing and vicariously suffering Bodhisattvas. Most people are just living under the stimulation of personal desires. That is, few in number are real Bodhisattvas and many indeed are those who are to be saved by them. When the matter is critically examined, vicarious sufferers grow less and less in number until we know two or three who are really such in the whole history of mankind.

If so, is the ideal Bodhisattva so rare that we have to consider him an impossible specimen of humanity? The thing is, however, to turn this critical way of judging human conduct and direct it on ourselves and not on a generality of people moving towards the gratification of their own egotistic passions. So when we criticize others we are really criticizing ourselves. To declare that there is no spirit of vicarious suffering in the world is to confess that we have no such spirit within our own hearts. The criticism must be directed on ourselves. It must be self-reflection. Now let us ask whence this self-reflection comes. It is no other than the working of the *bodhi* which makes the Bodhisattva vow to save all sentient beings. The subject of self-reflection is the Bodhisattva and its object is all beings. While in this concrete self itself we may naturally find the unity of subject and object, in our empirical consciousness the "I" as an objective existence is entirely individualistic. Some may think that even this "I" may not be lacking in the spirit of vicarious suffering, but here we find that the light of self-reflection has not yet penetrated deep enough into the recesses of consciousness where there lurks a trace of self-conceit which is really self-deception. The genuineness of the spirit is no longer there. However, if there is no Bodhisattva's vow lying, perhaps still dormant, deep in our hearts and not yet recognized by our self-reflecting consciousness, we shall have no occasion to lament our personal defects, nor may we be able to discover any vicarious sufferers however scarce they may come to us.

At the same time, the more this will become clear in our practical reason, the more will be the number of vicarious sufferers acknowledged as such until we come to recognize the meaning of vicarious suffering in the whole body of humanity. In other words, our self-criticism makes it wonderfully clear that all sentient beings are to be saved as well as ourselves, and also that the Bodhisattva of vicarious suffering is the taproot of their existence. However few may be exemplars of vicarious suffering, that which makes up the essence of vicarious suffering is no other than the *apriori*-self of all sentient beings. It is the maturest realisation of this *apriori*-self in the vicarious sufferers that we especially admire and respect; that is to say, that which we worship in all wise and holy beings is found reflected in our own souls while what constitutes our *apriori*-self is found realised in the Bodhisattva. This is the reason why in Buddhism the historical Buddha Śākyamuni is not recognised as the vicarious sufferer. All the innumerable Bodhisattvas referred to in the *sūtras* are the ideal of all sentient beings that makes up their transcendental ego. The names of the Bodhisattvas mean various desires and hopes of humanity. The name Samantabhadra in the *Avataṃsaka-sūtra* represents the virtue of the Bodhisattva in general, and Dharmākara-*bhikṣu* in the *Sukhāvatīvyūha-sūtra* means the most fundamental unity of all Bodhisattvas. The number of Bodhisattvas, whether one or many, is not to be predetermined. As far as each living individual is expression of a desire, or hope, or will, there must be so many corresponding Bodhisattvas, but when all those desires or hopes are regarded as unified in one fundamental will there is but one Bodhisattva. When we thus understand the meaning of Bodhisattva-hood, we are also able to comprehend the meaning of vicarious suffering.

We have understood the term "vicarious" in the sense of "representative." Of course these two concepts are to be distinguished the one from the other. As we recognize a deep meaning in the various stories of vicarious suffering, as told in the *Jātaka* tales, the former is not to be confused with the latter. If a man acts for others with the heart of a Bodhisattva, we can read here his desire to save all sentient beings. This is what we may call a "representative deed." So, the essential meaning of "vicarious suffering" must be sought in the idea of its being representative for all beings so as to bear their evil karma for them. And the real vicarious sufferer in this empirical life is no other than our transcendental ego itself, which constitutes the "not-I" in me.

Now we come to understand the explanation given by Genju and Chōkan that "Samantabhadra makes the spiritual universe his own body, which is constituted by all sentient beings; thus Samantabhadra is always the sufferer for all sentient beings, and in this sense his suffering is called "vicarious." What is the most direct sufferer in this vicarious suffering is not what we understand by "others," nor is it sentient beings themselves; it is Samantabhadra himself who suffers vicariously in sentient beings. In other words, when we are awakened to the sufferings we are actually experiencing and bear them, this is said to be suffering spiritually aided by Samantabhadra, for we by ourselves have no power of enduring sufferings. Forgetting Samantabhadra, however, who wants to suffer vicariously for us to an infinite degree, we externally seek for the means of removing our sufferings.

But to seek for the vicarious sufferer too near ourselves may seem to disregard the true sense of "vicarious suffering"; for each individual is a complete being by himself. In this case, that there is something still not quite clear in the meaning of "vicarious suffering" is because one understands it in the sense of "substitution"; when it is understood in the sense of "representative" the idea grows more intelligible, because the vicarious sufferer is near enough to us and in this again we are able to see such a vicarious sufferer in others. In those whom we esteem as vicarious sufferers there is no need to cherish the consciousness that they suffer for others. We see that the true vicarious sufferers have not such a self-conceit and move according to the vow and conduct of Samantabhadra. And we may take part in the great and sacred movement by aspiring for the deed and the vow of Samantabhadra. Herein we must seek for Life and Light Eternal.

Mahāyāna Buddhism and Japanese Culture

Yamabe Shūgaku

The Buddhism so far known to the West has been the Buddhism whose canonical literature is written in Pāli and generally known as belonging to the Hīnayāna. While the Sanskrit literature is not unknown yet it is to a limited extent. Even those who are acquainted with something of Mahāyāna are apt to regard it as a degenerated form of Buddhism. But in Japan it was from the very beginning Mahāyāna Buddhism that was introduced more than thirteen centuries ago, when Prince Shōtoku declared Japan to be the country most suited for the propagation of Mahāyāna Buddhism. Thus it came to pass that whenever Buddhism was mentioned in Japan it was the Mahāyāna form of it, and not the Hīnayāna. The study of the latter was not, however, neglected, it was part of the curriculum in Buddhist colleges. The Hīnayāna was a subject of study, not a religion in Japan. No wonder that it was in Japan that the Mahāyāna during its history of thirteen centuries has achieved most wonderful developments, dividing itself into many sects which represented the many-sidedness of the Buddhist doctrine, and that it also came to be most closely woven into the texture of Japanese life and culture. If Japan has anything contributive to the civilization of the world it is principally the product of Mahāyāna Buddhism.

Since the Restoration about sixty years ago Japan has learned to take many things from the West, especially its industry, machinery, and political organisation. The adoption was not of course a mere imitation but an assimilation which was carried out in an original manner. By this I mean that Western civilisation in Japan was modified according to the spirit of Mahāyāna Buddhism so as to promote life and culture in its most Oriental phase. In the adoption, therefore, there has been something quite original. To understand this spirit of originality peculiar to Japanese life, no earnest student of Japan can ignore the significance of Mahāyāna Buddhism.

The rise of Mahāyāna Buddhism is a long history, and we can say that it began to flourish at least two or three hundred years after the Buddha when the Prajñāpāramitā literature; began to be compiled, nay, even when the *Āgamas* were in the process of final redaction in which we have Subhūti as a representative of the doctrine of *śūnyatā*: From this we can infer that the so-called enlightenment attained by Śākyamuni contained much of what came to be recognised as Mahāyānistic though this fact never came to the surface in the consciousness of the Buddhists as distinguished from Hīnayānistic. The *Vimalakīrtinirdeśa*, the *Sukhāvatīvyūha*, the *Daśabhūmika*, the *Saddharmapuṇḍrīka*, and other *sūtras* mark no doubt stages of historical development, but we cannot deny the truth that they all endeavour to depict Enlightenment itself.

This conclusion may appear too dogmatic, but when we know the so-called *Āgama* texts are too abstract, too archaic, too poor in content, we naturally surmise the presence of something much deeper, more directly appealing to the heart of every Buddhist. Without this surmise we cannot explain the wonderful power contained in the discourses of the Buddha which he was supposed to have given on numerous occasions. This inspiring power was not concretely grasped by those compilers of the *Āgamas*. For instance, soon after the Enlightenment the Buddha was travelling with the group of his disciples in the neighbourhood of Magadha. When he saw a great fire he said,

> O monks, better embrace this big fire than falling in love with a woman; fire burns the body but lust leads us to hell. It is like drinking boiling metal to be the recipient of a charity yet to have no faith, no morality in him [and so on].

When this sermon was given the sixty disciples left the Brotherhood realizing the difficulty of religious training, sixty others prostrated themselves on the ground vomiting blood, while sixty others were cleaned of their spiritual defilements and attained enlightenment. The incident is told in the text in a detailed narrative, but to us there is a great discrepancy between the story itself which seems to be quite simple and the result achieved by the telling of the story by the Master. The whole narrative no doubt gives plain facts, but it utterly fails to give us the details of the most inspiring influence issuing from the personality of the Master himself.

To give another example, soon after the Enlightenment Buddha was sitting in the woods when thirty villagers each accompanied by his wife were enjoying themselves. One of the young men, however, happened to be a bachelor and his friends managed to get a courtesan for him as his temporary wife. After giving themselves to recklessness they all fell asleep. When they awoke they discovered that the courtesan had carried away all the precious stones and expensive dresses. They searched for her in all directions, and coming to the Buddha they asked if he did not see the guilty woman. Said the Buddha, "Which is more important, the precious stones or the mind that seeks them?" When they answered that the mind was more important, Buddha gave them a discourse on the subject. When this was finished, the thirty young men all abandoned their wives and at once became homeless monks under the Buddha. The sermon itself was quite simple but the wonderful result which was achieved surpasses the one recorded of any great historical personage. The sermon, whatever it might have been, must have been a most miraculous, most inspiring sort of music, which enrapturing every listener made him lose all the barriers of ordinary consciousness, directly looking into the inmost soul-fountain with its bubbling and gushing water. To depict this soul-effect, the plain narrations of the Hīnayāna style fail to do justice to the inner power beaming forth from the Buddha's sermon, The *Āgama* writers give us only an imperfect notation of the celestial music.

When the *Āgama*s are interpreted in this way, the texts are no more Hīnayānistic but Mahāyānistic. The Mahāyāna strives to catch the spirit that has been moving not only in the utterances of the Buddha but in his whole personality. This can never be described in words. It no doubt goes beyond them. But ours is to endeavour to catch this indescribable something in whatever form that is within human power, that is to say, the enlightenment attained by Buddha must be made to reveal its content somehow. It is no doubt mystical as it transcends our limited consciousness, but it is also rational because it sees everything in its aspect of *tathatā* or *śūnyatā*. *Śūnyatā*, or emptiness is something we cannot take hold of, but at the same time it is something before us that makes existence possible, that is *dharmatā*.

We generally live in the world of ideas and think this is everything; but in fact it is a kind of material which like a heap of coal requires to be ignited. We have to come in contact with facts themselves, and laws that govern them, that is, we are to acquaint ourselves with a definite arrangement of things which goes under the name, "cause and effect." This is scientific reasoning, corresponding to the Buddhist world of *tathatā*, or suchness. This explains how and why Buddha never contradicted science and thoughts based on it.

Mahāyāna Buddhism, however, goes one step beyond this by declaring that all that is discoverable by man is subject to the law of relativity, that anything explainable with words is thought construction having no permanency in it. This is the state of things as they are. Catch a fish and dissect it to find the life principle in it according to the so-called scientific method; but the fish thus brought on to the scientific table is a dead one. What is left in your hands is after all the shell of reality and not reality itself. The living fish must be studied, as it moves and swims and leaps.

The scientific method of study is, therefore, only one aspect of reality, and does not exhaust it. Its value is merely temporal.

To see reality as it is, as it lives, is the teaching of Buddha. To do this it teaches to leap, to leave science and intellection behind. When this leap is effected one is in the midst of reality, one gains a life of eternity. This is what is told by all those who have gone through the religious experience. By entering into the realm of suchness and reality the dualism of being and non-being, subject and object, reality and knowledge, existence and value, is altogether obliterated; we have jumped over the abyss, gone to the other side, but at the same time we are firmly standing on the very earth. The world originally neglected is affirmed once for all, this world of *saṃsāra* is not other than Nirvana.

This is the teaching and spirit of Mahāyāna Buddhism. In short the Mahāyāna teaches us to return into suchness, though this is no other than the world of particular facts. Our ordinary consciousness is under the control of science and every form of intellection, but Mahāyāna Buddhism wants us to realise a world of oneness which is the world of suchness, transcending idealism and materialism, realism and conceptualism. Suchness, in other words, is emptiness beyond human intelligence and discrimination, as it is on the other end of reality. When this suchness is grasped the whole domain of reality reveals its significance in the human personality, which is known as the value of religious experience.

The above delineation of the spirit of Mahāyāna Buddhism may appear somewhat difficult to comprehend intellectually, but an analogy may be found in art, which will facilitate our understanding. In the *Avataṃsaka-sūtra* we read that the artist does not know what he is painting, it grows out of himself, in spite of himself; he is moved or urged by something greater than himself; and what he does is no more than offering himself to the unconscious direction. To be a great artist, therefore, means that he is capable of offering himself as a more perfect and manageable instrument to a spirit. He does not try to analyze the spirit, he simply gives himself up to its control. When something comes between artist and spirit there is no artistic creation, for the product is maimed. The artist in this sense is an emancipated person, "one who thus comes," or "one who thus departs," that is Tathāgata.

The spirit of Mahāyāna Buddhism may thus be summarized in one word, *tathatā* or suchness; and those who have realized this suchness in any field of life as either a statesman or an artist or a capitalist or as a working man, he is a true follower of Mahāyāna Buddhism. He will build up his own world of suchness according to his own light in response to his environment. All that is specially considered religious—repentance, humility, gratitude, worship, and so on, will have its proper function as it is stirred in the bosom of a religious person. Without this grasp

Mahāyāna Buddhism will not yield its secrets to anybody. No scientific study of Buddhism will penetrate into this inner sanctuary of Buddhism. And when this spirit of Mahāyāna Buddhism is understood, the central force controlling the movements of Japanese culture will be seen in its full significance.

The Idea and the Man (A Response to Yamabe Shūgaku)

C. A. F. Rhys Davids

In his interesting article: "Mahāyāna Buddhism and Japanese Culture," of the July issue of this Journal, 1931, Shūgaku Yamabe has twice referred to passages as being of Hīnayāna Āgamas. I assume that by this is meant the Pāli Tipiṭaka. He omits to locate these references, which is regrettable. One of them is fairly accurately quoted from the Aṅguttara-nikāya (Pāli Text ed. IV, 128 ff.); the other is quoted with no less inaccuracy from Vinaya-piṭaka (Oldenberg ed. I, 22 ff.), so inaccurately that it seems possible he has had before him a later Sanskrit version.[1] I am not contending that, in the Pāli version either, we have a truly reported version, so corrupt it evidently is. But the opening words of this, the first lay-sermon of the Śākyamuni, are recorded in a true Upaniṣadic vein, very different from the later vein of the version quoted, yet unquestionably one that *would have been used* by the Hīnayāna editors of the record, if it had been in their tradition.

The Pāli version is, that certain *kṣatriya* gentlemen with their wives, at what we should call a picnic, find that a courtesan, included in the party, has made off with some property. (That she was as represented is probably a monkish error, so grotesque it is.) Seeking her, they meet with the solitary, as yet unknown *religieux*, the *kṣatriya* Gotama, and ask: Has he seen a woman pass by? The reply is; What have you, *kumāras*, to do with woman? Were it not better that you sought the self (*attānam*,[2] or "the man"; in the religious diction of the day *ātman* and *puruṣa* would be equivalents)? That the Self, the Deity within, should be sought, be inquired after, is a teaching in both the earlier Chāndogya[3] and the later Maitreya Upaniṣads, and as such, and as so worded, would not have been

---

1. Ed. In fact, as we know from his response, Yamabe had been using the Chinese Āgamas which only bear an approximate correspondence to the Pāli texts, having been translated from Sanskrit equivalents.
2. Ed. Here the author used the accusative, presumably because of the sense in the English sentence. The Pāli nominative *attan* would correspond to the Sanskrit *ātman* which follows.
3. *Tad anveṣṭavyam, tad vijñāsitavyaṃ.* Cf. my *Sakya, or Origins of Buddhism*, 1931, 201–213.

very palatable to *Piṭaka* monastic editors, and would in no case be a later gloss. Mr. Yamabe's version is:

> Said the Buddha, Which is more important, the precious stones or the mind that seeks them? When they answered that the mind was more important, Buddha gave them a discourse on the subject. When this was finished, the men all abandoning their wives became at once homeless monks under the Buddha.

Without dwelling on this deplorable termination, common to his version and the Pāli, I would only add that the discourse in Pāli was on "*dhamma*," not on "mind," but all we have in surviving records is alas, not the actual talk on seeking the "Self," but a set piece of stereotyped formula on a variety of subjects. No Indian teacher of that day would have dreamed of starting a life-mission on so relatively secondary a subject as the mind. As to that, has Mr. Yamabe's version for "mind," *manas*, or *citta*, or *vijñāna*? Each of these has a different force in the Piṭakas, and it is only the last that was then ever used to mean the man, and then only the man-in-survival. But as time went on *vijñāna* came to mean merely the man as receptive of impressions. It was still later that it was used in the comprehensive way we use "mind."[4]

But in the *vinaya* version of this crucially important utterance, the word is not "mind," but *attan*, the self, or man. The significance of the word as used then and there has been quite obscured by translations having the relatively weak Western meaning (which was also the later Pāli meaning) of "yourselves."

With the writer's general contention, that these *mantra*s were "winged words" beyond any power they may seem to have for us, I agree. Eloquence the Śākyamuni had not; he was not just an orator, but his will-power must have been compelling. That, however, the early *mantra*, spoken in a bookless world, had power transcending any dead *record* of it, belongs to the magic of the spoken word in such a world, a power which will have been less of a rare phenomenon than it is now. Much more than it is now will it have been felt to be, not the words alone, not mind alone, but the very man—let me use my word, the man-in-man—giving of himself to his fellowman. To call this-that-was-to-be-sought "the mind," is to hold up, not, (as in Upaniṣadic teaching) "the most precious thing in all the world" to me, to you;[5] it is to hold up the man in a Less, not in a More, much less in the Most. And it is here that I chiefly join issue with the writer.

All religion worthy of the name seeks to place before us man as a More. But we shall never worthily value man as that, if we quit hold of the

---

4. E.g. in the manual *Abhidhammattha-sangaha*.
5. Cf. *Bṛhadāraṇyaka Upaniṣad: Saṃyutta-nikāya* (Kosala).

man and glorify the idea. The Mahāyānist, when he extols *tathatā*, suchness, thusness, has in mind "truth," "reality," but ultimately he means *Man as and in* what is true, real. He means man as a More in so far as *he has these values*. Drop the man and you have but an abstraction, an idea in a general way. World religions do not begin with abstractions. Jesus never spoke of "brotherhood," nor did the Śākyamuni of "becoming," or of selfness, or of suchness. Prescind "such," "real," "true" from the man, and we have but a misty idea-world, a word-structure of what the man has been valuing "in" his minding. Ideas have in themselves no meaning, no reality save as works of Man, conceived, evolved by Man. It is only Plato and Platonists who would see in ideas a *prius* to the Man; or are Mahāyānists Platonists? They cannot be that if they are sincere in looking upon Śākya, the original teaching of Gotama Śākyamuni, as the cradle and foundation of their Buddhist faith. For then they must, as the reviewer of my *Gotama the Man* says in this issue,[6] "turn back from," I would say, get behind, "the monk-made Buddhism of the Analysts, and seek the true spirit of the Buddha's doctrine." And this they will find, not in Ceylon, not in Burma or Siam, but in that teaching of India which Gotama sought to expand in that seeking of the Self, the Man, even the Divine Man, who is the inner most inner of every man. There will they find no ideas transcending the Man, but the Man mandating himself in ideas about the Highest, that is, the Most, *by way of ideas about the More*. Always it is the imperfect man of earth striving to advance to, to become a More, a Better, not by clinging to some abstraction, but by a beholding a higher Self: Witness, Inspirer, Urger, the perfect actual He, Who the man as yet only potentially is.

As yet he can only conceive a More, call It Highest though he may. And no absorption in any abstract idea, be it Emptiness or Suchness or other, will transport him, the imperfect, into the Perfect. He is in process of becoming That Who he is potentially, and no "leap" to escape from reasoning, although it may aid him in becoming, will do more than this. I would echo the writer's words, only with an inversion of emphasis: "it is in the human personality that the grasped abstraction reveals its true significance."

Mr. Yamabe goes on to compare the man who is *tathāgata*—that is, as I understand the term, the Wayfarer, the man-in-the-Way, the Śākyamuni's Way[7]—to the artist working as "instrument to a spirit," I agree, but I hold it a lazy way to be so vague as all that about "spirit." Mr. Yamabe could find out more as to sources of inspiration if he would try.

---

6. Ed. i.e. "this issue" of *The Eastern Buddhist* 6, vol. 1, 1932.
7. That is, for me, not the late-interpolated "eightfold way," but the way-in-the-worlds, man's long process in Becoming, worded in the *suttas* as *magga* with *phala*.

Were such effort made with serious intelligent persistence, we should come to word our spiritual life more wisely. We should find, it may be, no encouragement to mistake abstractions as such for the true, the real. We might find, in both the artist's creations and our own inspirations, always the Man willing his instrument, the man willed.

Do I much offend if I say, that for me the weakness in Mahāyāna lies in the "more-worth" in which it holds abstractions, ideas? Herein it has strayed from the parent-stem of religion, and tends to lose itself, as do its *sūtras*, in a maze of the Word. The writer does not so remain lost. Once more, in closing, he makes the Idea subservient to the Man, showing the man as in the last resort the builder of his own becoming, his own world. But let this be a world of real "things," not of the abstraction *quā* abstraction: "reality."

I watch from our Pāli Society with reverent sympathy the new piety in Japan seeking to know better the oldest records we yet have found of that Indian movement, which a monastic vogue, as it grew, bore along and sadly altered. Japan will do justice to the *moral* values always kept to the front in Hīnayāna, even though it needed Mahāyāna to expand its *ethical* values. But religious values are, of the very Man, the man-in-man. And I look to Japan to realise this in the future, and to bring forward this, as the true heirs of the original Indian Śākya, and not rest content with abstract ideas. Then only will she place herself aright to conceive a More that is in man, in his nature and his destiny, while she awaits with the world the light that may yet come, the light that will be neither Hīnayānism nor Mahāyānism nor any other cultivated "ism," the light we shall one day be seeking in the new way, with the new values. Then indeed will she be, even in religion, the child of the Rising Sun.

A Rejoinder to Mrs. Rhys Davids' Comment
Yamabe Shūgaku

Regarding my article, "Mahāyāna Buddhism and Japanese Culture," Mrs. Rhys Davids wrote a sympathetic comment for which I am thankful. While I have to admit to my use of certain terms in a not very scientific way, I also wish to express what I think of Mrs. Rhys Davids' view of Mahāyāna Buddhism.

It is delightful to find that her Mahāyāna view is generally in agreement with mine; the difference however between us seems to lie in differences of emphasis, which come from a difference of standpoint, or from the different use of the same material.

First of all, I regret I was not quite exact in the use of the word "mind," which caused Mrs. Rhys Davids to make unnecessary inquiries into the original sources. The word "mind" occurs in the following passage of mine: "Which is more important, the precious stones or the mind that seeks them?" –this being my English version of the sermon of Śākyamuni given to the thirty-seven young men. If this question on the part of the Buddha is to be literally translated, "the mind" should be "yourself" as my critic suggests. For not only in the Pāli *Vinaya-piṭaka*, but in its Chinese version "yourself" is used. But my use of "mind" is justified, for my intention was not a scholarly study of the text, but to inquire into the thought of the Buddha which he had at the moment. "Yourself" in this case will not lend itself generally to the understanding of the real meaning which is behind his question, hence my interpretative phrase "the mind which seeks them." This may not be, strictly speaking, in harmony with the Buddhist idea, but when the general intelligibility of the statement is concerned I think my phrasing is clear enough. What I wished to emphasize in my telling the story of the young men was the following two points: 1. That Gotama's idea was to turn the attention of the young men from the stolen objects to what was going on within themselves, that is, from being troubled with earthly things to the consideration of the inner world; 2. That while the sermon taken in itself was not apparently sufficient to make all those thirty-seven young men join the Brotherhood, abandoning their family life, there was something behind the sermon emanating from the personality of the Buddha himself, which had a far greater spiritual effect on their young minds.

Mahāyāna Buddhism generally endeavours to explain why from an apparently plain discourse given by the Buddha which does not seem to be so very pregnant of weighty meaning such grave consequences result as, for instance, the abandonment of the family life. The Pāli-*piṭaka* is in a sense too fond of giving "a set piece of stereotyped formula," which fails to make one see into the inner meaning. I wish therefore to emphasize from the point of view of Mahāyāna Buddhism the significance of the events. The Mahāyāna is always intent on the inner value, which often makes it too neglectful of the outwardness of things.

As to Mrs. Rhys Davids' criticism of the conception of Mahāyāna Buddhism, I am sorry I have to express my complete disagreement. For the idea that the Mahāyāna is concerned only with abstract or metaphysical arguments and artistic inspirations and lacking in morality, seems to miss the mark. So long as she rests with this preconceived idea, it is very hard for her to accept the real teaching of Mahāyāna Buddhism. I cannot however help feeling delighted to know that Mrs. Rhys Davids, who has profound knowledge of the Hīnayāna *Tripiṭaka*, tries to come in touch with the great personality of Gotama Buddha himself, which, according to her, is far above "the monk-made Buddhism." This is important, for it is also the Mahāyāna point of view to think more of his personality than of the Brotherhood devoted to so-called Buddhist speculation. Being so, the Mahāyāna is very far from being Platonic or merely idealistic; those who take the Mahāyāna for metaphysical abstraction fail really to know what it stands for.

As I understand Buddhism, it not only teaches morality as defining human relationships but considers humanity in its broadest sense. It disciplines us to have a thorough control over our own small selves, which is equivalent to the abandonment of an ego-centred idea; it does this because it wants us to experience such religious feelings as joy, humility, and contentment, which are the outcome of spiritual regeneration. When viewed from these experiences the entire world assumes quite a different aspect from what it used to be, and this new aspect of existence presenting itself to the Mahāyānist eye is technically termed Suchness (*tathatā*). The moral life therefore in Mahāyāna Buddhism is something that grows out of such religious experiences, and there is in it no feeling of constraint or restraint, the conscious and the unconscious work harmoniously, which is a feeling of spiritual freedom, emancipation, that is to say, of having been released from the bondage of birth and death. While realizing that we are Buddhas even as human beings, we also know or feel that we are taking refuge in the great universal soul which is Buddha-nature (*buddhatā*). This is where the impersonal Dharma and the personal *dharmakāya* are unified in the form of the Tathāgata. This Mahāyāna conception of the Buddha or Tathāgata is more positive than Mrs. Rhys Davids's idea of "a More," and is also more personal and therefore of more effective significance.

Mahāyāna Buddhism as we have it today is the result of a steady evolution of the religious consciousness nourished in the Orient by the great experiences of so many strong Buddhist souls for so many years since its introduction to China and Japan. These souls have left records of the utmost spiritual importance in the form of literature, part of which can be viewed in the great Taishō edition of the Chinese *Tripiṭaka* edited by Drs. Takakusu and Watanabe. I regret that this short and therefore necessarily imperfect rejoinder to Mrs. Rhys Davids' comment on my article by no means does justice to my conception of Mahāyāna Buddhism as a whole, and my sincere wish is that someday I shall be allowed to give a much fuller expression in the present magazine as regards what Mahāyāna Buddhism really means to us people of the Orient.

Editorial of 1934

Anonymous

Recently, it was said by a friend abroad that he had heard that a revival of Buddhism in China was more likely than a revival in Japan. To us here in Japan this seems very strange, for we feel that the revival in Buddhism in Japan has already come and has been with us for some time. Persons who say this are not well informed. Buddhism has revived in Japan and is growing more and more flourishing.

I also read in a European journal that a certain Japanese priest in Berlin had said that he was obliged to go to Germany in order to learn pure Buddhism as Buddhism was degenerated in Japan. I cannot understand what he could have been doing or where he could have been staying in Japan, to have made such a statement, unless he was referring to strict Hīnayāna Buddhism.

Buddhism is not deteriorated in Japan. It is a living vital force, and, after its partial eclipse at the time of the Meiji restoration, has revived and become a vehicle of peace and power to thousands of its followers.

Let us consider some of the Buddhist activities in Japan. First of all the temples. They have many activities, perhaps one of the chief of which is consolation at the time of death. They conduct services for the dead and console the living. This, as with Christian denominations, is an important part of a priest's duties. There are the celebrations the death days of famous priests and patriarchs of the sect, and anniversaries of various kinds also make occasions for celebration. For example, as only one out of many, this year the 1100th anniversary of the death of Kōbō Daishi and the completion of the new Hall and Pagoda was celebrated at Kōyasan from April 2 to May 21. Thousands of people attended the services at this celebration.

There are many Buddhist societies for Buddhist propagation and dissemination. There are women's associations, also the Y.M.B.A. and Y.W.B.A.,[1] Sunday schools and philanthropic societies devoted to active charitable work. There are study classes, and many lectures are given by eminent speakers. Preaching Halls are established. Summer schools are held and group meditation periods are held for laymen. Pilgrimages to sacred places are frequent. As for books and magazines, they are issued in great quantities. There are a number of Buddhist colleges and schools where young people receive Buddhist instruction. Does all this imply deterioration? Buddhism, as Prof. J. B. Pratt states, is "emphatically the religion of Japan." He also says, "Whatever may come about in the next fifty years, certain it is today that Buddhism has a large, and, in some of the sects, an enthusiastic and devoted following."

---

1. Ed. Young Men's Buddhist Association, Young Women's Buddhist Association.

Prof. Pratt also remarks that "the last fifteen years have been marked by a notable advance. In education, propaganda, worship, and service it has taken great strides and we are witnessing today only the first fruits of its new sowings." He further states that in his opinion the Buddhism of Japan is "a religion of great present strength and pretty fair promise."

Prof. Addison of the Episcopal Theological School, Cambridge (USA), has a number of interesting things to say about what he calls the Revival of Japanese Buddhism. He states that behind the activity of Buddhist education and publication lies a genuine intellectual revival. Buddhist leaders with modern mental equipment are re-thinking and restating the doctrines of their religion. He also remarks "that partly as a result, partly as a cause of the Buddhist revival, there is widely observed, especially in the younger generation, an awakened idealism and a growing interest in religion. Far less enthusiasm is now manifested for the older type of materialism and scepticism represented by Herbert Spencer; far more general is the response to the stimulus of idealism in many forms—whether of the latest German philosophy, or of Christianity, or of the new Buddhism. Developing rapidly in such an atmosphere, the Buddhist revival, already accelerated, is likely to continue until far more radical changes have taken place than those we have here described."

There is no other place in the world where Buddhism in its Mahāyāna form can be so well studied in its theory or in its practice as in Japan. Indeed, I may go so far as to say that without a visit to Japan a certain spiritual grasp of Buddhism cannot be attained. But there are some who come and "seeing they see not" and do not understand. Generally these are persons who see but superficially, do not thoroughly investigate and study and come in contact with different classes of Buddhists. But those who do investigate know that the Japanese revival has already taken place, that Japan can give the follower the best Mahāyāna Buddhist teaching and initiate him into Buddhist activities of which he can only dream in other countries. Come to Japan, Buddhist aspirants, and witness for yourselves the Buddhist revival here. Study it in its various ramifications and activities and then you can truly assert that in Japan Buddhism exists, has revived from a temporary dull period, and is now pushing on to a new and deep spirituality.

Editorial of May 1949

Anonymous

The Eastern Buddhist Society has suspended its activities during the war-years, but we now intend to resume them in a smaller way. There are still many serious obstacles which we are not quite sure of having in control. With the political and economical reorientation of Japan caused by the fates of the War, Buddhism has also come to be evaluated newly. The War has indeed effected a thorough-going transformation of Japan in various ways, and here we wish to touch upon the spiritual life of the people.

Shintoism known as "Shrine Shintō" is under a ban now. It has been severed from the state to which it was hitherto closely attached and with which to a certain extent it identified itself, serving the state as a kind of operative principle. Hereafter, Shintō will have to endeavour to find the place where it fits best in the cultural scheme of the Japanese life, if it is not going to deteriorate into a mass of superstitions.

Christian activities will be accelerated and no doubt the Japanese people will thereby be benefitted. For one thing, they will learn a great deal about the social aspect of religion, which is one of the most distinctive characteristics of Christianity. While religion is essentially concerned with the question of the individual soul in relation to God, the individual has no sense when it is detached from society. The Japanese who have been used to the vertical hierarchic conception of a feudalistic community know nothing about the horizontal democratic relationship existing among its individual units. Christianity insists upon its members being directly, vertically, paternalistically connected with God yet it does not forget our horizontal fraternalistic connection among ourselves. It is possible that the democratic spirit cherished by the Christians is the offshoot of their political ideas.

The Orient has not fully learned the technique of systematisation or organisation, and in this respect Christianity representing Western culture and social institution will do much to stir up the Japanese mind along with its religious teaching.

While the militaristic regime was in full power, Buddhism was not very well countenanced, not because its followers were not willing enough to espouse its cause, but mainly because Buddhism is essentially a religion looking after the spiritual welfare of humanity, and not a system of teachings always ready to identify itself with the state and its egotistic assertion of power.

With the ending of the War, Buddhism is regaining its original status, though the feudalistic frame in which it has been set throughout its history in Japan is now proving the greatest possible obstacle for its re-adjustment. It will take years of internal and external struggles before it can present itself as a supreme spiritual force.

But it is Buddhist institutions and not the teaching that requires a total re-modelling. Our conviction is: Buddhism is a world-religion and has a mission of its own which cannot be replaced by Christianity. When the world is given up to the materialistic, mechanistic, economic, and scientific interpretation of Reality and has no time to reflect within itself and quietly to come in personal contact with God, Buddhism, we wish to state, has a great deal to say to Western people as much as to Eastern people.

The human mind eternally strives for synthesis or unification, which, however, can never be achieved as long as we remain in the intellectual plane. But it is our fate that we can never get away from rationalizing, which means in turn that we are to stay in this world of differentiation.

The two world religions, Christianity and Buddhism, will never be coalesced as one religion; they will serve humanity the best by each keeping to its own specific feature of spiritual experience. Let therefore each propound its teaching according to the light it has gained.

As facts stand, Buddhism is not properly understood in the West, that is, by the Christian nations. We mean here by Buddhism the Mahāyāna school of Buddhism as it prevails in China and Japan, especially in the latter at present. Most observers take the form for the content, the intellectual presentation for the experiential facts, the traditional and historical appendage for the reality itself. This may be generally unavoidable; and the duty of the Buddhists will be to elucidate its essentials to the fullest extent of their capacity so that the West will come gradually to comprehend what Buddhism really is and what the Buddhist life really means to humanity.

A scholarly interpretation of Buddhist history and philosophy is no doubt important in understanding Buddhism, but what is more urgently needed for the general public is to present its thought as based in life itself. Its followers may not know much about the Fourfold Noble Truth, the Twelve Links of Causation, the Eight-fold Path of Righteousness, or other doctrinal theories associated with historical Buddhism but they must face such problems of life as the meaning of the individual, its relationship to society and God, birth and death, "karmic bondage," "unthinkable (or mysterious) emancipation," Enlightenment, etc. These are eternal problems of life confronting every one of us and demanding final solution.

With the conclusion of the War, Japan has been made to emerge from her insularistic way of thinking and feeling. While she is at present economically and politically hampered in various ways and cannot express herself freely, she is allowed to enjoy spiritual liberty which is in fact the fountainhead of all kinds of worldly freedoms, and this spirituality—whatever it is that is left now in Japanese life—comes from Buddhism. For this reason, it is required of us Japanese Buddhists to be actively engaged more than ever in propounding Buddhist experience and its philosophical interpretation to the whole world. And we must present our views on them as best we can, however inadequate our best may be, and if possible in the light of modern thought so that they will be more readily comprehended by readers other than Buddhist.

This is the self-imposed mission of the Eastern Buddhist Society in resuming publication.

Part II

Two Presenters of Shin Buddhism

Shin Religion as I Believe it

Kaneko Daiei

Shin Buddhism was revealed by Shinran Shōnin (1173–1262), who founded it on the basis of the teaching of the *Larger Sukhāvatīvyūha-sūtra*. Its system of doctrine is set forth in the four fasciculi of the *Kyōgyōshinshō* which the founder himself has wrought, and this is said to be considerably abstruse. Its rather plain religion, however, may be traced in some more easily accessible works such as the *Tannishō* ("Refutations of Heterodoxies"), a tract which consists of Shinran's sayings and his disciple's comments. Now in this tract we find the following words which we can consider the excellent expression of the quintessence of Shin religion: "If we believe in the Original Vow of Amida, and say the Nembutsu, we shall become Buddha." In the succeeding pages I will endeavour to explain what is the significance of these words and attempt to communicate to the reader what I consider to be the general principles of Shin religion.

1

"If we believe in the Original Vow of Amida"

The Original Vow of Amida

We of this world must have something to rely on—something which is eternally true. The Shin maintains that this true something is Amida's Vow, except which there is nothing true. Amida is Amitābha Buddha, the Awakened One of True Light and Eternal Life. Amida is thus the Eternally True Being, the Knower of All the Truth of the particulars as well as the whole, and is our Light and Life.

The True Light represents the work of wisdom while Eternal Life signifies the cause of mercy; the one destroys all kinds of our delusions whereas the other alleviates all forms of our sufferings. Now in Amitābha Buddha wisdom and mercy is unified into one whole. From that source comes His Original Vow. And the Vow is the manifestation of His Wisdom-Mercy; His Wisdom being the enlightening working in His Mercy which wishes to save us from sufferings. For this reason it is not that we are to know Amida directly and immediately, but that we are led to become aware of His Mercy-Wisdom wrought upon us when the proclamation of His Original Vow comes home to our heart.

Now, the Original Vow of Amida is "the word" of His sincere wish. It expresses His Will. We who have heard this word proclaimed are sure to be pierced by His Will, and we come to have no doubt about the truthfulness of His Original Vow—this is called "faith" on our part. What, then, is the word of the Original Vow of Amida, and where is it to be found? It is set forth in the *Larger Sukhāvatīvyūha-sūtra* in the form of the Forty-Eight Vows of Amida. Among them, however, the most important, supreme and sovereign, is the Eighteenth Vow, in which the essence of the whole vow is contained. We may say, therefore, that Shin Buddhism is just the Eighteenth Vow realized. Now, it will require too much space to state to the full the deep significance of the Buddha's Vow, yet I can summarize its general purport by the help of the following word known as "the Epitome of the Eighteenth Vow."

The Epitome runs thus: "Any one who calls upon My name shall be reborn in My Land," Here we find that two things are said, by which we can learn the general principles of the Original Vow, and through which we can realize His Wisdom-Light and Mercy-Life. The first is, "any one who calls upon my Name"; and the second, "shall be reborn in My Land." I will take up the second in the beginning and make clear what is meant by those words, "shall be reborn in My Land." Our inquiry, then, is: What does the Buddha Land mean to us?

What does the Buddha Land mean to us?

The Buddha Land is the world of truth and eternity—the world where *byōdō* and *jakumetsu* prevail. *Byōdō*, meaning "equality," is that which the human being has long aspired after but never attained; while *jakumetsu* is the true peace, since it means "serenity of cessation," the state where there is no disturbance whatever. The Buddha has vowed that all sentient beings shall be reborn in His Land of Purity where equality and true peace prevail. The Buddha has thoroughly seen into the real nature of the world wherein we sentient beings are living, and knows full well that it can never be otherwise than the stage of discrimination and disturbance. We sentient beings, however, are ignorant of this state of things, and we would not deplore that we are in such a miserable condition; hence, our doom of eternal suffering. It is for this reason that the Buddha who was so much moved by pity for us sentient beings has vowed to make us to be reborn in His Land of equality and true peace. The Buddha has thus shown mercy and wisdom in His Vow, and there we are made aware of His sincere wish to save us from suffering and also of His constant activity to relieve us of delusion.

Now, according to Shin Buddhism, this world is a hopeless world, so long as it remains as it stands. There will neither be peace in its purest form, nor equality in its truest sense. Shin followers do not believe that real happiness can be attained by merely adjusting the outward conditions of this life. Neither do they admit that our perfection can be achieved merely through the discipline of our inward passions. To discipline our inward passions is the aim of morality. But morality is inevitably entangled in the meshes of the outward circumstances of life, so that it cannot lead us to thorough-going self-retrospection. This is why men are sometimes tempted to do evil in the name of good or to commit crimes in order to maintain themselves. Moreover, morality is accompanied by thought. Men differ in their opinions about what is right and what is wrong, and this difference in their opinions undermines morality. In Buddhist terminology, this kind of disturbance arising from the difference of opinions is called *ken-joku*, defilement by false views: whereas the other kind caused by the passions of love and hatred is called *bonnō-joku*, defilement by evil passions. Buddhists believe that ours is the world which is constantly being defiled by these two kinds of defilements.

This being the case, if there is anything capable of enlightening us who are painfully groping in the darkness of ignorance, it must be a Light shining out of a source which is beyond human wisdom and power. And the source is no other than the world of truth and eternity vowed by Amida in His Original Vow.

That on which life rests and to which death leads

The first thing we have to do here is both to define clearly and understand the meaning of the expression *jōdo ni umareru* or "to be reborn in the Pure Land."

Now, according to the Buddhist theory on the destiny of human souls, we human beings who go on accumulating our karma of good and evil, as these are caused by our passions of love and hatred, are eternally doomed to pass from life to death and from death to life, in order to undergo various kinds of sufferings.

Such transmigration being horrible, we sincerely long for the world where no longer any form of birth-and-death exists. The Buddha Land of truth and eternity is just such a desired world. For it is a higher realm, transcending birth-and-death, while yet including them.

Now, with this Buddha Land both behind his back and before his eyes, the Shin follower will live and die. He will make the world of truth and eternity the foundation on which his life rests and the goal to which his death leads.

To be reborn in the Pure Land, to which we have referred just above, is to attain the Buddha Land, the goal to which death leads. In other words, it means that we shall come to attain the world of truth and eternity where we suffer birth-and-death no more, and that this is occasioned in the moment when we die in this world, exhausting the human existence of suffering through the practice of the Nembutsu.

"To be reborn" in this expression, therefore, means not "birth" as it is generally understood, but the birth of no-birth or the birth of serene illumination caused by the death of serene cessation. The death of serene cessation, again, never means sheer annihilation. Though there is a sorrow for losing our life, yet there is an exulting joy in becoming one with the Eternal.

Thus, Shin Buddhism makes the Pure Land the goal to which death leads; in this respect, it is considered a teaching of future existence, and is regarded as a doctrine advocating salvation after death. Nevertheless, it should never be forgotten that Shin Buddhism also makes the Pure Land the foundation on which life rests, and for this reason it has much to do with our actual life. We who long for the Pure Land are constantly realizing the Buddha's Mind and the Buddha's Land in the midst of our human life. We who long for the Pure Land, though we are groping in the darkness of ignorance, yet are always being blessed with the True Light shining upon this world. This Light is of Mercy; it makes us contented with our present situation of discrimination, since behind our back there is a world of equality. This Light is of Wisdom; it makes us undisturbed in any circumstance of disturbance, since before our eyes there is a realm of the true peace. This Light still makes us repent of our one-sided love, hatred and anger, since Amida's proclamation of the Vow to save us universally reconciles us one another. Herein lies the significance of Shin Buddhism bearing upon our actual life—the significance the futuristic teachings alone can have, converting the goal to which death leads into the foundation by which life is firmly established. Now, it is through the power of the Original Vow of Amida that the Pure Land thus becomes the goal to which death leads and the foundation on which life rests; and, again, it is through "any one who calls upon My Name" that this power is realized in us. "Calling upon My Name"—this is the Nembutsu. Our next inquiry then is the subject of the Nembutsu.

2

"If we say the Nembutsu"

Practice with our bodies, through which Amida's Vow is realized in us

We have previously observed how Amida's Vow expresses His Will; and our faith consists in harbouring no doubt in our mind about the truthfulness of Amida's Will when we have heard the word of His Vow.

Faith then is the work of wisdom, since it means our having no doubt in the truth of the Original Vow of Amida; it is also a "nod of heart," since it means our obeisant accepting of His Will of Great Mercy. Hence, faith is said to be "Buddha's Wisdom" as well as "Buddha's Great Compassionate Heart." It is the truthfulness of Amida's Vow manifesting itself in our mind. Like the moon on the water, it is the Buddha's Will shining on our mind constantly to purify us sentient beings, who are always being defined by the passions of love and hatred.

Faith, however, is just the truthfulness of the Original Vow of Amida as perceived by our mind, and is not that as realized through our body. If the Original Vow is something not to be realized through our body, it will cease to function in us suffering mortals as the saving power. If the Original Vow is something ever meant to save us, it must realize its saving power on us through some practice with our body. And that practice with our body realizing the saving power of the Original Vow in us, is the Nembutsu, the calling upon the Name of the Buddha. If it were not for the Nembutsu, even the Mercy and Wisdom of the Buddha could never be realized as our Light and Life; neither could the Pure Land be the foundation on which our life rests and the goal to which our death leads. Consequently, if the Nembutsu were not practised, the Buddha's Original Vow would be rendered powerless; and our faith would be turned into mere thought. It is for this reason that the Buddha declares in His Vow that he will save those "who call upon My Name." It is thus only through the Nembutsu that the truthfulness of the Original Vow is rendered into a concrete fact.

Now, it is through the teachings of "the holy ones" that the truth of the Original Vow is made known to us. To hear "the good men's words," therefore, is the only way by which we can attain the truth of the Original Vow. This is why Shin Buddhism pays special respect to the tradition of the Nembutsu teachings, the main spring of which is the teaching of Śākyamuni the Awakened One. Nevertheless, if we do not practise the Nembutsu in conformity to these teachings, we shall never be able to become a faithful believer in the Original Vow of Amida. It is through the Nembutsu as direct cause and the holy teachings as indirect cause that we come to realize the purport of His Original Vow. Therefore, to believe in the Original Vow of Amida means to become one who practises the Nembutsu.

The practice of the Nembutsu consists in saying "*na-mu-a-mi-da-butsu.*" "*Na-mu*" of this phrase means "to direct towards and depend upon." To say "*na-mu-a-mi-da-butsu,*" therefore, is to express our sincere devotion to Amida Buddha, in which we direct ourselves towards Amida and depend upon Him. Here we see that the meditation on the Buddha (which is the original meaning of the word Nembutsu) and the calling upon His Name (which is the derived meaning of it) become one. Further the Nembutsu is the deed in accordance with the Original Vow of Amida, in which He declared that he would save "those who call upon My Name"; for this reason, the Nembutsu is regarded in Shin Buddhism as "the answer made by us to the merciful calling of Amida"; and, again, it is considered "the work pertaining to the Power of the Original Vow," This means that the Nembutsu is our bodily practice, through which channel Amida's Vow Power can flow into us sentient beings.

Nembutsu as the universal deed

The Original Vow, as we have mentioned above, wishes to save all sentient beings without exception; so, the deed that realizes the Vow should necessarily be something universally to be practised. It is for this reason that the Nembutsu is made the deed of the Original Vow. It can be practised by "any man," at "any time," and in "any place." In other words, the Buddha has singled out the Nembutsu as the deed of His Original Vow, just because He wished to carry those who are suffering in this world into the realm of equality and of the true peace by the vehicle of the Nembutsu which all of them can get on. Here in the Nembutsu the absolute truth of universal salvation vowed by Amida in His Original Vow is rendered into a concrete fact.

We now proceed to observe the significance of the universality of the Nembutsu practice.

The first thing we observe is the significance of the Nembutsu that can be practised by any man. Now, it is obvious enough that moral perfection is not something to be expected of all men. Even "the same level of moral excellence for all men" is never to be realized; for men each differ in their own capabilities and their social situations. Obviously, too, the achievement of those specially religious disciplines such as meditation and concentration is not to be expected for all men. Even though there are some people who can practise them according to their own capabilities, still they will find it difficult to demonstrate that all men shall be permitted through these practices to enter the realm of equality and of the true peace. In this respect, it is of really great significance that the following is said of the Nembutsu: "In calling upon the Name of the Buddha, no distinction is made between men and women, old and young, high and low, good and evil."

The second thing we observe is the significance of the Nembutsu that can be practised at any time and in any place. Now, it goes without mention that our religious sentiment is awakened by religious rites. But the religious rites need to be performed in some definite place and on some definite occasion, specially dedicated to the sacred. It is thus that we sit at the ceremony held in the temple and are removed from the cares of the world, being surrounded by the sacred atmosphere. Nevertheless, it is not restricted to the time when we sit at a ceremony in the temple that we are required to awaken the religious sentiment. It is rendered rather more necessary in our ordinary everyday times. When we are harassed by disorderly thoughts in our loneliness, or when we suffer from the conflicts of the passions of love and hatred in our intercourse with others—these are precisely the moments when we should practise the Nembutsu and be reminded of the Mercy of the Buddha. In these moments the Nembutsu will prove to be a deed of repentance or that of thanksgiving according to each circumstance. Herein lies the significance of the Nembutsu that can be practised at any time and in any place.

To practise the Nembutsu is to call upon the Name of the Buddha and listen to it quietly in one's heart. To say it much or to utter it loudly is not its purpose. What it aims at is "to achieve intimacy with the Name of the Buddha."

The virtue of the Nembutsu that purifies our karma and the world

Now let me explain why the realization of the Power of the Original Vow is to be found in the Nembutsu practice and not in so-called good works. It is because the Original Vow wishes to save all of us beings who are suffering from attachment to good and evil. In the eyes of Great Mercy, every mother's son is equally to be pitied, whether he is virtuous or wicked, either way being unable to get free from the bondage of the passions of love and hatred. It is for this reason that the Original Vow has not claimed moral virtues which could be relied on, neither has it demanded that evil natures are to be dreaded. It is also for this reason that it has recommended the practice of the Nembutsu without being trammeled in the idea of good and bad. In this connection, the following is one of the most impressive passages in the *Tannishō*.

> In believing this Vow, deeds of morality are not required, because there are no deeds of morality that can surpass the Nembutsu, neither should one be afraid of evil because there are no evils powerful enough to obstruct the way of Amida's Original Vow.

The apparent opposition between the Nembutsu and morality need by no means lead to any moral indifference. The Nembutsu will rather make us have much concern for morality, and help us to fulfill our moral obligations. The Nembutsu, inducing us ever to be mindful of the Buddha's Merciful Vow, gets us free from the attachment of good and evil and delivers us from the bondage of love and hatred. The Nembutsu thus purifies our mind and softens our heart. Herein lies the close connection between the Nembutsu and morality. The Nembutsu may not directly determine us in moral matters, but it will furnish the firm foundations on which a moral edifice will be brilliantly established.

Good and evil can only be talked of relatively. Therefore, if they remain as they stand and no reconciliation is made between them, the result will be constant disputes prevailing in the world; men will not cease to quarrel with one another, each contending that he is in the right. If self-vindication were carried out with a vengeance, no evil act would be found lacking something to justify it. If self-retrospection were made compulsory, each good deed would be found to have its dark side. It is for this reason that the contention, "I am in the right and you are in the wrong," may often be considered a grievously inconsiderate utterance. It is also for this reason that one's tears of repentance for evil conduct may often be regarded as a virtue softening the human heart. This being the case, one who has done some good deed should be thankful for the fortunate circumstances which enabled him to do so, and be careful not to fall into the error of self-conceit, taking himself alone for a virtuous man; and one who is conscious that he has done some evil deed should repent of his own sinfulness without vindicating himself with some plausible excuses. When we are thus aware of our real conditions, then the Light of Mercy-Wisdom will be realized to be shining on the virtuous as well as on the wicked. There the virtuous will get free from pride and the wicked from prejudice, and either of them will be awakened to the sense of brotherly love. And that which causes this is the Nembutsu. By the practice of the Nembutsu the passions of love and hatred are reconciled one to another, and the state of disturbance is quietened into the serenity of cessation.

Happiness and misery are said respectively to be the fruitions of good and evil. Accordingly, in the same way as good and evil are reconciled to one another through the practice of the Nembutsu, so happiness and misery should be harmonised one with another through the same practice of the Nembutsu. Indeed, it is the practice of the Nembutsu in our misery that makes us realize the boundless depth of Amida's Mercy and also the unfathomable abyss of our own wickedness. It is obvious enough that our spiritual life begins with our experience of suffering, so that it is said that without suffering one would be entirely a "lost soul" who cannot walk in the way of religion. When viewed from this standpoint, one who lives a so-called happy life cannot be said to be "happy" in the real sense of the word. For he is not given the occasion to know what real happiness is. It is the Nembutsu that induces such a person to examine himself in such a way as to repent of his own forgetfulness of the True Light ever shining on him. In this way the Nembutsu, as the liberator from the attachment to good and evil, induces us to turn to the fulfillment of moral obligations; and, again, as the deliverer from the bondage of happiness and misery, causes us to awaken to the sense of the real inner happiness.

3

"We shall become Buddha"

Ōsō and Gensō (Aspect of "going-into" and "coming-back")

The practice of the Nembutsu, as I have repeatedly said, is the work establishing life on firm foundations and for attaining the goal to which death leads; and it is because of this constitution of the Nembutsu that it can bestow the benign Light upon actual life. In other words, it is just because the Nembutsu will make us attain the Pure Land that it can give us the True Light in this world, and, when this is stated by us, from the Nembutsu followers' stand-point, it is just because we are blessed with the Light in our daily life of this world that we become assured of being reborn in the Pure Land. Shin Buddhism describes this state as *jūshōjōju hisshi metsudo*—"being established among the order of the steadfast and sure to attain the serenity of cessation."

Now the word "*metsudo*" (serenity of cessation) is the Chinese equivalent for the Sanskrit word "Nirvana."[1] Being specifically Buddhistic, the idea is considered to be most difficult to grasp. It means the serenity of cessation of life; hence it suggests death. It is a kind of death, indeed; nevertheless, the death it suggests is not that suffered by ordinary mortals but that experienced by the truly religious man. In the death of ordinary mortals the serene cessation of life can never take place, because they are sure to continue their transmigration, as they adhere to the idea of good and evil and also to the principle of happiness and misery. The serenity of cessation is attained only when good and evil, happiness and misery, are reconciled with one another owing to acceptance of the Vow through the practice of the Nembutsu.

Buddhists take delight in the "serenity of cessation." It is a kind of death in which human existence is exhausted. But, to die the death exhausting human existence necessarily means to be reborn in the eternally true world. Therefore, to lose "self-hood" in this world is to attain "Buddhahood" in the Pure Land. We are to become one with the Buddha by the death exhausting human existence through the practice of the Nembutsu. Thus becoming one with the Buddha, we ourselves come to participate in Amida's work, and contribute to the enhancement of the function of His Original Vow. Now, in Shin Buddhism, this process is called "*gensō-ekō*,"

---

1. Ed. That is, in Japanese pronunciation. This term was a translation into Chinese as *mièdù* 滅度 (J. *metsudo*), while a transliteration following the sound was *nièpán* 涅槃 (J. *nehan*).

representing the aspect of our coming back to this world from the Pure Land; while the other process is called "ōsō-ekō," representing the aspect of our going into the Pure Land from this world. Either of these processes is due to the power of the Original Vow; hence, "ekō."

In this way it is in our daily practice of the Nembutsu that we realize that we are being supported by our forefathers who are doing their work of *gensō-ekō*; and in it also we are reminded how our forefathers got through their own life of suffering through the same practice of the Nembutsu. Here again we look forward to the future when we, who become one with the Buddha to participate in His work, shall be able to support those who will come after us by means of our work of *gensō-ekō*. We are expecting this.

In this way, the tradition of the Nembutsu, the source of which is the Pure Land eternal and true, has taken possession of the minds of millions of people in the Orient from generation to generation; and, constituting the core of spiritual life, it will continue to exist as the undercurrent of human history, keeping its course silently but steadily, and exercising its influence on the surface world where all kinds of disturbances and vicissitudes will take place in the form of rise and fall and peace and war.

Jiri and Rita (the work of self-profiting and that of others-profiting)

To be reborn in the Pure Land through the practice of the Nembutsu is to achieve one's own salvation; hence, it is the *jiri* work of profiting one's own self. To do the work of *gensō-ekō* after having become one with the Buddha is to support those who will come after us; hence, it is the *rita* work of profiting others. This being the case, when "we believe in the Original Vow and say the Nembutsu, and attain Buddhahood," we shall have made complete both the *jiri* work and the *rita* work.

The question will naturally arise, what are the mutual relations between one's own self and other selves. As to this, we should remember that on the one hand one's own self is one's own self to all intents and purposes: for, there is no denying the existence of the individual. On the other hand however, we must recognize that one's own self is closely related to other selves in such a way as to represent the whole of mankind. We are the members of society, each representing the whole of mankind. Hence it follows that we each should be responsible for each and every event which takes place in our society. For this reason we feel that, as long as there are in our society some people who commit crimes, we cannot afford to call ourselves virtuous. The social situation is a mirror reflecting our own image. So long as moral decadence actually exists, we cannot say, "I for one am blameless."

Human wisdom, however, sets a limit to the scope of human responsibilities, and tries to make each individual responsible only for his allotted share. In one sense, this is inevitable; for, if it were not arranged in this way, neither politics nor morality would be rendered practicable. And we see here the reason why it should be said that all the mundane matters are only relative, including all the talks on right and wrong and on good and evil. To us, the Nembutsu followers, it seems that all these limitations and apportionments of responsibilities are mere compromises set up for convenience' sake. We are convinced that we, each representing the whole of mankind, should take all responsibilities upon our respective shoulders; and also that one who ought to bear all responsibilities should be one's own self which is the individual. Therefore, it comes to this that where one is awakened to his own self which is the individual, there he comes to answer for the whole of mankind.

This being the case, the concrete fact of the salvation of the individual necessarily involves the principle by which the whole of mankind can be saved; and the principle capable of saving the whole of mankind is evidenced by the concrete fact that the individual is saved. Consequently, it must be said that it is no other than the salvation of the individual which opens the way for the universal salvation of the whole of mankind. Nevertheless, the salvation of the individual as it is actuated by the Other Power of the Original Vow of Amida is not to be extended to others by our own efforts. We cannot declare, "I have achieved my own salvation, now I shall extend it to others." For, we are always living in the world where salvation is essentially impossible except by the Original Vow of Amida. Here lies the reason why we confine ourselves to our own salvation, as long as we are living in this world; and, as to the salvation of the whole of mankind, look forward to the future when we come back to this world and do the work of *gensō-ekō*.

Further, it is here implied that the Nembutsu follower dares not to take himself for the leader of the world. He is convinced that that which can save the world is the tradition of the Nembutsu teachings caused by the Power of the Original Vow of Amida. On this account, the propagation of the doctrine conducted by the Shin follower consists solely in clarifying the purport of the Original Vow and in making oneself and others to hear it. He does not attempt to force others to believe it. Men are saved only when the cause and condition of their salvation are brought to maturity. This being the case, the sense of joy the Nembutsu followers embrace when they welcome a new brother to the same practice of the Nembutsu is all the more great; for, truly mutual and heartfelt friendship is to be enjoyed only through the agency of that same practice of the Nembutsu. We take it indeed that, except for the Original Vow of Amida, there is no universal principle capable of saving all humanity. Nevertheless, we feel that, as to the attestation of this truth, we have no other way than this, that we shall become conscious of its work in our own practice of the

Nembutsu. We feel that the fundamental principle of true peace of the world has long been prepared in the Orient; only it is a great regret that Japan has not yet realized this as a fact—still in the present day.

The present age and our present situation

Lastly, let me observe how Shin followers take the present age and men's present situation.

Now, the Shin followers claim their religion to be "the only religion in conformity with the times and men's capacities." In these words is suggested their awakened attitude towards the prevailing conditions of the times. It may be said it is their sense of the times which will constitute the basis of their world view. We feel that we of the present age can have no hope, both within and without. We have keenly felt this these last ten years.[2] We are living in an age when salvation is quite impossible except by the Original Vow of Amida.

History moves beyond our will. As to the stream of the times, we cannot swim against it, nor can we remain its unconcerned spectators. To swim against it is to lose one's life to no purpose, while to remain its unconcerned spectators is to lose touch with the times. And yet, the power of the times is actually controlling us. We have no other way than to follow it. We must say, therefore, that if the present situation does not permit us to live like human being, it is inevitable for us to live like an animal. We have no choice. Argumentations are all idle talks.

However, we Nembutsu followers cannot but feel that we are sinful, for it is indeed due to our karma that we are destined to live in an age such as this. And our view of sin consists in proving ourselves blamable. We ourselves are blamable, because we ourselves are through our own karma the makers of all the evils of the times. Here we are convinced that we ought not to take advantage of the times. Those who do so seize every opportunity afforded by the times and busy themselves in making money and in gaining honours. The so-called ideologies are advocated from the same motive. But these are the doings of men who do not believe in the Eternally True World. We who are awakened to its presence will do nothing but to obey the dictate of the times and do what we think the best in the circumstances under which we are placed. And this "best" does exist even in an animal-like existence. The practice of the Nembutsu will open the way for us to go serenely. In this sense, it may be said that the Nembutsu followers are given a freedom that knows no obstacle in any age whatever.

But it is due to the fact that they always concentrate their minds on the serenity of cessation even while they are obedient to the dictate of

---

2. Ed. That is, since 1941, the beginning of Japan's involvement in the Second World War.

the times, that the Nembutsu followers are thus blessed with the way of freedom. Śākyamuni who had his mind set upon Nirvana, said, "I do not contend with the world, neither do I become defiled by the world." All systems of thought hinge on attachment to life. But the Buddhist doctrine rests on the serenity of cessation of life. A doctrine of this kind may not directly lay down how society should be but, if society disregards this kind of doctrine, it will not be able to stand strong and firm. For this reason, I should like to say, with Shinran the founder of Shin Buddhism, "May Peace reign in the world, and the Dharma be diffused."

The Meaning of Salvation in the Doctrine of Pure Land Buddhism

Kaneko Daiei

It goes without saying that, for all its profound philosophical systems, Buddhism is essentially a doctrine of liberation. In Buddhism, no salvation is conceivable except the liberation through Enlightenment from the bondage of ignorance and suffering. But does this apply equally to the doctrine of Pure Land Buddhism (the Shin and other Pure Land schools of Buddhism) in which faith in Amida (Amitābha Buddha) has prime importance, or is Pure Land Buddhism virtually a soteriological religion, despite its Buddhist background?

In this article, I, as a Buddhist thinker, shall attempt to make clear the meaning of salvation in the doctrine of Pure Land Buddhism.

1

Suffering

Semantically, the term "salvation" means the liberation or emancipation of someone from the predicament into which he is fallen. This is equally true of the Japanese term *sukui* or *kyūsai*.[1] In other words, "salvation" semantically presupposes some predicament, whatever it may be. What, then, is the human situation which Buddhism envisages as the predicament from which man should be liberated? The Buddhist answer to this question is widely known: "The suffering of life." But the term "suffering of life" is vague and indefinite in meaning. It needs further definition and clarification. What does it specifically mean? To make its meaning clear, we should turn our eyes to human life as an ever flowing duration or continuum.

One thing to be noted about our life is that it flows on, ever alternating between "doing" and "undergoing." This alternation between doing and undergoing, however, is by no means a lawless, order-less movement. It

---

1. *Kyūsai* 救済 is a compound of the Chinese characters, *kyū* 救 which means "to keep one from harm," and *sai* 済 which means "to ferry one across."

is ruled by a kind of law, so to speak, a law of inter-causation or mutual conditioning. We do, and our "doing" inevitably makes its influence felt on our way of feeling, sensing and thinking, directly as well as indirectly (through its effects on our environment). Our way of feeling, sensing and thinking, thus influenced, then inevitably conditions the further steps of our doing.

It is true that an awareness of this law has been expressed very early in mythology and folklore, and later in religion, philosophy and psychology. It is, indeed, one aspect of wisdom that underlies the process of human civilization. Broadly speaking, however, the bearers of this wisdom have been those who have naively affirmed life with its impulses, cravings and desires, and have sought to gratify life's wants ever better; that is, they applied their awareness of this law for the better enjoyment of life. Life itself was never radically questioned. They remained strangers to the tragic sense of life and to the negation of life. Their wisdom had something analogous to the "wisdom of instinct," as Fabre called it.

Buddhism started with a keen sense of the painfulness of life and sought in all seriousness to penetrate to the nature and origination of the suffering of life. It declared that no human experience could be free from suffering. In other words, the life as we actually live it is, after all, suffering. This declaration may sound bold and too pessimistic. However, it should be remembered that the declaration is made from the viewpoint of Enlightenment, from a penetrating insight into the origination of suffering.

Buddhism teaches that all sufferings of life originate in delusion (*kleśa*). Intellectually, delusion is ignorance (*avidyā*), that is, the ignorance of the emptiness (*śūnyatā*) or suchness (*tathatā*) of things and events. Emotionally, delusion is primarily a thirsty craving (*tṛṣṇā*). Possessed by delusion, we are irresistibly involved in matters of love and hate, gain and loss, honour and dishonour, aggression and defence, in short, in things and events of the world. The result is that we suffer.

The process of our life alternating between doing and undergoing referred to above is thus seen by Buddhism as a vicious circle under the spell of delusion between doing (karma) and suffering. Delusion causes us to do deluded things in our actual life; the deluded things done cause us to suffer; and the suffering tends to cause us to become more and more deluded, and so on endlessly. The law that rules over this process is the law of karmic causation.

The origination of suffering as stated above makes the nature of suffering clear. In Buddhism, suffering primarily means the painful uneasiness or anxiety of being deluded. As such, suffering is pregnant with an urge, even if subconscious or semiconscious, to break through delusion. It is precisely in this sense that suffering is declared to be universal in human life. Some one might be conscious of such suffering, but very feebly and only in the exceptional moments of affliction or depression. Another might have no experience of it. Nevertheless, no one is exempt from such suffering, as long as he is human. In other words, everyone is potentially a sufferer.

2

Our Inner Togetherness

One thing should be remembered in connection with the problem of suffering: everyone of us human beings is deeply interrelated with fellow beings in an *inner togetherness*. It can hardly be doubted that we are so born as to be sensitive of our inner togetherness. Do we not implicitly mean this when we use the term "we"? In this sense, our inner togetherness may be called "we-ness." As long as our fellow beings are unhappy, none of us can remain aloof from them. We cannot but share the unhappiness with them. Because of the inner togetherness of man, sympathy can be awakened within us.

The consciousness of the inner togetherness of man finds its fullest and most sublime expressions in the sphere of religion. Mahāyāna Buddhism is especially emphatic about the principle of "seeking for emancipation from suffering together with fellow beings." In the *Vimalakīrtinirdeśa* we read, "I [Vimalakīrtī] suffer, because my fellow beings suffer." This is precisely what the term compassion (*karuṇā*) means. The Mahāyāna principle of "together with fellow beings" may naturally lead to the vision of the Dharma: The Dharma through which I am truly saved from suffering must be the same Dharma through which all my fellow beings are equally saved, that is, the Dharma that is adequate to all the human beings. But what, then, is meant by the term "adequate"?

We actually live in a world in which we find ourselves bound to others by family, neighbourhood, occupational, religious, political and other countless ties. Our life situation is largely conditioned by these ties. Above all the family tie has a fundamental importance in conditioning our life situation. Most men and women are actually living a home life. No one doubts that home life is the normal way of living. The life of the homeless one, secluded from family and society, however sublime its purpose may be, is exceptional. Most people make much of their home and family, and are ready to accept all the cares accompanying their home life. They believe that man is so born as to live and love home life for all its cares and troubles. It is true that home life is exposed to the danger of disintegration in the highly industrialized society of today. Nevertheless, the home does not seem to have lost its primary importance in human life.

However, it is definitely in the home as well as in social life that we experience the full strength of delusion over us. The foliage of delusion is exuberant on the soil of home and social life. The delusive passions such as attachment, hatred, anger, fear, jealousy, enmity, perverseness and aggressiveness become intensified in the tensions of human relationships. It is undoubtedly such delusive passions and their results that afflict us. Suffering is thus inevitable for us beings in the world. To suffer because of being submerged in the world—this is precisely our existential situation.

The Chinese Buddhist master, Shàndǎo,[2] undoubtedly had this existential situation in mind when he wrote as follows:

> I am actually an ordinary, sinful being who has been, from time immemorial, sunken in and carried down by the current of birth-and-death. Any hope to be helped out of this current has been wholly denied to me.[3]

Some commentary may be needed on those words. By the term "I" Shàndǎo definitely means the we-ness or inner togetherness referred to above. He represents here all the human beings in the world. Otherwise, this sentence is not meaningful. The "sinfulness" mentioned here does not refer to any personal sin, but to the sinfulness of the delusion of human existence itself. The phrase "from time immemorial" may be taken to express how long the delusive circle between karma and suffering has been repeated up to the present. In short, this passage expresses a penetrating insight into the existential situation in which man is inevitably bound to suffering, and as such still has a vital meaning for the present day world. The doctrine of Pure Land Buddhism has appeared as the Dharma that is truly adequate to such an existential situation of man, the Dharma through which alone we can be saved as we are in the world, that is, without deserting home or social life.

3

The Dharma adequate to all ordinary beings

The doctrine of Pure Land Buddhism has a long history of transmission throughout India, China and Japan. Among the masters who transmitted the doctrine, Tánluán[4] and the above-cited Shàn Dǎo were exceedingly

---

2. Shàndǎo 善導 (613–681, known in Japanese as Zendō), an eminent Chinese Buddhist master, especially important in the Pure Land traditions of Buddhism in China and Japan.

3. Shàndǎo, *Kangyōsho* 観経疏 *A Commentary on the Meditation-sūtra* (Ed. Abbreviation for *Kanmuryōjukyōsho /Guānwúliàngshòu jīngshù* 觀無量壽經疏), Vol. 4: Exposition of the goods that are meant for the practically minded (not the contemplatively disposed) to practice.

4. Tánluán 曇鸞 (476–542, known in Japanese as Donran), an eminent Chinese

influential over their own times and over posterity. But the fundamental significance of the Pure Land doctrine as the Dharma truly adequate to all ordinary beings was for the first time positively established by the Japanese master, Hōnen 法然 (1133–1212),[5] who resolutely declared the independence of the Pure Land doctrine from all other Buddhist schools. The depth of Hōnen's faith which remained as yet unexpressed by himself was subsequently fully grasped and given a profound and most thoroughgoing expression by Shinran 親鸞 (1173–1262).[6] The mark that distinguishes both these masters is their decided preference of "our" salvation to "my" emancipation. They firmly stood on the ground of the inner togetherness of man.

In his childhood, Hōnen was exhorted by his dying father, who was murdered by his jealous competitor, to become a Buddhist monk and quest for the Dharma through which is emptied every discrimination between friend and foe, love and hate, and through which true peace is attained. He followed his father's dying will and became a monk of the Tendai sect of Buddhism. His elaborate study of the *sūtra*s and *śāstra*s, as well as his rigorous disciplinary practices for many years in the monastery on Mt. Hiei, were exclusively devoted to the purpose of attaining that Dharma. But all his efforts brought him no light. This is no wonder, considering that the Buddhist quest which had been traditionally undertaken in the monastery was fundamentally directed to the personal emancipation of each monk, while Hōnen's quest was exclusively for the salvation of all human beings in the world. Had his chief concern been personal emancipation, he would have believed that he was steadily marching on the right path to the goal.

The sinfulness of man was continually a problem that confronted Hōnen. The popular belief of the day that sinfulness can be expiated by the virtue of leaving home and becoming a Buddhist monk was unacceptable to him. Sinfulness was nothing other than the deluded-ness because of which man endlessly alternates between evil karma and suffering, thus afflicting others as well as himself. As such it was definitely a problem of man, not a mere personal problem. The personal solution of

---

Buddhist master, especially important in the Pure Land traditions of Buddhism in China and Japan. His main work is *A Commentary on Vasubandhu's Treatise on the Pure Land* (往生論註 *Wǎngshēnglùn zhù*).

5. Hōnen, the founder of the Pure Land (Jōdo) school of Buddhism in Japan and teacher to Shinran. His main work is the *Senjakushū* 選択集 Ed. Short for *Senjakuhongannenbutsushū* 選択本願念仏集, *Selected Passages on the Nenbutsu of the Original Vow*. The short title is pronounced *Senchakushū* in Jōdo Shin-shū contexts.

6. Shinran, the founder of the Shin (Jōdo Shin) school of Buddhism. The most important of his numerous works is the *Kyōgyōshinshō* 教行信証.

this problem might be conceivable, of course, and in fact a great number of Buddhist monks have sought a solution of this sort. The sense of our inner togetherness, however, makes this sort of solution less meaningful. Unless "we" can be saved, what is the meaning of "my" emancipation? Hōnen thus exclusively sought the Dharma through which all the human beings can be equally saved, and at last he discovered this Dharma in the Pure Land doctrine.

In this connection, reference may be given to the critical view that faith in the Pure Land is dominantly motivated by the desire for happiness or enjoyment after death. As regards the deteriorated and secularized form of the Pure Land cult which is observable among the masses, this criticism is irrefutable. Regarding the genuine form of faith in the Pure Land, however, it is completely wrong. As stated above, in Pure Land Buddhism and, accordingly, in the genuine faith in the Pure Land, the prime concern is the salvation of all of us human beings from the predicament of suffering. This concern is really furthest from the egocentric desire for happiness and enjoyment. The spirit of Mahāyāna Buddhism which emphasizes "seeking Enlightenment together with all fellow beings" is most vitally and thoroughly embodied in Pure Land Buddhism.

4

The Pure Land and the Original Vow

In the first section I made a reference to suchness, stating that suchness is emptiness, and vice versa. In other words, suchness is the reality of things and events. Beyond suchness no Ultimate Reality is conceivable. It is primarily because of ignorance that we remain blind to suchness and are attached to the illusory images and views of things and events.

It is, however, the common faith of all Buddhists that suchness is attainable for everyone. In this respect, the Pure Land Buddhists are no exception. But the Pure Land Buddhists have something unique in their view of suchness. For they believe that while suchness is attainable in principle for everyone, one would never be able to embody suchness in one's own personality as long as one remains in the world. To remain in the world means not to be liberated from the power of delusion. With this thought, they paid keen attention to the dynamic aspect of suchness. What, then, is the dynamic aspect of suchness?

In the first place, guided by the *sūtras* relating to the Pure Land, they learned to comprehend suchness in terms of land, namely, as the Pure Land. As the land of suchness which illumines, empties and purifies our delusion, the Pure Land is the land of Wisdom (*jñāna*, as flowing out of *prajñā*). Shinran defined it as the land of infinite light (Wisdom). Suchness now appears as the land of infinite light. Illumined by the light of

The Meaning of Salvation in the Doctrine of Pure Land Buddhism

the Pure Land, we come to know the delusiveness of this world. Such is the basic conception of the Pure Land. But the dynamic aspect of suchness cannot be fully expressed by the idea of the Pure Land alone.

Secondly, the Pure Land masters further learned to comprehend the dynamic character of suchness in terms of personality, namely, as the Original Vow of Amida Tathāgata. The term "tathāgata" means "the one who emerges out of suchness." "Amida" means "infinite," being derived from *amitayūs* and *amitābha*.[7] As such Amida Tathāgata symbolizes the dynamic operation of suchness which is expressed as infinite compassion and Wisdom, even though he appears as an individual Buddha in the *sūtras* relating to him. According to the *Larger Sutra of Eternal Life*,[8] out of the sincerest desire of delivering all beings from suffering Amida took an incomparably excellent vow when he was in the original, disciplinary stage as a Bodhisattva (Dharmākara by name), which he has already fulfilled. This vow is called the Original Vow. The Original Vow is thus Amida's fullest self-expression and, accordingly, the sublimest self-expression of suchness in terms of tathāgata-hood or bodhisattva-hood.

The *Larger Sūtra* shows that the Original Vow is differentiated into forty-eight items. They are interrelated with each other in a subtle way. They cannot be discussed fully in this paper, but for the present the following should be remembered as the essentials of the Original Vow:

1. It is vowed that Amida's Name should appear as embodying all the virtues or efficiencies that have any bearing whatever on the salvation or deliverance of all human beings, and, when the Name appears, it should sound throughout the lands in ten directions.[9]

2. It is vowed that anyone who, hearing Amida's Name praised, awakens faith in Amida's Sincerity and keeps Amida's Name with him, should be assuredly reborn in the Pure Land.

3. It is vowed that the Pure Land should be completed as the land in which all the reborn ones should attain nirvana.

We notice from the descriptions above that two important things are vowed in the Original Vow regarding the problem of our salvation: one

---

7. Ed. The Sanskrit names Amitayūs and Amitābha mean "immeasurable life" and "immeasurable light" respectively.

8. Ed. I.e. the *Daimuryōjukyō*, also referred to in brief as the *Larger Sūtra*, cf. Synoptic List of Text Titles.

9. In the tradition of Pure Land Buddhism, the term "Name" as applied to Amida Tathāgata is something much more than name in the usual sense of the term. According to the tradition, Amida's Name stores all of his virtues or efficiencies and, when uttered, the virtues are actualized in the utterer himself. How to interpret the actualization of the virtues has been a problem for the nembutsu-adherents to tackle existentially.

is the rebirth in the Pure Land; the other is the awakening of faith in Amida's Sincerity.

The rebirth in the Pure Land that is held to take place after death has been the central concern of most Pure Land masters as well as followers for a long time. It was really inconceivable for them to attain Enlightenment in this life. The Buddhist monastic disciplines were so difficult to accomplish. They wished to attain Enlightenment after death in the Pure Land, relying on Amida's Original Vow. As a general tendency, faith in Amida's Original Vow was regarded merely as a requisite to the rebirth. They hardly realized the profound significance of the awakening of faith. It is, indeed, Shinran who for the first time realized this in its full significance. He was revolutionary in shifting the prime importance, hitherto attached to the problem of rebirth or Enlightenment, to the problem of the awakening of faith. Faith is essential; once true faith is awakened and established, the rebirth in the Pure Land will take place as a natural result. For Shinran, the awakening of faith in Amida's Sincerity really meant salvation.

5

The Awakening of Faith in Amida's Sincerity

Shinran coped in all seriousness and tenacity with the problem of faith. He suffered long in his search for pure faith. Any form of faith, so long as it remains an expression of the will to believe, can never be pure. It is branded with a self-willed character. It is mixed and defiled with calculation, self-interest, suppressed doubt, etc. Pure faith must be something cleared of all this defilement and mixture. As such genuine faith is most difficult to attain, because it could not take place without some otherness coming from beyond and working upon us. How, then, does pure faith in Amida become possible for us?

Influenced by Shàndǎo's *Commentary on the Meditation Sūtra*, Shinran came to hit upon the "Sincerity" of Amida. He learned to see all that Amida did—and does—as the expression of Amida's Sincerity. The Original Vow itself is the loftiest, most sublime expression of his Sincerity. Suchness has now appeared as Sincerity in the Tathāgata-hood of Amida. Ever disclosing himself in the sound of his Name, Amida the All-Sincere One untiringly works upon us. He turns himself over us. His Sincerity radiates itself as boundless illumination and compassion. Precisely as a genuine response called forth by his Sincerity, the awakening of faith in Amida's Original Vow takes place in us, when the time is fully ripe.

In the awakening of faith, we experience a breaking through at the root of the delusion. We realize how delusive, insincere and sinful we have been. Our self-complacency breaks down at this moment. We are emptied through and through. At the same moment, however, we find ourselves decisively taken in by Amida's Sincerity. We for the first time attain true restfulness, because the deepest root of our existential anxiety or suffering, namely, ignorance, is cut through for ever. It is still true that the foliage of actual sufferings does not perish; so long as we remain in the world, there is no escaping them. We have to undergo them. But they no longer disturb the fundamental restfulness and serenity. Further, in this experience of awakening we find ourselves firmly standing on the way which leads straight to the Pure Land. It is the way of nembutsu or going with Amida's Name.

What, then, is the nembutsu? It is definitely *our* act, *our* practice, which has been chosen by Amida for *us* to do in the Original Vow. Regarding the nembutsu as our act, Hōnen declares as follows:

> By nembutsu I do not mean the practice of contemplating as engaged in by the sages of China and our country. Nor is it the recitation of the Buddha's name practised as the result of understanding the meaning of the term *nen* 念 (thinking). It is just to recite *Namu-Amida-Butsu* without doubting that this will issue in rebirth in the Pure Land.[10]

Both the contemplative form of nembutsu and the vocal form of nembutsu as resulting from some special understanding are rejected by Hōnen, because they are after all, distortions into special forms of nembutsu capable of being practiced only by the gifted ones. None of these practices can be our act as originally intended by Amida. The nembutsu intended by Amida himself as *our* act, Hōnen concludes, consists of reciting "*Namu-Amida-Butsu*," that is, calling Amida's Name, out of faith in his Original Vow. As such, the nembutsu originates in Amida's Sincerity itself. Its significance is clear: it is meant to be that which everyone of us can easily practice. It is precisely that which enables us to go straight along the way of "no hindrance." Shinran, too, when he developed a profound comprehension of the nembutsu, took the same position as Hōnen.

6

The maturing of the time for the awakening of faith

Our next problem is: How do we come to be awakened to Amida's Sincerity and surrender ourselves to it? How does the time become mature and full for the awakening of faith? From the viewpoint of practice, I would like to emphasize that the time is matured for faith through—and only through—the nembutsu.

According to Kiyozawa Manshi, it is not that we believe in the Tathāgata because of his existence but the Tathāgata exists because of our faith in

---

10. From Hōnen's *One-Sheet Document* (*Ichimaikishōmon* 一枚起請文). Ed. *Namu-Amida-Butsu* 南無阿弥陀佛 i.e. the *nenbutsu*.

him.[11] This is basically true of the relationship between the Tathāgata's existence and the practice of the nembutsu: It is not that we practice the nembutsu because of the Tathāgata's existence; the Tathāgata exists because of our practice of nembutsu.

In the last analysis, nembutsu, and nothing but nembutsu, makes us realize what the Tathāgata is in reality. It is true that we are attracted to the nembutsu by hearing of Amida Tathāgata, but it is even more true that Amida's Sincerity becomes really understandable and appreciable to us through the nembutsu. It is more than probable that it was from this insight that Amida himself specifically chose, in his Original Vow, the nembutsu as *our* practice. In this sense, I would prefer to say: "In the beginning, the nembutsu was."

In the process of the life of nembutsu, time is matured for the awakening of faith. At the outset, however, the nembutsu expresses our urgent need for salvation from suffering. Under the pressure of existential suffering, we cry, so to speak, for salvation while calling the Name of Amida. But there is no hope of this need being satisfied from without by, say, some saviour god. The need is not the kind of need which can be satisfied in such a way. What we can do in this situation is, in so far as we are existentially inclined to the teaching of nembutsu, patiently to seek to realize the deepest meaning of the teaching, while intently practicing the nembutsu.

A revolution takes place in our nembutsu-mindedness itself when the time is ripe. The nembutsu is no more a mere expression of our desire for salvation this moment; it now appears as the very vehicle through which Amida's Sincerity of awakening and receiving us becomes fully audible and understandable. We who have been calling Amida's Name for salvation now turn out to be the ones who, all the while, have been called by Amida to awake and take refuge in him. The well-known definition of religion by Schleiermacher as the "feeling (or consciousness) of absolute dependence" becomes acceptable to the Pure Land Buddhists, too, on the ground of this revolutionary experience. Shinran himself has written: "The Tathāgata has already taken his Vow and turned over the Act (that is, the nembutsu completed by himself) to us for our Act."[12]

As mentioned in the previous section, so long as we still live in the world, the actual sufferings of life do not cease to press upon us even after we are awakened to Amida's Sincerity. But we do not now des-

---

11. Kiyozawa Manshi (1863–1903), an eminent Buddhist leader in Japan in the Meiji Era. As for his thought, refer to S. Yamabe (ed.), *Selected Essays of Manshi Kiyozawa* (tr. by K. Tajima and F. Shacklock), 1936.

12. Shinran, *Kyōgyōshinshō* 教行信証 (*Teaching, Practice, Faith and Enlightenment*. Full title: *Collection of Passages Revealing the True teaching, Practice and Enlightenment of the Pure Land*), Vol. 2: The collection of passages relating to the practice that is true and real.

perately grope for the liberation from suffering. We are always with Amida's Name, that is, with nembutsu, wherever we may be or wherever we may go. We never call Amida's Name without returning at that same moment to the fundamental restfulness and serenity of being saved by Amida's Sincerity. This return to the original experience of the awakening of faith refreshes us and enables us to brace ourselves for natural but courageous living. We are thus, through nembutsu, enabled to pass the impassable current of sufferings in every moment. To be enabled to pass the impassable—this is precisely what salvation means in the Pure Land doctrine. This life of nembutsu is designated as the way that leads straight to the Pure Land.

7

The fruits which faith bears in actual life

What fruits does faith in the Pure Land bear in actual life? Does it introduce something novel into life?

As already observed, Pure Land Buddhism has disclosed itself as the Dharma which is truly adequate to *our* existential situation. From this fact it naturally follows that the Pure Land doctrine makes its adherents all the more sensitive of the inner togetherness and interrelatedness of human beings. Once we are awakened to the Original Vow that has been vowed for all beings, we can no more look on others' follies or evil deeds with coldness; we can no more look on other's suffering with indifference. In a similar situation or under similar conditions, each of us might have done the same thing. We are all "ordinary beings," as Prince Shōtoku has declared. With this thought we are emptied of all unreasonable contempt for evil-doers and actors of folly. Arrogance now gives place to humility. What we can do is, first of all, to pray heartily that all our fellow beings, including the persons in question, might awaken to Amida's boundless Sincerity and boundless compassion, as expressed in the Original Vow; then we must do all that we can do to help bring about this awakening.

It is the experience of the awakening of faith which, emptying and purifying us of delusive thoughts and emotions, enables us to live in accordance with suchness, that is, to live naturally. This life of naturalness is lived in and through the practice of nembutsu. The humility just mentioned is one aspect of the life of naturalness. Another aspect of this life is *tenderness* or tender-heartedness. The boundless compassion of Amida, when we awaken to it and accept it, melts away to tenderness our deep-seated obstinacy and self-complacency. We are thus enabled to confront every problem open-mindedly, flexibly and without prejudice.

This reminds us that in Buddhism any wrath whatsoever is rejected as sin. Even if the wrath is an emphatic expression of the justice of God, that makes no difference to Buddhism. Wrath is a violent, destructive emotion. It must be melted and transformed into tenderness by the boundless compassion of Amida.

In its expression in human relationships, tenderness may bear something in common with tolerance. This something should not, however, be confused with the toleration which is based on the temporary, political suppression of the impulse to justify oneself and blame the other. The tolerance on the part of the nembutsu-adherents is essentially rooted in repentance and humility for the fact that the same evil (which is "tolerated") is finally characteristic of us all. Further, the selflessness of repentance and humility exerts an immense influence upon others. It naturally calms others and induces them to reflect upon themselves. It thus helps to purify others. The repentance and humility spring from faith in Amida's boundless Sincerity and are renewed every moment through the nembutsu. It is in this sense that the nembutsu is called the "purifying act." The nembutsu purifies not only the nembutsu-adherents themselves but also those who come into contact with them.

In this connection, a reference may be made to Shinran's assertion that "the nembutsu is the way of no-hindrance."[13] A careless reading might suggest that Shinran is here emphasizing the overwhelming supernatural power of the nembutsu to clear away every hindrance and obstacle blocking the nembutsu-adherent's way to the Pure Land. But this is a sheer misunderstanding. The word "no-hindrance" should be interpreted never in terms of *power* but always in terms of *spirituality*. Shinran's statement should be interpreted as follows: The nembutsu-adherent naturally confronts with tenderness and humility every problem that comes about. The tenderness and humilty themselves make for no-hindrance. Consequently, Shinran's idea of no-hindrance bears no colour of licence or antinomianism.

All of the above has a vital bearing on the problem of morality. What, then, is the basic attitude of the nembutsu-adherent to the problem of morality? They all pay due respect to the importance of morality. It is a pity, however, that we can never do good in the complete sense of the term, considering the fact that our impulse to justify ourselves and to blame others is finally characteristic of us all. This fact shows how deep we have been submerged in the current of birth-and-death, as deplored by Shàn Dǎo. Therefore, we need by every means to listen to, to awaken to, and thus to be purified by the Original Vow.

Not out of the consciousness of moral obligation or duty, but immediately out of the humility which arises from being awakened to Amida's Sincerity, the nembutsu-adherent seeks to attain a warm reconciliation

---

13. *Tannishō* 歎異抄 *Notes Lamenting Differences* (recording sayings of Shinran by Yuienbō, one of Shinran's direct disciples), Section 7.

and communion with others. It has often been the case with excellent nembutsu-adherents that the humility, tenderness and gratefulness to Amida which shine out of their personality, quite naturally influence others around them and thus bring about genuine peace in their local community. Is not such virtue surely what morality envisages as its ideal? Bearing this in mind, Shinran says, "There is no good that surpasses the nembutsu."[14]

World peace is our urgent, serious problem. It goes without saying that it can never be brought about by any temporizing measures. Political toleration or appeasement will not avail much. The foundation of peace must be firmly laid in the depth of human nature. In this situation, the doctrine of Pure Land Buddhism may well be rediscovered as a valuable source for bringing peace. I do not mean that the awakening to the Original Vow of Amida Tathāgata is a panacea for all the problems of man. However, it should never be overlooked that Pure Land Buddhism has long been, and continues to be in the present, the Dharma that is adequate to the existential situation of all ordinary beings, and, further, that it has borne to the nembutsu adherents above described spiritual fruits, all of which have great importance for the problem of peace.

(English adaptation by Hiroshi Sakamoto)

---

14. *Tannishō*, Section 1.

Goodness and Naturalness

Kanamatsu Kenryō

1

In Book V, the "True Buddha-land," of the *Doctrine-Work-Faith-Attainment* (*Kyōgyōshinshō*),[1] which is the fundamental text-book of the Shin-shū or the Shin sect of Buddhism, Shinran Shōnin 親鸞聖人 (1173–1262), the founder of the sect, declares, quoting from the *Larger Sūtra on Amitābha* (*Daiamidakyō*):

> The Light of the Buddha Amida[2] is the Supreme Good, and the brightest and nicest of all good. It is so pleasant that it is unparalleled and unsurpassed in its pleasantness. The Light of the Buddha Amida is pure and clean; flawless and undefiled. And it never wanes nor diminishes. The Light of the Buddha Amida is so excellent that it is infinitely superior to the light of the sun and the moon... There is no human being, no mollusk that does not see the Light of the Buddha Amida. There is no one who, having gazed upon the Light, does not feel blissful and joyous. Of the people in this world who are given to debauchery, or ablaze with anger, or obscured with ignorance, there is no one who, having gazed upon the Light of the Buddha Amida, does not do good... The Light and the Name of the Buddha Amida pervades the immeasurable and innumerable Buddha-lands in the eastern, southern, western, and northern quarters, above and below, in the cardinal and intermediate points. Of all the celestial and human beings there is no one who does not hear the Name of the Buddha Amida, and there is no one who, having heard it, does not attain deliverance.

Or again in Book VI, he says: " 'The Ground of Good' is no other than the Blessed Name of the Nyorai.[3] In the Blessed Name is perfectly em-

---

1. Or *Teaching, Practice, Faith and Enlightenment*.
2. That is, the Buddha of Infinite Light and Eternal Life. Amida is the Japanese reading of the Sanskrit Amitābha, which means the "Infinite (*amita*) Light (*ābhā*)," or Amitāyus, which means the "Eternal (*amita*) Life (*āyus*)."
3. Nyorai (Tathāgata in Sanskrit) is an epithet of the Buddha. Nyo (*tathā*) means

bodied all good. The Blessed Name is the ground of all goodness. It is therefore called the 'Ground of Good.'"

The morality of the ordinary people is founded on the sound opinions inculcated in them by education. Their virtue is steadfast loyalty to established tradition which they have imbibed from *outside*, i.e. from their social environment, not loyalty to the claims of a *summum bonum* grasped by *inward* sight. It will be characteristic of their experience that there should be conflicts of desire with the tradition of loyalty, and that a sort of chivalrous sentiment should be required to act as the reinforcement of loyalty to tradition. But a man who has directly gazed for himself on the Supreme Good necessarily desires the good he has beheld. So long as man is holding converse with outward and bodily things through his senses and opinions, and does not withdraw into himself and learn to know his own life, who and what he is, he can never become truly virtuous, good or happy. "Going out were never so good, but staying at home were much better."

True goodness lies in one thing alone, and nothing else. And if ever man is to be made good, that one thing alone must be in his heart. Now what is that one thing? It is the Supreme Good. It is neither this good nor that; which we can name or perceive or show; but it is all and above all things. Moreover it need not enter into the heart, for it is the real ready, only it is unperceived, being hidden under so many layers of vile and wicked passions. And since it is One, unity and singleness is better than manifoldness, for goodness lies not in much and many, but in One and oneness. Therefore we must wait only on Amida and His work, and leave on one side all beings and their works, and first of all ourselves, and must love, know, taste, and feel within us only the working of the One Good Will in and through us. In other words, goodness lies not in any being, or work of the beings, but it lies alone in Amida and His work. Therefore, Shinran Shōnin declares in The *Tract on Deploring the Heterodoxies* (*Tannishō*):[4]

> I do not know at all what is good nor what is evil, for if I knew something good as completely as the Nyorai knows it [to be] good, then I

"thus," and rai (*āgata*) "is come" or "is arrived." Hence, the Nyorai 如来 (Tathāgata) is the "One who has thus come." On the other hand, "tathāgata" can be divided also into tathā (*nyo*): "thus," and gata (*ko*): "gone" or "departed." Hence, the Tathāgata has also the meaning of *nyoko* 如去 or the "One who has thus gone." There is no doubt the *tathā* is connected with the Mahāyāna conception of the Ultimate Truth as Tathatā (Suchness or Thusness). Therefore, the Tathāgata is the "One who has the nature of *thusness* or *suchness* in his coming and going," that is, the One who is neither coming nor departing, whose being is not subject to the category of being and non-being.

4. Ed. *Tannishō* 歎異抄, *Notes Lamenting Differences*.

> could say that I know it [to be] good. And if I knew something evil as completely as the Nyorai knows it [to be] evil, then I could say that I know it [to be] evil. But I am a wretched sinner utterly blinded by vile and wicked passions, and this world is transitory and changeable as if it were a burning house. All is vain and false, and nothing is true. True remains, however, the Nembutsu[5] alone. (Chapter 18)

Or:

> The Nembutsu is the One Unimpeded Path, for a man who practises the Nembutsu with firm faith is not only respected by the gods in heaven and on earth, but he is hindered neither by evil spirits nor by anti-Buddhists, and sin itself can have no influence upon him. Therefore, the Nembutsu is the One Unimpeded Path, as it supersedes all goodness. (Chapter 7)

However, let no one suppose that we may attain to this One Unimpeded Path by much questioning, or by reading and study, nor yet by high skill and great learning. The Nembutsu or the union with Amida stands not in any man's *self-power* (*jiriki*), in his working or abstaining, perceiving or understanding, nor in that of all the beings taken together, for this union is that we should be purely, simply and wholly at one with the One Eternal Good Will, or altogether without will, so that the *self-will* (*hakarai*) should be swallowed up and lost in the Eternal Will, so that the Eternal Will alone should work in us. Now neither exercises, nor words, nor works, nor any being, nor any being's work can help or further us towards this end. Therefore we must renounce and forsake all things, and must not imagine or suppose that any words, works, or exercises, any skill, or cunning, or contrivance can help or serve us thereto. We must suffer these things to be what they are, and enter into the union with Amida simple-heartedly. So the *One-sheet Document* (*Ichimaikishōmon*) written by Hōnen Shōnin, the teacher of Shinran Shōnin, declares:

> By the Nembutsu I do not mean such practice of meditation on the Buddha as is referred to by the wise men of China and Japan, nor is it the invocation of the Buddha's Name, which is practised as the result of study and understanding as to the meaning of the Nembutsu. It is just to utter the Name of Amida: *Namu-Amida-Butsu!*[6] without doubting

---

5. Nembutsu (*buddha-anusmṛti* in Sanskrit) means literally, "thinking of (*nen* 念, *anusmṛti*) the Buddha (*butsu, buddha*)." But it has come to be synonymous with *shōmyō* 称名/稱名 or "reciting or uttering (*shō*) the Name (*myō*)." For the followers of the Shin teaching of Buddhism, Nembutsu means *shōmyō*, and to think of the Buddha Amida is to utter His Name: *Namu-amida-butsu!*

6. *Namu-amida-butsu* is the transliteration of the Sanskrit, *namomitābhāya buddhāya* or *namomitāyuṣe buddhāya*. *Namo* or *namas* (=*namu*) means "adoration" or "salutation," and *amitābhāya* (or *amitāyuṣe*) *buddhāya* means "to the Buddha of Infinite Light (or of Eternal Life)." So "adoration to the Buddha of Infinite Light (or of Eternal Life)"

that this will issue in the believer's *Rebirth* (*ōjō*[7]) in the Pure Land (*jōdo*). ..Those who believe in [the Unthinkable Power of] the Nembutsu, however learned they may be in all the teachings of Śākyamuni, shall behave themselves like an ignoramus who knows nothing, or like a simple-hearted woman-devotee: avoid pedantry, and utter the Buddha's Name with singleness of heart.

Or Shinran Shōnin says:

> A man who opines that good deeds are helpful towards attaining Rebirth, while evil deeds are harmful to it, does not trust the Unthinkable Power of the Vow[8] [of Amida], but, counting upon his own self-power, endeavors to accumulate various merits for the sake of Rebirth, and thus makes the Nembutsu, which he utters, a practice for his own sake.[9]

Now a man who is in union with Amida and walks the One Unimpeded Path is in a state of absolute *fearlessness*, because he has lost the fear of pain or hell, and the hope of reward or the Pure Land, but is living in pure submission to the Eternal Goodness, in the perfect freedom of fervent love. Thus Shinran Shōnin declares:

> As far as I, Shinran, am concerned, I simply and purely do believe what my good teacher Hōnen Shōnin told me: "Leave your salvation with Amida by uttering his Name with singleness of heart." I don't know at all whether the Nembutsu is the cause of Rebirth in the Pure Land or of descent into hell. I shall never regret, even if, deceived by Hōnen

---

is the meaning of *Namu-amida-butsu*. But in the Shin sect, the full form of "*Namu-amida-butsu*" is regarded as the Name of the Buddha Amida, because in it is embodied His Eternal Good Will to enlighten and deliver us from the night of ignorance. It is the Buddha Amida (*Amidabutsu*) that causes us to trust or have faith in (=*namu*) Him as our Light and Life. "*Namu*" and "*Amidabutsu*" are therefore essentially inseparable, being the two aspects of the One Eternal Power. *Namu* is *Amidabutsu* and *Amidabutsu* is *namu*.

7. *Ōjō* 往生 means literally "to go (*ō*) and be born (*jō*)" an other world, that is, in the Pure Land of Amida. In the Shin teaching, Rebirth (*ōjō*) or Nirvana is used in the sense of Enlightenment. Rebirth and Nirvana and Enlightenment are synonyms.

8. The Vow (*gan* 願 or *seigan* 請願 in Japanese; *praṇidhāna* in Sanskrit) or more precisely, the Original Vow (*hongan* 本願 in Jap.; *pūrvapraṇidāna* in Skt.) of Amida, which is mentioned in the "Myth of Bodhisattva Dharmākara" told by Śākyamuni in the *Larger Sukhāvatīvyūha-sūtra* (*Daimuryōjyukyō*), is in essence as follows: "If, after my obtaining Buddhahood, all beings in the ten quarters should not desire in sincerity and trustfulness to be born in my Country, and if they should not be born by repeating my Name even for ten times only, may I not attain the Highest Perfect Enlightenment." The Vow expresses Amida's immovable determination to carry out His Eternal Will to deliver us from this world and make us attain Enlightenment in His Land of Purity and Bliss.

9. *Notes Lamenting Differences* (*Tannishō*), Chapter 11.

Shōnin, I should descend into hell because of my practising the Nembutsu. The reason is as follows. If I should descend into hell because of my practising the Nembutsu, while I am so constituted that I can attain Buddhahood by steadily performing other good deeds,-then I might regret having been deceived by Hōnen Shōnin. But in truth I am so constituted that I can perform no good work, and therefore I am doomed to hell, which will be my ultimate dwelling place anyway.[10]

It goes without saying that this *fearlessness* is spiritual, not merely moral. It is not the sort of courage demanded of the good soldier, which is absolute loyalty to a code of honour, but it is a state of *absolute dependence* or *absolute Passivity*, which is nothing less than *absolute activity*; for a man who, bereft of the self-will, is obedient, resigned and submissive to the One Good Will, is also resigned, obedient and submissive to all things, in a spirit of yielding, and not of resistance, and takes them in silence, resting on the hidden foundation of his soul, and having a secret inward patience that enables him to take all chances or crosses willingly, whatever may befall him, neither calls for nor desires any redress, or deliverance, or resistance, or revenge, but is always in a loving sincere humility.

> Once we obtain firm faith, our Rebirth [in the Pure Land] will be left entirely to the Will of Amida, and therefore no room will be left for our self-will to take part in the matter. The more we realize our wickedness, the more we shall come to rely upon the Power of Amida's Vow, and then it is that we become persevering and meek of heart as a natural result. As regards our Rebirth, we had best in all things abandon sagacious contrivance, and affectionately recollect His Boundless Grace, day in day out. Then the Nembutsu will rise of itself from the depths of our hearts. This is *naturalness* (*jinen* 自然). Where there is no self-will, there is *naturalness*. In other words, *naturalness* is the working of the Other Power[11] (*tariki* 他力).[12]

Indeed the good soldier has a courage which no fear of pain or death and no bait that can be offered to cupidity are able to overcome. Clearly courage like this will carry a man over the top, make him volunteer for a desperate enterprise or win him a decoration for gallantry in action. But there are situations in life which make a demand for a higher degree of fortitude. It is a matter of experience that the self-devotion of the good soldier may not be equal to the task of duty imposed, for example on a priest whose business it is to tend daily the last hours of the victims of some foul pestilence in a plague-smitten city. Or again a brave soldier,

---

10. *Notes Lamenting Differences*, Chapter 2.
11. Amida's power which is wholly *other* than our self-power.
12. *Notes Lamenting Differences* (*Tannishō*), Chapter 16.

who will face deadly peril when his blood is up and the eyes of his comrades and his commander are on him, may not have the nerve of the scientific man who will quietly inoculate himself with some loathsome disorder to study its symptoms, or try the effects of some new and powerful anaesthetic upon himself, in order to decide on its possible utility in medicine. This is the sort of courage which is only possible to a man who realizes the relative insignificance of the duration of any individual personal life from his habitual contemplation of all time and all existence. Both in the case of the priest and in the case of the man of science, the agent is inspired by an absolutely assured conviction about the universal order and his own place in it. Without this absolute assurance of conviction, one is never wholly free from liability to illusion about one's own personal importance, and so never quite *free* and *natural* in his conduct.

Therefore, in the soul of the man who sees by *spiritual insight* the Whole and the Perfect clearly, all the fragments and parts which have been distinguishable at a lower level of moral development will be finally fused. His life will have only one spring of action or active-principle, his vision of the Supreme Good itself. The forms of virtue, at its highest level or in the realm of *spirituality*, will therefore lose their distinction. Indeed it might be possible for the average good citizen as well as for the good soldier of the State to be characterized by one form of goodness more than by another, but it is not meant that so long as the shop-keeper or the farmer is temperate, it does not matter whether he is a coward. He could not be a good man at all, if he were that, and a society in which no one had any courage except the members of the army and police would be morally in a bad way. But if a man is inspired in all the acts of his life by the vision of the Supreme Good, he will be equal to all the emergencies of life alike; in having *one* virtue, he will necessarily have *all*.

> Once you have faith in the Original Vow, you need not seek after any other sort of goodness, for there is no goodness that is better than the Nembutsu; nor need you fear evil, for there is no evil powerful enough to obstruct the way of Amida's Original Vow.[13]

Only the man who is inspired by the direct vision of the Supreme Good can *create* the national traditions by which the rest of society is to live, for he has a goodness which is not simply the product of those conditions themselves.

> The Light of the Buddha Amida is the Supreme Good.[14]
>
> As His Light surpasses that of the Sun and the Moon,
> He is known as the Sun-and-Moon-Surpassing Light;

---

13. *Notes Lamenting Differences* Chapter 1.
14. The *Doctrine-Work-Faith-Attainment* (*Kyōgyōshinshō*), Book V.

> Śākyamuni could not praise Him enough:
> Take refuge in the One who is peerless.[15]
>
> As His wondrous Light transcends form and description,
> He is known as the Buddha of Inexpressible Light;
> His Light has the power to enlighten all beings:
> So He is praised by all the Buddhas."[16]
>
> The Unimpeded Light that pervades the ten quarters,
> For ever enlightening the night of ignorance,
> Opens the Way of Nirvana
> To those who rejoice even for once only in His Grace.[17]

The Supreme Good or the Sun-and-Moon-Surpassing Light is to the objects of inward sight and to inward sight itself what the sun is to visible objects and to outward sight. As the sun both makes the colours we see and supplies the eye with the source of all its seeing, so the Supreme Good supplies the objects of inward sight with their being and renders them visible to inward sight. And as the sun is neither the colours we see nor the eye which sees them, so the Supreme Good is something even more exalted than being. It "transcends form and description." It transcends, and is *wholly other* than, every particular real thing. It is the *Other Power* (*tariki*) which, indestructible and imperishable, holds everything together and is thus the cause of all order in the universe. So:

The Light is called the Indestructible; the Indestructible is called the Nyorai. The Light is also called the Wisdom.[18]
And further:

> Deliverance (*gedatsu* 解脱) is called the "Empty Nothing (*komu* 虛無)."
> The Empty Nothing is Deliverance; Deliverance is the Nyorai; the Nyorai is the Empty Nothing; for it is not the effect attained by any human work. Or: True Deliverance is beginning-less and endless, and therefore it is the Nyorai. The Nyorai is also beginning-less and endless, ageless and deathless, and indestructible and imperishable; it is not a reality subject to vicissitudes... Nirvana is called "Deliverance," the Empty Nothing is called the "Non-Good," and it is also called Unimpededness.[19]

---

15. Psalms (*wasan*) by Shinran. Ed. *Hymn on the gāthā Praising Amida Buddha* (*Sanamidabutsuge*) Verse 15. Cf. *The Jōdo Wasan* (*The Hymns on the Pure Land*), Ryukoku Translation Series IV, Kyōto 1965.
16. Psalms (*wasan*) by Shinran. Ed. *Hymn on the gāthā Praising Amida Buddha* (*Sanamidabutsuge*) Verse 14.
17. Psalms (*wasan*) by Shinran. Ed. *Hymns on the Pure Land Masters* (*Kōsōwasan*) Verse 38 (among the verses praising Tánluán). Cf. *The Kōsōwasan* (*The Hymns on the Patriarchs*), Ryukoku Translation Series VI, Kyōto 1965.
18. The *Kyōgyōshinshō*, Book V. Shinran's quotations from the *Nirvāṇa-sūtra*.
19. The *Kyōgyōshinshō*, Book V. Shinran's quotations from the *Nirvāṇa-sūtra*.

The distinguishing characteristic of the Supreme Good is that it is the transcendent source of all the reality and intelligibility of everything other than itself. It is rightly regarded as distinct from and transcendent of the whole system of its effects or manifestations. And it transcends the distinction, valid everywhere else, between value and existence. It is the supreme value and the source of all other value and at the same time it is, though *wholly other* than being, the source of all existence. And since the distinction between value and existence falls away in the Supreme Good, it should no longer properly be called a "value" or a "reality," and hence it is called the "Non-Good" or the "Empty Nothing." No one could tell what the Supreme Good is except negatively, or he can only characterize it positively by imperfect analogy, because it can only be apprehended by the most incommunicable and intimate personal insight-*faith* or the "*wisdom* of the believing heart (*shinjin no chie*)."

The Good is only seen by the man who lives it, who keeps adapting himself to it, who "affectionately recollects His Boundless Grace, day in day out," to make himself conformable to His Will. Thus when a modern biologist explains the structure of an organism by the notion of "adaptation" to its environment, by proving that it is *best* that it should have just that structure and no other, he is using on a small scale the supreme universal principle of unification. Only, of course, the biological conception of "adaptation" stops short with a relative "best"; the particular environment of a particular species is taken as (relatively) constant and independent; the "best" realized in the development of the species is adequate adaptation to that given environment. When the principle is made universal, the "best" becomes an *ethical* and *absolute* best, since no place is left for an "environment" of everything. The Goodness of Amida takes the place of the fixed "environment" as that to which the structure of things is conceived as "adapted."

It is needless to say that Shinran Shōnin did not imagine Enlightenment or Rebirth or Nirvana as capable of actual execution by human beings. He says: "There are some who hold the view that a man of faith attains Enlightenment here in this present life even before he is bereft of the mortal body filled with vile and wicked passions. But such a view is absurd and out of the question."[20] Now as often as and as long as a man dreams that he is already firm in faith and given up wholly to the Other Power alone, there arises a false peace and satisfaction, and then it follows that he thinks he has already attained Enlightenment and abides in a state where he suffers nothing and is moved by nothing, whether things fall out well or ill. But this puffed-up feeling of exaltation or elation is a form of self-assertion. We must be ever watchful about this. So Shinran Shōnin says:

---

20. *Tannishō*, Chapter 15.

> If it happens that we are so joyful as to leap to our feet and very anxious to make an early start from this world for the Pure Land, we may well ask our selves: "Why this feeling of exaltation? Because I am already bereft of vile and wicked passions?"[21]

In truth a human being, with respect to himself and his own power, is nothing, has nothing, can do and is capable of nothing but only infirmity and evil, so long as this mortal life lasts. Hence, once he is awakened to this, thorough humility and poorness of spirit is the true state of his mind, for he finds himself altogether unworthy of all that has been or ever will be done for him, by the Other Power or the other people, and that he is a debtor to all and nothing is owing to him, so that he will be ready to bear all things from others, and also, if needs be, to do all things for others. It is only in the man who is awakened to his nothingness that the Eternal Good works, and then it is that *naturalness* or *absolute passivity*, which is no other than *absolute activity*, pervades his conduct. And when the man in whom the Eternal Good works, has and ought to have a will towards anything, his will and endeavor and works are for no end, but that the Good may be seen and manifested. In him is no willing, no working, nor desiring but that which has for its end goodness as goodness, for the sake of goodness; and he has no other wherefore than this. He would say:

> I must do this, and cannot do otherwise, for it is my duty; but this my duty, and the work I do, is not of myself, and I do not call it mine.

just as Shinran Shōnin says:

> The Nembutsu is "non-deed" and "non-good" for those who practise it. It is "non-deed" because when they practise it, the practice does not originate in their self-will. It is "non-good," because it is not an act of goodness originating in their self-will. Since it is entirely the working of the Other Power (*tariki*) and free from their self-power (*jiriki*), it is "non-deed" and "non-good" for those who practise it."[22]

Now it should be unnecessary to dwell on the point that the man who is illuminated by the vision of the Supreme Good is not a mere contemplator divorced from practical social activity, for the Good is only seen by the man who *lives* it. He is necessarily a missionary and a sort of lesser Good Will to man-kind, because the Good cannot be seen without drawing all who see it into its service. And his social activity is all the more effective that it is not pursued directly for its own sake, in the spirit of well-meaning but tiresome persons of our own day who take up

---

21. *Tannishō*, Chapter 9.
22. *Tannishō*, Chapter 8.

social work as they might take up typewriting or civil engineering, but issues naturally and inevitably, as a sort of by-product, from his aspiration after something else, just as the great inventions of modern times regularly issue from discoveries of men who were not thinking at all of the applications of science to convenience and commerce, or as art, literature and social life have all owed an incalculable debt to Shōtoku Taishi (572–621)[23] who had no other end than goodness as goodness, for the sake of goodness.

---

23. Shōtoku Taishi: the second son of the Emperor Yōmei. He was surnamed Umayado, because his mother, whilst walking in the Palace, was suddenly seized with the pangs of child-birth and brought forth her child in the Imperial stables (*umaya*). At the accession of his aunt Suiko to the throne (593), he was named "heir to the throne" (*taishi*) and in reality exercised a regency. He is one of the great figures of Japanese history, especially on account of his activity in the propagation of Buddhism. He followed the teaching of Eji, priest from Koma (Korea). As soon as he came to power, he selected three *sūtra*s of the Mahāyāna doctrine and ordered them to be taught everywhere; he built the temples Shitennōji, Hōryūji, Chūgūji, Hōkōji, etc., and at the time of his death, Buddhism numbered already 46 temples (*tera*), 820 priests (*sō*), and 560 nuns (*ama*) in Japan. It was Shōtoku Taishi who promulgated a Code of Laws in 17 chapters based on the Buddhist spirit of compassion and tolerance (604) and who adopted the Chinese calender (604). It was also he who for the first time sent an embassy to China (607). With the help of Soga no umako, he published two historical works, the *Tennōki* and the *Kokuki* (620). He died the following year, at the age of 49. Shinran Shōnin praises him as follows: "Kannon (Avalokiteśvara), the Great Bodhisattva who is the Saviour of the world, was made manifest in this world as Shōtoku the Prince, who, like Father has not forsaken us, and like Mother is ever among us. Since the beginning-less past until today, Shōtoku the Prince has been dwelling among us like Father and Mother, for ever exercising his Compassionate Heart."

Part III

Three Western Responses to Shin Buddhism

The Concept of Grace in Paul, Shinran and Luther

Fritz Buri

Despite the manifest differences between Paul, Shinran, and Luther, and their differences from us today, these three religious thinkers have something in common which, over and beyond time, unites them not only with each other but also with us.[1]

First, they are all at home in religious world-views, which are, to be sure, very different, but which intend to show men the way to salvation from the meaninglessness of existence. That is, generally speaking, the essential intent of religious world-views. Paul's spiritual home is Judaism or Jewish Christianity; Shinran's is Buddhism in the form of the teaching of the Pure Land of Amida; Luther's is the Christianity of the Catholic Church. Furthermore, through personal experience all three became convinced of the insufficiency of their respective religious traditions, and in creatively establishing their own lines of thought within these traditions, all became reformers who produced new forms of their respective religions. Characteristic of their transformations of religious tradition, granted that this activity is found in each in a different way,

---

1. A German version of this article has been published in *Theologische Zeitschrift*, Jahrgang 31, 1975. The opportunity to do this study was provided through the publication of two important works: D. T. Suzuki's English translation of Shinran's chief work, The *Kyōgyōshinshō*, and his *Collected Writings on Shin Buddhism* which were published by the Eastern Buddhist Society in Kyoto in 1973 on the occasion of the celebration of Shinran's 800th birthday. I used parts of the subject matter of my present treatise for lectures given in the winter semester of 1974–1975. The present treatise, which is a summary of those lectures, was presented in August, 1975, at the International Congress for the History of Religions in Lancaster, England. As far as I know, this material has not been dealt with before in any other publications. In their comparative studies, G. Mensching and H. Butschkus referred only to Shinran and Luther, and their approach is different from mine. Albert Schweitzer, whose interpretation of Paul I have generally followed, does not make such comparisons at all even in his unpublished manuscripts on the history of religions. Catholic and Protestant theologians, as far as they are concerned with Buddhism, are generally interested in Zen, although, regardless of philosophy, they should have very good reason for confronting Shinran.

is that for each salvation is understood as being unattainable through striving but won only through trust in a divine power. In none of their cases does this mean that man works together with the divine power to attain salvation; it means that his salvation is to be wholly understood as the grace of the divine giver.

This trust in the grace of God in Christ or in the promise of the All-embracing Mercy of Amida Buddha moves all three reformers to a new interpretation of the holy tradition to which each wants to remain true, and it brings all three into conflict with traditional belief; but, at the same time, it produces certain difficulties in their own thought. From their emphasis on grace as opposed to works, problems arise, especially for ethics, and each of them has to defend his doctrine of grace against possible misunderstandings in that sphere. We could in fact say that the schemes of the respective world-views and anthropologies through which their doctrines of salvation are expressed actually block the unfolding of their true intention, and instead of solving problems, actually create new ones.

This similarity among these three religious thinkers makes their comparison not only interesting for the history of religions but also significant for the philosophy of religion or theology. The question about the meaning of existence and the question about the possibility of an answer are no less important for us than they were for Paul, Shinran, and Luther, even if we do not share, or no longer share, their presuppositions. Those who pursue the question about existence on the basis of the Bible, as Luther did, or as Shin Buddhists did in emulation of Shinran and his interpretation of the *sūtras* which he regarded as authoritative, cannot overlook the changes with regard to the age and mental environment which separate us from them. Even if the historically and secularly oriented person of today is very attuned to these differences, his awareness of the dissolution of the old world-views in which the question about existence earlier found its answer by no means resolves the question itself. In fact, for those of us who live in a graceless age, the question about grace moves us rather more than it did those who seemingly had grace constantly at hand. That holds true even when we say that the concept of grace has become rather foreign to us today. That briefly is why I wish to discuss here the concept of grace in these three figures.

The starting points for our inquiry are the religious traditions in which Paul, Shinran, and Luther were situated, as well as the experiences they had within their traditions by which they became reformers.

1

Paul, Shinran, and Luther appeared out of definite spiritual contexts. Paul's was late Jewish-early Christian apocalypticism which had already been transformed in part into Hellenistic mystery religion. Shinran's was Buddhism in the form of Amida belief. Luther's was the institution of salvation as re-presented by the Catholic Church at the end of the Middle Ages. Each context had its own long history and in each of these histories the original driving impulse was certainly no other than the attempt to realize the meaning of human existence in a world beset by meaninglessness. It is true that within this commonality of original, universal religious striving, the question of meaning is put and answers are sought in fundamentally different ways in Far Eastern Buddhism and in Judaism. In Buddhism all existence is seen as trapped in a cycle without beginning or end. Salvation means escape from this cycle. In Judaism all being and all events have a beginning as the creation of a God who stands outside the world, a God who leads history toward a goal which consists in a new and perfect creation in which only the elect shall live. In Buddhism the difficulty lies in man's lack of knowledge about the true state of things and, resulting from this, his captivity within the world. In Judaism man's difficulty stems from his disobedience of God's command and the resulting entanglement in sin and guilt. In Buddhism salvation consists in knowledge and in following the way of that knowledge. In Judaism it consists in the reconciliation of the sinner with God. The Buddhist arrives in Nirvana, while in Biblical belief man arrives in the Kingdom of God.

In the course of their histories the aforementioned basic concepts of Judaism and Buddhism took on very different forms. So, for instance, in the late Jewish apocalypticism which forms Paul's world of thought, it is out of the transformation of an originally somewhat earthly rule of God that a new aeon comes into being. With the coming of this aeon the Messiah puts an end to the existing world, and if the yet living and the dead successfully withstand the trial of the end-time, there will be transformation or resurrection into a non-earthly way of being. With the early Christians, who saw in Jesus the promised Messiah who through his death on the cross atoned for the sins of all believers, Paul expects the resurrected Jesus to return soon in all his glory to establish the Kingdom of God.

As a consequence of the fact that the Kingdom did not come, the church arose among those who, in believing in Christ's return, had expected the end of the world. The church continued to hope for the return of its Lord and the completion of his work of salvation, but it removed this final event into the indefinite future. It did this in the same way that it understood itself to be the institution of salvation as established in the world by God, through Jesus. In time not only did the pope take over the representation of Christ on earth, but in endowing the altar sacraments with the power of imparting salvation the church found a surrogate even for the non-arrival of the new aeon. The effect of this was that instead of the arrival of the Kingdom of God on earth, the soul rose to heaven. This was made possible through good works, which in turn were made possible through the sacraments.

The changes which occurred in the belief of the Christian church from the time of its unanticipated origins into the time of Luther are no greater than those which were experienced in Buddhism from the time of its establishment by Śākyamuni to the time of Shinran. In the historical development of Buddhism, there were two essential moments. The first was the formation of the Bodhisattva ideal in the Mahāyāna. In this concept, the Mahayanist no longer endeavours simply to free himself from the samsaric cycle of endless births through self-effort, as in Hīnayāna Buddhism, but may count on the help of merciful spirits, above all, the help of Buddha himself. The second was the transformation of the historical Buddha, Śākyamuni, into Amida Buddha. Amida Buddha made the vow that he would not enter Nirvana until he had saved all living beings. Here it became necessary and sufficient for salvation to put one's complete trust in this promise of Amida, and this trust was given attestation through the continuous repetition of the formula, *Namu-amida-butsu*.

That, briefly, is the Amidist belief in the attainment of the "Pure Land in the West"—in contrast to the "way of holiness"—as it was taught to Shinran by his teacher Hōnen. It forms the basis for Shinran's development of the idea of a Buddhism of faith or trust, just as Jewish Christianity provides the ground on which Paul developed his specific idea of salvation through Christ which later as the sacrament and work piety of the Catholic Church originating in Paul, became the object of Luther's reformation. In Paul and Luther as in Shinran the relation to tradition is characterized by a radicalization of a pre-existent moment of grace, a radicalization in which the respective tradition is given the pronounced character of a religion of grace. In spite of their very real and decisive transformations of previously valid concepts of faith, none of them wished to be an innovator, but rather hoped to reaffirm through radical revaluation, as they saw it, some lost or misunderstood meaning original to their tradition.

The followers of Paul, Shinran, and Luther, however, were not content with merely honoring their teachers as reformers, but made them, at least Paul and Shinran, saints. As such, they were imagined to have been brought to their reformative activity through supernatural occurrences, which is in general accordance with a pattern commonly encountered in the legends of saints.

Such legendary motifs in the lives of saints, of visitations by good and divine powers or of struggles with evil demonic forces, appear in the lives of all three, if in different forms. In the Catholic Church Paul is revered as one of the highest of saints. His conversion on the Damascus road in the Book of Acts is attributed to an appearance of Christ, and his life is, generally speaking, depicted throughout as surrounded by miraculous events (Acts 9:1-31; 22:3-21; 26:9-20). In his own letters he asserts that his authority lies in divine revelation (Galatians I:19-24; 2:2) and he speaks of himself as being plagued by demonic powers (2 Corinthians 12:1-10).

In the life story of Shinran (*Godenshō*), especially significant is the vision of the Bodhisattva Avalokiteśvara who appeared to him in Rokkakudō Temple in the form of a beautiful woman and promised assistance in all his struggles.[2] This account, recorded by his great-grandson along with similar supernatural experiences and events,[3] and which may possibly derive ultimately from Shinran himself, is given credence by followers in the Shin sect, some of whom revere him as an incarnation of Amida.[4]

Luther confesses that he entered the monastery because, in the midst of a terrible thunderstorm, he made the vow, "Help, holy Anna—I will become a monk!" The reaction of Luther's father is equally interesting for he scorned his son, saying that what Luther had thought to have been a heavenly event was actually a deception of the devil.[5] It is well known that Luther, not only in the monastery but also in later life, often had dealings with the devil.[6] The good and evil spirits with which Paul, Shinran, and Luther had to do in their lives belong to the idea of the end-time or latter-day, a period in which all three thought they lived. Such experiences and ideas can of course be explained historically and psychologically with reference to this belief in the end-time. The significance of such ideas, however, consists doubtlessly in the fact that the consciousness of a divine mission is being reflected in them, a consciousness which arose out of their insight and which was likewise perceived by those who let themselves be moved by such preaching or teaching. We might say that such visions are erruptions of truth out of a prior concealment into symbolic form while legends are an articulation of the experience of having been moved by the power of such revelations. Such things happened to Paul, Shinran, and Luther as they thought and lived through the question about the meaning of existence, a process which while occurring within their respective holy traditions at the same time reached beyond those bounds. Today, as we attempt to trace their thinking on this question, we are able to understand something of what they have to say about merciful grace and come to see it as a possibility for

---

2. "The Life of Shinran Shonin," trans. D.T. Suzuki and Sasaki Gesshō, in *Collected Writings on Shin Buddhism* (hereafter referred to as *Collected Writings*) (Kyoto: Eastern Buddhist Society, 1973), 170 f.
3. "The Life of Shinran Shonin," 165 f.
4. "The Life of Shinran Shonin," 171.
5. Otto Scheel, *Dokumente zu Lutbers Entwicklung*, 1929.
6. H. Obendiek, *Der Teufel bei Martin Luther*, 1931.

salvation, a possibility that resulted from their thorough and serious contemplation of their situation.

2

Paul knew the grace of God through earliest Christianity's idea of the sacrificial death and resurrection of Christ. By virtue of that sacrifice, God withdraws the penalty for the former sins of believers in order that they may take part in the glory of the Lord upon his return (1 Corinthians 15:3f. cf. Acts 2:14f). But for earliest Christianity the command of the holy law was still valid. Anyone breaking these laws became guilty all over again and would not be able to successfully withstand final judgment.

Paul, the first theological thinker of early Christianity,[7] explains that if Christ was resurrected, the arrival of a new aeon can no longer belong simply to the future; in the victory of Christ over death the passing to a new aeon has begun. The world of the resurrection with its spiritual power realizes itself even in the midst of the temporal continuum of this world through the baptism of believers, who die in Christ and arise with him in a new existence. "If anyone is in Christ, he is a new creation; the old has passed away, behold, the new has come" (2 Corinthians 5:17).

Death has no dominion over the resurrected body. Sufferings which have yet to be endured only bind those who share in Christ's body more closely to their crucified and ascended Lord (Romans 14:7-8). The requirements of the law can no longer frighten the believer, for they belong to the old aeon that was overcome through Christ. Their place has been taken by the Spirit of God which works in the believer and enables him to ready himself inwardly for the joyful fulfillment of God's will (Romans 8:1f). Therefore, the justice of the believer is wholly a gift of grace and yet at the same time his own work, but it is without any merit for himself independent of God. It rests entirely on the grace which works in him.

The apostle Paul emphasizes that his understanding of grace must appear to the world as foolishness because the world either is not acquainted with or will not allow the presuppositions of his understanding (1 Corinthians I:18f). He knows, too, that for the Jew as well as the Christian who holds to Jewish law, his understanding of grace must seem a blasphemy against God. They do not attribute to the cross and resurrection the significance these had for him resulting as a consequence of his thought and in accordance with his experience.

When we turn to Shinran, we find a very similar doctrine of grace, even to the extent of a parallel structure, although the circumstances in which Shinran's doctrine was formed were extrinsically completely different and with partly differing presuppositions. As Paul's idea of the divine

---

7. Albert Schweitzer, *Die Mystik des Apostels Paulus*, 1930, 4, and 365 f.

event of grace resulted as a consequence of his thought on the figure of Christ as given in tradition, so too are Shinran's radical conclusions drawn from a given doctrine of grace, conclusions whereby he became the founder of a particular form of Amida Buddhism. Paul's relation to Judaism or to Jewish Christianity corresponds to Shinran's relation to the Amida Buddhism brought from China to Japan. Just as Paul radicalized the salvific significance of death and resurrection, Shinran radicalized the trust in the promise of the All-embracing Mercy of Amida.

The differences we find in the beliefs of Jewish Christianity and Amida Buddhism as they later developed are basically differences of their respective saviour types. At the center of Christian belief stands a historical personality. Amida, on the other hand, is a mythological figure, or as Suzuki Daisetz in his commentary on the *Kyōgyōshinshō* says, a metaphysical reality, a product of the religious consciousness.[8] Insofar as the Messianic title "Christ" and the Bodhisattva-being of Amida are indicative of their functions as saviours, one may speak of a correspondence between the two saviour types. They do have great differences, however, and this is seen, for example, in the respective ideas regarding incarnation, which will be but mentioned here.[9]

According to the earliest Christian-Pauline notion, Jesus, as the Christ or the one destined to be the future Messiah, dies and is resurrected in order to atone for the sins of believers and to bring about the cosmic turning to the new aeon. Faith is directed toward this historical-suprahistorical event in the end-time. For the Amida believer, salvation is based on the promise Amida Buddha made not to enter Nirvana until all beings are freed from their ignorance in samsaric existence and enabled to replace their evil karma with good karma, which makes entry into the Pure Land possible. In spite of the once and for all character of Amida's promise, it does not have or is not given the significance of a sacred event in time or at the end of time, as is the case in the New Testament with regard to the crucifixion and resurrection of Jesus. The nature of grace with regard to Amida's vow lies not so much in a once and for all temporal happening as it does in the timeless, eternally valid truth of its content. The grace of Amida is spoken of not in a category of facticity but in the category of Dharma, which means "teaching," but also refers to being or reality.[10] One can therefore say that in Christianity the teaching is grounded on a historical fact, while in Buddhism it is the teaching of the sacred fact which matters.[11]

---

8. The *Kyōgyōshinshō*, trans. D. T. Suzuki (Kyoto: Eastern Buddhist Society, 1973), 204.
9. The *Kyōgyōshinshō*, 252.
10. The *Kyōgyōshinshō*, 260 f.
11. *Collected Writings*, 201.

Another fundamental difference in the respective ideas of sacred history is seen in the fact that in Biblical-Christian eschatology history comes to an end with the arrival of the Kingdom of God, while in Buddhism each ended *kalpa* is followed by another in an endless repetition. However, despite the basic difference between Paul and Shinran, the decisive changes which they introduced into their traditions have in their structures much in common.

Paul argues that since Christ has risen, the new aeon has already broken forth into reality. He derives from this event all his statements concerning the essence of grace and its effects upon the relation of man to God and of man to man. Similarly, for Shinran all is decided through complete trust in the authenticity of Amida's vow or promise. The content of this promise is for him the basis of his belief just as the message of the resurrection is the basis of belief for Paul. For Shinran, too, there are certain inner and outer experiences in which the working and therefore the reality of Amida's mercy is evident. Certainly for Shinran these experiences are not unimportant, but they are in fact no more a determining factor for him than they are for Paul. Even if a person never experiences Amida's mercy, even if one is sceptical of it, it still remains true.[12] *Karuṇā* is absurd only as far as a reasoning faculty which demands proof is concerned. By virtue of this essentially undemonstrable nature of grace, Shinran can comfort the despairing with the idea—often encountered in Amida belief—that as a consequence of Amida's All-embracing Mercy not only will the good be saved but also the evil. He can state that in the paradoxical formulation, "if even the good can become blessed, how much more so the evil."[13] Good works are not necessary for blessedness, not even in the form of cultic practices, such as the recitation of the Nembutsu, for example. The recitation of the Nembutsu can, at best, serve for training in faith. Fully-arrived faith, however, consists in the pure inwardness of enlightenment in which the believer is already in Nirvana, and which, therefore, cannot be rationally grasped. At best, it can be brought to expression in paradox.[14]

When the Jesuit missionary Francis Xavier, on his visit to Japan in 1549, encountered what seem to have been followers of Shinran, he thought to his shocked surprise that the country had been penetrated by Lutheran

---

12. *Tannishō*; VIII, included in *Collected Writings*; cf. *Tannishō* (Kyoto: Ryukoku University, 1962).

13. *Tannishō*; VIII, III.

14. These ideas are found in their most concentrated but also simplest form in the *Tannishō*, which is something like a catechism of the Shin sect. Ed. To avoid misunderstanding, it may be noted that in fact the *Tannishō* is a collection of remembered sayings of Shinran, but it is neither a comprehensive doctrinal checklist nor is it in question-and-answer form.

heresy, which is understandable in view of Shinran's emphasis of grace alone being the path to blessedness. In fact, Shinran's radicalization of Amida belief is very similar to Luther's reform of Catholicism. Shinran's Jōdo Shin sect is related to his teacher's Jōdo sect in much the same way as Luther's thought is to the Roman Catholicism of his time. Shinran's radicalization of Amida Buddhism precisely corresponds to Luther's assertion of *sola gratia, sola fide* (through grace alone, through faith alone) against Catholic synergism. Luther argues, just as Shinran does, if grace, then grace alone. As a pope was later to remark of the Jesuits, "*sint ut sunt, aut non sint*" (be just as they are, otherwise not be at all)[15] so Shinran against his tradition and Luther with reference to Paul against the Catholic Church would say: trust in grace alone or there is neither grace nor trust. Similarly, one can compare Shinran's criticism of Zen Buddhism with Luther's criticism of the mystics of the late Middle Ages and the spiritualists of the Age of Reformation.[16] Luther's delimitation of the boundary between himself and the spiritualists has its parallel in Shinran's criticism of the way of salvation through self-effort typified by Zen. Just as Paul stands between Judaism and the early Jewish-Christian community with his idea of grace, so Shinran stands between Jōdo and Zen with his idea of grace, and Luther between Catholicism and mystical spiritualism with his evangelism. All three reformers had to face similar opposition on two fronts.

The spiritual landscape in which each of these men developed his position and within which he carried forth his criticism and belief, is in each case very different. Nevertheless, their common concern for salvation through grace alone and their common struggle against every form of self-salvation—as Buddhists say, the opposition of *tariki* and *jiriki*—binds these men together over and beyond all limitations of time and space. It is again understandable how Karl Barth in his *Church Dogmatics*, with no less astonishment than Francis Xavier, speaks of the remarkable relationship between Shinran's teaching and Luther's doctrine of justification. He reproaches Shinran only for using the wrong name to designate the center of his teaching: instead of Amida, Barth says, he should say Christ.[17]

Barth's comment suggests a possible Christianization of Shinran, but we wish no more to engage in that than we do in an Amidaization of Pauline or Lutheran theology. The reason for our refusing to do so is not due to "the power of the name" of the saviour, Christ or Amida; a power which does not allow any other name to be surrogated for it, and which

---

15. Ed. More literally: "May they be as they are, or else not be."
16. In this regard, see, for example, the Marburg dissertation of Ueda Shizuteru, *Die Gottesgeburt in der Seele und der Durchbrucb zur Gottbeit. Die mystische Anthropologie Meister Eckbarts und ibre Konfrontation mit der Mystik des Zen-Buddhismus*, 1965.
17. Karl Barth, *Kirchlicbe Dogmatik* 1/2, 372 f.

Barth, no less than Shinran, believes in. One main reason for refusing a Christianization of Amida or an Amidaization of Paul and Luther is that exactly in their similar concepts of grace, what we might call "grace-monism," a problem common to Paul, Shinran, and Luther emerges which is of central importance and which cannot be overlooked. This problem has two aspects. The first regards their reference to holy tradition. The second regards ethical difficulties which arise from their doctrine of grace.

3

We turn first to their reference to holy tradition. Each of them makes appeal to scriptures of a holy tradition for their belief. It is not their intention merely to proclaim their own experiences and insights, or to speak of the revelations and enlightenments which they have had. They are conscious, to be sure, of the singular character of immediate inspiration and of the limits of its communicability. They encounter such limits for example in interpretations of texts by others which differ from their own understandings, and in misunderstandings of their statements by friend and opponent alike. They, however, both wish to and are convinced that they teach nothing but what is contained in the holy writings. For this reason the proofs of scripture which they collect and interpret from the Bible or from the *sūtras* are very important for them. Paul is a Jewish scribe. Luther translates the Bible and wishes to be nothing other than a Biblical theologian. Shinran's chief work, the *Kyōgyōshinshō*, consists mainly of a collection of texts from *sūtras* and excerpts from commentaries on the *sūtras*. Paul quotes Christian hymns in his letters. Luther composes church hymns on the basis of Old Testament Psalms and stories from the Gospels. Shinran incorporates Buddhist faith into his *wasan* songs.[18]

Yet certainly the individuality of all three is also clear even as they maintain a relation to tradition. Each evaluates his respective documents differently although all three actually bring only the parts of the documents forward as suits their purposes. They leave extensive parts unmentioned. One can, however, not really reproach Paul for that, since the Biblical canon was not established until after his time by the Christian church. Luther's depreciatory judgments of certain canonical books are well known. His personal experience plays a large part in the formulation of his criterion of the canon as "that which has to do with Christ." This parallels the rejection of knowledge of Christ *kata sarka* (according

---

18. Examples of the songs (*wasan*) of Shinran, along with commentaries on them, are found in two articles by D.T. Suzuki: "The Songs of Shinran Shonin" and "Infinite Light" in *Collected Writings*, III f. and 129 f. respectively.

to the flesh) in favour of Christ *kata pneuma* (according to the spirit) by Paul (2 Corinthians 5:16). Similar to this is Shinran's concentration on the 48 promises or vows of Amida contained in one of three primary *sūtras* which he selected out of all those in the Buddhist canon. He bases his understanding of grace on these 48 promises.[19]

Just at this point, however, one sees the problem of such an approach to tradition. Paul, Shinran, and Luther add to and change the traditional texts both in their wording and in their subject matter. That unjustly conditions the life and continued effectiveness that these texts legitimately have. It is characteristic, furthermore, that all three reformers furnish us with evidence enough to show that their manipulations of the texts they use are directly related to the exposition of their idea of the essence of grace.

Paul, for instance, supports his eschatological idea of the cancellation of the law by reference to the gnostic concept of the law as having been given by evil angelic powers, who through the law enslaved mankind (Galatians 3:19; cf. Acts 7:38 and 53, Hebrews 2:2). That stands in complete contradiction to the Old Testament-Jewish and to the traditional early Christian interpretation, both of Moses's reception of the law on Sinai and of the purpose of the giving of the Mosaic law. It also supplied one basis for Luther's misunderstanding of the Pauline *abrogatio legis* (abrogation of the law).

To prevent a new works righteousness from developing out of Paul's questionable transformation of the law of works into the "law of faith," Luther adds to the wording of his translation of Romans 3:28 the famous and notorious little word "alone." This word can effect a displacement of Paul's meaning, and in fact it did so in suggesting the belief that faith without works makes for blessedness and that good works are, indeed, even harmful for blessedness.

Discussion of the formation and fate of the doctrine of "justification through faith alone without works of the law" in Luther and his followers would lead us too far away from our central theme. It is only to be mentioned that in the *theologia crucis* (theology of the cross) of his early period, in the despairing belief that he had been damned by God because he could not find peace of mind in the monastic life and in the sacraments, Luther found salvation in the *se ipsum resignare ad infernum pro Dei voluntate* (to resign oneself to hell if God so wills). This same thought is also found in Shinran. According to a passage in the *Tannishō*, Shinran is supposed to have said that he, as an unlearned man, did not care if Hōnen—and consequently also he himself—were in error about Nembutsu and must go to hell because of it. Since he could not, in any case, per-

---

19. The 48 promises of Amida in the *Sūtra of Eternal Life* have been translated with commentary in Collected Writings, 42 f. Cf. The *Kyōgyōshinshō*, 184 f.

form meritorious works, he belonged in hell anyway. But, he continues, if the promise of Amida, which had been handed down from Śākyamuni to Hōnen, is true, then Nembutsu will suffice.[20]

If these stages of comforted despair as found in Luther and Shinran are not identical, they are, in any case, more alike than Luther's experience of grace in his theology of the cross and the final form which his doctrine of justification took in the forensic idea of a *nonimputatio peccati* (nonimputation of sin) and an *imputatio* of the *aliena justitia Christi* (imputation of the foreign justice of Christ) in the believer. But Shinran came to a similar notion in the imputation of foreign merit. He did it, however, by intentionally misreading the Chinese text of the 18th promise of Amida in the *Sūtra of Eternal Life*. The usual, literal sense of the reading, found as such even in the Jōdo sect, was completely reversed. In the usual reading of the text, the believers bring their merits to Amida and thereby enter the Pure Land.[21] In the *Kyōgyōshinshō*, Shinran interprets this passage to mean that Amida transfers all the merit he possesses to anyone who, hearing his name, has only a single thought of pure belief. On the basis of Amida's merit the believer is reborn into the Pure Land.[22]

In this way, Shinran tries, as do Paul and Luther, to demonstrate that his grace-monism stands in agreement with holy tradition. All of them believe strongly in authority and therefore it is important for them to make this demonstration. It is trust in the "foreign power" which is the material side of both Christian and Amidist belief in the idea of "through grace alone." That is complemented formally by reference to a foreign authority.

For all three men, it is clearly a matter of personal struggle for salvation as the fulfillment of meaning in their lives. It is just as clear, however, that their recourse to holy tradition to give authority to what they had won through personal struggle, a gain which goes far beyond holy tradition, is a very questionable matter. Their chosen way of salvation through grace alone has even worse consequences for ethical practice. The ethical problem is already apparent in the fact that they have to refer to a foreign authority for affirmation of truth, the proof of which is quite fragile.

It is a fact of experience that the more a faith supports itself through reliance on an infallible outer, foreign authority, instead of relying simply on its own inner and fallible self-certainty, the more intolerant it will be towards those who go in another way. It does that simply for the

---

20. *Tannishō*; II.

21. Ed. In spite of the new accentuation brought in through Shin Buddhism, the idea of actually bringing merits to Amida to ensure entry to the Pure Land can probably not really be documented. Even in Jōdo Buddhism, it is the *nenbutsu* which counts, i.e. thinking of or calling on the name of Amida.

22. The *Kyōgyōshinshō*, 89, and 293. *Collected Writings*, 45, 50, and 72.

sake of validating such authority and legitimatizing its own subjugation to it. In order to safe-guard itself from admitting any error, it is forced to regard those others as enemies of the true faith, unbelievers, men sunken in depravity. This attitude is hardly rare in Christianity, as is well known. In fact, it seems to be the rule rather than the exception. It also appears in Shinran and his followers, which is in striking contrast to Buddhism's otherwise tolerant attitude. It is a curious fact that for all their intolerance, Paul, Shinran, and Luther emphasize their own humility and unworthiness before God or Amida. Yet this dual personality is hardly an accidental peculiarity. It results necessarily from their understanding of grace.

4

If grace-monism has the above consequence by virtue of its formal basis in the authority of holy tradition, its effect on ethics in general is even worse. What has man to do if grace does everything? Does his behaviour have any significance at all? Does not the distinction between good and evil become untenable, or if it is maintained, does it not indicate a mistrust of the grace which is valid for sinners but not for the just? As Paul asked in Romans 6:1, "should we persist in sin in order that grace increase?"

Our three authorities, in any case, do not think so. When they encounter such ideas in friends and opponents they see in them only a misunderstanding of their teaching. But are they not the ones responsible for that through their own exaggerated formulations? Perhaps the most fatal of all such exaggerated formulations is Luther's pastoral advice to a prince, advice which he certainly did not intend for the public: *pecca fortiter sed fortius fide et gaude* (sin strongly but strongly in faith and joy).[23] But can life really be divided in this way into separate spheres, into an existence in sin and an existence in grace? Are the usual commands of the law valid in the sphere of sin, which they uncover or keep within limits, while grace cancels these commands or gives them a new function? But where and how does faith function as the fulfillment of the law?

Paul, Shinran, and Luther are acquainted with these questions from their own deliberations as well as from their intellectual environments. Their ways of dealing with them, however, only puzzled their followers. All three recognize the distinctness of three different areas: an unsaved area, an area in which grace is already effective, and an area in which salvation has reached completion. The first is the existing world in which man in need of salvation finds himself. For Paul this is the world of death

---

23. Ed. This classic quotation seems to have become confused. The phrase should continue with the words *in Christo*, hence: Sin strongly, but believe and rejoice in Christ more strongly. However, it is often misleadingly reduced to *pecca fortiter* (sin strongly).

which is destined to pass away. It stands under the rule of evil powers and men in this world are, through the law of those powers, subject to sin (Romans 7:7f.) and they sigh with all creation for salvation (Romans 8:19f.). According to Shinran, all life has always been in the circle of karma, i.e., each life is in a condition corresponding to its behavior in its preceding form of existence.[24] For Luther, God's good creation has been ruined through the fall into sin of the first Men. Their progeny stand under the curse of original sin, cannot fulfill God's command, and therefore cannot withstand the final judgment.

Biblical and Buddhist faith also know of a salvation out of this calamitous world through the Messiah of divine and sacred history or through the appearance of the Buddha. In Biblical as in Buddhist faith the saviour has different forms. The Messiah of the Old Testament is not the Christ which the New Testament recognizes in Jesus, and the Buddhology with regard to Amida belief is unique within Buddhism. But Christ and Amida have in common an effect on the life of the believer in the existing world. That holds true even though their activity of salvation aims at what lies beyond this world, the Kingdom of God or Nirvana, which for the Amida believer means ultimately the extinction of the Pure Land.

By virtue of being bound with Christ, Paul knows himself, with all believers, in his "inner self," to be already removed into the world of the resurrection, although he yet lives "according to the flesh" in the world of sin (Romans 7:22f.). Likewise, Shinran says of the believer that although he is still under the compulsion of karma, he is, in spirit, already freed from it in Nirvana.[25] The literal distinction of two such areas and, simultaneously, the maintenance of the identity of the believer within them are also found in Luther's idea of the Christian being both "justified and a sinner at the same time." It is also found in the elaboration of this idea in Luther's doctrine of the two kingdoms and in the division of the function of the law into a civil function, which orders the common life, and into an elenctic function, which shows men their sinfulness and the necessity of the forgiving grace of God.

With reference to Paul's requirement of works of faith as the fruit of a free and joyful fulfillment of the law made possible by the new being of the believer, Luther adjoins his *tertius usus legis* (third use of the law) to the civil use of the law and to the elenctic use of the law which

---

24. On karma and being partially freed from it, see discussions in Glossary to The *Kyōgyōshinshō*, 257 f.
25. In reference to the effectiveness of Amida's name; "So says Shinran in the *Tannishō*: 'While my body is in the world of karma, my mind (spirit) is in the Pure Land of Amida,'" D.T. Suzuki *Collected Writings*, 74. On the basis of this statement Suzuki arrives at a *hōs me* similar to Paul's in I Corinthians 7:24, and with the corresponding ethical consequences.

prepares one for the acceptance of grace. This *tertius usus legis* has its parallel in the Amida believer's idea of becoming a Bodhisattva. He, like Amida, leaves the Pure Land in order to take up mercifully those yet in ignorance and to lead them to the way of salvation.[26]

One cannot say that Paul or Luther are any more successful than Shinran in making clear how the believer, who belongs both to this world and to the world of salvation, maintains his identity. Nor are they any more successful than Shinran in demonstrating the necessity and possibility of good works proceeding from grace, where these works can not belong to the merit of the believer. The conflicts about nomism in Lutheranism demonstrate all of these points no more and no less than do the charges of libertinism against which Paul and Shinran had to defend themselves.

More obviously and with greater portent than in their theories of knowing and of metaphysics, the problem of their common doctrine of salvation is demonstrable in its practical ethical consequences. One may, of course, ask whether the ethical problem is the consequence of their theory or whether their theory is formulated to serve the practical purpose of answering the problem of meaning. In any case, there is a very close relation here between theory and practice. The fact of the matter is that this relation has a disastrous effect on any religious mythology or philosophical speculation which in any way tries to locate the answer to the question about the meaning of existence in a teachable, doctrinal form. To state but one aspect of the problem, in religious mythology and philosophical speculation about existence, three dimensions are given consideration: the world in which man finds himself; man, who seeks for meaning; and the transcendence of the divine, which functions to reconcile the former two. None of these can be objectified. Not the world, for it is something we can never really grasp as a whole. Not man, because we men are always something other than what we know ourselves to be. Not transcendence, because it is no longer transcendence if we can make statements about it. Nevertheless, we must ask the question about the meaning of existence, and we have to try to find an answer and to live according to this answer. And we can do none of these without speaking objectively about what cannot be objectified, without treating them as objects for us, the thinking subjects.

The unavoidability of confronting this state of affairs becomes all the more distressing the more we become aware of the subjectivity of our thought. It becomes less and less so to the degree that we are able to extinguish our consciousness of ourselves as subjects. On the one hand, the state

---

26. Suzuki opposes this idea of the return of the Bodhisattva, which is found in all forms of Mahāyāna Buddhism, to his understanding of the Christian belief in the beyond. See his deficient polemic in *Collected Writings*, 61 f.

of being self-conscious of the subjective problem carries within itself the stimulus to ever new searches for and attempts at possibilities of meaning and their realization, even if these possibilities remain only partial and their realizations ever questionable. The state of the extinction of consciousness of oneself as subject, on the other hand, seems to have already reached its goal, to be participant in salvation through freedom from the question about salvation. As regards the former, it is to be asked if one should really speak of salvation where there is only an endless, unceasing striving for salvation. With regard to the latter it is to be asked, who would want to receive grace if grace means the extinction of its recipient?

5

One might be tempted to find the subject-object type of thought in Paul and Luther or generally in a Western-Christian understanding of grace and way of life, and to find the type of thought which extinguishes awareness of the subjectivity of thought in Shinran or generally in the Far Eastern Buddhist understanding of grace and way of life. Consequently, one might be inclined as a Buddhist representative, with reference to Buddhists' antipathy to the Biblical-Christian history of the passion and resurrection in mind,[27] to become convinced of one's superiority, even perhaps to the point of wanting to set about refuting and converting Christians belonging to the other type. One might be tempted as a Christian representative to do the same thing, with the assertion that Buddhism has to do only with forms of world-fleeing self-salvation or non-salvation. The inclination to such attitudes might be strong, but the attitude is inappropriate and only leads thought astray.

In all attempts to understand spiritual traditions different from one's own—and in an attempt to understand one's own tradition as well—it ought to be considered that concepts of one tradition always have, for those who live within that tradition, a definite significance and value which are not immediately comprehensible and can be easily misunderstood by persons of another tradition. We ourselves should regard our own interpretation, not only of Shinran but also of the Gospel of the apostle Paul and of the reformer Luther, with the same reserve.

Even with this concession, however, we still refuse to see, on the one hand, Paul, Luther, and their spiritual world as representative of that type of thought characterized by conceptual-objective thinking and its consequent active realization of meaning, and on the other hand, Shinran and his spiritual world as representative of the nullification of the subject-object scheme in the mystical void of enlightenment and the

---

27. Cf. Suzuki's remarks on the impression which the image of the crucified Christ and blood theology makes on the Buddhist (*Collected Writings*) 59 f.

consequent unworldliness of the one so saved. The origin, form, and aim of grace in Christianity are very different from what we find in Buddhism. While they thus show different fundamental tendencies, they also have fundamental tendencies in common. In the Christian and Buddhistic concepts of grace two types of thought and ethical consequences may be discerned, albeit in various forms.

For this reason a Christianization of Buddhism or a Buddhaization of Christianity comes into question only if we can thereby gain a deeper insight into the problematics of the concept of grace in the three religious thinkers. Mutual fertilization can, in fact, prove very fruitful. In order to indicate how that might proceed, we shall cite in conclusion two possibilities. One has to do with theoretical perception, and the other with the sphere of ethics.

In contrast to the necessity of reference to the holy act of Christ in history for the grace of God and the uncertainty and ambiguity of its asserted historicity, an enviable timelessness and clarity is characteristic of the promise of Amida that provides the basis of believing trust. For Shinran, salvation is not bound, as it is for Paul and Luther, to an event occurring once in time, an event dimensionally different from all other human history and to be believed, against all other experience, as a miracle. Certainly the promise of Amida in which Shinran trusts presupposes the incarnation of Amida and the statement of the promise. To be sure, this is also a unique and supernatural event, just as Christ is for Paul and Luther. But the object of Shinran's faith is not the facticity of Amida's promise not to enter Nirvana until all beings have been saved, but the content of that promise alone. This content is nothing but the complement to Shinran's own entanglement in karma, an entanglement from which he wants to be freed. If he first asked if the promise really were given by Amida, he would no longer be wholly trusting in the promise. To believe that Amida really made the promise means to trust in it completely. Wherever and whenever the Nembutsu is thought or spoken in this sense, even if only once, there is in it, in every place and in every time, the content of truth and reality. The name of Amida stands for a timelessly valid content, and that is the acknowledgment of guilt and its forgiveness. The person who accepts himself as he is, who is reconciled with himself, has done enough penance and is able to bring others to their own reconciliation. He has become a Bodhisattva.

There is also a Christian faith which understands itself in this way, even if it is not the faith of the churchly institution of salvation and its official confessions. But Paul knew such faith when he said that, speaking of one "who does not work but trusts him who justifies the ungodly," "his faith is reckoned as righteousness" (Romans 4:5). And the young Luther knew it, too, in his *theologia crucis*, in which he knew himself embraced by the love of God even in hell. Perhaps their followers in Christianity can gain strength in facing the risks inherent in the immediacy of grace through the example of Shinran's piety. On the other hand, the followers of Shinran in Buddhism could learn from the difficulties which Christianity has fallen into as a consequence of its historicizing and institutionalizing of grace. They could learn to set aside the vestiges of such misunderstanding regarding Amida's promise and become more aware of its complete immediacy.

We turn from discussion of historical origins of grace to that of the problem of the working of grace in history. The mode of this working is not independent of the idea of history which the believer has, the idea of the historical frame in which grace effects itself. Paul, Shinran and Luther expect the completion of the effect of grace not within but beyond history. Paul expects it in the coming of the kingdom of God. Luther expects it partly in the coming of the Kingdom, but above all in heaven. Shinran expects it in being reborn in the Pure Land. It already occurs for him in enlightenment or at the moment of death, but in any case it means an escape from the eternal cycle of endless births. In this sense all three have a negative attitude toward the existing world and its future. And yet there are fundamental differences to be seen. Paul expects the end of the world and the dawning of the Kingdom of God in the immediate future. Luther shares this expectation in its negative part, but he distinguishes between the two kingdoms of worldly and spiritual rule, as has already been mentioned. In Buddhism, however, history has no end and no aim, just as it never had a beginning. According to Paul, one should act in this world as if one no longer belonged to it, and one should not think that one's own act, influenced by the reality of the Kingdom, can or should change the existent world. In spite of its wholly different basis, the Bodhisattva-being of Amida belief comes to a similar ethical orientation. Luther, on the other hand, with his two distinct ethical spheres, reckons with the continued existence of this world, something Paul did not allow for. Out of his own experience Luther rejects monasticism, which had earlier in a specific way taken the place of the Kingdom of God which did not come, and he revaluates the Christian life in worldly vocations by calling it a service to God.

Although the concept of secularism had appeared originally in connection with the rejection of monasticism and the disowning of the church by the state, the concept today is used in the more comprehensive sense of designating all forms of that thought which brings the supernatural into the worldly. This process began in Christianity along with its emergence into the world. That led at first, to be sure, to the arising of the church and its belief in the beyond. Only in the modernity of the Western world has this process moved beyond that churchly *ersatz* for earliest Christian eschatology. Belief in the future, which gives wings to modern Western culture, rests in large part on the Biblical expectation of the Kingdom of God, a belief which the Buddhist world, because of its different idea of history, does not share.

Unlike Hīnayāna Buddhism, which is actually a religion for monks, Mahāyāna represents a secularization, and it is significant that Shinran, just as Luther did, left the monastery and married. Because Amida Buddhism knows neither a supernatural teleology nor a natural one as it developed in the West, it is content with the salvation of the individual and sees this salvation in terms of becoming free of the evil world, not in its betterment. If Amida Buddhism today sees itself challenged in its contact with old and new forms of Western secularism, it is also faced with the question of whether it can better validate the grace of Amida than can Christianity the grace of Christ.

With this very aspect of the matter in mind, it should be clear that the question about the concept of grace in Paul, Shinran and Luther, with which we have occupied ourselves here, is truly far more than a question for the history of religions. It should also be clear that the ultimate destination of the forces which were generated by those men and, therefore, our common future as well, is to be decided on the basis of our understanding of grace.

Nembutsu as Remembrance

Marco Pallis

Were someone to put the question wherein consist the differences between Theravāda, the Buddhism of the Pāli Canon, and Mahāyāna, with its vast variety of schools and methods, one might for a start mention the particular emphasis laid, in the Mahāyāna teachings, upon the cosmic function of the Bodhisattva: saying this does not mean that in relation to the Theravāda the Bodhisattva ideal constitutes some kind of innovation; it suffices to read the *Jātaka*s or stories about the Buddha Śākyamuni's previous births in order to find those characteristic postures which the word "Bodhisattva" came to imply in subsequent centuries here prefigured in mythological mode.[1] These stories were current long before the distinction Theravāda-Mahāyāna came in vogue; since then they have remained as common means of popular instruction extending to every corner of the Buddhist world. Nevertheless it is fair to say that, with the Mahāyāna, the Bodhisattva as a type steps right into the centre of the world-picture, so much so that "the Bodhisattva's Vow" to devote himself consciously to the salvation of all beings without exception might well be considered as marking a man's entry into the Mahāyāna as such; viewed in this light, whatever occurs at a time prior to his taking this decisive step must be accounted an aspiration only, one

---

1. The epithet "mythological" has been introduced here advisedly, in order to draw attention to an important feature of traditional communication which modern terminological usage has tended to debase. The Greek word *mythos*, from which our word derives, originally just meant a story and not a particular kind of story, supposedly fictitious, as nowadays. It was taken for granted that such a story was a carrier of truth, if only because, for the unsophisticated mentality of people brought up on the great myths, anything different would have seemed pointless; the idea of a fictional literature intended as a passing means of entertainment was quite alien to that mentality, and so was allegory of a contrived kind however elevated its purpose. As a factor in human intelligence a "mythological sense" corresponds to a whole dimension of reality which, failing that sense, would remain inaccessible. Essentially, myths belong to no particular time; there is an ever present urgency about the events they relate which is the secret of their power to influence the souls of mankind century after century.

waiting to be given its formal expression through the pronouncing of the vow, when the hour for this shall have struck.

By its root meaning the word "Bodhisattva" denotes one who displays an unmistakable affinity for Enlightenment, one who tends in that direction both deliberately and instinctively. In the context of the Buddhist path it indicates one who has reached an advanced stage;[2] such a man is the dedicated follower of the Buddha in principle and in fact. If all this is commonly known, what we are particularly concerned with here, however, is to extract from the Bodhisattva vocation its most characteristic trait, as expressed in the words of the Vow which run as follows:

> I, so and so, in the presence of my Master, so and so, in the presence of the Buddhas, do call forth the idea of Enlightenment.... I adopt all creatures as mother, father, brothers, sons, sisters, and kinsmen. Henceforth...for the benefit of creatures I shall practise charity, discipline, patience, energy, meditation, wisdom[3] and the means of application... let my Master accept me as a future Buddha.

It can be seen at a glance that this profession of intent anticipates, by implication, the vow taken by the Bodhisattva Dharmākara from which the Pure Land teaching and practice stem. He who first had vowed to dedicate himself wholeheartedly to the good of his fellow-creatures, "down to the last blade of grass" as the saying goes, after treading the Path from life to life or else, in an exceptional case like that of Tibet's poet-saint Milarepa, in the course of a single life, finds himself clearly set for the great Awakening; his unremitting efforts, canalized thanks to

---

2. In Tibet the word for Bodhisattva, side by side with its more technical uses, is often loosely applied where, in English, we would use the word "saintly"; this is not surprising really, since a saintly person evidently exhibits traits appropriate to an incipient Bodhisattva-hood.

3. The six *pāramitās* or Transcendent Virtues: according to Mahāyāna convention *dāna*, the readiness to give oneself up to the service of others, charity in the broadest sense, heads the list as being the "note" whereby a Bodhisattva can be recognized. It is, however, unlikely that a man would have reached such a pitch of self-abnegation without previously espousing a religiously inspired life of discipline, *śīla* under its double heading of conscious abstention from sin and positive conformity with the ritual, doctrinal and other prescriptions of the religion in question; such conformity does not go without effort, *vīrya*, the combative spirit. As complement to the above outgoing virtues, *kṣānti*, contentment, repose in one's own being, follows naturally. It is after a certain blending of these three virtues that the urge into *dāna* may be expected to be felt strongly, thus pointing the way to a Bodhisattva's vocation. The last two *pāramitās*, namely *dhyāna*, contemplation, itself implying discernment between what is real and what is illusory, and *prajñā*, that transcendent wisdom which is a synthesis of all other virtues, completes their scheme of life for followers of the Mahāyāna: obviously this general pattern is applicable in other religions besides Buddhism.

the proper *upāya*s (means) matching each successive need, have placed him in possession of *prajñā*, that wisdom whereby all things in a formerly opaque world have been rendered transparent to the light of *bodhi*—it is at this crucial point that the Bodhisattva renews his vow to succour all beings. This time, however, he gives to his vow a negative as well as a more intensive turn by saying that "I shall *not* enter Nirvana unless I be assured that I can draw after me all the other creatures now steeped in ignorance and consequent suffering": through this vow the Bodhisattva's compassion becomes endowed with irresistible force; aeons of well-doing pass as in a flash; countless creatures are lifted out of their misery, until one day the cup of Dharmākara's merit overflows, and lo! we find ourselves face to face with Amitābha radiating in all directions his saving light. By this token we are given to understand that the vow has not failed in its object; the Buddha himself stands before us offering tangible proof of the vow's efficacy through the communication of his Name under cover of the Nembutsu; henceforth this will suffice to ferry across the troubled waters of *saṃsāra* any being who will confidently trust his sin-weighted body to this single vehicle, even as Zen's stern patriarch Bodhidharma one time trusted the reed he picked up on the water's edge and was borne safely upon its slender stalk across to the other shore. Such is the story of the providential birth of Jōdo-shin.

Reduced to bare essentials Nembutsu is first of all an act of remembrance, whence attention follows naturally[4] thus giving rise to faith in, and thankfulness for, the Vow: from these elementary attitudes a whole program of life can be deduced.

Given these properties comprised by the Nembutsu as providential reminder and catalyst of the essential knowledge, it should cause no one any surprise to hear that comparable examples of the linking of a divine Name with an invocatory *upāya* are to be found elsewhere than in China and Japan; details will of course be different, but the same operative principle holds good nevertheless. To point this out is in no wise to impugn the spiritual originality of the message delivered by the agency of the two great patriarchs, Hōnen and Shinran Shōnin within the framework of Japanese Buddhism with effects lasting even to this day; on the contrary, this is but further proof of the universal applicability of this method to the needs of mankind, and more especially during a phase of the world-cycle when the hold of religion on human minds seems to be weakening in the face of a vast and still growing apparatus of distraction such as history has never recorded before. The fact that the obvious accessibility of such a method does not exclude the most profound in-

---

4. In the Islamic world the word *dhikr*, remembrance, is used of the invocation practised by members of the Sufi confraternities with the Divine Name as its operative formula; the Buddhist term *smṛti* and the Sufic *dhikr* bear an identical meaning.

sights—indeed the contrary is true—has turned Nembutsu and kindred methods to be found elsewhere into potent instruments of regeneration even under the most unfavourable circumstances: this gives the measure of their timeliness as well as of their intrinsic importance.

As an example of mutual corroboration between traditions I have chosen a form of invocation current in the Tibetan-cum-Mongolian world where, however, it is not, as in Japan, associated with any particular school but is in fact widely used by adherents of all schools without distinction: other examples might also have been chosen belonging to non-Buddhist traditions, but it has seemed best to confine one's choice to places nearer home both because one can continue to use a common terminology and also, more especially, because in the Tibetan version the Buddha Amitābha figures in a manner which makes this tradition's kinship with Jōdo-shin clearly apparent.

The operative formula in this case is the six-syllable phrase *Om mani padme Hum* of which the acknowledged revealer is the Bodhisattva Chenrezig (Avalokiteśvara in Sanskrit, Kannon in Japanese). It is his intimate relationship with the Buddha Amitābha which provides the mythological link between the two traditions in question: in order to illustrate this point it will be necessary to hark back to the moment when the Bodhisattva Dharmākara became transfigured into the Buddha of Infinite Light; what we shall have to say now will be something of a sequel to the history of Dharmākara's ascent to Buddhahood as previously related.

If one stops to examine that history somewhat more closely one will become aware of a fact replete with meaning, namely that it would be possible without the least inconsistency to reverse the emphasis by saying that it is an Amitābha about to be who has been replaced by a Dharmākara fulfilled. In other words, if Buddhahood as such represents a state of awareness or knowledge, Bodhisattvahood when fully realized, as in this case, represents the dynamic dimension of that same awareness, it is that awareness in dynamic mode. It is moreover evident that this latter mode of awareness can only be realized in relation to an object in view; if the rescue of suffering beings be its ostensible motive, then this dynamic quality will necessarily take on the character of *compassion*, the Bodhisattva's virtue as already specified in the elementary version of the vow; such a virtue moreover postulates a given world for its exercise, apart from which compassion would not even be a possible concept.

As the dynamic expression of *that* which Buddha-hood is statically, Bodhisattva-hood belongs to this world; it is with perfect logic that the Mahāyāna teachings have traditionally identified compassion with "method." Method is the dynamic counterpart of "wisdom," the quality of awareness: try to separate these two ideas and they will forfeit all practical applicability; hence the Mahāyāna dictum that Wisdom and

Method form an eternal syzygy[5] excluding any possibility of divorce. The Bodhisattva incarnates method as exercisable in saṃsāra; the Buddha personifies wisdom as ever-present in nirvana: this leaves us with two complementary triads namely "Bodhisattva—this world—method" and "Buddha—Buddha-field (= Pure Land)—wisdom." "Human life hard of obtaining" is the opportunity to realize these complementary possibilities; if the saying be true that at the heart of each grain of sand a Buddha is to be found, it is no less true to say that in every being a potential Bodhisattva is recognizable, in active mode in the case of a man, in relatively passive mode in the case of other beings but nonetheless realizable by them via the prior attainment of a human birth.[6]

From all the above it follows that a Bodhisattva's activity on behalf of beings does not lose its necessity once Buddhahood is attained; the ascending course from Dharmākara to Amitābha, as confirmed by the Vow, must needs have its counterpart in a descending course under a fresh name. This name in fact is Chenrezig or Kwannon[7] who, as the story tells us, took birth from the head of Amitābha himself thus becoming the appointed dispenser of a mercy which is none other than a function of the nirvanic Light; in Chenrezig we see a Dharmākara as it were nirvanically reborn, if such an expression be permissible. Here again the story of this celestial event is illuminating, since we are told that Chenrezig, in his exercise of the merciful task laid upon him by his originator and teacher Amitābha, began by leading so many beings towards the promised Buddha-land that the very hells became emptied. However, when this Bodhisattva looked back upon the world, just as his predecessor Dharmākara had done prior to taking his vow, he perceived the horrifying fact that as quickly as one lot of beings climbed out of the infernal round of birth and death, following in his wake another lot of beings, in apparent unconcern, hastened to fill the vacant places, so that the mass of samsaric suffering remained virtually as bad as ever. The Bodhisattva was so overcome by disappointment and pity that his head split in fragments, whereupon the Buddha came to the rescue with a fresh head for his representative. This same thing happened no less than ten times until, with the bestowing by Amitābha of an eleventh head, the Bodhisattva was enabled to resume his mission without further hindrance.

---

5. Ed. This somewhat unusual word means a coordination or an alignment, as for example of heavenly bodies.
6. For an unusually illuminating commentary on the relationship Bodhisattva—Buddha the reader is referred to Part III of *In the Tracks of Buddhism* by Frithjof Schuon, published by Allen and Unwin, a work to which the present writer gratefully acknowledges his own indebtedness.
7. Ed. An older transcription for Kannon, left here to retain the flavour of the original.

In the Tibetan iconography Chenrezig is frequently portrayed under his eleven-headed form, appropriately known as the "Great Compassionate One"; multiple arms go with this portrait, as showing the endless ways in which the Bodhisattva can exercise his function as helper of beings. The most usual portrait of Chenrezig, however, is one with four arms, the whole figure being coloured white; in one hand he holds a rosary and it is this object which symbolizes his communication of the *mani* as invocatory means.[8] Some details of how the invocation with *mani* is carried out by the Tibetans will serve to relate the practice to other similar methods found in Japan and elsewhere.

Firstly, about the formula itself: the most usual translation into English has been "Om, jewel in the Lotus, Hum." Obviously, such words do not immediately lend themselves to logical paraphrase; one can reasonably assume, however, that since in the traditional iconography Buddhas are normally shown as seated upon a lotus, that serene flower resting on the waters of possibility and thereby evocative of "the nature of things," the jewel must for its part represent the presence of the Buddha and the treasure of his teaching inviting discovery, but this by itself does not get one very far. As for the initial and concluding syllables, these belong to the category of metaphysically potent ejaculations whereof many figure in the Tantric initiations; one can safely say, with this kind of formula, that it is not intended for analytical dissection, but rather that its intrinsic message will spontaneously dawn upon a mind poised in one-pointed concentration. This view moreover was confirmed by the Dalai Lama when I put to him the question of whether the *mani* would by itself suffice to take a man all the way to Deliverance. His Holiness replied that it would indeed suffice for one who had penetrated to the heart of its meaning, a ruling which itself bears out the saying that the *Om mani padme Hum* contains "the quintessence of the teaching of all the Buddhas." The fact that the Dalai Lama specifically exercises an "activity of presence" in this world in the name of the Bodhisattva Chenrezig, revealer of *mani*, renders his comment in this instance all the more authoritative.

As in all similar cases an initiatory *lung* (authorization) must be sought by whoever wishes to invoke with *mani*, failing which the practice would remain irregular and correspondingly inefficacious. Once the *lung* has been conferred it is possible to invoke in a number of ways, either under one's breath or, more often, in an audible murmur for which the Tibetan word is the same as for the purring of a cat. It is recommended, for one invoking regularly, that he precede each invoking session by a special poem of four lines and likewise repeat a similar quatrain by way of conclusion. Here is the text:

---

8. Ed. *Mani* means jewel and also refers to the invocation in which the word is contained, as explained below.

> Unstained by sin and white of hue
> Born from the head of the perfect Buddha
> Look down in mercy upon beings
> To Chenrezig let worship be offered.
>
> By the merit of this (invocation) may I soon
> Become endowed with Chenrezig's power.
> Let all beings without even one omission
> In his (Chenrezig's) land established be.

No need to underline the reference to Amitābha in the first verse and the reference to the Buddha Land in the second in order to show how close to one another *Mani* and Nembutsu stand as regards their basic purpose.

Mention should also be made here of the standard treatise on the *mani* invocation, in which are outlined the various symbolical correspondences to which the six syllables lend themselves, each of which can become a theme for meditation. These sixfold schemes range over a wide field, starting with deliverance from each in turn of the possible states of sentient existence and the realization one by one of the six *pāramitās* or transcendent virtues (see again note 3); the latter parts of this treatise lead the mind into still deeper waters which it is beyond the scope of this essay to explore.

To turn to more external features of the *mani* invocation, it is common practice to use some kind of rhythmical support while repeating the words of the *mantra*, which can be either a rosary or else an appliance peculiar to Tibet which foreign travellers have rather inappropriately labelled as a "prayer-wheel," since no idea of petition enters in; this wheel consists of a rotating box fixed on the end of a wooden handle and containing a tightly rolled cylinder of paper inscribed all over with the *mani* formula. A small weight attached by a chain to the box enables the invoking person to maintain an even swing while repeating the words; sometimes, especially with elderly people, the practice becomes reduced to a silent rotatory motion, with the invocation itself taken for granted.

Very large *mani*-wheels are commonly to be found at the doors of temples which each person as he enters will set in motion; likewise, rows of smaller wheels are often disposed along the outside walls so that those who carry out the *pradakṣina* or clockwise circuit of the sacred edifice may set them revolving as they pass. But remembrance of the *mani* does not stop there; immense *mani*-wheels ceaselessly kept going by waterfalls exist in many places, while flags bearing the sacred words float from the corners of every homestead. Lastly, flat stones carved with the formula and dedicated as offerings by the pious are to be found laid in rows on raised parapets at the edge of highroads or along the approaches of monasteries. These "*mani*-walls" are so disposed as to allow a passage on either side, since reverence requires that a man turn his right side towards any sacred object he happens to pass, be it a *stūpa* or one of these *mani*-walls; being on horseback is no excuse for doing otherwise. The popular dictum "beware of the devils on the left hand side" refers to this practice.

If it be asked what effect all this can amount to, the answer is that it serves to keep people constantly reminded of what a human life is for; reminiscence is the key to a religiously directed life at all levels, from the most external and popular to the most interior and intellectual; "popular" may often be allied with deep insights, of course, the above distinctions are not intended in a social sense. Certainly in the Tibet we visited while the traditional order there was still intact the whole landscape was as if suffused by the message of the Buddhist Dharma, it came to one with the air one breathed, birds seemed to sing of it, mountain streams hummed its refrain as they bubbled across the stones, a dharmic perfume seemed to rise from every flower, at once a reminder and a pointer to what still needed doing. The absence of fear on the part of wild creatures at the approach of man was in itself a witness to this same truth; there were times when a man might have been forgiven for supposing himself already present in the Pure Land. The India of King Aśoka's time must have been something like this; to find it in mid-twentieth century anywhere was something of a wonder.

Moreover a situation like this was bound to be reflected in the lives of individuals despite inevitable human failings; piety was refreshingly spontaneous, it did not need dramatizing attitudes to bolster it up nor any rationalized justifications. Each man was enabled to find his own level without difficulty according to capacity and even a quite modest qualification could carry him far. Among the many people using the *mani* one can say that a large proportion stopped short at the idea of gathering merit with a view to a favourable rebirth; the finality in view, though not entirely negligible in itself, remained essentially samsaric: it did not look far beyond the limits of the cosmos. More perceptive practitioners would resort to the same invocation for the general purpose of nourishing and deepening their own piety, the finality here was "devotional" in the sense of the Indian word *bhakti* as implying a comparatively intense degree of participation; such a way of invoking represents an intermediate position in the scale of spiritual values. Rarer by comparison is the kind of person whose intelligence, matured in the course of the practice, is able to envisage that truth for which the invocation provides both a means of recollection and an incentive to realize it fully: this is the case to which the Dalai Lama was referring when he spoke of penetrating to the heart of the teaching which the Six Syllables between them enshrine.

In a more general connection, the question often arises as to how much importance should be attached to the frequent repetition of a formula like the *mani* or the nembutsu as compared with a sparser use of it; here one can recall the fact that in the period when Hōnen was preaching the Pure Land doctrine in Japan many persons, carried away by their enthusiasm, vied with one another as to the number of times they were able to repeat the formula as if this were the thing that mattered; in the face of these extravagances Shinran Shōnin applied a wholesome corrective by showing that the value of Nembutsu is primarily a qualitative one, with number counting for nothing in itself as a criterion of effectiveness. The essence of a thing, that which makes it to be what it is, and not something else, is not susceptible of multiplication: one can for instance count one, two or a hundred sheep, but the quality of "sheepness" becomes neither increased nor sub-divided thereby. The same applies to nembutsu or *mani*; each represents a unique and total presence carrying within itself its own finality irrespective of number. This is an important principle to grasp; were one able to penetrate as far as the very heart of the sacred formula a single mention of it would be sufficient to bring one home to the Pure Land; the various steps that have led one as far as the threshold become merged in fulfillment.

At the same time, on the basis of an empirical judgment, one is not justified in despising the man who finds frequent repetition of an invocatory formula helpful; to estimate the value of such repetition in purely quantitative terms is certainly an error, but to feel an urge to fill one's life with the formula because one values it above everything else and feels lonely and lost without it is another thing. To rise of a morning with nembutsu, to retire to bed at night with its words on one's lips, to live with it and by it, to die with its last echo in one's ear, what could in fact be better or more humanly appropriate? As between one who invokes very often and another who does so with less frequency there is little to choose provided attention be focused on the essential. It is the effects on the soul which will count in the long run, its alchemical transmutation in witness of the Vow's power, thanks to which the lead of our existential ignorance is enabled to reveal its essential identity with the gold of Bodhi, even as Dharmākara's identity with Amitābha is revealed in the Vow itself.

There is one more question of practical importance for all who would follow a contemplative discipline outside the monastic order, which here is not in question, namely the question of how one may regard the interruptions imposed by the need to transfer attention, during one's working hours, to external matters either of a professional kind or else, in the majority of cases, as means of earning a livelihood. Does not this, some may well ask, render the idea of a lifelong concentration on nembutsu virtually unrealizable? And if so, what result will this have in regard to the essential awakening of faith? Some such question has in fact always worried mankind in one form or another, but has become more pressing than ever as a result of the breakdown of traditional societies formerly structured according to religiously linked vocations. The individual is now left in so-called freedom to make choices which his ancestors were mercifully spared. Nevertheless, there is sufficient precedent to enable one to answer this question in a way that all may understand.

The criterion which applies in all such cases is this, namely that so long as a man's work is not obviously dishonest, cruel or otherwise reprehensible, that is to say so long as it conforms, broadly speaking,[9] to the definitions of the Noble Eightfold Path under the headings of Proper Ordering of Work and Proper Livelihood, the time and attention this demands from a man will not, *per se*, constitute a distraction in the technical sense of the word; rather will the stream of contemplation continue to flow quietly like an underground river, ready to surface again with more animated current once the necessary tasks have been accomplished for the time being. Here "necessary" is the operative word: activities undertaken needlessly, from frivolous or luxurious motives such as a wish to "kill time" because one expects to feel bored when not actually working, cannot on any showing be ranked as "work" in the proper sense. A vast number of so-called "leisure activities" fall under this condemnable heading: these do, on any logical showing, constitute distractions in the strict sense of the word. One would have thought that the briefest portion of a "human life hard of obtaining" could have been put to better uses; yet nowadays such abuse of the human privilege is not only tolerated but even encouraged on the vastest scale by way of tribute to the great god of Economics, Māra's fashionable alias in the contemporary world. By rights most of these time-wasting practices belong to the category of noxious drugs, addiction to which comes only too easily.

Apart from this question of man's occupational calls and how these properly fit in, the invocation with nembutsu or its equivalents in other

---

9. "Broadly speaking": this reservation was necessary, inasmuch as no person is in a position to assess all the repercussions of his work or his livelihood in an ever changing world. All he can do is to avoid practices of a self-evidently wicked kind, while conforming to a reasonable degree with the circumstances in which his karma has placed him. In earlier times, when vocations were more clear-cut and also religiously guaranteed, discrimination was relatively easy though by no means infallible in practice. Nowadays, with the bewildering complications which beset almost everybody's life in the modern world, a man can but do his limited best to conform to the ideal prescriptions of the Eightfold Path under the two headings in question; there is no call for him to scrape his conscience by looking far beyond what lies obviously within reach of a human choice. This does not mean, of course, that one need have no scruples as to what one does or does not undertake; where discernment is still possible, it should be exercised in the light of the Buddhist teachings.

traditions will always offer a most potent protection against distractions of whatever kind. A life filled with this numinous influence leaves little chance for Māra's attendant demons to gain a footing. I remember one Lama's advice when he said "finish the work in hand and after that fill the remaining time with *mani* invocation"; this sets the pattern of a life's program, details of which can be left to settle themselves in the light of particular needs.

The heart-moving tale of Dharmākara's journey to Enlightenment, on which our own participation in the teachings of Jōdo-shin depends, may at first sight appear to record events dating from long, long ago. It is well to remember, however, what has already been said about the timeless nature of mythological happenings (see note 1), whereby they are rendered applicable again and again across the changing circumstances of mankind, as means of human illumination. There are certain truths which are best able to communicate themselves in this form without any danger of entanglement in the alternative of belief versus disbelief which, in the case of historical claims, is all too likely to be raised by the very nature of the evidence on which those claims rest: question the factual evidence, and the truths themselves become vulnerable as has been shown in the case of Western Christianity during recent times where the attempt to "demythologize" its sacred lore, including the Scriptures, has only made the situation worse for present-day believers. Historical evidence of course has its own importance, no need to deny this fact. In relation to history a traditional mythology provides a factor of equilibrium not easily dispensed with if a given religion is to retain its hold over the minds of men.

As it stands, the old story of Dharmākara represents the Wisdom aspect of a teaching whereof the Method aspect is to be found when this same story comes to be re-enacted in a human life, be it our own life or another's, thanks to the evocative power released by the original Vow, following its confirmation in the person of Amitābha Buddha. Hence the injunction to place all our faith in the Other Power, eschewing self. The consequences of so doing will affect both our thinking and feeling and all we do or avoid doing in this life.

Here it is well to remind ourselves of what was said at the outset, namely that the Bodhisattva's compassion, his dynamic virtue, needs a field for its exercise as well as suffering beings for its objects, failing which it would be meaningless. For a field one can also say "a world" either in the sense of a particular world (the world familiar to us, for example) or in the sense of *saṃsāra* as such, comprising all possible forms of existence, including many we can never know. A world, by definition, is a field of contrasts, an orchard of karma replete with its fruits black or white which we ourselves, in our dual capacity of creators and partakers of these fruits, are called upon to harvest in season, be they bitter or sweet. This experiencing of the world, moreover, also comes to us in a dual way, at once external and internal: for us, the external world is composed of all beings and things which fall into the category of "other," while to the internal world there belong all such experiences as concern what we call "I" or "mine," the ego-consciousness at every level. One can go further and say that man, in this respect, himself constitutes something like a self-contained world; it is not for nothing that the human state has been described, by analogy with the Cosmos at large, as a "microcosm," a little world. It is in fact within this little estate of ours that the drama of Dharmākara and Amitābha has to be played out if we are truly to understand it, this being in fact the Method aspect of the story which thus, through its concrete experiencing, will reveal itself as Wisdom to our intelligence. It is with this, for us, most vital matter that the present essay may fittingly be concluded.

The three principal factors in our symbolical play are firstly, the psycho-physical vehicle of our earthly existence which provides the moving stage and, secondly, the faculty of attention under its various aspects including the senses, reason, imagination, and above all our active remembrance or mindfulness—these between them represent the Bodhi-sattva-ic dynamism in relation to our vocational history; thirdly and lastly, there is the illuminative power of Amitābha as represented by the un-embodied Intelligence dwelling at that secret spot in the centre of each being where *saṃsāra* as such is inoperative[10] or, to be still more accurate, where *saṃsāra* reveals its own essential identity with nirvana (to quote the *Heart Sūtra*): but for this Eye of Bodhi[11] within us, able

---

10. By way of concordant testimony one can profitably recall the teaching of the great medieval Sage of Western Christendom, Meister Eckhart, when he said that "in man is to be found something uncreate and uncreatable and this is the Intellect" to which he adds that were man entirely such, he too would be uncreate and uncreatable. Substitute "Eye of Bodhi" for the word "intellect" and you have there a statement any Buddhist might understand. In the traditions issuing from the Semitic stem, where the idea of creation" plays a dominant part, to say of anything that it is "uncreate" is the equivalent of "beyond the scope of samsaric change." It should be added that, at the time when Meister Eckhart was writing, the word "intellect" always bore the above meaning, as distinct from "reason" which, as its Latin name of *ratio* shows, was a faculty enabling one to relate things to one another apart from any possibility of perceiving their intrinsic suchness which only the Intellect is able to do. The modern confusion between intellect, reason and mind, to the practical emasculation of the former, has spelt a disaster for human thinking. The above example can be paralleled by another, taken this time from Eastern Christianity, where it is said that the crowns of the Perfected Saints are made out of "Un-created Light" or as we might also say, the diadems of the perfected Bodhisattvas are made from Amitābha's own halo.

11. Ed. The author's rather difficult expression "Bodhic Eye" has been replaced

to read the Bodhi message which all things display to him who knows where to look, human liberation through Enlightenment, and the liberation from suffering of other beings via a human birth, would not be a possibility; the door to the Pure Land would remain for ever closed. Thanks to Dharmākara's example, culminating in his Vow, we know that this Pure Land is open, however; herein consists our hope and our incentive, what more can one ask of existence than this supreme opportunity the human state comprises so long as that state prevails? Before quitting this discussion one other question calls for passing consideration, affecting the manner of presenting Jōdo-shin ideas in popular form today: writers on the subject seem much given to stressing the "easy" nature of the Jōdo-shin way; faith, so they say, is all we really need inasmuch as Amitābha, Dharmākara that was, has done our work for us already, thus rendering entry into the Pure Land as good as assured, with the corollary that any suggestion of responsibility or conscious effort on our part would savour of a dangerous concession to Own Power and is in any case redundant. In voicing such ideas a sentimentally angled vocabulary is used without apparently taking into account the effect this is likely to have on uncritical minds. Though this kind of language is doubtless not actually intended to minimize the normal teachings of Buddhism it does nevertheless betray a pathetically artless trend in the thinking of authors who give vent to it. Some will doubtless seek to defend themselves by saying that the writings of Shinran and other Jōdo-shin luminaries also contain phrases having a somewhat similar ring; those who quote thus out of context are apt to ignore the fact that a teaching Sage, one who is out to win hearts but not to destroy intelligences (this should not need saying), may sometimes resort to a schematic phraseology never meant to be taken literally. Lesser persons should show prudence in how they quote from, and especially in how they themselves embroider upon, such statements of the great.

  When for example Nichiren, that militant saint, declared that a single pronouncing of the nembutsu was enough to send a man to hell, he was obviously exaggerating for the purpose of goading his own audience in a predetermined direction; religious history offers many such examples of rhetorical excess, albeit spiritually motivated. The proper reply to such a diatribe would be by saying, in the tone of respect due to a great Master, "Thanks Reverend Sir, your warning brings great comfort; for me Hell, with nembutsu, will be as good as Heaven; without nembutsu paradise would be a hell indeed!"[12]

---

    throughout with "Eye of Bodhi," i.e. for which "eye of enlightenment" would be a simple English alternative.

12. My friend Dr. Inagaki Hisao has supplied a quotation from Shinran's teachings as embodied in the *Tannishō* (Chapter II) where the same sentiment is expressed con-

Let us, however, for a moment, as an *upāya* nicely matched to the occasion, carry the argument of the very people we had been criticizing a little further by putting the following question: if Dharmākara's compassionate initiative, culminating in the Vow, has come to the aid of our weakness by completing the most essential part of our task for us, leaving it to us to take subsequent advantage of this favour, how best can we repay our debt of gratitude for the mercy shown us? Surely an elementary gratitude requires, on the part of a beneficiary, that he should try and please his benefactor by doing as he has advised and not the contrary. The Eightfold Path is what the Buddha left for our life's program; in following this way, whether we are motivated by regard for our own highest interest or by simple thankfulness for Amitābha's mercy, makes little odds in practice, though this second attitude may commend itself to our mentality for contingent reasons. To bring all this into proper perspective in the context of Jōdo-shin one has to bear in mind its operative principle, namely that the Nembutsu itself comprises all possible teachings, all methods, all merits "eminently," requiring nothing else of us except our faith which must be freely given. A genuine faith, however one may regard it, does not go without its heroic overtones; how then are we to understand it in relation to the finality of Jōdo-shin, as symbolized by the Pure Land? Surely, in this same perspective, faith is there to act as a catalyst of all the other virtues whether we list them separately or not. In this way an attitude that may sometimes seem one-sidedly devotional can still rejoin Buddhism's profoundest insights; for one who does so, the way may well be described as "easy."

What is certain, however, is that no Buddhist, whatever his own personal affiliations may happen to be, can reasonably claim exclusive authority for the teachings he follows; as between an "Own Power" and an "Other Power" approach to salvation we can perhaps say that if the latter may sometimes take on a too passive appearance as in the cases previously mentioned, the former type of method, if improperly conceived, can easily imprison one in a state of self-centred consciousness of a most cramping kind. The best defence against either of the above errors is to remember that, as between two indubitably orthodox but formally contrasted teachings, where one of them is deliberately stressed the other must always be recognized as latent, and vice versa. This excludes, moreover, any temptation to indulge in sectarian excesses. No spiritual method can be totally self-contained; by definition every *upāya* is provisionally deployed in view of the known needs of a given mental-

---

sonantly with Jōdo tradition and using its typical dialect: "I would not regret even if I were deceived by Hōnen and thus, by uttering the nembutsu, fell into hell... Since I am incapable of any practice whatsoever, hell would definitely be my dwelling anyway."

ity; there its authority stops, and to say so of any particular teaching implies no disrespect.

The stress laid on "Other Power" in Jōdo-shin provides a salutary counterblast to any form of self-esteem, a fact which makes its teachings peculiarly apt in our own time when deification of the human animal as confined to this world and a wholesale pandering to his ever-expanding appetites is being preached on every side. In the presence of Amitābha the achievements of individual mankind become reduced to their proper unimportance; it is in intelligent humility that a truly human greatness is to be found.

One important thing to bear in mind, in all this, is that the Buddha's mercy is providential, but does not, for this very reason, suspend the Law of Karma: if beings will persist in ignoring that law while coveting the things mercy might have granted them, the mercy itself will reach them in the guise of severity; severity is merciful when this is the only means of provoking a radical *metanoia* (change of outlook), failing which wandering in *saṃsāra* must needs continue indefinitely. The Nembutsu is our ever present reminder of this truth; if, in reliance on the Vow, we abandon all wish to attribute victory to ourselves, the unfed ego will surely waste away, leaving us in peace.

Apart from all else, reliance on "Other Power" will remain unrealizable so long as the ego-centric consciousness is being mistaken for the real person; it is this confusion of identity which the great *upāya* propounded by Hōnen and Shinran Shōnin was providentially designed to dispel. Let Nembutsu serve as our perpetual defence against this fatal error, through the remembrance it keeps alive in human hearts. Where that remembrance has been raised to its highest power, there is to be found the Pure Land.

Shinran's Way in Modern Society

Alfred Bloom

Introduction

It is a common practice when discussing the significance of a religious or philosophical system to put it in the context of the times and spend most of the period discussing contemporary problems rather than the nature of the teaching which will resolve those issues. It is as though we went to the doctor and got a diagnosis and then thought we were cured. We will not analyze the contemporary situation in detail except where it is immediately relevant to consider a point in Shinran's teaching.

We are all aware of the variety of problems that confront the modern world from even the most casual reading of the newspaper. When all the problems are reduced to their most fundamental character, they focus upon the problem of the ego. A recent work exploring the meaning of Shinran's teaching for the contemporary world states:

> What is the cause of this modern dilemma? Can we blame science which is at the base of technological advances? The answer is no, because science in itself is neither good nor evil. The problem lies in the manner in which we utilize the results of scientific research; it is man, and not science, who ultimately decides on how scientific knowledge shall be used. Thus, the responsibility for the dark aspect of modern civilization rests with man himself.[1]

According to this text, modern people have become alienated and dehumanized as a result of the very freedom they sought in the assertion of ego that emerged from the Renaissance, Reformation and other modern western developments in philosophy and politics. Egoism, whether of individuals or nations and groups, is the fundamental issue of our time. However, it is easy to look out at the world and see the problems, but not recognize that they lie within each of us.

---

1. Nishi Honganji Commission on the Promotion of Religious Education, *Shinran in the Contemporary World* (Kyōto; Jōdo Shinshū Nishi Honganji, 1974), 6.

Alfred Bloom

Before taking up Shinran's thought directly, we should make some observations concerning Buddhism and religion in general. Although we assume that religion can help us solve our problems, we must recognize frankly and honestly that religion is also the cause of some problems.

As a result of the complicity of religion and political authorities throughout history and in the modern world, religion itself has become a problem. Freedom from despotism has frequently required refuting the religious views of society. In Europe political oppression was carried out on the basis of "the divine right of kings." In Japan there have been similar tendencies and problems leading to disaster. Further, religion has frequently resisted the progress of modern knowledge and has given rise to the conflict of science and religion. Religious sectarianism has produced wars as in Ireland, Palestine, Philippines, sometimes in India, and in pre-modern Europe. Even in Japan during the ancient and medieval periods there was petty strife between temples seeking their own privilege. Persecution, bigotry, dogmatism and hatred have often been the marks of religion from ancient to modern times in every culture and nation. We must understand that there is religion which cloaks egoism or masks it with high sounding terms, and there is religion which penetrates the deceptions of the ego and liberates everyone for a fuller life.

We should also point out that for people everywhere religion has become a spiritual problem, because they confuse matters of formality and ceremony with the true essence of religion as life and a way of living. Religious traditions are highly conservative. The problem of tradition is well illustrated by the story of a man from Chǔ in ancient China who dropped his sword in the river. In order to be able to find it again, he marked the edge of the boat where it fell, never realizing that the boat itself was moving in the current.

We must also recognize that religion has become a personal problem with the collapse of traditional social structures that enforced obligatory religious participation. A person can now choose his own religion. However, individuals are now more at a loss to discover meaningful insight in the face of the enormous diversity of religious viewpoints that circulate in our time. They may become fanatic, or indifferent. The spread of some movements indicates a yearning on the part of individuals for meaning, but also a gullibility to believe anything soothing. We are living in an age described by the Japanese proverb: *Iwashi no atama mo, shinjin kara*—"Even a sardine's head can be an object of worship."

Further, secularization in all areas of society is pushing religion to the fringes of life. It has become an occasional event or is relevant only in crisis. It is resorted to only when all else fails. Religion appears to mark the dead ends of life, or it is like an aspirin to cover over symptoms, but not to provide fundamental cure. In many cases, Buddhism has suffered from such views of religion, and its real potential to contribute creatively to modern issues has been obscured.

Despite its many problems, Buddhism, among the many competing world philosophies, is relevant to our age because it focuses primarily on the problem of the ego that afflicts humanity. The Buddhist concepts of Delusion, Non-soul, and Voidness have great importance in breaking through prejudices, preconceptions, dogmatisms and egoism. There are many aspects to Buddhism, but it is important to concentrate upon the more reformist and dynamic features of Buddhism as a living spiritual experience.

We are all familiar with the fact that Gautama rejected the comfortable ways of life in his aristocratic society in order to seek enlightenment. The enlightenment he attained enabled him to see deeply into the self-deceptions people nurture in making their lives secure and stable. Buddhism is a reforming and iconoclastic, truth-seeking approach to life. Buddha challenged the pursuits of permanence, pleasure and possessions as the means to security and meaning in life. He faced egoism realistically and uncovered the false consciousness which makes us seek our own benefit even at the expense of others. In modern terms, we might say Buddhism was a "consciousness-raising" effort—enabling people to become aware of their true natures to such a degree that they would be liberated from the domination of passion and egoism.

In Mahāyāna Buddhism, as it later developed, the doctrine of Voidness carried forward this same task of breaking through the superficialities of our perceptions and graspings by rejecting the belief that our minds could comprehend any true absolute. All our experience is limited and relative to our own egos. When we are blind to this fact, we engage in competitions and conflicts in order to secure our own desire.

In the teaching of Voidness, Buddhism has a self-renewing principle which enables it to bring new insights and fresh experiences to play in the modern world, since it is freed from bondage to the past. Buddhism teaches, through the concept of Voidness, that nothing, however absolute it may appear, can, or should, stand in the way to deeper enlightenment. Nothing that we conceive or establish in thought or organization can replace or exhaust true enlightenment. Religion, theology and institutions are only a means to the greater end of enlightenment and truth. Buddhism embodies a spirit of self-criticism and reform which must be given application in our own time. Buddhist iconoclasm comes most clearly in the symbol of the sword of wisdom seen throughout the tradition, and is given most profound expression in the words of the Chinese Zen master Línjì (J. Rinzai). He declared Buddhist emancipation from all limiting structures:

> Seekers of the Way, if you want to achieve the understanding according to the Law, don"t be deceived by others and turn to [your thoughts]

> internally or [objects] externally. Kill anything that you happen on. Kill the Buddha if you happen to meet him.... Kill your parents or relatives if you happen to meet them. Only then can you be free...and at ease. ...I merely put on clothing and eat meals as usual and pass my time without doing anything. You people coming from the various directions have all made up your minds to seek the Buddha, seek the Law.... Crazy people!..."Buddha" and "Patriarchs" are *terms of praise and also bondage*. Do you want to know where the Three Worlds are? They are right in your mind which is now listening to the Law.[2]

The critical temperament which will not allow structures, distinctions, concepts, or theory to obstruct the deeper inner reality of experience was also present in Shinran. He declared that the Original Vow made no distinctions such as humans employ in organizing their lives, societies and religions. He declared in the *Kyōgyōshinshō*:

> As I contemplate the ocean-like Great Faith, I see that it does not choose between the noble and the mean, the priest and the layman, nor does it discriminate between man and woman, old and young. The amount of sin is not questioned, and the length of practice is not discussed. It is neither "practice" nor "good," neither "abrupt" nor "gradual," neither "meditative" nor "non-meditative," neither "right meditation" nor "wrong meditation," neither "[ideational]" nor "[non-ideational]," neither "while living" nor "at the end of life," neither "many utterances" nor "one thought." Faith is none other than the inconceivable, indescribable, and ineffable Serene Faith. It is like the *agada*[3] which destroys all poisons. The medicine of the Tathāgata's Vow destroys the *poisons of wisdom and ignorance*.[4]

The bondage of patriarchs and Buddhas in Línjì and the poisons of wisdom and ignorance pointed to by Shinran suggest that all aspects of religion must be scrutinized to prevent liberation from becoming a form of enslavement. From these suggestions we understand that Buddhism is not a belief, a system, or an institution. It is a continual process of growth in life which comes about as we keep ourselves open to discover further and deeper truths and as we subject our "truths" to the brilliant light of the wisdom of Voidness.

We have already called attention to the fact that Buddhism, throughout its long history, has been most concerned with the problem of ego-

---

2. Wing-tsit Chan, *A Source Book in Chinese Philosophy* (Princeton University Press, 1963), 447–448. Italics added.
3. Ed. The Sanskrit term *agada* means "free from disease" and refers to a medicine which cures all diseases. Cf. note in the source of the citation.
4. *The Kyō Gyō Shin Shō*, Ryukoku Translation Series v (Kyōto; Ryūkoku University, 1966), 113–114 (hereafter cited as RTS). Italics added.

ism and how it may infect all activity, thought, and even religion. Shinran, as an heir of Buddhist teaching, also focused upon this problem and even more intensely as *his own problem*. Consequently, Shinran's experience and teaching is directly relevant to our contemporary situation in society and religion. A major interest today centers around understanding how the ego functions and how to gain liberation from its bondage. There are mind control systems, human potential programs, behaviour modification theories, sensitivity approaches, psychiatric analysis, and studies of consciousness. Interest in Oriental traditions which also take up the problem of ego has been strong because of these developments. While the ancient Hindu traditions primarily seek to demonstrate the relation of our limited egos to the ultimate reality of *Brahman*, Buddhism concentrates on the process of the ego and the worlds it constructs for its own advantage. It is at this point that Shinran's perception of the ineradicable egoism that distorts our every activity, however idealistic it may appear to be, is extremely pertinent.

Shinran is also important because he was an existentialist who faced the concrete realities of his life and struggled with his own destiny. In the deepest sense Shinran reveals himself in his writings as a true personality. His teachings mirror his own struggle to gain emancipation from the bondage of egoism after long years of fruitless monastic discipline. His many confessions of imperfection and evil are among the most keen and real in all religious literature. Shinran was a therapist in assisting people on the basis of his own experience to become liberated from fear and anxiety or despair concerning their lives and destiny. He was a true teacher, because he could identify with his students and share his life and experience with them.

We may also note that a major issue of our time is interest in the occult and authoritarian religion. Shinran negates the need for magic and occult by proclaiming the all-embracing and all-sufficient compassion of Amida Buddha for whom no good surpasses and no evil can hinder. Magic is a reflection of fear and anxiety; an attempt to impose our egoistic wills on reality. When we see the true foundation of our lives in the compassion of Buddha, there is no more anxiety and no need to impose our will. Shinran also developed a non-authoritarian religion. He shares truth but does not impose it; he exhorts and encourages, but he does not coerce or condemn. While Shinran did not face problems identical with ours in modern society, he offers a perspective which can assist us in the discovery of solutions by bringing a deeper sense of compassion and self-understanding into all areas of human activity and relationships.

There are two other points of importance in establishing the perspective of this study. One concerns the otherworldly nature of Pure Land teaching, and the other is the problem of the meaning of life in modern society.

Pure Land teaching is widely considered to be an otherworldly teaching directed to life after death. Consequently, it appears to have little relevance to affairs of this life. While evidence for this view can be seen in the historical development of Pure Land tradition, it is rather incomplete as a basis for judging Pure Land teaching. Without going into great detail, we should note that in China the teaching was severely criticized by Confucianists who misperceived the attitude which Pure Land teaching held toward life in the world of suffering. There is a social awareness built into Pure Land doctrine in its offer of salvation and purity in the other world. More important is the teaching of the *Sūtra of Eternal Life* itself which exhorts people to fulfill virtue in this life:

> Cultivate widely the field of virtue in this world! Share a warm heart with others, give alms, and do not break the ways of life! Know forbearance, spare no effort, and with one mind and wisdom teach each other! Cultivate virtue, do good, and with right mind and will keep your own self clean and pure for a full day and night. This will be superior to practising good for a hundred years in the Country of the Buddha of Eternal Life.[5]

Rather than otherworldliness being advocated, ethical social life in this world is commended over life in another world. As the text goes on to point out, it is no problem to do good in other worlds where the environment is just right. It all comes naturally. In this world where evil reigns, it is a challenge to pursue the good. Throughout Shinran's writings there are also numerous references to ethical action as an integral part of religious life. According to Shinran, Faith and recitation of Nembutsu transform the person and create deeper relations with one's fellows:

> Signs of long years of saying the nembutsu and aspiring for birth can be seen in the change in the heart which had been bad and in the deep warmth for friends and fellow-practisers; this is the sign of rejecting the world.[6]

That Shinran did not consider the end of religion merely salvation to live in another world is observable in his emphasis on *gensō*, the aspect of the Bodhisattva's return to this world to work for the salvation of all beings. Shinran, as well as other Pure Land teachers, had in view the welfare of people in this world as well as the next.

Finally, there is the problem of the meaning of life in modern society as it relates to our present discussion. In the upheavals of modern

---

5. Kōshō Yamamoto, *Shinshū Seiten* (Honolulu; Honpa Honganji Mission of Hawaii, 1955), 65.
6. *Mattōshō* xix, *from Letters of Shinran*, Shin Buddhism Translation Series x, i (Kyōto; Honganji International Center, 1978), 58.

life, individuals have been driven to question the value of their personal existence. It is peculiarly a problem for western societies, and it is also a modern problem which did not exist in this form in earlier societies, east or west. The meaning of life has become an issue with the discovery of the individual as a real element of the world, capable of independent action. Earlier societies were communal and tribal. No independent, personal decisions could be allowed to threaten the existence of the group. In western tradition, the group became the Church, and the goal was the kingdom of God. Each person was to play his role in bringing about its realization in the process of history. Hence, according to western thinkers, history had a meaning as it was directed by God toward the fulfillment of his purposes.

Protestantism individualized the role of the person in assisting the fulfillment of God's will. According to this interpretation, each individual can find God's plan for his life, and thereby perceive its meaning within the totality of God's plan for history. In its own way it was a grand affirmation of the importance and value of each person.

However, the succession of wars and destruction, and the futility of individualism in modern times has led to a breakdown in confidence in this theory of meaning. Thus the question has arisen: what is the meaning of life? It becomes more poignant when history has no meaning and the individual is cut off from sources of direction and assurance.

In this context the Oriental teachings of Hinduism, Taoism, and Buddhism have had great attraction for contemporary people. Rather than a historical meaning of life, they offer an ontological meaning. Ontological meaning of life stresses that all potentiality and value lie within ourselves, though it may be covered by ignorance and delusion. When we enter into the depth of the mystery of our own beings and the world we have constructed from it, we contact the very root of reality that energizes all life. In Buddhism this means to realize our Buddha natures, and in Shinran's teaching it is interpreted as the awareness of the two types of deep faith: the awareness of our fundamental imperfection and the awareness of the illuminating vision of Amida's compassion which embraces us without regard to our imperfections. It is also *jinen hōni*, the natural-ness of life, which is perceived beyond or within all the conditions of life.

In essence, Buddhism turns our attention to the inner nature of our lives. It does not look to the process of history for justification and meaning. It does not deny the present for an imagined future. Rather, it means to develop a sensitivity to all that is around us for the direction our experiences offer. It means to be open to others, to work with them, to share with them. Finally, it means not so much to ask: what is the meaning of *my* life? But rather to ask: *How meaningful am I to others?* In contributing to the building up of others, we attain our own stature.

We have been thinking theoretically and generally about Buddhism and Shinran. We wish now to concentrate on Shinran as a model for our age. Our youth lack attractive and commanding models who exhibit in their lives the qualities and character that radiate meaning. Although Shinran did not attempt to display his own character for all to see, we do catch glimpses of his personality in his writings and the reflections of his disciples.

Shinran as a model for our time

The life of Shinran provides a clue to the way in which a person can approach his life. Victor Frankl in his book *Man's Search for Meaning* (Boston 1959), points out that, as a result of his experience in the German concentration camps, the one freedom left to a person is the ability to determine one's attitude to existence even when one is left without a shred of hope. The struggle to retain one's humanity in the face of the negation of humanity is the key to the meaning of existence. It is from this perspective that we wish to look at the life of Shinran as a guide for our own lives.

It is important to look at the life of a teacher, as well as his teaching, because more than the abstract word, it is example that moves people. The massive depersonalization of modern life tends to highlight the strength of extraordinary personalities who transcended their environments to chart new directions for the human spirit. We can see this easily in political personalities and the great followings they command. For good or ill, this is the age of the personality cult in which people try to discover a focal point for their lives. Consequently, any claims for the validity and significance of a teaching must be able to point to its realization in the life of persons.

Shinran's life has many affinities with our own time. He lived in an age of social turmoil and upheaval. There were natural disasters and wars, as well as religious corruption throughout the Kamakura era (1185–1333). Like many of his contemporaries, Shinran became deeply concerned about his own destiny—or in modern terms, the meaning of life. His dissatisfaction with life and with himself became more intense and eventually led him on a desperate search to solve his problem. During this period, Hōnen, Dōgen, and Nichiren had also passed through times of profound spiritual search.

In Shinran's case, he had been made the ward of a monastery and later became a monk on Mount Hiei. Although he participated in serious religious discipline for twenty years, he could not attain assurance of his own spiritual liberation. Rather, he became more keenly aware of his passionate nature. Finally, he concluded that monastic regulations and spiritual discipline were not suitable for him or the time in which he lived. Looking back over his life in later years, he declared:

> The reason is that, if I could become Buddha by performing some other practice and fell into hell by uttering the Nembutsu, then, I might feel regret at having been deceived. But since I am incapable of any practice whatsoever, hell would definitely be my dwelling anyway.[7]

More poignantly he says of himself:

> Even though I take refuge in the Pure Land as the True Teaching,
> It is difficult to have a mind of truth.
> I am false and untrue,
> And without the least purity of mind.
> We men in our outward forms
> Display wisdom, goodness, and purity.
> Since greed, anger, evil, and deceit are frequent,
> We are filled with naught but flattery.
> With our evil natures hard to subdue,
> Our minds are like asps and scorpions.
> As the practice of virtue is mixed poison,
> We call it false, vain practice."[8]

As a consequence of his deep spiritual dissatisfaction and search, Shinran joined the hermitage led by Hōnen. He discovered his spiritual release there which he noted in the latter volume of the *Kyōgyōshinshō*. With persecution and banishment, Shinran found himself in Echigo in a difficult and cold climate where he had to live like a peasant without the privileges of a monk. He married and began to raise a family. The experience of family life deeply influenced his thought about the life of lay people and the reality of Amida's compassion.

After his exile was over in 1211, Shinran settled in Eastern Japan (Kantō) where he began quietly to teach the Pure Land way. Never again did he meet his master Hōnen, nor apparently other companions from that time of study. Responding to the conditions of his new life, he probed more deeply into his faith in an effort to help the peasants and samurai he met. These efforts and their reflections in his writings indicate that he had personal qualities that promote and enhance life. He became for his followers a virtual manifestation of Amida's compassion in action. Consequently, though he is a figure of the distant past, having recently celebrated the 800th anniversary of his birth and the 750th anniversary of the establishment of his doctrine, he witnesses to us of a faith in life and truth which we need today.

---

7. The *Tannishō*, RTS II (Kyoto, 1966), 20
8. *Shinshū Shōgyō Zensho* II (Kyōto; Kōkyō Shoin, 1957), 527 (hereafter cited as SSZ).

We do not wish to over-idealize or modernize an ancient, historical person. As we draw new insights from his life and teachings, we must understand that the implications or possibilities were there from the beginning, though Shinran himself was not directly aware of our problems.

A singular feature of Shinran's experience of exile from Kyōto and his later teaching career was his marriage. Of course, it is known that other monks had concubines or even wives in contradiction to the discipline they professed. Shinran differed from them because he instituted this as the way of life for the leaders of his community, making it the consequence of his teaching rather than a contradiction to it.

Shinran married a young woman, Eshinni, and by her had several children. This act symbolised his identification with the full range of human emotions and problems. Some have criticized his act as a negative capitulation to the power of passion, based as it was on the doctrine of Mappō where, with the decline of Buddhism in history, human defilement increases. Nevertheless, whatever the doctrinal background of the relationship might be, it does not undermine its importance in the reconciliation of people with themselves and their world. Through Shinran's involvement in married life and the social responsibility attending it, the way was opened for the ordinary person to participate in, and have full assurance about, his own spiritual enlightenment despite his worldly involvements. For Shinran, as his letters show, the true renunciation of the world was to live compassionately *in the world*, not to reject or leave it.

The conversation between Yuienbō[9] and Shinran concerning Yuienbō's lack of desire to go to the Pure Land has great importance in observing Shinran's relation to individuals and for an understanding of his approach to alienation. After Yuienbō relates his sad complaint and doubt about his faith, Shinran responds tenderly, "Even I, Shinran, once had this doubt."[10] In the *Kyōgyōshinshō* Shinran records his own lament:

> I know truly how sad it is that I, Gutoku Shinran, am drowned in the broad sea of lust and wander confusedly in the great mountains of fame. I do not rejoice that I have entered the company of the truly assured; I do not enjoy (the fact) that I am approaching the realization of the true attainment. O how shameful, how pitiful! [11]

It is important to note here how Shinran identified with his disciple's problem. He did not stand above him as a sainted master. He acknowledged the reality and seriousness of the issue. However, he also got Yuienbō to look beyond his problem to something deeper hidden in it.

---

9. Ed. The name may also be seen as Yuien; the suffix -bō indicates that the name Yuien is an alias.

10. *Tannishō* ix.

11. SSZ II, 80 (author's translation).

He helped Yuienbō to accept himself and to realize that his very awareness of his own evil was the witness to Amida's compassion.

In a sensitive way Shinran tells us that alienation is not overcome by ignoring or rejecting it, but by accepting it. The modern psychiatric method holds that mental illness is remedied only when brought to consciousness and accepted for what it is. Repression never cures, but merely shifts the mode of expression. In human relations, the only way to solve problems is by accepting them as real and accepting the person for what he is.

This touching incident is related to another problem confronting Shinran and his early community. He had to face factionalism and differences of opinion in his own group. When he was called upon by some disciples to reject those whose opinions differed from them, Shinran refused to take the authoritarian position of the teacher and demand that others follow him or be excluded. He maintained: "I have not even one disciple." He recognized deeply the compassion of Amida in bringing people together. Such community was ultimately not the property or monopoly of one person. Amida created faith, not the teacher. He explained:

> The reason is, if I should lead others to utter the Nembutsu by my own efforts, I might call them disciples. But it is truly ridiculous to call them my disciples, when they utter the Nembutsu through the working of Amida Buddha.[12]

Shinran's identification with his followers and his refusal to stand over them as an authority points the way to the solution of many problems of personal and even social conflicts in our contemporary society. A major aspect of any problem is the issue of authority and the power it wields. Power over another person creates a distrust and a separation which make dilemmas even more difficult to solve.

Shinran's tragic disowning of his eldest son also reveals much about his character. Apparently, Zenran attempted to assume control of the fellowship by claiming he had special teachings from Shinran. This situation naturally raised questions in the minds of the disciples about Shinran's fairness and honesty. When the problem became clear to Shinran, he took decisive, though painful, measures in disowning his son and maintaining his sincerity toward his disciples.

Many problems arose in the early Shin-shū community which had necessitated sending Zenran as an emissary to deal with the issues. Shinran's letters give much information on the disputes that arose, particularly on those radical interpretations of his teaching that because Amida saves without consideration of how sinful one might be, it is all right to sin or do evil intentionally. Shinran had to deal firmly and considerately

---

12. The *Tannishō* vi, RTS II, 28.

with these questions. He shows himself to be of an open mind, but also firm in stating his own position.

Interspersed throughout Shinran's letters, we can see that his relations to his disciples were warm, affectionate and sympathetic. He gave kindly counsel. They consulted and asked for direction. He never forced himself upon them; never condemned or coerced them. Some made trips to be by his side, some even wished to die there; such was their intense devotion to him.

Pure Land teaching had frequently experienced persecution and restriction by political authorities. While Shinran saw these conditions as fulfillment of the prophecies of Buddha, he cautioned his disciples not to provoke or give any reason for the authorities to interfere with their teaching and faith. He was, however, aware of abuses of power. He could register his disapproval of government action:

> Lords and vassals who opposed the Law and justice bore indignation and resentment (to the Nembutsu teaching). Thus Master Genkū, the great promulgator of the True Teaching, and his disciples were, without proper investigation of their crime, indiscriminately sentenced to death, deprived of their priesthood and exiled under criminals" names. I was one of them.[13]

Shinran not only could be critical of political action, but also of the traditional culture in which he stood. The exclusive commitment and faith he had in Amida Buddha rendered all other spiritual allegiances unnecessary. Shinran unequivocally rejected Japanese folk religion and its magical beliefs. Thus he wrote in the *Kyōgyōshinshō*:

> By discerning the true and false teachings based on the *sūtras*, I shall caution people against perverted and wrong views of non-Buddhist teachings.
>
> The [*Nirvana Sūtra*] says: "Once you have taken refuge in the Buddha, you should never turn to other gods for refuge."
>
> The [*Pratyutpannasamādhi-sūtra*] says:"If, O Upāsaka, you hear of this *Samādhi* and want to attain it . . . you should take refuge in the Buddha, take refuge in the Dharma, and take refuge in the Sangha. You should not follow other paths, should not worship the gods in heaven, should not enshrine spirits, and should not weigh lucky or unlucky days.[14]

For Shinran, Buddhism was superior to secular institutions, powers and customs. Though he counseled respect for the state and society, he approvingly quoted the *Sūtra of Bodhisattva Precepts* to show that Bud-

---

13. The *Kyō Gyō Shin Shō*, RTS v, 206.
14. The *Kyō Gyō Shin Shō*, 204.

dhism was not to be subservient to society. It states: "The monk does not revere the king, or parents, nor serve the six near relations, nor worship the spirits."[15]

When we assemble various hints throughout Shinran's writings, we can discover the outline of a person who was deeply concerned with the meaning and end of human existence in its most universal scope. He was critical of a system of politics and religion which claimed to provide meaning, but actually obscured it through injustice and by cultivating fear and anxiety. Shinran was committed by his own experience to seek a new way. He was not negative in rejecting the traditional path, but constructive and creative in his thorough-going reinterpretation of Pure Land doctrine. He was an existentialist in the truest modern sense, because he did not settle for fine theories and high abstractions. Rather, he permitted his doctrine to arise from his experience of life. Consequently, he introduced new perspectives on religious existence to make real the compassion he saw at the heart of reality. He demonstrated throughout his relation with his disciples the virtues of concern, commitment, constructiveness and compassion. These are qualities which all of us must embody if any of our contemporary problems and issues are to be resolved. There can be no true meaning in life beyond the fulfillment of these qualities.

Sometime ago in Japan there was an interesting controversy surrounding a statement by a government official that Japan must not rely on "other power" in dealing with her affairs, but must be self-powered. The implication was that other power represented weakness and ineffectiveness or otherworldliness. Of course, there is much in Japanese tradition and in other traditions that would support this criticism. We hear all the time that religion is just a crutch which usually means something exterior to life and useless.

However, when we observe Shinran, his life, his personality and his teachings, we see that he was a person of strength; that he could withstand the pressures and oppression of his time and retain his dignity and humanity. Shinran never gave up in despair nor became cynical when those he dealt with were even to disappoint him. Shinran was mild, but not weak; he was not self-assertive but also not ineffective. Shinran was a true person at one with himself and also a person for others. He lived a long time ago, but his qualities are timeless, making him a fitting model for our time.

---

15. *Kyōgyōshinshō*, SSZ II, 191–192 (author's translation).

Part IV

Broadening Perspectives for Shin Buddhism

Freedom and Necessity in Shinran's Concept of Karma[1]

Ueda Yoshifumi

The concept of karma existed prior to the rise of Buddhism, and though quickly adopted into Buddhist thought, its precise role in the early tradition and its relationship to such concepts as the five aggregates and dependent origination remain topics of controversy among modern scholars. It may be said, however, that in Mahāyāna tradition, the major significance of karma lies in its expression of temporal existence from the stance of the no-self nature (*anātmatā*) of all things.[2] The bodhisattva, in realizing *prajñāpāramitā*, thoroughly breaks through discriminative thinking and comes to stand in suchness. At that time, he attains *dharmakāya* or "reality-body," but he does not simply remain in the realm of the formless, where the subject-object dichotomy has been completely obliterated. *Dharmakāya* holds within itself the non-duality of the karma-created (*saṃskṛta*) and the uncreated (*asaṃskṛta*), the temporal and the timeless, and thus develops from itself the subsequently attained non-discriminative wisdom that, while never parting from suchness or the uncreated, sees and acts in the world of *saṃsāra*, working to save igno-

---

1. Author's note: This article is based on *Bukkyō ni okeru gō no shisō* (Kyoto, 1957), 7–39; its present form and much of the detail in content, however, have emerged from discussions with the translator, Dennis Hirota.

2. Various concepts are used in the history of Buddhist thought to express no-self. Among them, the five aggregates in early Buddhism and emptiness in the Prajñāpāramitā *sūtra*s, while including temporal implications, do not give direct expression to the element of time. The temporal side of emptiness was clarified by Nāgārjuna through the concept of mutual dependence, by which he showed theories of time as linear succession to be untenable. In terms of the relationship of action and recompense, there can be neither simple continuity nor interruption, neither permanence nor impermanence. The positive implications of karma for the bodhisattva's temporal existence were articulated in the early Yogācāra of Maitreya, Asaṅga, and Vasubandhu through the concept of the simultaneous, reciprocal causation of *ālayavijñāna* and defiled dharmas. See my *Bukkyō ni okeru gō no shisō*, 42–79.

rant beings. The functioning of karmic causation is the foundation of the existence of the bodhisattva—who has transcended birth-and-death—in the realm of *saṃsāra*, and the self-realization of the karma-created (false discrimination between subjectivity and world)[3] as karma-created is the content of, and inseparable from, non-discriminative wisdom.

While in Mahāyāna thought in general the concept of karma is taken up from the stance of the transcendent, as an aspect of existence in the world of the enlightened being, in Shinran's thought—in his concepts of karmic evil (*zaigō, tsumi*) and past karma (*shukugō*)—it expresses rather the stance of the person who has awakened, through insight, into the fundamental nature of human existence, to the impossibility of transcendence. Nevertheless, Shinran's concept of karma shares with that of Mahāyāna tradition the nature of being established in the immediate present, in which time is itself timelessness, as the content of the personal realization of Buddha's wisdom or of no-self—in his case, as the content of the "nembutsu of wisdom" or "wisdom of *shinjin*."[4] Below, I will discuss the central elements of Shinran's concept of karma as an expression of religious awakening in his teaching.

The great path of unobstructedness

Shinran states: "The person of the nembutsu is [one who treads] the great path free of all obstruction" (*Tannishō* 7).[5] These words express the remarkable freedom of the person who has realized *shinjin*—the person whose blind passions have become one with the wisdom-compassion of Amida Buddha. Shinran goes on to explain, "The evil he does cannot bring forth its karmic results." Does this mean that the person of the nembutsu does not fall into karmic causation? Or is it an example of religious hyperbole, meant to be understood only figuratively?

Causation is a cornerstone of the Buddha's teaching. Śākyamuni states, "He who sees dependent origination (*pratītyasamutpāda*, i.e., causation) sees me (Buddha)." Even the enlightened one is subject to the law of action-recompense and cannot violate or circumvent it. Thus, Shinran uses the term "karmic power of the great Vow" to express the strength of Amida's salvific activity. This working is not simply a matter of Amida's will or compassion; mere aspiration to save others would be futile

---

3. Ed. The word "between" has been added to complete the sense.
4. *Shinjin* 信心 is the "true, real, and genuine mind" (*makoto no kokoro*) in which a person's mind and the mind of Buddha have become one without their duality and mutual opposition being eradicated. This term expresses the core of Shinran's religious awakening.
5. Quotations from *Tannishō* are from Dennis Hirota, trans., *Tannishō: A Primer* (Kyoto: Ryūkoku University, 1982); portions have been adapted.

without the aeons of practice performed as Bodhisattva Dharmākara. The working of the Vow is manifested from *dharmakāya* as suchness, but without the creation of karma through practice, no means to save can be devised and no results achieved.

If even Buddha must realize that all volitional acts fall within the working of action-consequence, what does it mean that the evil acts of the person of the nembutsu "cannot bring forth their karmic result"? It does not mean that a person eradicates his karmic evil through saying the Name, for Shinran rejects such practice as based on attachment to one's own powers. Neither can it be taken to mean that, because birth into the Pure Land in the future is assured, *ultimately* his evil acts will not have the effect of continuing samsaric existence. There is nothing to imply that this freedom belongs only to the future, and elsewhere Shinran states,

> We have been able to encounter the moment when *shinjin*, firm and diamond-like, becomes settled . . . so that we have parted forever from birth-and-death. (*Kōsōwasan* 77)[6]

In addition to this assertion of the radical freedom of the person of *shinjin*, there is another notable passage treating karma in the *Tannishō*:

> Good thoughts arise through the prompting of past good; evil comes to be thought and performed through the working of evil acts (karma). These words were among those spoken by the late master: "You must realize that there is never [any act]—even so slight as a particle on the tip of a rabbit's hair or sheep's fleece that is not evil that we commit and [the working out of] past karma (*shukugō*)." (*Tannishō* 13)

According to this passage, in all our activity—our thoughts and feelings, words and deeds we do not commit good and evil according to our own judgments and decisions, but merely obey the working of our past acts. Shinran here attributes absolute control over the conduct of our lives to karmic causation, implying a complete denial of moral responsibility and freedom of will in the present. Surely such an awareness of karma might be called fatalistic, for in the thorough necessity of all our acts, whether good or evil, the present self is completely powerless.

Moreover, the karma from our past that rules our lives is always evil. In the first sentence of the passage quoted above, evil indicates the opposite of good, but in the words of Shinran that follow, both "good thoughts" and "evil acts," good and evil as determined in the moral and ethical dimensions of human life, are "evil that we commit and caused by past karma." "Evil" in the latter sense encompasses both good and evil as we normally consider them; that is, even acts we usually deem

---

6. In *Shinshū shōgyō zensho* (hereafter as SSZ; Kyoto: Ōyagi Kōbundō, 1941), 510.

good are seen as rooted in evil.

Karma, as a general Buddhist term, denotes both good and evil acts. According to the law of karmic causation, past acts, whether good or evil, become causes manifesting their effects in the present, and likewise, present acts become causes of results that will appear in the future. Good causes necessarily result in good and evil in evil: this necessity between cause and result is the essential characteristic of karma. For Shinran, since he states that both "past good" and "evil acts" are in fact evil, necessity leads entirely from evil as cause to evil as result. "Good thoughts" that arise through the prompting of past good are also included in the statement, "There is never [any act]...that is not evil that we commit and [the working out of] past karma." This necessity from evil to evil lies at the heart of Shinran's concept of karma. According to it, we lack the potential to do anything that is not evil. If whatever we do—even acts we consider to be good and virtuous—is in fact evil, then whatever our subjective thoughts, in reality we have no moral freedom of choice. We can do no other than evil.

For Shinran, evil is not foremost an issue of social life, but rather of a person's attainment of Buddhahood. In order to realize enlightenment, one must perform various religious practices to rid oneself of false thinking and the blind passions that arise from it. The person bound about by his passions, however, cannot keep from committing acts that they motivate and cannot, therefore, realize Buddhahood. Any act other than practice that makes Buddhahood possible—however virtuous according to our usual standards—is evil from the stance of Buddha. If it does not bring one closer to enlightenment, then it only involves one further in endless birth-and-death. Shinran terms the good we do in our daily lives "good acts variously poisoned" by falsity and passions. Even the human capacity to love, which sometimes seems a gift that brings a person to transcend himself, is seen to harbour egocentricity at its core, and only the Buddha's "heart of great compassion is replete and thoroughgoing" (*Tannishō* 4). Perhaps the clearest expression of the extent to which Shinran's concept of evil encompasses all aspects of life may be seen in his statement, "Not wanting to go quickly to the Pure Land, or becoming forlorn with thoughts of death when even slightly ill, is also the activity of our blind passions" (*Tannishō* 9). When a person in sickness comes to realize that death is near, it is natural—however good or evil he may be—that he should feel loneliness and pain at parting from life. Even such natural human feelings Shinran labels "blind passions." In its depths, then, the evil we commit transcends the realm of human interaction, and extends to the very limits of human existence.

Shinran states, on the one hand, that as a human being one is so bound by one's past acts that all that one does in the present is defiled by evil, whatever one's conscious intentions; and on the other, that as a person of the nembutsu, one has broken free from the bondage of such karma, so that the evil one has done cannot bring about its retribution. Moreover, these two assertions do not concern two different kinds of people—for example, those who have not yet realized *shinjin* and those who have; nor do they describe two stages in the religious life of a single person, such as before and after the realization of *shinjin*. Both these statements apply to the same person—the person who has realized *shinjin*—simultaneously. Both articulate the nature and content of his religious awakening. How are we to understand this absolute bondage simultaneous with absolute freedom? First, let us consider Shinran's understanding of the basic elements of the concept of karma, temporality and causality.

Temporality: karma is always past karma

In Shinran's concept of karma, all that we do, think, or feel is instigated by past action; in other words, all that we are in the present has been determined by the past. What does this mean for the future? Most Buddhist and Shin scholars state that the concept of karma differs from a kind of fatalism in that one can freely exert one's will in determining the course of the future, so that it is possible, through effort in the present, to anticipate betterment. Though this may be acceptable in general Buddhist thought, it does not represent Shinran's thinking. Whatever we may seek to do in the present, our future is determined, and there is no room whatever for any change or improvement through our present activity. Our acts, whether morally good or evil, are all seeds that send us to hell, and there is nothing we can do to change this and direct ourselves toward attainment of Buddhahood.

According to the general Buddhist concept of karma, all the painful or happy circumstances that we experience in this world are the results of past volitional acts; only our present good and evil thoughts are not caused by past karma. Acts are classified into good, evil, and neutral, with the first two types bringing recompense. The pleasant and painful circumstances in the present are the results of past good and evil acts, but they themselves are karmically neutral with regard to the future. Concerning karmic causation, "Causes are good or evil; results are neutral": this is an ironclad rule in both the Hīnayāna and Mahāyāna traditions. Shinran, however, teaches not this general Buddhist insight, but rather that the good and evil we commit in the present are brought about by past karma. This clearly departs from the fundamental Buddhist concept of causes as good and evil but results as karmically neutral.

That our physical, mental, and verbal acts in the present are all induced by past karma means that not only the present but the future also is determined by the past. In the general Buddhist concept of karma, the present holds both the results of the past and the causes of the future. If, however, the present thoughts and actions that become the cause of the future are all determined by past acts, then not only the present but even the future is encompassed within past karma. There is no power in the present to give birth to the future.

Fundamentally, the future is distinguished from the past in its potentialities in contrast to the determinedness of the past, but if the present is completely conditioned by the past and there is no possibility in the present newly to give rise to the future, the present holds no meaning as the present and, accordingly, the future also lacks the significance of the future. Not only the present, but even the future into its furthest reaches is controlled by past karma and lies within its determinedness, and good or evil acts performed in the present lack the power to alter this. Thus, only the acts committed in the past possess the original significance of karma as an act—a free exercise of will—influencing later life and circumstances. By contrast, acts committed in the present or the future do not possess the significance of new karma. Since there is no creation of karma in the present, there is no present as we usually think of it.

Ordinarily we conceive time as existing objectively as a regular, linear progression that transcends our subjectivity. It forms a framework within which we and all things exist, and all our thoughts and acts arise within it. From the Buddhist perspective, however, such time, like the other aspects of the dichotomized, objectified world that we see standing apart from us, is the product of false thinking based on egocentric discrimination. If we seek to grasp time at its very ground-source—time in which we as true subjectivity are actually living—we must abandon objectified concepts of time. The self as true subjectivity takes now—the immediate present—and actual existence to be identical; objective time cannot enclose it. In other words, our true subjectivity cannot be illuminated through such concepts of time. The self that exists within conceptualized time is not the actually living and thinking self, but nothing more than the objectified self or subjectivity. Linear time advancing mechanically and inexorably apart from ourselves is merely a conception of genuine time, a shadow projected by it. Actual time is that time in which the subjectivity itself stands. There is no framework existing beforehand; rather, time is established and moves moment by moment through the activity of the subjectivity. Our thoughts, words and deeds do not occur within time; rather, time is established where the three modes of activity take place. Where acts are being performed is the present, where they have ended is the past, and where they have yet to begin is the future.

If the present is robbed of all sense of our performing acts, there is nothing to be called present karma, and the present cannot be established. Without the present, nothing different from the past can be created; hence, the progression from the present into the future becomes a continuation of the past, and the future also fails to be established. In this concept of past karma, present and future are meaningless; the past alone dominates all. For all eternity there is only the past. Further, where there is no meaningful present and future and all is merely the burden of the past, neither can there be a past in the ordinary sense. The past-ness in Shinran's concept of karma—the endless future being controlled by the past—is not a past relative to present and future, but is eternal, pervading the temporality called past, present, and future; it is beginningless and continues endlessly. It is, in other words, samsaric existence that is essentially unchanging however far one goes into the past or future. The eternalness of past karma is none other than this samsaric-ness. In this way, Shinran's concept of past karma expresses the temporal dimension of the total lack of any condition for salvation in human beings.

Karmic causality and free will

The concept of karma is commonly understood to teach that one reaps the fruits of one's own acts. Through good acts one obtains favorable life-conditions, through evil acts one undergoes pain. As the subject of moral freedom, one accepts as one's own responsibility that present pain is the consequence of evil karma created through one's decisions and acts of will in the past and, at the same time, seeks to accumulate good karma in the present in order to gain happy conditions in the future. This popular conception of the working of karma may not be mistaken with regard to Buddhism in general, but, as we have seen, it differs from Shinran's understanding.

At the foundations of the popular conception of karma lies the subject that exercises free will. An example of this thought may be seen in the *Dhammapada*, which belongs to early Buddhism:

> An evil act that has been committed, like milk, does not congeal immediately. It is like fire covered with ash; smoldering, it accompanies the foolish one. (71)
>
> The foolish person commits evil acts but is unaware; dull and ignorant, he suffers according to his own acts, just as though burnt by fire. (136)

It is not clear whether such sayings are spoken with focus on the past, present or future. They may be taken as teaching the relation of past to present, or again of present to future. But their general intent concerns the present; it is the message that we should refrain from evil acts and strive to perform good:

> Like the wealthy merchant with few companions who shuns dangerous roads, like the person who, cherishing life, shuns poison, so you should shun evil acts. (123)
>
> Be prudent in speech, control your will, and do not commit evil with the body. Purify these three kinds of activity. [In this way] you will attain the path taught by the sages. (281)

Shinran, however, states, "Good acts are not necessary...nor is there need to despair of the evil one commits" (*Tannishō* 1). Our moral decisions in the present are irrelevant; good and evil are not at issue. In fact, there is no question of the nature of the acts we perform, and no room for any intervention of personal effort and ideals. As we have already seen, both the "good" and "evil" committed in the present are prompted by past evil acts. The karmic evil of the self is fathomless and forms the core of the self itself. However we might strive, it is impossible for us to improve our circumstances in the future. This concept of past karma is established in the realization that the self as the subject of free will cannot extricate itself from falsity, delusional thinking, and fierce attachment to an unreal self, and that it is powerless in any efforts to awaken to true reality.

Since good and evil thoughts in the present all arise determined by past karma, our decisions and efforts in the present—and, indeed, the subject of free will seeking to suppress evil and nurture good thoughts—are completely bereft of meaning. This denial of the self of free will applies to the past also, for any point in the past when an act was performed was, at that time, the present, and was already conditioned by what preceded. Past karma has been accumulated from the depths of the past, and together with ignorance extends back into the beginning-less past. Hence, our good and evil acts in the past were also prompted by past karma that existed from before, not the free will of our subjectivity. However far back we go, no acts escape the fundamental character of dependence on preceding evil past karma. The unfolding of this abysmal past-ness expresses in temporal terms the delving into the depths of the self. This negation of the self and its potential for good in the past and present reaches, of course, into the future as well. In this way, the concept of past karma denies the validity of the self-determining ego and its attachment to its own goodness and moral judgment throughout the past, present, and future.

In the case of reaping the fruits of one's own acts, karmic causality functions as the basis for the continuity of the freely acting self as temporal existence. The present forms the nexus of the past and future, and there the subject of free will stands, acting as the central axis of causality. Facing the past, the person sees good and evil acts as the causes of the happy or painful results of the present, and facing the future, he sees pain and pleasure as the result of present good and evil acts. What integrates and sustains these two aspects of causality—from past to present and from present to future—and forms their pivot is the subject existing and freely exercising its will in the present. On the basis of these two aspects of causality, time as past, present, and future is established.

In Shinran's thought, however, the causal relationship of karma is single: from past to present *and* future. Here, causality has a twofold significance. Negatively, it breaks through the common notion of "reaping the fruits of one's own acts" based on the subject performing acts of moral judgment and free will in the present. It is the past, not the present, that forms the center of causality. The ego-self in the present, as the result of past karma, is dominated completely by the working out of past acts and possesses no freedom. However far back into the past one goes, it is impossible to say "I do this" in the sense of the self acting freely according to one's own intents. The focal point of causality in past karma is not the subject of personal will. Rather, past karma transcends the time termed past, present, and future in the direction of the past, and thereby transcends the self as temporal existence. There is a similarity here with the concept, or realization, of original sin in Christianity. While original sin is founded on the common ancestor of all individuals, however, the concept of past karma points directly to the individual himself. Herein lies its positive significance. Although past karma transcends the self as the subject of free will, it works to bind the self to its own past acts; hence, its significance as the acts of one particular individual is never lost. In past karma as "karmic evil that I have performed," "I" points not to a freely acting subject, but rather to the bonds of one's own karmic evil. Since one is brought to act through the past karma one bears, there is no act one commits that does not arise from one's own karmic evil.

Causality in Shinran's concept of past karma, then, is related not to the self as the subject performing acts in the present, but rather to the self as the bearer of karmic evil from the past. Its fundamental nature is not temporality, as in the case of the two aspects of causality in general Buddhist thought, but rather the bond between oneself in the present and immeasurable karmic evil in the past. Thus, its significance lies not in the moral action of the self committing good or evil, but rather in the awakening to the self as karmic evil.

Transformation: karma is no-karma and no-karma is karma

The person who has realized *shinjin* is fettered by his past evil and, at the same time, is free and unobstructed, for his past acts cannot bring forth their results. This does not mean that he stands apart from the working of causation. To borrow phrases from the Zen kōan of Hyakujō 百丈 and the fox, "he does not obscure karma" (*fumai inga*) he abides in its working and is clearly aware of this—and yet "he does not fall into karma" (*furaku inga*).⁷ Shinran articulates the nature of karma as experienced by the person of *shinjin* through the concept of "transformation":

> Without the practiser's calculating in any way whatsoever, all his past, present, and future karmic evil is transformed (*tenzu*) into good. To be transformed means that karmic evil, without being nullified or eradicated, is made into good, just as all waters, upon entering the great ocean, immediately become ocean water.⁸

Our karmic evil remains just as it is, and at the same time it is transformed into the Buddha's virtues; hence, we are bound to the world of birth-and-death, and yet we do not experience the unfolding of our karma as bondage, but rather as the free activity of wisdom-compassion in genuine self-awareness. Freedom here is not a matter of being able to exert our egocentric will. Such freedom is in reality the constraint of blind passions and false self, what Jaspers calls "self-will" (*Ich-Will*) or "apparitional freedom" (*Scheinfreiheit*).⁹ True freedom lies rather where the demands of ignorant self-will fall away in the awakening to the working of karma; hence, Shinran states, "It is when one simply leaves both good and evil acts to karmic recompense and entrusts wholeheartedly to the Primal Vow that one is in accord with Other Power" (*Tannishō* 13). Here, the natural working of karmic causation (*gōdō jinen*), by which we live leaving all to karmic recompense, and the natural working of the power of the Vow (*ganriki jinen*), by which we tread the path of necessary attainment of enlightenment guided by the Buddha's wisdom, function as a single natural working.¹⁰ True freedom—the power to act in accord with things as they truly are—can only be the activity of wisdom-compassion taking what stands opposed to itself (necessary working of karmic evil) as itself. As D. T. Suzuki states, "Karma is no-karma and no-

---

7. Ed. *Fumai inga* 不昧因果, *furaku inga* 不落因果.
8. Ueda Yoshifumi, ed., *Notes on 'Essentials of Faith Alone': Yuishinshō mon-i* (Kyōto: Shin Buddhism Translation Series, Honganji International Center, 1979), 32–33. Many of the quotations from Shinran in this article are from other volumes of this series: *Letters of Shinran: Mattōshō* (1978; hereafter as Letters), *Notes on Once-calling and Many-calling: Ichinen-tanen mon'i* (1980), and The True Teaching, Practice and Realization of the Pure Land Way: *Kyōgyōshinshō* (Volume I, Chapters on Teaching and Practice, 1983; Volume II, Chapter on Shinjin, 1985). Portions have been adapted.
9. Ed. Scheinfreiheit: deceptively false freedom.
10. For a discussion of the working of *jinen*, see my article, "The Mahayana Structure of Shinran's Thought," Part II, *Eastern Buddhist*, Vol. XVII No. 2 (Autumn 1984), 51–52 (and below in this volume).

karma is karma."[11]

The awareness that karma renders us incapable of doing other than evil—that all our thoughts, whether normally judged good or evil, arise through the prompting of immense karmic evil from the past—is not fatalistic, for it is not attained through intellectual reflection, as an objective truth about the world around us, but only through the wisdom of Buddha unfolded in us in the realization of *shinjin*. Thus, it does not spawn resignation or passivity; rather, vital and positive life is born from it, for awareness of one's karmic evil is also awareness of one's salvation, and is established only as the Buddha's wisdom-compassion taking the defiled as itself. In abandoning one's clinging to a relative freedom, which is in fact subjugation to evil, one becomes aware that the necessity of evil is encompassed by the freedom of wisdom-compassion. As the Tang dynasty Pure Land master Shàndǎo teaches, the deep mind of *shinjin* has two aspects: that with regard to the practiser or self (*ki no jinshin*), in which one realizes that there is no condition within oneself for release from *saṃsāra*, and that with regard to dharma or Primal Vow (*hō no jinshin*), in which one entrusts oneself to the necessary attainment of birth through Amida's wisdom-compassion. These are two faces of a single religious awakening. The transformation of karma is, at its core, the transformation of awareness. It is the awakening of the true subjectivity free of egocentric will or, in general Buddhist terms, the realization of no-self. Shinran clearly expresses this transformation in the following verse:

> When, into the vast ocean of Amida's Vow of wisdom,
> The waters of the foolish beings' minds, both good and evil,
> Have returned and entered, then immediately
> They are transformed into the mind of great compassion.
> (*Shōzōmatsuwasan* 40, SSZ II, 520)

Shinran annotates this verse: "'Transform' means that the evil mind becomes good." "Evil mind" refers to blind passions and embraces both the good and evil, morally and ethically judged, mentioned in the verse. "Good" refers not to moral goodness, but to complete freedom from blind passions. It is "the mind of great compassion" or, in the verses quoted below, the "ocean water of virtues" and "ocean water of wisdom." Transformation is not, however, simply a conversion of blind passions into enlightenment; hence, Shinran also uses the expression "become one taste":

> The ocean waters of the inconceivable Name are such
> That even the corpses of grave offenders and slanderers of dharma do
> not remain as they are;

---

11. *The Essence of Buddhism* (Kyoto: Hōzōkan, 1968), 30–32.

> When the myriad rivers of all evils have returned,
> They become of one taste with the ocean water of virtues.
>
> (*Kōsōwasan* 41)
>
> When, to the ocean waters of the great compassionate Vow
> Of unhindered light filling the ten quarters,
> The streams of blind passions have returned,
> They become one taste with the ocean water of wisdom.
>
> (*Kōsōwasan* 42) (SSZ II, 506.)

Our blind passions are transformed into great compassion—they become wisdom-compassion—and in the mind that results, blind passions and wisdom are of "one taste." If blind passions have become wisdom, however, there should be only wisdom; it should not be necessary to speak of the two as becoming "one taste." We see here that the mind in which blind passions and wisdom-compassion have become one has two aspects. First, it is the Buddha's "good" mind. Our "good and evil" mind, on returning to and entering the ocean of the Vow, becomes the "mind of great compassion," which is also great wisdom. Second, this good mind is not good alone, but at the same time embraces within itself the "evil mind," the blind passions. Thus the two—wisdom-compassion and blind passions—while they stand opposed as pure and defiled, form the single "good" mind, which is *shinjin*, or the mind that is true, real, and sincere (*makoto no kokoro*).

This self-contradictory structure of transformation on the one hand together with oneness that includes duality on the other is also clarified by Rennyo. He states, concerning the aspect of becoming one (transformation):

> Already the practiser's mind of evil is made the same as the Tathāgata's good mind. This is what is meant when it is said that the Buddha's mind and the mind of the foolish being become one.
>
> (*Gobunshō* II, 10; SSZ III, 440)

Our minds become the same as Amida's good mind; nevertheless, our blind passions do not simply disappear or change utterly into wisdom-compassion. To clarify this point, Rennyo states:

> Amida Buddha mends sentient beings. "To mend" means that, while leaving the mind of the sentient being just as it is, Amida adds the good mind (Buddha's mind) to it and makes it good. It does not mean that the mind of the sentient being is completely replaced, and is distinguished and taken in as Buddha-wisdom only.
>
> (*Goichidaikikikigaki* 64; SSZ II, 548)

Here, there are both wisdom and blind passions. The mind of the foolish being, before becoming one with the Buddha's mind, is blind passions, and on realizing *shinjin*, it changes into the same mind as the Buddha's. This transformed mind, however, has not ceased to be blind passions, for it holds within itself the mind of the foolish being. For this single mind, blind passions are not something other than itself. That is, the good mind (*shinjin*) that is the same as the Buddha's mind, established through the Buddha's mind and the mind of the foolish being becoming one, has awakened to itself as blind passions and karmic evil. Stated conversely, the mind that has been able to awaken to itself as blind passions is the same good mind as the Buddha's. To know oneself as blind passions is to become one with the Buddha's mind. The following two verses articulate the whole of what we have seen above: Buddha's mind and the mind of the foolish being becoming one, and the complex structure of the one mind—the good mind—thus established.

> (4) Through the benefit bestowed by unhindered light,
> One realizes the *shinjin* of vast transcendent virtues:
> Unfailingly the ice of blind passions melts
> And immediately becomes the water of enlightenment.
>
> (*Kōsōwasan* 39)

> (5) Obstructing evils have become the substance of virtues;
> It is like the relation of ice and water:
> The more ice, the more water;
> The more hindrances, the more virtues.
>
> (*Kōsōwasan* 40) (SSZ II, 505–506)

Through the working of the Vow, we realize *shinjin*, and our blind passions become the Buddha's mind of great wisdom and great compassion (verse 4). In this mind, blind passions and the good mind make up one whole (verse 5: our "obstructing evils have become the substance of virtues"), but they do so while standing in a relationship of mutual opposition ("the more hindrances, the more virtues"); hence, our passions, just as they are, have become one with great wisdom and, in addition, through the working of that wisdom, they are gradually transformed like ice melting to become water. *Tannishō* 16 also speaks of this interaction after the realization of *shinjin*:

> If *shinjin* has become settled, birth will be brought about by Amida's working, so there must be no designing on our part. Even when our thoughts and deeds are evil, then, if we thereby turn all the more deeply to the power of the Vow, gentleheartedness and forbearance will surely arise in us through the working of *jinen*.

Through the working of wisdom-compassion, our blind passions are transformed into the same good mind as the Buddha's; this occurs at the moment of realizing *shinjin* and, further, continues to occur throughout life. This is the path of perfect unobstructedness.

The emergence of the authentic present

Realization of *shinjin* takes place in "one thought-moment" (*ichinen*), which Shinran explains as "time at its ultimate limit" (*Once-calling and Many-calling*, 32). This one thought-moment, like other moments, occurs within samsaric time, but in it, the mind of blind passions becomes one with the trans-temporal mind of the Vow. Hence, that which is timeless fills this moment of the practiser's life, and for him samsaric time reaches its end: "We have parted forever from birth-and-death." Perhaps the most illuminating discussion of the structure of this one thought-moment is that of Prof. Nishitani Keiji in "The Problem of Time in Shinran."[12] Nishitani delineates the religious nature of this moment as the emergence of true existence, unfolding it as the place of the simultaneity of 1) the time in which Amida fulfilled the Primal Vow to save all beings throughout history—this is the past prior to any being, further back in the past than any point in the historical past, 2) the time of the establishment of the Pure Land, which is the future for each being, however far into the future it exists, and 3) the historical present of the realization of *shinjin*. These three times, while remaining distinct and sequential as past, present, and future, are brought into simultaneity in the practiser of *shinjin* through the working of the Primal Vow. Further, in the religious existence of *shinjin*, the practiser delves into the depths of the present moment, which, as the place of simultaneity, opens bottomlessly into the Trans-temporal that penetrates it and makes it the true present. It is such reflection that is expressed in Shinran's statement, "When I consider deeply the Vow of Amida, which arose from five *kalpa*s of profound thought, I realize that it was entirely for the sake of myself alone!" (*Tannishō*, "Postscript"). This nonduality or simultaneity of the temporal (historical time of the practiser) and the trans-temporal (working of Buddha) is the focus of Nishitani's article.

From the perspective of our concerns here, however, it must be added that the content of the practiser's reflection inevitably involves past karma. Shinran's statement above continues: "How I am filled with gratitude for the Primal Vow, in which Amida settled on saving *me, though I am burdened thus greatly with karma*." To delve into the depths of the present in *shinjin* is none other than to delve back into the immense burden of karmic evil one has borne for beginning-less *kalpa*s into the distant past,

---

12. In *The Eastern Buddhist*, Vol. XI, No. 1 (May 1978), 13–26.

and also to realize that this karma will continue to disclose itself in the future. "Our desires are countless, and anger, wrath, jealousy, and envy are overwhelming, arising without pause; to the very last moment of life they do not cease, or disappear, or exhaust themselves." (*Once-calling and Many-calling*, 48). Thus, "When the karmic cause so moves us'" when past karma functions as the cause or condition for some act—"we will do anything" (*Tannishō* 13).

Passage of time is ordinarily experienced as a progression from past into present and present into future; as potentiality, it flows out of the future and recedes into the past. For the person of *shinjin*, however, the course of time is not merely linear, but cyclical and repetitive—not merely historic, but samsaric—for he realizes that the working of evil past karma constrains him and deprives him of all possibility for new and free activity. His heart and mind, as great compassion established through the transformation of his blind passions, has broken free from birth-and-death, but since this mind (the good mind) includes blind passions within itself, even though he has entered the timeless ocean of the Vow and gained immeasurable life, simultaneously he lives samsaric time and has, in fact, for the first time genuinely awakened to the nature of his existence as blind passions and karmic evil. This awakening corresponds to deep mind with regard to self, which is essentially the realization that "hell is to be my home whatever I do" (*Tannishō* 2). This necessity of karmic evil is apprehended temporally as all-prevailing past-ness. The relative past and present, and thus future also, conceived in terms of acts performed according to our will, are not actual time, but time encompassed within the past-ness of karma. Karma, as primal, fundamental evil, transcends the good and evil acts that constitute relative existence and possesses temporal absoluteness. Thus, when past karma is seen to be evil, evil is understood to form the root-foundation of the person as relative existence. All acts of good or evil throughout the past, present, and future—that is, human life as temporal existence—through being dominated by past karma, are evil from their source. For this reason, Shinran, from his stance within the realization of *shinjin*, teaches not the creating of karma in the present, but only karmic recompense.

At the same time, however, the fulfillment of salvation is also seen in terms of an encompassing past-ness in the establishment and fulfillment of the Primal Vow to save all beings. Dharmākara has become Amida Buddha, and the Name, *Namu-amida-butsu*, in which each being is already included and called to as "*Namu*," pervades the ten quarters. The realization of this past-ness "further back in the past than any point in the past" corresponds to deep mind with regard to dharma or Vow. The prevailing past-ness of karmic evil (samsaric existence of the sentient being) and the past-ness of the fulfillment of the Vow (Amida Buddha) are established for the practiser only in self-contradictory fusion and interpenetration with each other; this fusion takes place in the present as genuine time, and its first emergence is the thought-moment of the realization of *shinjin*, in which the mind of the being and the mind of Buddha become one.

The person who has realized *shinjin*, looking to the past, finds both the fulfillment of the Primal Vow and the depths of his past karmic evil; at the same time, he apprehends his future as the certain plunge into hell, and as the Pure Land. The futurity as the Pure Land differs from the future within samsaric time, which is in fact no more than repetition of the past. It is genuine futurity or freedom, which means that in it bondage to temporal existence as birth-and-death has been broken and the oppressive burden of the past has been lifted. The future that is apprehended as the Pure Land, then, is trans-temporal; it cannot be confined to the future of samsaric time. In every present moment of the life of *shinjin*, obstructing karmic evil is transformed into virtue, and the two aspects of the future fuse into one. For this reason, Shinran speaks of realization of *shinjin* as itself the immediate attainment of birth occurring in the present.[13] While the Pure Land remains the future, the person of *shinjin* immediately attains birth, and while to the very last moment of life anger and envy arise without pause, he has parted forever from birth-and-death and his heart "sports in the Pure Land."

The fulfilled Pure Land is the land of immeasurable light and the fulfilled Buddha—Amida, or the mind of the Vow—is the Buddha of inconceivable light; both are in essence boundless light or wisdom that surpasses conceivability and transcends time. While the karmic past gives rise to samsaric time, that which transcends time—immeasurable light, or the ocean of the Vow—as the past-ness of the Vow's fulfillment, penetrates and fuses with samsaric past-ness to form the genuine present of the practiser of *shinjin*, and as the futurity of the Pure Land, it imparts to each present moment of the life of *shinjin* its character as authentic time. The eternal (timelessness) does not stand solely beyond samsaric time in the future, but fuses with the present; the present (hence the relative past and future also) is not merely impermanent or temporal, but is established on the foundation of the timeless that pervades it. True time—not an objectified reflection of time, but time that encompasses the subjectivity—is established only as the interpenetration of time and timelessness. It is here—where the past is, on the one hand, samsaric existence burdened by karmic evil and, on the other, the fulfillment of the Primal Vow; where the present is the fusion of these two kinds of past in

---

13. For a discussion of the two meanings of "birth" in Shinran, see my article, "The Mahayana Structure of Shinran's Thought," Part I, *Eastern Buddhist*, Vol. XVII No. 1 (Spring 1984), and further below in this volume.

the realization of *shinjin*; and where the future is both bondage that leads inexorably to hell and freedom in which that bondage has been broken through—that the true subjectivity of no-self, which is free of egocentric will, lives and thinks and acts. Past and present, while remaining distinct, are one; further, present and future, while distinct, are one. This is the temporal aspect of the mutual opposition of sentient being and Buddha simultaneous with their identity, or of the grounding of karma in the working of the Primal Vow. The present of the person of *shinjin*, as both past and future, necessity and freedom, holds at once the two contradictory aspects of deep mind, for leaving both good and evil (temporal existence) to karmic recompense—awakening to the karmic evil that pervades the past, present, and future—takes place in the realization of *shinjin*. Samsaric past-ness (necessity), while remaining necessity, gives itself up totally and comes to stand within the future (freedom): "The heart of the person of *shinjin* already and always resides in the Pure Land" (*Letters*, 27). Each moment of his life may be envisioned as a point on the circumference of a circle. Every act up until death is dominated by the past, and this domination moves him along the circle of samsaric time, in which nothing new can arise. Simultaneously, however, he is encompassed by the Vow, and through the Vow's power, he is brought beyond the circle into a trajectory directed to the genuine future, which is the Pure Land. Each moment is transformed (*tenzu*), so that every new present possesses the newness or originality that cannot arise from karma. In the life of *shinjin*, each day is new and fresh. The future in such life lies not along the circumference of samsaric time, but in the constant transformation by which the direction of karma-ridden time is broken and the practiser is brought to face the Pure Land. Thus, in the interpenetration of time and timelessness in *shinjin*, we come to know true and real time—the self-aware, impermanent existence that is living and, accordingly, that is dying. Although samsaric time merely stretches out endlessly, the time of the subjectivity, while it flows, does not flow, and while it moves, is still. It is time, and it is eternity or timelessness. Life and death do not simply stand in mutual opposition; within life there is death, within death there is life. Such life is true life, such death true death.

Radical shame: the awakening to karmic evil

Shinran terms effort to desist from evil and perform good *hakarai* ("deliberation," "calculation," "contrivance"), referring to the working of intellect and will, in all its facets, to attain salvation. He states:

> Sages of the Mahāyāna and Hīnayāna and all good people, because they take the auspicious Name of the Primal Vow as their own roots of good (i.e., say the nembutsu out of their own judgment and will to do good),

are incapable of awakening *shinjin*, of understanding Buddha-wisdom, and of understanding the [Buddha's] establishment of the cause [of birth in the Pure Land].

(*Kyōgyōshinshō*, Chapter on Transformed Buddha and Land, SSZ II, 165–166)

Those who strive to be virtuous, believing themselves capable of doing good and shunning evil, are engaged in *hakarai* or designing born of attachment to their own worthiness and capabilities; hence, *shinjin* cannot open forth in them and they cannot understand the Buddha's wisdom. To become free of attachment to one's own powers (self-power) and to entrust oneself to the Primal Vow are no more than different expressions for the same thing.

As long as there is self-working, it is not Other Power, but self-power.... Self-working is the *hakarai* of the person of self-power.

(*Goshōsokushū* 10, SSZ II, 712)

Moreover, "Other Power means to be free of any form of *hakarai*" (Letters, 39). As long as *hakarai* remains, one does not entrust to the Primal Vow. Further, it is because one does not grasp the nature of past karma that this *hakarai* does not fall away.

Only when a person knows that he cannot do other than evil, however much he might strive to do good, does he realize that he lacks any means to extricate himself from samsaric existence; his judgment and will being poisoned by self-attachment, nothing remains to him but utter entrusting of himself to the Primal Vow. It may be thought that realization of *shinjin* involves a decision or personal commitment; Shinran's expressions reveal it in negative terms, not as a "leap of faith," but simply as the thorough dissolution of *hakarai*. Further, among early Shin Buddhists, there were those who felt that it was natural for the genuine practiser to fear committing evil; such an attitude is criticized in *Tannishō* 13 as "the thought of one who doubts the Primal Vow and fails to understand the working of past karma in our good and evil acts." If the karmic conditions exist, we cannot avoid evil however we may strive to. When we grasp the nature of our karmic past, it becomes impossible for us to believe that a person must despair of his evil; finding ourselves powerless, we cannot but abandon our self-will and "leave both good and evil to karmic recompense."

Hakarai includes both the will to cease from evil and do good and the discrimination that judges. Both aspects are accompanied by our feelings and emotions. In terms of human intellect, *hakarai* is ignorance of genuine good and evil. Although burdened with karmic evil, we are not aware of its working; believing ourselves capable of choosing good over evil, we value as essentially worthy our aspirations to perform good as best as we can. To become free of *hakarai*, then, is to awaken to our karmic evil and to our actual ignorance of good and evil. Shinran states:

I know nothing of what is good or evil. For if I could know thoroughly, as is known in the mind of Amida, that an act was good, then I would know the meaning of "good." If I could know thoroughly, as Amida knows, that an act was evil, then I would know "evil." But in a foolish being full of blind passions, in this fleeting world—this burning house—all matters without exception are lies and gibberish, totally without truth and sincerity. The nembutsu alone is true and real.

(*Tannishō*, "Postscript")

In the realization of *shinjin*, a person awakens to his own ignorance; thus, one aspect of *shinjin* is wisdom: "When one has boarded the ship of the Vow of great compassion...the darkness of ignorance is immediately broken through" (*Kyōgyōshinshō*, "Chapter on Practice" 78).

Karmic evil, however, cannot rise to self-awareness by itself, and the intellect alone cannot discern its own profound ignorance. For a person to realize that, though he had assumed he could choose between good and evil, in fact he cannot, he must first distinguish intellectually between good and evil. Animals and infants, who cannot make this distinction, can have no awareness of karmic evil. In addition, the will must be exerted in action.[14] Shinran states, after instructing a disciple to kill in order to attain birth in the Pure Land:

"If we could always act as we wished, then when I told you to kill a thousand people in order to attain birth, you should have immediately gone out to do so. But since you lack the karmic cause enabling you to do this, you do not kill even a single person. It is not that you keep from killing because your heart is good. In the same way, a person may wish not to harm anyone and yet end up killing a hundred or a thousand people." Thus he spoke, referring to our belief that the good of our hearts and minds is truly good and the evil truly evil, not realizing that Amida saves us through the inconceivable working of the Vow.

(*Tannishō* 13)

The phrase, "If we could always act as we wished," means "if it were in our power to act according to our *hakarai*." That we do not kill means not that we will not kill because we are good; rather, we cannot carry it out merely because we lack the karmic conditions. When this is realized, it is clear that though we considered ourselves good and morally upright, in fact we cannot genuinely be called good. Acts that we judged intellectually to be good are not really so.

Our intellectual judgment of good and evil and our conviction that we can accomplish good through our will (even if not perfectly, at least to

---

14. For a discussion of the process of realizing *shinjin*, see my article, "How is Shinjin to be Realized?" *Pacific World* (Institute of Buddhist Studies, Berkeley), New Series, No. 1 (1985), 17–24.

some extent) is *hakarai*. As long as we remain in the stance of *hakarai*, we cannot know that "Amida saves us through the inconceivable working of the Vow." Unless this *hakarai*—this resolve to make ourselves morally and spiritually worthy—reaches a total impasse and all room for design and effort vanishes, entrusting to the Primal Vow will not arise. When we have exerted all our will and intellect in seeking what is good and true, and thus reached our limits—if we have earnestly listened to the teaching—a conversion or turnabout occurs. This is an awakening, a returning. Shinran calls it "the equal of perfect enlightenment" (*tōshōgaku*). Here, our intellect, will, and feelings are transformed into true wisdom that knows—and great compassion that grasps—karmic evil as itself.

It is commonly said that being human inextricably involves evil. This view does not, however, constitute realization of oneself as a "person in whom karmic evil is deep-rooted and whose blind passions abound" (*Tannishō* 1). Realization of karmic evil is not accompanied by feelings that evil is "natural" or "unavoidable"; rather, it is felt to be deeply shameful. This shame is not a form of regret that includes feeling that one can reform in the future. Rather, all expectation of moral or spiritual progress is gone; there is nothing but shame and lament. Regret or remorse tends to arise in the ethical and moral dimensions of human existence. The shame born of awakening to one's karmic evil goes deeper, to the roots of one's personal existence itself, and belongs to religious life; in this sense, it is radical and pervasive. Shinran states:

> With our snake's or scorpion's mind of wickedness and cunning,
> It is impossible to perform good acts of self-power;
> And unless we entrust ourselves to Amida's directing of virtue,
> We will surely end without shame, without self-reproach.
>
> (*Shōzōmatsuwasan* 99, SSZ II, 528)

To reflect on one's own evil and be filled with regret is still to be "without shame," which is impossible without wisdom. If to feel regret means to pass judgment in the present on an act committed in the past, then the past act may be seen as evil, but the present is no longer so. From the perspective of karmic evil, however, not only the past but the present also is evil, and the future holds no possibility for anything but evil. Simple repentance over a single a past act is meaningless. In the consciousness of karmic evil, there remains no room for remorse, but only the realization that one is a "being possessed of blind passions" or "deep-rooted karmic evil."

An example of such realization may be seen in the *myōkōnin* Shichisaburō of Mikawa province. When he discovered that he had been robbed of some firewood, feelings of gratitude toward the thief arose in him. He understood the theft to be the result of his having stolen from the thief in the past. Thus, he was moved to profound shame for his past offense, and further, realizing that the person had come to take back stolen property because he, Shichisaburō, had no idea of how to return it, he wanted to thank him. He did not merely accept the theft because it was retribution for his own past misdeed; in fact, he did not see the act as a theft. Through it he was awakened to his own karmic evil, and since this awareness was the activity of great compassion in him, he felt joy rather than resignation, gratitude rather than vindictiveness. The self that takes an egocentric perspective and self-love as its fundamental nature had been transcended, as had the objectively moral or ethical stance that judges the thief as a criminal. In the belief that we merely reap the fruits of our own acts, there is only causality and no transcendence of it; there is never more than *saṃsāra*, and no salvation. Shichisaburō's subjectivity, however, is no-self in which egocentric will has fallen away and religious love emerges as gratitude toward the thief. As Shinran states, "Obstructing evils"—karmic recompense—"have become the substance of virtues." With a subjectivity in which blind passions that arise moment by moment are transformed into no-self through genuine self-awareness—through the mind of Buddha—the person of *shinjin* acts in accord with his nature and circumstances, manifesting the working of compassion in the occurrences and interactions of ordinary life. In awakening to his karmic evil, he carries on his life subject to causality and, further, has transcended it. Thus Shinran states that he "constantly practices great compassion" (*Kyōgyōshinshō*, "Chapter on *Shinjin*", 65).

(Translated by Dennis Hirota)

The Concept of the Pure Land in the Teaching of Nāgārjuna

Yamaguchi Susumu

In Mahāyāna Buddhist literature reference is sometimes made to the "Pure Land"; in pre-Mahāyāna Buddhist literature such references are not to be found. Is then the Mahāyānist idea of Pure Land a mythological element which is essentially alien to Buddhism? Or is it firmly rooted in the soil of Buddhist religion and philosophy? In this article I want to make the answer to these questions clear by examining Nāgārjuna's concept of the Pure Land, as a representative case of the Mahāyānist conception of the Pure Land.

Śākyamuni's awakening to Mahāyāna depicted in his biography

Before dealing with Nāgārjuna's thought, I would like to call attention to a significant part of Śākyamuni's life which depicts how the Buddha came to start his preaching activities, for it will throw light on the problem of the Pure Land in Mahāyāna Buddhism. The Mahāyānist conception of the Pure Land is inseparable from the preaching activities of Buddhas and Bodhisattvas, as will be discussed later.

According to Śākyamuni's life stories, he was absorbed in deep contemplation (*samādhi*) after Enlightenment, a contemplation said to have lasted four weeks, during which time he changed his sitting place four times. He pondered over the possibility of teaching and awakening others to the ultimate truth he himself had realized. The result was that the ultimate truth, the truth of interdependent origination (*pratītyasamutpāda*) was so profound and so despairingly difficult for people to understand that, even if he were to preach it, no one would understand it. He thought it better to keep silent and continue enjoying the blissful state of Enlightenment. Brahmā, lord of the world, was shocked to learn the Buddha's mind; to him the Buddha's silence meant the spiritual devastation of the world. He immediately appeared before Śākyamuni, entreating him, "Please, be beneficent enough to begin preaching. There must be some people who are wise enough to understand you." Śākyamuni at first declined but, on Brahmā's repeated and earnest request, made up his mind to start preaching despite his anticipated difficulties. Thus the Buddha gave his first sermon in the Deer Park.

In the contemplation immediately after Enlightenment Śākyamuni was, so to speak, standing at the crossroads of life. Should he live a secluded life, enjoying the blissful serenity of Enlightenment and detached from any thought of awakening others? This is the way of the *pratyekabuddha*.[1] Or else, should he resolutely set out to preach and awaken others, despite all difficulties? This is the way of the Buddha as Tathāgata.[2] As stated above, Śākyamuni finally decided to start preaching activities, upon the request of the Lord of the World, that is, for the sake of all human beings. In other words, the Buddha now appeared as the Tathāgata in the midst of the world.

The lofty motive underlying the Buddha's steps from contemplation to the beginning of preaching activities is definitely the same motive that underlies the development of Buddhism as "Mahāyāna," [i.e. "great vehicle", Ed.]. This motive finds expression historically in the "original vow" of Bodhisattvas which is said to drive them to their respective preaching activities. In other words, the original vow is an unequivocal expression of that lofty motive, namely the Mahāyāna spirit, in the form of taking the vow.

Nāgārjuna and his *Mūlamadhyamakakārikā*[3]

Let us go into Nāgārjuna's Mādhyamika system of thought, the first philosophical exposition of Mahāyāna Buddhism, and examine what historical contribution he added in making clear the significance of "Mahāyāna." The importance of the Mādhyamika system as representing Mahāyāna Buddhism has long been an established historical fact. Yìjìng 義淨, a Chinese Buddhist scholar who travelled to India in the seventh century, writes as follows: "The so-called Mahāyāna does not exceed the following two: one is the Mādhyamika and the other Yogācāra."[4] As mentioned before, the aim of the present article is to make clear Nāgārjuna's Mahāyānist conception of the Pure Land. For that purpose I would like in

---

1. Japanese *dokkaku* 独覚, a Buddha who lives in seclusion and obtains emancipation for himself only.
2. Japanese *nyorai* 如来. Usually this term is taken to mean "the one who emerges out of suchness (*tathatā*)." But it should be remembered in this connection that the term has another meaning, "the one who preaches (the truth of) suchness" (*tathāgata*), as referred to in the *Vimalakīrtinirdeśa*.
3. Ed. The original refers to *Mūla-mādhyamika-kārikā*.
4. Cf. *Nankaikikinaihōden* (Ch. *Nánhǎijìgūinèifǎzhùan*) 南海寄帰内法伝, "Record of the Journey across the Southern Sea to seek the Dharma" (by Yìjìng 義淨/义净).

the first place to recapitulate the central thought of his teachings as set forth in the *Mūlamadhyamakakārikā*[5] and then discuss its bearings on his concept of the Pure Land as brought forth in the *Jūjūbibasharon*.[6]

At the beginning of the *Mūlamadhyamakakārikā* comes the *gāthā*, or verse-song, confessing faith: "I heartily bow before the Buddha who has disclosed the truth of interdependent origination which results in the 'eightfold negation' and the emptying of *prapañca*.[7]" According to Candrakīrti,[8] any work beginning with the *gāthā* of confessing faith may well be regarded as the author's principal work and the *gāthā* itself as a symbol of the importance of the work concerned. If so, the present *gāthā* may be said to disclose the quintessence not simply of the *Mūlamadhyamakakārikā*, but of the author's thought as a whole. Bearing this in mind let us examine the purport of the *gāthā*.

First of all we should remember that Nāgārjuna bowed before the "Buddha who had preached the truth of interdependent origination." The truth of interdependent origination is, as mentioned above, the very truth to which Śākyamuni was enlightened under the Bo tree.[9] This Enlightenment is indeed the *sine qua non* of Buddhism. Its importance needs no discussing, but it is extremely difficult to understand intellectually, because it is beyond word and thought. Zen Buddhism, in particular, emphasizes this aspect of Enlightenment and exhorts men immediately to penetrate it. The Buddha who attained Enlightenment under the Bo tree is especially significant for Zen Buddhists as their ideal. No wonder a most intensive training called *rōhatsu sesshin* 臘八接心 is held annually in every Zen monastery from the first to the eighth of December in commemoration of Śākyamuni's Enlightenment which is said to have taken place on the eighth of December.

It is the Buddha of the Bo tree who earned Nāgārjuna's adoration, the Buddha who, after long deliberation, resolutely started his preaching activities; in short, the Buddha who preaches.

---

5. I.e. the verses by Nāgārjuna. Incorporated in the Middle Treastise, *Chūron*中論.

6. A Commentary on the first two of the *daśabhūmi* (ten stages) in the *Avataṃsaka-sūtra* by Nāgārjuna. Ed. The author refers to *Daśabhūmikavibhāṣya-śāstra;* however this is not known in Sanskrit and in reality refers to the *Jūjūbibasharon* 十住毘婆沙論.

7. *Prapañca* semantically means "words." It is used by Nāgārjuna to denote deluded words and thoughts. Ed. These verses are also extant in Sanskrit, so the terminology is not speculative.

8. Candrakīrti (Japanese: Gesshō 月称), an Indian scholar and one of the commentators of Nāgārjuna's *Mūlamadhyamakakārikā*.

9. Ed. I.e. the Bodhi Tree, the Tree of Enlightenment.

The emptying of *prapañca*

The *gāthā* of confessing faith refers to "the truth of interdependent origination which results in the 'eightfold negation' and the 'emptying' of *prapañca*." Because of the limitation of space I will confine myself to the discussion of interdependent origination as emptying of *prapañca*, omitting the description of the "eightfold negation." That should suffice for the purpose of clarifying Nāgārjuna's basic thought.

In early Buddhist *sūtras* the truth of interdependent origination (*pratītyasamutpāda*) is put into a group of conditional propositions as follows: "(Under the condition that) *this* is, *that* is; (under the condition that) *this* comes into existence, *that* comes into existence": And negatively: "(Without the condition that) *this* is, *that* is not; (under the condition that) this falls away, that falls away." From these propositions it follows that this and that are interdependent and correlative, and neither of them is self-existent. This truth was later given a further predication by the introduction of the term "empty" (*śūnya*): "Because of their interdependent origination, all existents are not self-existent. Because of their non-self-existence, they are empty."

Once I was asked by a learned person who happened to hear a lecture of mine, "Can the truth of interdependent origination be as simple as you explain it? It is inconceivable that Śākyamuni really became the Buddha by merely awakening to such a simple truth." Simple indeed, in so far as the form of expression is concerned. The meaning it conveys, however, is tremendously difficult to realize, because its meaning is primarily and deeply concerned with the existential problem of man.

The central problem to Buddhism is always the problem of the man who is actually living here and now. Categories such as the "five *skandhas* (five aggregates: the corporeal element and four psychic elements, namely; perception, imagination, emotion and act of consciousness)," the "twelve *āyatanas* (six sense-organs and six senses)," and the "eighteen *dhātus* (six sense-organs, six sense-objects and six senses)," invented and used since the early days of Buddhism, were really tools with which to grasp the nature of the human existence here and now, however static their way of analyzing may seem to be. Yet I have no space here to dwell on these categories.

In the *Mūlamadhyamikakārikā*, Nāgārjuna viewed man's actual existence here and now as bearing on the *kartṛ* (maker) and—*karman* (the made) relationships, such as those between the knower and the known, the speaker and the spoken, the maker and the made; in other words, the relationships between the functionally subjective and the functionally objective. As a matter of fact, man functions as the knower, speaker or maker as against the known, the spoken, or the made. Functionally, man is *kartṛ*. This Nāgārjuna admitted as a matter of "empirical practice" (*laukikavyavahāra*).

Despite this fact, however, an entanglement arises. In subject-object relationships of every kind, we as the subject work upon and grasp something as the object. This experience makes us affirm or reaffirm that "I," as the subject, really exist and possess this grasped thing as "mine." Here we have at once belief in, and attachment to, "I" and "mine." Our attachment to "I" and "mine" is more and more deepened and strengthened as our daily experience continues. The bearing of "I" on "mine" may be likened to that of fire burning wood. The actual state of our life is also "burning" with the fire of suffering. According to Shinran, the founder of Shin Buddhism, human life is "love and hate, and gratification and frustration (of thirsty cravings)," a fact of life equally true in the contemporary world.

The suffering of love and hate, the gratification and frustration of thirsty craving, originates in and is intensified by the illusory discrimination of, and attachment to, "I" and "mine." Such discrimination and attachment, together with the resultant sufferings, Nāgārjuna named *prapañca*. Semantically, the term *prapaña* means "word." Word presupposes thought and vice versa, so by this application of the term, Nāgārjuna emphasized the importance of thought in the life situation of man and accordingly regarded man's suffering actuality itself as a meaningless play of deluded words and thoughts.

As stated above, the discriminative attachment to the subjective and the objective as "I" and "mine" makes the flames of love and hate burn more and more fiercely. Yet, the truth is that the functionally subjective and the functionally objective are interdependent and correlative, just as fire and wood are interdependent and correlative in the burning. Neither of them is independent and self-existent in nature. Ontologically, they are empty. By awakening to this truth, *prapañca*—the attachment to the subjective and the objective as self-existent—is emptied. The emptying of the attachment means emancipation from the suffering of love and hate.

Once emancipated from suffering, one realizes clearly how long he has been suffering. In other words, the truth of interdependent origination (*pratītyasamutpāda*) is precisely that truth by the awakening to which one is forever emptied of *prapañca* and thus emancipated from the suffering of love and hate. As such it is tremendously difficult to understand for us who, from time immemorial, have been deluded by *prapañca* and who have been suffering from love and hate. Anyone who takes the truth as being simple and easy to understand is taking it in a shallow theoretical way. He is neglecting the fact that he himself is fallen in *prapañca* and suffering. In spite of the difficulty of understanding it, we should by all means awaken to the truth of interdependent origination, in other words, the emptiness of *prapañca*.

Śūnyatā in three aspects

The truth of *pratītyasamutpāda*, interdependence and non-self-existence of all existent beings, is designated as *śūnyatā* or "emptiness," in the sense that any hypostatizing apprehension of "I" and "mine" turns out to be empty in the awakening to this truth. It is further denoted as *tathatā* or "suchness," in the sense that all existent beings are seen as they really are. The one who has realized *śūnyatā* or *tathatā* is called "Buddha," the enlightened one. Śākyamuni became the Buddha the very moment he attained Enlightenment under the Bo tree.

Śākyamuni at this moment, however, was not yet the Tathāgata by which Nāgārjuna means "the Buddha who preaches the truth of interdependent origination," that is to say, "the tathatā which, by way of preaching, has reached, or emerged in the midst of, the world of sentient beings." If the Buddha were to remain in the enjoyment of *śūnyatā* or *tathatā*, he would have been a *pratyekabuddha*, which implies "Hīnayāna" [i.e. "lesser vehicle", Ed.]. Nāgārjuna emphasized the "Buddha who preaches."

Since his lifetime, Nāgārjuna has been exposed to adverse criticisms, most of which rest on the misunderstanding of his Buddhist thought. Some critics regarded his *śūnyatā* theory as nihilistic and *śūnyatā* as meaning mere vacuity. Others criticized him, as well as Buddhists in general, as being world-denying and escapistic for exclusively devoting himself to the union with *tathatā*. These critics were ignorant of the Nāgārjuna who emphasized the Buddha who preaches, and who devotes himself to others-benefiting activities.

Nāgārjuna comments on the various contemporaneous misunderstandings of his *śūnyatā* theory thus: "In the last analysis these misunderstandings arise from a failure to distinguish the three aspects of *śūnyatā*." According to him, the first of these three is *śūnyatā*, the real nature of existent beings, the experience of which empties one of *prapañca*. It is utterly beyond word and thought.

The second is "the operation of *śūnyatā*," that is, *śūnyatā* as it empties *prapañca*. Its original term, "*śūnyatāyām prayojanam*" can be translated in two ways: Kumārajīva translated it as "to cause (awakening to) *śūnyatā*" and meant by this translation that the emptying of *prapañca* is necessary for *śūnyatā* to be realized. It can also be translated as "to apply *śūnyatā* in actual practice" and so interpreted as to mean that the emptying of *prapañca* is effected as the result of the operation of *śūnyatā*. The former is certainly a reasonable translation. We should, however, bear

The Concept of the Pure Land in the Teaching of Nāgārjuna

in mind that Nāgārjuna set forth this term in connection with *śūnyatā* and its expression in thought in passages dealing with misapprehensions of *śūnyatā* as something nihilistic. It then seems more probable that he meant by *śūnyatāyām prayojanam* that the emptying of *prapañca* is effected ever anew by the activities of the Buddha, the one who fully realized *śūnyatā*. This is the reason why I prefer the latter translation to the former and why I retranslate the term as the "operation of *śūnyatā*."

The conception of "the operation of *śūnyatā*" thus presupposes that a self-examination or self-criticism should be made by the enlightened one as to whether he is not in danger of viewing *śūnyatā* statically and becoming attached to its enjoyment. In reference to "Mahāyāna" in this connection, the awakening to Mahāyāna takes place as a result of such self-examination or self-criticism. Therefore a number of Mahāyāna *sūtras* attach great importance to the problem of self-examination, lest the enlightened one should fall into Pratyekabuddha-hood, that is, in order that the enlightened one may start his practice of Bodhisattva-hood. This emphasis upon the Bodhisattva practice may be said to be generally characteristic of Mahāyāna *sūtras*.

Nāgārjuna stated the purport of "the operation of *śūnyatā* in other words: "*Śūnyatā* is also to be emptied." Attachment to *śūnyatā* changes into something in the domain of *prapañca*, and so is no longer *śūnyatā*. Attachment to *śūnyatā* thus needs to be critically broken through ever anew. Through this repetition of emptying, the *jñāna* (wisdom) of the Buddha is more and more purified and deepened. This is one thing meant by the statement above: "*Śūnyatā* is also to be emptied." It can be said to be the *jñāna* aspect of the principle. But the statement has another aspect. As mentioned above the enlightened one clearly sees how he has been submerged in delusion and suffering from time immemorial. The enlightened one, being emancipated from attachment to "I" and "others," now fully realizes the truth of non-self (*anātman*), that is, the truth of the equality of "I" and "others." The moment he realizes that he has been immersed in delusion and suffering, he equally realizes that all sentient beings have been and are now immersed in delusion and suffering. Then an aspiration arises in him to break up the delusion and suffering, namely, *prapañca*, that captivates all sentient beings. *Prapañca* is to be emptied repeatedly and limitlessly. The principle, "*śūnyatā* is also to be emptied," thus develops as the practice of *mahākaruṇā* (great compassion); preaching, instructing and emptying all sentient beings of *prapañca* and suffering. This is, then, the *karuṇā* aspect of the principle.

These two aspects remind us of the conception of "limitless light" and "eternal life" as set forth in the *Larger Sūtra of Eternal Life*. The "limitless light" is symbolic of the *jñāna* aspect and the "eternal life" the *karuṇā* aspect of "*śūnyatā* as it empties itself." A movement full of such light and life which necessarily evolves out of Buddha's Enlightenment is called the "original vow" in terms of inwardness, and the "Bodhisattva practice" in terms of behavior. The original vow is the long-cherished vow,[10] intended to put the emptying of *prapañca* into practice untiringly and ever anew. It is the vital expression of *śūnyatā* as it operates.

How then will the compassionate vow be fulfilled? It is, in the last analysis, through the Buddha's turning over to human beings of the teachings of the Dharma, so that they may be awakened and emptied of *prapañca*. The Buddha's raising of the original vow and his putting it into practice are illustrated in the biography of Śākyamuni by his resolution to preach at the request of Brahmā and by the delivery of his first sermon at the Deer Park, resulting in the awakening and emancipation of the five mendicants.

For the Buddha, to preach means to awaken and empty sentient beings of *prapañca* through teachings consisting of words and thoughts. The words and thoughts of ordinary beings, as stated before, are *prapañca* and as such they cause attachment to "I" and "mine," bringing about *saṃsāra* and suffering, love and hate and the indulgence and frustration of restless desires. The Buddha's words and thoughts differ, in being thoroughly emptied and purified. They make up the teachings of the Dharma which, as something necessarily flowing out of *tathatā*, empties us of *prapañca* and thus takes us to the realm of *tathatā*.[11] The teachings, from the part of the Buddha, mean something which he, as Tathāgata, turns over to sentient beings. From our part, the teachings mean something turned over to us by Tathāgata which enables us to go to the realm of *tathatā*. In the Pure Land doctrine, the former aspect is called the "returning aspect," in the sense that the seeker for the ultimate truth now "returns" to the world of his fellow beings carrying with him the teachings to awaken and save them; the latter aspect is called the "going aspect" in the sense that we are enabled to "go" by the teachings. Underlying both aspects we see the natural, necessary flowing out of *tathatā*. Within teachings of the Dharma are comprised both the Buddha and sentient beings; the former as the one who turns over the teachings and the latter as the recipient of the Buddha's teachings: both are inseparably combined in the teachings.

As stated above, Nāgārjuna named the teachings of the Dharma "the expression of *śūnyatā* in thought" (*śūnyatā-artha*)[12] in his

---

10. There are two Sanskrit terms for the "original vow": *mūlapraṇidhāna* (fundamental vow) and *pūrvapraṇidhāna* (long-cherished vow). I prefer the latter to the former, for the latter is more expressive of the vow's enduring, untiring and prayerful nature.

11. The necessary flowing out (of *tathatā*) is named "*niṣyanda*" (necessary consequence) in Sanskrit, děngliú 等流 in Chinese.

12. The term "*artha*" means "actuality of things." *Śūnyata-artha* is thus taken to mean that things are re-examined and put right in accordance with the truth of *śūnyatā*.

Mūlamadhyamikakārikā. According to Nāgārjuna, *śūnyatā* seeks to express itself by the means and resources available. In other words, *śūnyatā* provisionally borrows the worldly means and resources of words, thoughts, categories, etc. for the purpose of expressing itself. The categories of the knower and the known, the speaker and the spoken, and the maker and the made, as discussed above, cause man to be attached to "I" and "mine," and thus result in *prapañca* and suffering. Their *prapañca* character is thoroughly broken through and emptied in the experience of *śūnyatā*. Even then, they can be and are provisionally, but reasonably rehabilitated as the means and resources by which deluded sentient begins are awakened to *śūnyatā*. In short, words and thoughts are provisionally used to express to a considerable extent the ultimate truth which is after all beyond word and thought, and to lead sentient beings to this truth. As a result we have the expression of "*śūnyatā* in thought," which is actually given as the teachings of the Dharma.

What matters in listening to the teachings of the Dharma is to be emptied of *prapañca*, and not to cling to the words as something absolutely authoritative. To cling to the teachings as unconditionally authoritative is to reduce them to a ruling force. When reduced in such a way, the teachings may keep alive, but they cease to be the expression of *śūnyatā* in thought. This is doubtless a distortion of what the teachings of the Dharma really means.

The conception of the Pure Land as set forth in *Jūjūbibasharon*

Bearing the foregoing discussions in mind, let us now examine Nāgārjuna's conception of the Pure Land in his *Jūjūbibasharon*. The Pure Land, as defined by him, is the realm in which there is no impurity. By impurity he means the wickedness of both *sattva* (sentient beings as the subjects of karma) and karma (made by them). The wickedness, however, can be "denied and transformed"[13] into the corresponding merits of both sentient beings and karma in the realization of *śūnyatā*. These two kinds of merits themselves, he holds, make up the Pure Land.

We here again deal with the problem of subject and object. As long as we are attached to the subject and the object as independent and self-existent, we are caught in *prapañca*, which inevitably makes ourselves and our karma wicked. As a result we find ourselves in the realm of im-

---

13. The Chinese term for "to deny and transform," as pronounced in Japanese, is *tensha* 転遮. As for the original Sanskrit term for the phrase, we cannot but guess from the Chinese translation, for neither the Sanskrit text nor the Tibetan translation of the present *śāstra* is now extant. The term "*sha*" is easily traced to *pratiṣedha* or *niṣedha* both of which mean "to prohibit" or "to deny." As prefixed to "*sha*," "*ten*" may be taken to mean "over again" or "unceasingly." "To transform" is merely an implication of the term *tensha*.

purity (saṃkleśa).[14] But the moment *prapañca* is broken through in the light of the truth of interdependent origination, we experience *śūnyatā*. *Śūnyatā*, however, does not mean void or nothingness, but is dynamic and creative with the inexhaustible merits of the enlightened one. *Śūnyatā*, definitely for this dynamicity and creativity, comes to be represented as the Pure Land standing beyond the turmoil of *prapañca*. The representation is made in terms of thoughts and categories of common use which are emptied of *prapañca* and then rediscovered as effective means and resources of instructing people. As such the Pure Land means neither a mythological reality nor a metaphysical reality; nor is it a negative nothingness. Nāgārjuna defines the Pure Land as the realm of purity or purification (*vyavadāna*), meaning that the Pure Land is precisely *śūnyatā*, represented in terms of the realm which stores inexhaustible merits or possibilities of operating, instructing and purifying people by the means and resources mentioned above.

In this connection, a few words should again be given to the *Larger Sūtra of Eternal Life*, the *sūtra* of first importance in the Shin school of Buddhism. The purport of this *sūtra* is essentially the same as Nāgārjuna's conception of the Pure Land. In the introductory part of the *sūtra*, we find passages relating the excellent signs reflected in the person of the Buddha that foretell the wondrous teachings to come. The Buddha's beaming countenance at that time tells that he abided in the stillness of *śūnyatā*. Accordingly, Shinran, resorting to another version of the *sūtra*, praises the Buddha in one of his hymns of the Pure Land as follows: "In the vast stillness of *samādhi* the Tathāgata's countenance was wondrously beaming." The stillness symbolizes the emptying of *prapañca*, namely, *śūnyatā* itself. *Śūnyatā* is, as repeatedly stated, tremendously difficult for people to understand intellectually. Nevertheless, the enlightened one is urged to step out of the stillness of *samādhi*. It was in this way that Śākyamuni disclosed Dharmākara Bodhisattva's Original Vow, his Bodhisattva practice according to the vow for innumerable *kalpa*s and his foundation of the Pure Land as the fulfilment of his Original Vow. This story of Dharmākara Bodhisattva depicts the operation of *śūnyatā* in terms of the Bodhisattva's vow and practice.

Further, Śākyamuni's proceeding from the stillness of *samādhi* to the sermon disclosing the establishment of the Pure Land is definitely what Nāgārjuna means by the term "to deny and transform over and over again" (*tensha*).

What is to be noted of the Pure Land thus established is its description in that *sūtra* as follows:

---

14. The term *saṃkleśa*, as well as *kleśa*, has the connotation that defilement or impurity, once arising, becomes more and more aggravated.

The Pure Land is filled with lotus flowers made from many different jewels; each petal of the flowers sheds innumerable beams of light, from each beam of light appear countless buddhas. Each of these buddhas in turn sheds hundreds of thousands of light beams and each preaches the wonderful Dharma for the sake of all sentient beings in the ten directions. The buddhas thus set countless sentient beings firmly on the right path to Buddhahood.

From this it is clear that the significance of the foundation of the Pure Land lies in that numberless buddhas thence emerge into the world in the ten directions (Śākyamuni, as one of them, emerged in this world) and empty and purify all sentient beings of *prapañca* boundlessly and endlessly. That is nothing other than *tathatā* emerging in this world and reaching us, namely Tathāgata. The very fact that the teachings of the Dharma are actually disclosed before us and we can listen to it as we like makes the teachings of the Pure Land inexhaustibly meaningful.

On this dynamic aspect of the Pure Land, the aspect of sending forth innumerable Buddhas and teachings, awakening and purifying sentient beings of *prapañca*, Nāgārjuna laid special emphasis. For him the teachings of the Pure Land are after all one form, the loftiest form, of expressing the dynamic nature of *śūnyatā* in thoughts and categories of common, worldly use. In this sense his concept of the Pure Land is truly a development of his Mahāyānist theory of *śūnyatā*.

(English adaptation by Hiroshi Sakamoto)

The Mahāyāna Structure of Shinran's Thought[1]

Ueda Yoshifumi

Part I[2]

All forms of Buddhism take as their foundation going out from this world of suffering (saṃsāra) and attaining the transcendent (nirvana). This is often assumed to entail a renunciation of ordinary life, an idea reinforced by the figure of Śākyamuni, whose abandonment of family and throne presents a thoroughgoing repudiation of the values of secular life. During Śākyamuni's lifetime, however, there were strong bonds between the disciples who had renounced home life and the laity that remained in the secular world, and in the person of the Buddha, who embodied the transcendent, both his mendicant disciples and his lay followers were able to find salvation. Still, the negative aspect of Buddhism—that of transcending the mundane world—is strong in Śākyamuni's teaching, and after Śākyamuni's death the distinction between lay and monk solidified.

Mahāyāna Buddhism arose as a movement to reunite the laity and the monks and nuns by overcoming the distinction between lay and monk, the world of ordinary life and the world of nirvana. Mahāyāna saw the earlier Buddhism as one that sought nirvana by abandoning the world of

---

1. This is a translation of Prof. Ueda's widely-read article, "Shinran no ōjō no shisō," in *Dōbō gakuhō* 18–19 (February 1968), 335–383, and reprinted with minor revisions in *Shinran kyōgaku* 13 (November 1968), 97–117, and 14 (June 1969), 105–128. Material has been incorporated from a number of Prof. Ueda's other books and articles; these are identified in footnotes. Many of the quotations from Shinran are from the Shin Buddhism Translation Series (Honganji International Center, Kyoto; distributed by Asian Humanities Press, Berkeley) edited by Prof. Ueda: *Letters of Shinran: Mattōshō* (1978; hereafter as *Letters*); *Notes on 'Essentials of Faith Alone': Yuishinshōmon'i* (1979, *Essentials*); *Notes on Once-calling and Many-calling: Ichinentanenmon'i* (1980, *Once-calling*); and *Notes on the Inscriptions on Sacred Scrolls: Songōshinzōmeimon* (1981, *Inscriptions*); portions have been adapted. For definitions of Shin terms, see the glossaries to these volumes.

2. Ed. The text was originally published in two parts, both in Japanese and in *The Eastern Buddhist*, and these are therefore indicated here.

saṃsāra and thus knew nothing of benefiting others, that is, leading the laity to enlightenment. It therefore labeled such Buddhism "Hīnayāna," the small vehicle, while proclaiming itself the great vehicle. Mahāyāna does not teach abandonment of *saṃsāra*. It considers it an error to seek the transcendent apart from the secular world, and is established at the point where the dualistic thinking of Hīnayāna is broken through. The true transcendent realm also transcends the distinction between *saṃsāra* and nirvana, and is attained not through renouncing everyday life but through transforming it at its roots. To borrow Dōgen's words, "Realize that *saṃsāra* is none other than the life of Buddha" (*Shōbōgenzōshōji*). Living ordinary life is itself the life of Buddha. In attaining this mode of existence lies the fundamental character of Mahāyāna.[3]

That *saṃsāra* is not abandoned must not be understood superficially, for one does indeed go out from *saṃsāra*. But while the person who simply dwells in *saṃsāra* is attached to it and does not seek nirvana, the one who has abandoned *saṃsāra* to dwell in nirvana (Hīnayāna sage) is attached to nirvana. The true transcendent realm is free of all forms of attachment. Moreover, the person who has realized nirvana experiences the sameness (*samatā*) of sentient beings in *saṃsāra* and himself, that is, the fact that the minds of sentient beings and his own mind are one. When the mind thus awakened turns towards sentient beings in *saṃsāra*, it is called great compassion. One goes out from *saṃsāra* and reaches nirvana, but without abiding in nirvana compassionately re-enters the world of *saṃsāra*. Since the awakened one abides neither in *saṃsāra* nor nirvana, there is nowhere that he abides. Hence, the Mahāyāna concept of nirvana is "nirvana of no abiding place" (*apratiṣṭhita*-nirvana).

In order to reach the transcendent, Mahāyāna Buddhists practiced the "three learnings" (precepts, meditation, wisdom). In other words, they walked the path of renunciation of secular life. This did not mean that one could not reach the transcendent unless one entered a life of monastic discipline and practice; renouncing home life was significant only as a tested method for transforming the world of ordinary life and grounding it in the transcendent. Monastic life is unnecessary if one is able to attain the transcendent while living in the mundane world. This is the Mahāyāna spirit, typically expressed in the *Vimalakīrti-sūtra*, in which the layman Vimalakīrti is depicted as superior to bodhisattvas who have renounced the world. But even though the distinction between monk and lay was erased in spirit, it was not until the Pure Land Buddhism of twelfth century Japan that a reliable method to replace the three learnings was established. Hōnen (1133–1212), the central figure in this development, states:

---

3. For a discussion of the concept of transformation in Buddhist tradition, see Ueda Yoshifumi, "Bukkyō ni okeru tenkan no shisō," *Dōbō bukkyō* 4 (November 1972), 53–72.

> Although Buddhism is vast, in essence it is composed of no more than the three learnings... But as for precepts, I myself do not keep a single one. In meditation, I have not attained even one. In wisdom, I have not attained the right wisdom of cutting off discriminative thinking and realizing the fruit.

Nevertheless:

> Without distinguishing between wise and foolish, the upholding of precepts and the breaking of them, Amida Buddha comes to welcome us.[4]

It is in Hōnen's disciple Shinran (1173–1262), however, that we see the full development of the Mahāyāna position, for in marrying, Shinran completely transcended the distinction between monk and lay that originated in Śākyamuni's day.

Evidence that a foolish person (*bonbu*) can become a buddha without observing precepts and performing meditative practices is afforded by the appearance of many *myōkōnin*, "wondrously excellent people," often uneducated, who have attained a wisdom beyond the reach of ordinary learning. There is no question of the greatness of Zen Buddhism, but the history of Zen affords no example of bringing to "the sage wisdom of awakening to self"[5] a person like Asahara Saichi (1850–1932), a *geta*-maker,[6] *while he was carrying on his day-to-day life in his work*. There are, of course, stories in Zen of common laborers without special education attaining *satori*, but in such cases, they attained wisdom by observing precepts and practicing meditation, so in fact they walked the path of a monk. Shinran, however, states:

> Not choosing the learned or those of pure precepts,
> Nor rejecting the violators of precepts or those of karmic evil:
> With that person who simply says the Name,
> It is as though rubble were transformed into gold.[7]

Such a statement is impossible from the standpoint of Zen. The path of Hōnen and Shinran is not that of abandoning home life. Neither is it a lay Buddhism distinguished from the path of monks. Shinran's self-

---

4. Words addressed to Kenkōbō, *Hōnen shōnin zenshū*, (Kyoto: Heirakuji shoten, 1955), 569.

5. *Jikaku shōchi* 自覚聖智; *pratyātmāryajñāna*. D. T. Suzuki states: "Saichi always emerges forth from the 'sage wisdom of self-realization.' Whatever Saichi is ultimately expressing, it is always one with Amida's perfect enlightenment." (Foreword to *Myōkōnin Asahara Saichi-shū*, Tokyo: Shunjūsha, 1967, 19). The term *pratyātmāryajñāna* occurs often in the *Laṅkāvatāra-sūtra*; Suzuki equates it with *satori*.

6. Ed. *Geta* are traditional wooden sandals.

7. *Tamon Jōkai erabarezu / hakai zaigō kirawarezu / tada yoku nenzuru hito nomi zo / garyaku mo kon to henjikeru (Jōgai wasan);* see Murakami edition, *Shinshū seiten* (Kyoto: Nagata, 1956), 590.

description as "neither monk nor lay" sweeps away this distinction. The person who can "hear" the teaching can actualize it—whether he has abandoned home life or not, whether wise or foolish, whatever his character or livelihood.[8]

Pure Land Buddhism is often seen as a future-oriented religion of salvation that offers a path from this defiled world to the world of purity, to be attained at physical death. The compassion that forms the foundation of Pure Land Buddhism, however, is but another name for the wisdom that lies at the heart of all Mahāyāna; thus, as a form of Mahāyāna, Pure Land Buddhism must share the character of transformation and not consist merely of a linear progress in which this world is negated and the future world is affirmed. In fact, it is in the teaching of Shinran that we see the complex structure of transformation common to all Mahāyāna Buddhism clearly manifest in Pure Land thought. Shinran brought the Pure Land tradition, which up to his day had been nothing more than a side current in Mahāyāna thought, into the mainstream of the Mahāyāna tradition by adopting this structure of transformation as the core of his teaching. Even in traditional Shin scholarship, however, important facets of Shinran's thought have been neglected or misunderstood because of a superficial understanding of this general Mahāyāna concept in his thought. Below, I will consider the structure of transformation in Mahāyāna tradition and then delineate its place in Shinran's Buddhism.

Transformation

In Mahāyāna thought, a person goes out from *saṃsāra* and attains nirvana, and this at the same time means that he transcends the distinction of *saṃsāra* and nirvana. Thus, attainment of nirvana must, on the one hand, imply the negation or transcendence of *saṃsāra*, and on the other hand, it must be non-dual with *saṃsāra*. In that the bodhisattva has eradicated discriminative thinking and feeling, he has attained nirvana, but since for him there is no distinction between *saṃsāra* and nirvana, he does not abandon *saṃsāra* (he is in *saṃsāra*). This is expressed as "not dwelling in nirvana." Since he is in *saṃsāra*, he "gives rise to discrimination," but

---

8. Shinran himself was well aware of the monumental significance of this. He states that the Pure Land teaching leads all beings to the attainment of the One Vehicle, which is supreme *bodhi*, and further that the One Vehicle signifies the Vow only. All other paths exist only to bring beings to enter the One Vehicle: "The One Vehicle is the great vehicle. The great vehicle is the buddha vehicle. To attain the One Vehicle is to attain highest perfect enlightenment. Highest perfect enlightenment is the realm of nirvana.... In the great vehicle there are no 'two vehicles' or 'three vehicles.' The two vehicles and three vehicles lead one to enter the One Vehicle. The One Vehicle is the vehicle of highest truth. There is no One Vehicle other than the one buddha-vehicle of the Vow." (*Kyōgyōshinshō*, "Chapter on Practice," *Shinshū shōgyō zensho* II [here-after as SSZ], Kyoto: Ōyagi Kōbundō, 1941, 38).

though he does so, he does not part from nirvana (non-discrimination, suchness). In this sense, he does not dwell in *saṃsāra*.[9] This world of non-discriminative wisdom (*nirvikalpa-jñāna*) is and is not *saṃsāra*, it is and is not nirvana. "*Saṃsāra* is itself nirvana" is also "neither *saṃsāra* nor nirvana," and at the same time each of these phrases implies the radical transformation by which one transcends *saṃsāra* and realizes nirvana. Moreover, these two contradictory aspects—the identity of *saṃsāra* and nirvana and the change or transformation by which *saṃsāra*, through being negated, becomes nirvana—are united throughout the various stages of practice.

Śākyamuni was able to transform ordinary life by perceiving the four noble truths and dependent co-origination, that is, by seeing all things—the self and the world that surrounds it—just as they are. To see things as they truly are means having cast off all self-centered, discriminative thinking. Such seeing is not mere seeing but at the same time a kind of practice, and the wisdom established through this seeing-practice is called supreme *bodhi*, or emancipation, signifying liberation from the bonds of *saṃsāra*, or nirvana, meaning that suffering has been extinguished.

Historically, the earliest Mahāyāna concept of the wisdom established through seeing-practice is *prajñāpāramitā* (lit. wisdom that has gone to the other shore). It is described in the Prajñāpāramitā *sūtra*s, which are considered the foundation of all Mahāyāna thought, as the seeing-practice of "not seeing" any objects. Not to see any objects means to cut off the dichotomous thinking (*vikalpa*) that takes all things as objects in relation to self, and this means at the same time that all things that become objects of thought do not really exist. For the bodhisattva practicing *prajñāpāramitā*, there is nothing, whether material or mental, to become the object of any act of perception, thought, or imagination; thus, "all things are empty" (*śūnya*) or non-existent. "Empty" is used with regard to things seen and "not seeing" with regard to perception of them. That things do not really exist and that the bodhisattva's perception does not see or discriminate them are one and the same. This means that there is no object apart from the subject: seer and seen are one. The wisdom that functions when object and perception have thus become one is *prajñāpāramitā* or non-discriminative wisdom; emptiness and *prajñāpāramitā* are different terms for the same thing.

In *prajñāpāramitā*, the term emptiness means that there are no objects. It does not, however, mean simply that the absence of objects is wisdom; the non-existence of the object of illusory discrimination is at the same time no-discrimination or no-seeing. When no seeing of any kind of object is established, that is, when non-discriminative wisdom has arisen,

---

9. *Shōdaijōronshaku*, T31, 247b.

the bodhisattva perceives things as they really are. The seeing of non-discriminative wisdom is, therefore, seeing of no-seeing. By practicing *prajñāpāramitā*, the bodhisattva reaches the fundamental reality of all things, the true world of existence just as it is. This means that he "sees suchness (*tathatā*)." Hence, emptiness is also synonymous with suchness or true reality. The mental faculties of a person lacking wisdom perceive objects that are not really existent and may be labeled illusory discrimination (*vikalpa*); the mental faculties of the person of wisdom that arise where all such discrimination is eradicated and all objects have vanished is called non-discriminative wisdom or *prajñāpāramitā*. The objects of discrimination include all things—forms, sensations, thoughts, feelings, consciousness; the object of non-discriminative wisdom is the emptiness of all things. This emptiness is things as they truly are."[10]

The Identity of Opposites

In the Prajñāpāramitā *sūtras*, the transformation in which the world of ordinary life (*saṃsāra*) is completely uprooted and at the same time unfolded as the transcendent realm (true existence, *tattva*)—is implied in the expression, "Form is itself emptiness." "Is" (*soku*, which literally indicates identity) is not the mere equation of form and emptiness; it implies the process by which form (ordinary life) becomes established on the foundation of true existence by passing through a complete negation. Form (self and all things) sinks into emptiness (no objects and no seeing), and at the same time emptiness (reality or suchness), limiting itself as form, becomes the seen; here, *prajñāpāramitā* as not-seeing and at the same time seeing (things as they are) is established. Because emptiness is not mere non-existence but also true reality, "Form is itself emptiness" is reversed: "Emptiness is itself form." All things of the world of *saṃsāra*, which are indicated by the term form, are pervaded by emptiness; all things are like phantasms or mirages. In the formulation of the *Diamond Sūtra*, "A is not A, and therefore it is A"; this signifies that A is negated and at the same time affirmed by emptiness. A is penetrated by emptiness, and it is this A that is true reality or suchness. This structure of *prajñāpāramitā* has been termed by D. T. Suzuki "the logic of *soku-hi*" (identity-mutual negation).[11]

---

10. For a more detailed discussion of *prajñā*, see Ueda Yoshifumi, *Daijō bukkyō no shisō* (Tokyo, 1977), 9–24.

11. The self-contradiction embodied in *soku*, indicating the identity of two elements that stand in a relation of mutual negation, is not merely a logical contradiction; it is an expression of the simultaneous negation and affirmation practiced as non-discriminative wisdom. Here, the self-contradiction seen in "form is emptiness" or "*saṃsāra* is nirvana" cannot be resolved by any logical thought, and to understand it as not self-contradictory cannot be a correct understanding of the thought it

The self-identity of opposites realized in the transcendence of discriminative thinking is also expressed, "Saṃsāra is itself nirvana." Nāgārjuna states: "Saṃsāra is without any distinction from nirvana; nirvana is also without any distinction from saṃsāra" (Madhyamakakārikā XXV, 19). Here, saṃsāra and nirvana are brought into a relationship of non-duality through the negation of each with reference to the other. In Nāgārjuna's thought, the identity of saṃsāra and nirvana holds two aspects. One is dual negation; as mentioned above, "Saṃsāra is nirvana," as the identity of opposites, is also "neither saṃsāra nor nirvana." This stance is possible, however, only through the religious experience in which nirvana is established through the eradication of saṃsāra. The second aspect, then, is the turning of saṃsāra into nirvana. Although the Prajñāpāramitā sūtras formulate the structure of prajñāpāramitā as the non-discrimination of opposites (soku), they do not fully articulate the transformation implied in the realization of such wisdom. In order to clarify the practice of prajñāpāramitā, Nāgārjuna teaches the process of thoroughgoing negation by which form (saṃsāra) is eradicated and made empty (nirvana), for example, in his exposition of the eighteen types of emptiness in Mahāprajñāpāramitāśāstra.[12]

Since Nāgārjuna takes the Prajñāpāramitā sūtras as his fundamental standpoint, however, the ontological aspect expressed in the concepts of existence (form; self and all things) and non-existence (emptiness) constitutes the basis of his thought, and explanation from the epistemological side is weak. The early Yogācāra thinkers—Maitreya, Asaṅga, and Vasubandhu—opened up a new field in Mahāyāna thought by analyzing the practice of non-discriminative wisdom as "seeing only"(vijñaptimātratā). Before Yogācāra, the basic issues in Buddhism were organized around contrasting terms: sentient being and buddha, blind passions and enlightenment, saṃsāra and nirvana, all dharmas and thusness. Yogācāra, however, in order to treat the working of the mind, divided "saṃsāra" or "all things" into the seer and the seen, developing the theory of three natures (tri-svabhāva).

The seer (discriminative mind, vikalpa) is termed "other-dependent nature" (paratantra-svabhāva), for it arises from causes and conditions. The seen is termed discriminated nature (parikalpita-svabhāva), since it is that which is differentiated and conceptualized by the seer as its object. For the unenlightened being, the objects perceived with defiled discrimination arising from the seeds (bīja) of karma and blind passions are thought to be real. For the bodhisattva or tathāgata who has attained non-objectifying, non-discriminative wisdom, however, all things that

---

expresses. See Ueda Yoshifumi, "Ui Hakuju to Suzuki Daisetz," *Suzuki Daisetz zenshū geppō* 21 (June 1982), 1–5, and 22 (July 1982), 1–10.

12. Ed. This presumably refers to the *Daichidoron*. See list of texts.

are the objects of discriminative perception are "always non-existent" (*nityam asat*) or "not existent" (*na vidyate*). Further, since there is no object to be grasped, neither can there be discriminative perception that grasps. In other words, both the seer and the seen are empty. Since there is no seer, the term no-mind (*acitta*) is used, and since there is no seen, it is said that there is "no object to be perceived" (*anupalambha*).[13] As stated above, the seen (discriminated nature) is always non-existent; hence the seer must also always be non-existent. That is, discriminative mind exists (*sat*) in that, as other-dependent nature, it arises from causes and conditions, but since its object (the seen), as discriminated nature, is always non-existent, it is non-existent. This is stated: "Other-dependent nature, through discriminated nature, is empty (*śūnya*)."[14] This emptiness of all things (both seer and seen) is consummated nature (*pariniṣpanna-svabhāva*). It is non-discriminative wisdom, suchness, emptiness, *dharmakāya*, or nirvana. It is things as they truly are.

Nāgārjuna states simply that all things arise from causes and conditions and therefore are empty. In Yogācāra thought, however, the seer (other-dependent nature, which itself constitutes *saṃsāra* or all dharmas), since it arises from conditions, exists, and at the same time, through the nothingness of all objects, it is empty or non-existent. This emptiness of both the seer and the seen is, as stated above, consummated nature or nirvana. In other words, the pure non-discriminative wisdom of the bodhisattva includes within it defiled discrimination (*vikalpa*). D. T. Suzuki therefore states, "Karma is no-Karma and no-Karma is Karma." (*The Essence of Buddhism*). In this way, other-dependent nature is both existent and nonexistent, and the theory of three natures, while indicating the content of

---

13. "Always non-existent" (*Madhyāntavibhāgakārikā* III, 3); "not existent" (*Triṃśikā*, verse 20); "no-mind," "no object to be perceived" (*Triṃśikā*, verse 29, and Sthiramati's commentary to it).

14. Sthiramati's commentary to *Triṃśikā*, verse 22. That the nonexistence of both seer and seen is consummated nature is taught in *Madhyāntavibhāga* I, 5. Further, Sthiramati's commentary to *Triṃśikā*, verse 24, states: "Consummated nature takes nothingness as its nature." There is a slightly different definition of consummated nature in *Triṃśikā* 21: "In other-dependent nature, there is always separation from what precedes (i.e., discriminated nature); this is consummated nature." This does not mean that other-dependent nature is separated from discriminated nature so that they become two, but rather that in other-dependent nature (the seeing mind), there is no object. Other-dependent nature and discriminated nature together as a whole make up consummated nature.

When it is said that the non-existence of the seer and the seen is consummated nature, the existence of other-dependent nature, which arises from conditions, is not excluded, for the nothingness that is consummated nature is absolute and harbours other-dependent nature within itself. Since consummated nature is non-discriminative wisdom or suchness, it holds within it the discriminative mind (*vikalpa*), which is not true or real.

"Form is itself emptiness, emptiness is itself form" or "Saṃsāra is itself nirvana," at the same time illuminates the relationship between the seer and the seen that occurs in non-discriminative wisdom.

The Logical Structure of Transformation

In order to probe further how such non-discriminative wisdom is possible, the theory of three natures was developed in a new direction by Asaṅga in Mahāyānasaṃgraha. In addition to the three natures described above, Asaṅga proposed a version based not on the dichotomy of seer and seen, but on the relationship of the impure and the pure. This second version of the three natures constitutes a unique exposition of the concept of change or transformation underlying the structure of Mahāyāna thought and provides perhaps the most fully articulated model of it. According to this second theory, other-dependent nature signifies the "mutual dependence" of saṃsāra and nirvana or defiled and pure. The relationships of these two aspects, which are unified in "mutually other-dependent nature," are explained on the basis of passages from two sūtras, with each passage clarifying one face of the relationship. First:

> The Brahmaparipṛcchā-sūtra declares: "With what meaning does the World-honored one say, 'The Tathāgata does not see saṃsāra, does not see nirvana'?" In other-dependent nature (paratantra-svabhāva), through its discriminated nature (parikalpita-svabhāva) and its consummated nature (pariniṣpanna-svabhāva), saṃsāra is nirvana; this follows from their non-difference. The reason is that other-dependent nature, through its aspect of discriminated nature, gives rise to saṃsāra, and through its aspect of consummated nature, establishes nirvana.[15]

Asaṅga states that the identity of saṃsāra and nirvana arises from their non-difference, which is expressed, "Tathāgata does not see saṃsāra, does not see nirvana." In his non-discriminative wisdom, the bodhisattva perceives no distinction between saṃsāra and nirvana. This is the same concept as in Nāgārjuna's verse quoted above. The two opposing aspects of mutually other-dependent nature are non-dual in their basis, and at the same time, each is negated by the other. These relationships of identity and dual negation express the nature of nirvana of no abiding place, but like the formulations of the Prajñāpāramitā sūtras, they fail to provide a basis for explaining the dynamics of awakening. In order to clarify the structure of transcending saṃsāra and attaining nirvana, Asaṅga, based on the Abhidharma-sūtra,[16] identifies discrimi-

---

15. Mahāyānasaṃgraha. See Ueda Yoshifumi, Shōdai jōron kōdoku, (Tokyo: Shunjūsha, 1981), 265.
16. Ed. There is no extant text with precisely this title. Ueda is quoting from the Abidatsumadaijōkyō 阿毘達磨大乘経 which in turn is known only from citations

nated, consummated, and other-dependent nature as defiled, pure, and defiled-pure,[17] and then introduces the concept of transformation (*āśrayaparāvṛtti*, lit. "transformation of the basis" of the unenlightened person into that of an enlightened one):

> The nirvana of no abiding place has as its characteristic (*lakṣaṇa*) the transformation of the two kinds of basis, parting from discriminative thinking (*saṃsāra*) and not parting from *saṃsāra*. In this, *saṃsāra* takes as its essence the impure aspect of other-dependent nature, nirvana the pure aspect. The fundamental basis is other-dependent nature that possesses the two aspects of pure and impure. Concerning transformation: When remedy occurs, this other-dependent nature, in its impure aspect, changes forever its fundamental nature, and in accord with its pure aspect, its fundamental nature is established forever.[18]

Here, Asaṅga states that the nirvana of no abiding place, in which both *saṃsāra* and nirvana are negated, is characterized by transformation or "remedy (*taiji*)." Remedy refers to the three learnings, by which blind passions are eradicated. If the time when it occurs is taken as a boundary line, then the two aspects of other-dependent nature—the impure aspect (*saṃsāra*) and the pure aspect (nirvana)—are in a relation such that the establishment of one side implies the nullification of the other. When remedy occurs, the impure aspect disappears, and dependent nature is established as that which is pure, nirvana or buddha-body. Since the impure is eradicated, and through this eradication the pure is consummated, the impure and the pure are unified by passing through an absolute negation. This is the structure of transformation.

The *Brahmaparipṛcchā-sūtra* states that in other-dependent nature *saṃsāra* and nirvana are non-dual, while the quotation concerning transformation indicates that all things (discrimination) are transformed and become emptiness or suchness. Thus, other-dependent nature holds two different meanings: first, *saṃsāra* and nirvana are in a relationship of non-duality founded upon a dual negation, and second, they are in a mutually exclusive relationship such that when one is established the other is nullified. In this way, the aspects of other-dependent nature indicated in the

---

in the *Shōdaijōron* 摂大乗論. To maintain the original flavour, i.e. the suggestive reference back to a presumed Indian source, we leave the author's references to *Abhidharma-sūtra* in this context.

17. "In the *Abhidharma-sūtra* the Buddha, the World-honored one, teaches, 'There are three kinds of dharmas: 1) the defiled, 2) the pure, 3) the defiled-pure.' What is the meaning of teaching these three? Within dependent nature, the discriminated nature forms the defiled, the consummated nature forms the pure, and the other-dependent nature itself forms the defiled-pure. With this meaning the three are taught"; T31, 121a; see also *Shōdaijōron kōdoku*, 268.

18. T31, 121a–b; see *Shōdaijōron kōdoku*, 208.

two *sutra* passages also stand in a contradictory relationship: that *saṃsāra* and nirvana are completely without distinction and that they are such that at all times only one or the other is established cannot both be logically affirmed simultaneously. Hence, other-dependent nature cannot be considered a simple combination of discriminated nature and consummated nature. It is a totality of complex structure such that two elements, in spite of the fact that their interrelationship or mutual connection has been completely sundered through absolute negation, make up a single whole. This is the logical structure of the attainment of nirvana.[19] The structure of the path to Buddha-hood is clearly indicated by this transformation.

The Process of Practice

The phrases "Form is itself emptiness" and "*Saṃsāra* is itself nirvana" have two aspects, reflecting the two sides—identity and transformation—of the attainment of emptiness or nirvana. One is that the phrases can be reversed: "Form is itself emptiness, emptiness is itself form," "*Saṃsāra* is itself nirvana, nirvana is itself *saṃsāra*." Simultaneously, however, these phrases imply a single direction, a movement "toward emptiness through eradicating form," "toward nirvana through freeing oneself from *saṃsāra*." The reversible aspect of emptiness is clearly expressed in the Prajñāpāramitā *sūtras*: "It is not that form is emptied through emptiness; the self-nature of form is emptiness." The irreversible aspect is seen in Nāgārjuna: "Form is broken through and made empty." The irreversible aspect, as the dynamic application of the double negation of "neither being nor emptiness" or "neither *saṃsāra* nor nirvana," expresses the deepening of the practice of non-discrimination that continues to eradicate discrimination and blind passions. This constantly moves toward the ultimate stage of *tathāgata*. The reversible as-

---

19. "Form is emptiness, emptiness is form" in the Prajñāpāramitā *sūtras* corresponds to the concept "*saṃsāra* is nirvana" in the *Brahmaparipṛcchā-sūtra*; it must also be seen to imply, therefore, the transformation by which "form disappears and becomes emptiness," which is expressed in the *Abhidharma-sūtra* as going from *saṃsāra* to nirvana. In the Prajñāpāramitā *sūtras*, however, only the identity of form and emptiness is emphasized. Nāgārjuna teaches both the identity of form and emptiness and the process by which form is eradicated. Nāgārjuna's disciple Āryadeva inherited this thought that emptiness breaks through all things and makes them empty, and brings the practicer to reach the inconceivability of all things. This thought was adopted by Jízàng and became the basis of the Sānlùn school in China. In this tradition, the identity of form and emptiness, which is the original concept of the Prajñāpāramitā *sūtras*, was weak. Both aspects of negation and identity together were developed in China in Tiāntái and Huáyán thought, but the latter, because it emphasized identity and was weak in practical negation, was absorbed into Ch'an. In these forms of Chinese Buddhism, the concept of transformation developed by Asaṅga and Vasubandhu approximately two centuries after Nāgārjuna was not incorporated at all.

pect signifies that this practice of absolute negation, through the realization of suchness with each step, reaches the ultimate at every stage of advance, and that the direction of the former aspect is eliminated so that all things become established in their true form. This is the meaning of Nāgārjuna's statement, "Because of emptiness, all things become established." The directional aspect, through its conformity with the non-directional aspect, constantly loses its directionality, and going from saṃsāra to nirvana is actually to return to saṃsāra—or rather, it is never to go anywhere from the very beginning. At the same time, the non-directional aspect, through its conformity with the directional aspect, signifies the movement of deepening and purifying ever more the nirvana or absolute nothingness that forms the basis of saṃsāra or being. The practice of these mutually contradictory aspects together is prajñāpāramitā or non-discriminative wisdom.

The transformation I have outlined above is not an experience that occurs suddenly only once, but involves a long process, from first hearing the teaching and undertaking practice to the final attainment of the stage of tathāgata. Since it is a process, the negation or transcendence of ordinary life through the perfection of no-seeing occurs gradually; nevertheless, at some point the eradication of blind passions becomes thoroughgoing, so that complete liberation from saṃsāra is accomplished and one enters the true transcendent realm. This point is called attainment of the stage of non-retrogression and forms the core of transformation. Here one realizes non-discriminative wisdom, or the seeing of no-seeing. Non-retrogression means that one who has attained the true transcendent realm, upon once entering, never falls back.

In Mahāyāna thought in general, even after entering the stage of non-retrogression one continues practice, and the entire process of practice until one attains the rank of ultimate buddha-hood is called transformation. Through the non-discriminative wisdom attained with non-retrogression in the first of the ten bodhisattva stages, one eliminates all attachments and sees suchness; hence, the bodhisattva there realizes *dharmakāya* and attains the three bodies of *tathāgata*, and non-discriminative wisdom reaches its consummation. However, a residue from blind passions still remains, so absolute negation (non-discrimination, practice of eradicating the traces of discrimination) continues to deepen. This is represented by the ten stages, from the second stage to the stage of *tathāgata*. In each of these stages, not only the stage of *tathāgata*, it is said that the bodhisattva reaches the ultimate, for the bodhisattva sees suchness at each stage, and the suchness thus seen is always identical, without any distinctions whatever. Since the true transcendent realm is beyond all speech and thought, after one has entered one emerges again into the world of words and thoughts, but again re-enters the realm in which thought is eradicated: this is repeated over and over. By repeatedly entering the realm beyond thought, the deep root of *saṃsāra* and blind passions is gradually cut through. In all of this, the stage of non-retrogression is the first seeing of suchness; hence it is termed *kendō* (the path of seeing). After this, the seeing of suchness is repeated a number of times; this is called *shudō* (the path of practice). *Shu* 修 (*bhāvanā*) means to practice repeatedly.

In Shinran, the attainment of the stage of non-retrogression occurs at the moment of realizing *shinjin* 信心. *Shinjin* is the mind of Amida Buddha given to and realized in a person. Shinran interprets *shin* 信 to mean "truth, reality, sincerity,"[20] and also states, "Sentient beings, who are filled with blind passions, lack a mind true and real" (*Inscriptions*, 33). When *shinjin* is realized, the mind of Buddha and the mind of blind passions become one. This is a oneness of the pure and the impure together; further, since the impure becomes the pure, it has the complex structure of transformation outlined above. For a sentient being to realize *shinjin* is for his mind of blind passions to be transformed (*tenzu*) into the mind of Buddha while remaining as it is. Shinran states: "Transform means that the mind of evil becomes good." The mind of evil here is the entire human mind, including the moral consciousness that seeks to avoid evil and to do good; "good" refers to great wisdom-compassion. Since a person's mind becomes the mind of Buddha, to realize *shinjin* has the significance of becoming Buddha; hence, for Shinran, it signifies attainment of non-retrogression. He also calls it "immediate attainment of birth."

The Two Meanings of Birth in Shinran

The presence of the structure of transformation in Shinran's thought is revealed in his concept of birth (*ōjō*). In its traditional usage beginning with Indian scriptures, birth meant to be born in the other world (Pure Land) at the end of life in this world (the defiled world). In the Pure Land, one attains the stage of non-retrogression through performing practices, and thereafter continues to practice until attainment of the supreme Buddha-hood . In Shinran, however, birth came to signify attaining supreme Buddha-hood . At the moment life in this world ends, one becomes supreme Buddha. To express this, Shinran states that the person of *shinjin* is the same as Maitreya:

> Truly we know that the mahāsattva Maitreya has realized the diamond-like mind of the stage of equal enlightenment, and therefore will attain the supreme enlightenment... Beings of the nembutsu, because they have attained the diamond-like mind of the crosswise leap, will attain great nirvana at the moment of death. Hence it is said that they are the same. (Chapter on Shinjin, SSZ II, 79)

---

20. *Kyōgyōshinshō*, "Chapter on Shinjin," SSZ II, 59.

This change in the meaning of birth in Shinran is inseparably connected with his teaching that the attainment of the stage of non-retrogression occurs not in the Pure Land after death, as traditionally taught, but at the moment a person realizes *shinjin*. Since one already dwells in the stage of non-retrogression in the present life, the Pure Land as a place for practice is no longer necessary. The practiser of *shinjin* is said to have attained the equal of perfect enlightenment and to have reached the same level as Maitreya; at the end of life in this world, he will attain supreme Buddha-hood . Concerning the relationship between non-retrogression and birth, Shinran states:

> When we are grasped by Amida, immediately—without a moment or a day elapsing—we ascend to and become established in the stage of the truly settled;[21] "this is the meaning of *attain birth*." (*Once-calling*, 32)
>
> To dwell in the stage of non-retrogression is to become established in the stage of the truly settled. This is also called the attainment of the equal of perfect enlightenment. Such is the meaning of *they then attain birth*. (*Essentials*, 35)

Thus, to realize *shinjin* and dwell in the stage of non-retrogression is to attain birth. Further, as stated above, to realize great nirvana at the end of life is also attaining birth. The term "birth" in the following passages, since it is attained after *shinjin* has become settled and one has entered the stage of non-retrogression, signifies the realization of great nirvana at the time of death:

> Since one dwells in the stage of non-retrogression until being born into the Pure Land, one is said to be in the stage of the truly settled."
>
> (*Letters*, 42)
>
> "The person of true *shinjin* abides in the stage of the truly settled, for he has already been grasped, never to be abandoned. There is no need to wait in anticipation for the moment of death, no need to rely on Amida's coming. At the time *shinjin* becomes settled, birth too becomes settled. (*Letters*, 19–20)

---

21. The "truly settled," in Mahāyāna tradition, refers to bodhisattvas who have reached the stage where supreme enlightenment will be attained without fail. In the Pure Land tradition prior to Shinran, it refers to those born in the Pure Land, who will attain enlightenment through religious practices in the ideal environment there. Shinran uses the term for people who have realized *shinjin* in the present. Shinran's position with regard to the tradition may be seen in his understanding of Tánluán's passage: "If a man simply hears of the purity and happiness of the Pure Land and earnestly desires to be born there, he shall obtain birth and thereupon enter the stage of the truly settled." Shinran, asserting that one immediately becomes truly settled on attaining *shinjin*, interprets Tánluán to read: "The man who simply hearing of the purity and happiness of that land, earnestly desires to be born there, and the one who attains birth immediately, enter the stage of the truly settled" (*Once-calling*, 35–36).

Shinran's first usage of birth is uniquely his own, and is not found even in Hōnen.

In Shinran's writings, the same word—"to be born" (*ōjō suru*)—is used to indicate two different attainments: birth in the Pure Land at death (which signifies for Shinran the realization of supreme enlightenment)[22] and attainment of the stage of the truly settled in the present. To realize enlightenment and to attain the stage of the truly settled through realizing *shinjin* are related as result and cause. Although cause and result are clearly different, a binding relationship exists between them. Nevertheless, for birth to refer to both means that it harbors a self-contradiction. If one takes both meanings of birth together, then the person who has been born (one who dwells in the stage of the truly settled) has not been born (has not reached nirvana, the result). Or, the person who has already been born (the person in the stage of the truly settled) will be born in the future (unfailingly attain nirvana).

Because of this self-contradiction, sectarian scholars sometimes argue that birth in the Pure Land is the true meaning, while Shinran's second usage does not really mean "to be born," but rather that one's birth has become certain.[23] In other words, birth has only one meaning, realizing nirvana. Shinran, however, bases his understanding on the passage from the *Larger Sūtra* that teaches that the Eighteenth Vow has been fulfilled:

> Sentient beings, as they hear the Name, realize even one thought-moment of *shinjin* and joy, which is directed to them out of Amida's sincere mind, and aspiring to be born in that land, they then attain birth and dwell in the stage of non-retrogression.[24]

Shinran explains the phrase "they then attain birth" (*sokutoku ōjō*)

> Then (*soku*) means immediately, without any time elapsing, without a day passing. *Soku* also means to ascend to and become established in a certain rank. Attain (*toku*) means to have attained what one shall attain. (*Once-calling*, 33)

---

22. Prior to Shinran, birth in the Pure Land did not signify immediate realization of nirvana, and although the concept of attainment of enlightenment upon birth seen in Shinran is not entirely absent in Shàndǎo and Hōnen, it was not developed. The distinction between *sokuben ōjō* 即便往生 and *tōtoku ōjō* 当得往生 by Shōkū (1177-1247), founder of the Seizan branch of the Pure Land School, bears some similarity with Shinran's two usages, but what is noteworthy in Shinran is his assertion that non-retrogression is attained with realization of *shinjin*.

23. This is asserted in spite of the fact that, as the quotation above shows, Shinran is perfectly familiar with the expression "birth becomes settled," or in other words, that he distinguishes between "birth becomes settled" and "attains birth."

24. T12, 272b. This passage was traditionally interpreted, "When sentient beings hear the Name, say it even once in trust and joy, sincerely direct their merits toward attainment of birth, and aspire to be born in that land, then they shall attain birth and dwell in the stage of non-retrogression."

Shinran points out that the word *soku* has two meanings, which taken together signify "immediately becoming established in a rank." *Toku* means "to have attained what one shall attain," that is, having already attained birth. The meaning of "they then attain birth" becomes:

> When one realizes true and real *shinjin*, one is immediately grasped and held within the heart of the Buddha of unhindered light.... When we are grasped by Amida, immediately—without a moment or a day elapsing—we ascend to and become established in the stage of the truly settled; this is the meaning of *attain birth*. (*Once-calling*, 33)

As long as one takes "birth" to mean being born into the Pure Land at the end of life in this world, it is impossible to state that entering the stage of the truly settled is "to attain birth." In this passage of the *sūtra*, however, the Buddha refers to reaching the stage of the truly settled as "they then attain birth," and Shinran takes note of this.

Shinran was not forced into the statement that reaching the stage of the truly settled is attaining birth out of some necessity to interpret the words of the *sūtra*, however; rather, he is positive in his belief. This is clear from the fact that passages in the *sūtras* or the writings of the Pure Land masters that may be interpreted as teaching that attainment of the stage of the truly settled is birth are consistently so interpreted by Shinran. For example, there are the following passages from Shàndǎo: "The foolish being, when he thinks on Amida, is immediately brought to the attainment of birth,"[25] and "In the preceding thought-moment life ends, in the succeeding thought-moment one is born."[26] In both of these passages, Shàndǎo intended the term "birth" to mean birth in the Pure Land at the end of life. Shinran, however, based on the Buddha's statement in the *Larger Sūtra*, found in these passages the teaching that to reach the stage of the truly settled is to attain birth. That is, birth in these passages is attained upon realization of *shinjin* in the present.

If the importance of this idea were not great, surely Shinran would not have felt the need to repeat it as often as he does.[27] In fact, it represents

---

25. From *Fǎshì zàn* 法事讚 J. *Hōjisan*; discussed in *Once-calling*, 46–47.
26. *Wǎngshēng lǐzàn*, J. *Ōjōraisan* 往生礼讚. Shinran's interpretation is made clear in *Gutokushō*, where the *sūtra* passage on the fulfillment of the Vow is divided into "hear [the Name] and realize even one thought-moment of *shinjin*" and "they then attain birth," and "In the preceding thought-moment life ends" is matched with the first part, "in the succeeding thought-moment one is born" with the second.
27. In *Once-calling*, *Essentials*, and other works. *Once-calling* is dated the second month of Kōgen 2 (1257), when Shinran was eighty-five; *Essentials* was written in the eighth month of the same year (a variant text is dated the first month). Even though Shinran wrote these works around the same time, he not only gives a detailed exposition of the passage on the fulfillment of the Vow in the first, but repeats himself in abbreviated form in the second, even though the passage does not occur in the

an epochal development in the history of Pure Land Buddhist thought. It might even be said that the core of Shinran's thought is manifest in it. No one before Shinran, whether in India, China, or Japan, including even Hōnen, had asserted that one attains birth in the present, while carrying on one's life in this world. But it is precisely this that Shinran boldly and persistently declares.

Suchness

The line of thought expressed in the two meanings of birth is also taught in other terms. For example, Shinran asserts that both *shinjin* (cause) and nirvana (result) are suchness:

> Great *shinjin*. ... is the ocean of entrusting that is suchness or true reality. (*Kyōgyōshinshō*, "Chapter on Shinjin," SSZ II, 48)

> This *shinjin* is Buddha-nature. Buddha-nature is dharma-nature. Dharma-nature is *dharmakāya* (i.e., suchness). (*Essentials*, 42)

> True and real enlightenment ... is the ultimate fruit, supreme nirvana. ... Supreme nirvana is the uncreated ... *dharmakāya* ... suchness ... oneness.
> (*Kyōgyōshinshō*, "Chapter on Enlightenment," SSZ II, 103)

From the standpoint of suchness, there is no distinction between a sentient being and buddha. When things are known just as they are (being such, *nyo*), both the wisdom that knows and all things thus known, including the self, are true and real. That sentient being and buddha are not different means that there is no distinction between cause and result. It is also true, however, that this perspective of suchness is arrived at through performing practices. In other words, there are those who have awakened to suchness and those who have not. Maitreya discusses this in *Mahāyānasūtrālaṃkāra*:

> In suchness, all beings are non-differentiated; nevertheless, one who has attained purity (i.e., suchness) is a *tathāgata*. For this reason, all sentient beings are beings as *tathāgata-garbha* ("*tathāgata* embryo").[28]

From the perspective of suchness, all things are non-differentiated; buddha and sentient beings are one. In spite of this, there exists a distinction between "one who has attained purity" (*tathatā-gata*, "has arrived at suchness") and one who is still impure (sentient beings), that is, between *tathāgata* and potential *tathāgata* or *tathāgata-garbha*. These two may be viewed as result and cause. Where this distinction stands, there is a basis for practice aimed at attaining purity. In suchness, however,

---

work to which he is providing commentary.

28. IX. 37. Ed. The expression is more frequently translated "*tathāgata* womb"; it means that a sentient being is the matrix for the appearance of a Tathāgata.

where cause and result are non-different, practice has no basis. According to the Mahāyāna teaching, although a person is originally a buddha, through performing practices he becomes a buddha, and when he has reached the absolute, then for the first time he returns to his true self.

Shinran's idea that both cause (*shinjin*) and result (enlightenment) are suchness is fundamentally the same as Maitreya's expressed above. Traditional Shin exegesis, however, ignores the non-difference and sees only differentiation. It claims that although both cause (*shinjin*) and result (enlightenment) are labeled "suchness," there is a distinction between suchness in the causal stage and suchness in the stage of realization. In order to express this distinction, the term "inner virtue" or "working" (*naitoku*) has been introduced. The suchness of the causal stage is said to be the virtue residing within the Name. This virtue manifests itself simultaneously with birth in the Pure Land and becomes the realization of enlightenment. To ignore non-difference in this way, however, fails to arrive at a true understanding of the concept of suchness, and of course this distinction regarding suchness cannot be found in Shinran.

Enlightenment

Shinran's understanding of enlightenment or realization (*shō*) provides a third example of the structure of his thought. In explaining that enlightenment "is the ultimate fruit, supreme nirvana," he states:

> When a sentient being realizes the mind (*shinjin*) and practice directed to him for his going forth, he immediately enters the group of the truly settled. Because he dwells in the stage of the truly settled, he necessarily attains nirvana. To necessarily attain nirvana is eternal bliss. Eternal bliss is tranquility...supreme nirvana...*dharmakāya*, true reality... dharma-nature...suchness...oneness. (SSZ II, 103)

When Shinran states here that enlightenment is "the ultimate fruit, supreme nirvana," he is speaking of the result. When, in further clarifying this result, he states that "to necessarily attain nirvana is eternal bliss," he is explaining that the result is already present in the cause.

What is expressed in the two meanings of the term birth is also expounded as the view that both *shinjin* and enlightenment are suchness, and that enlightenment is nirvana (result), and at the same time this nirvana is non-dual with the stage of the truly settled (cause). In short, result differs from its cause, and does not differ. This self-contradiction inevitably appears when one attempts to read Shinran's words literally. We find that one who has been born has not been born, or that one who has in the present already been born will be born in the future. This self-contradictory thought was inherited by Rennyo (1415–1499). A record of Rennyo's words states:

The Mahāyāna Structure of Shinran's Thought

When asked whether one should say the nembutsu out of gratitude for having been saved or out of gratitude because one will be saved, Rennyo said: "Both are good. From the standpoint of the stage of the truly settled, one rejoices at having been saved; from the standpoint of the enlightenment of nirvana, one feels gratitude because one will be saved. In both cases, one rejoices at becoming a buddha, which is good."[29]

"To say the nembutsu out of gratitude for having been saved" and "to say the nembutsu out of gratitude because one will be saved" are both to "rejoice at becoming a buddha"; hence, both are affirmed. "Becoming a buddha" is the simultaneous establishment of "having been saved" and "will be saved." When one becomes a person who "has been saved"—one who has already reached the stage of the truly settled—then for the first time one can rejoice that one "will be saved." In other words, the person who can rejoice that he will be saved—will "necessarily attain nirvana"—must be one who already "has been saved"—has attained the stage of non-retrogression. Without having already been saved (dwelling in the stage of non-retrogression), it is impossible that one "will be saved" (necessarily attain nirvana). If we substitute "attain birth" for "be saved," then without already having attained birth in the present, it is impossible that one necessarily "will attain birth" in the future. The person who necessarily "will attain birth" (realize nirvana) is one who in the present has attained birth (reached the stage of the truly settled). We see, then, that Shinran's thought as indicated by the two meanings of birth is taught by Rennyo using the words "being saved." In both cases the content is "to become a buddha"; hence, it is characterized by the self-contradictory structure of simultaneous identity and transformation.

Part II[30]

Non-duality of Cause and Result in Mahāyāna Tradition

In Shinran, the term "birth" (*ōjō*) encompasses two meanings: attainment of the stage of non-retrogression at the moment one realizes *shinjin*, and attainment of enlightenment or buddha-hood at the moment of death. His concept of birth, therefore, is inherently self-contradictory: the person who has attained birth (non-retrogression) has not yet attained birth (enlightenment); the one who has already been born (attained the cause) will be born in the future (result, buddha-hood). In fact, it may be said generally that if the experience of becoming a

---

29. *Goichidaikikikigaki* 19; SSZ III, 537.

30. *Ed.* The text was originally published in two parts, both in the original Japanese and in *The Eastern Buddhist*, and these are therefore indicated here. For general indications applicable to both parts see note 1 above.

buddha is expressed intellectually, this self-contradiction results. Stated conversely, an experience that can be expressed in terms that are not self-contradictory is not attainment of buddha-hood. Self-contradictory thought arising from the complex structure of wisdom outlined in Part I— the identity of *saṃsāra* and nirvana or sentient being and buddha simultaneous with the transformation of the former into the latter—is one of the hallmarks of the Mahāyāna tradition. The idea that result (nirvana) at once differs and is non-different from its cause appears in the Prajñāpāramitā *sūtra*s, Nāgārjuna's concept of *śūnyatā*, and Maitreya, as we have seen earlier. Below, I will consider representative formulations of this concept in Huáyán and Tiāntái thought.

In *Húayán wǔjiàozhāng* (On the five teachings according to Huáyán), Fǎzàng (643–712) divides the One Vehicle teaching into two gates—the special teaching and the common teachings. Concerning the former, he states:

> The [special teaching] may be further divided into two. First, the result, the ocean of reality. This is inexplicable, for it is not tied to the teaching. It is the realm of the ten Buddhas. Therefore Vasubandhu's commentary on the *Daśabhūmika-sūtra* states: "Cause is explicable, result is inexplicable." Second, the cause, co-dependent origination; this is the realm of Samantabhadra. These two [aspects of the teach-ing] are non-dual; there is the total inclusion of each in the other. They are like waves and water.[31]

The special teaching, the Huáyán One Vehicle teaching, takes as fundamental a non-duality of two aspects: the non-duality of explicable and inexplicable—what Nāgārjuna terms worldly truth (*samvṛti-satya*, truth expressed in terms of human discourse) and supreme truth (*paramārtha-satya*)—and that of cause and result. The non-duality does not deny the distinctive natures of these elements; rather, it has a self-contradictory structure in which they are two and not-two, not-two and two. (The two meanings of birth correspond to the non-duality of cause and result. I will take up Shinran's treatment of the explicable and the inexplicable in connection with his contrast of form and the formless.)

The distinction between cause and result is based upon the difference between buddha and sentient being, the distance between them, and expresses the path or process that leads from one to the other. Every person at any point along this path is called a "person in the causal [stage]," or in the passage quoted above, "Samantabhadra." A commentary states concerning this passage that Samantabhadra is a *mahāsattva*[32] of perfect enlightenment (*tōgaku*), at the head of all "people of the causal [stage]."

---

31. T45, 477a.
32. Ed. Literally "a great being," a common epithet for a bodhisattva.

It further states that he also signifies "all practisers as Samantabhadra":

> Without distinguishing the ordinary person and the sage, all are called Samantabhadra—because they have faith in the universal dharma, because they understand the universal dharma, because they practise the universal dharma, because they realize the universal dharma.[33]

Those of the stage of faith on the path toward buddha-hood, as well as those of the stages of understanding, practice, and realization, are all called Samantabhadra. Even the place furthest from buddha-hood, the first step along the path, is non-dual with the goal. This is expressed in: "the moment one first awakens the mind [of enlightenment], one attains perfect enlightenment." From the opposite perspective, the result is non-dual with every point of the path toward it. This means that "buddha" is non-dual with every sentient being—whether it be an ordinary person, a sage, or a *mahāsattva* of perfect enlightenment.[34] This non-duality of cause and result implies a negation of the path from sentient being to buddha and any basis upon which practice can be established. Sentient beings, without awaiting the fulfillment of practice, are from the very beginning buddhas. We are, however, unaware of this. To become a buddha is none other than to awaken and return to the original self. Buddha, as a marker showing the direction in which the sentient being should advance, does not exist apart from the sentient being; buddha is none other than the sentient being who has awakened to his true self. For the establishment of this "awakening" our unenlightened thinking must be eradicated; this is the significance of practice. When, through the elimination of non-enlightenment (ordinary being), attained enlightenment (buddha) is established, one awakens to the fact that one has possessed this enlightenment from the beginning. The non-duality of cause and result is identical in structure to the concept expounded in *The Awakening of Faith* of non-enlightenment-acquired enlightenment (the path from cause to result) and original enlightenment (result that is non-dual with this path).

Nāgārjuna states that both *prajñāpāramitā* and *śūnyatā* are different names for the reality of things. In *śūnyatā*, the sense of "breaking form and making it empty" and that of "form is originally empty" are united. "Original emptiness" corresponds to "original enlightenment" in the

---

33. *Tsūroki* 通路記 by Gyōnen 凝念 (1240–1321), T72, 306b.
34. Shinran interprets the *tō* 等 of *tōgaku* (perfect enlightenment) to mean "equal," and states that a person of *shinjin* in the stage of the truly settled has attained the equal of perfect enlightenment (*tōshōgaku*)—that is, has become the equal of a perfectly enlightened one; hence, he may be seen as the same as a *mahāsattva* of perfect enlightenment. Shinran also states that he is the same as Maitreya, who has reached the fifty-first of fifty-two stages, the final stage being the supreme enlightenment.

The Awakening of Faith, and "making empty" to acquired enlightenment. In each instance of "emptying" there is original emptiness. Since every point of the path is originally empty, discrimination of places along the path is meaningless. Every step from sentient being to buddha-hood has the significance of returning to the origin, that is, of dissolving the path. It has been common to interpret *śūnyatā* to mean that when all forms have been broken through, and further *śūnyatā* has also been broken through and made empty, so that true emptiness in which nothing at all remains has been attained, then wondrous existence manifests itself. Such an understanding is mistaken. As Jízàng (549–623) of the Sānlùn school states, breaking through the false is itself the manifesting of the true; that is, each instance of breaking through falsity is always simultaneously the immediate manifestation of truth.

One of the most telling expositions of this concept is the six *soku* (non-dualities) of the Tiāntái school, which are six stages of the path to enlightenment.[35] "Six" here corresponds to cause in Huáyán thought, "*soku*" to result. These two are non-dual, and the term *soku* is used to express this. A commentary states: Because of *soku*, before and after are both affirmed. "Because of the six stages, there is no confusion in the order of before and after."[36] Here, the non-duality of before and after—the mutual interpenetration of illusion and enlightenment—is stated. Further: "Because reality (*ri*) is always the same, it is *soku*. Because things (*ji*) differ, there are six stages." Here, the non-duality of *ri* and *ji* or of essence and function is explained. The non-duality of cause and result is first of all the non-duality of before and after (the negation of the path), but since "after" is result, it is nirvana, and since it is non-dual with cause (things), the non-duality of before and after is also the non-duality of individual things and ultimate reality or suchness (*jiri funi*). It is further the non-duality of the karma-created (*ui*) and the uncreated (*mui*), of the impermanent (time, *mujō*) and the eternal (timeless, *jōjū*). Hence, *saṃsāra* and nirvana, which are in a relation of mutual negation (with before and after distinct) are one (*soku*).

By Dōgen, this concept is taught as the "oneness of practice and realization" (*shu shō ittō*). Practice corresponds to cause, realization to result. In Zen, much emphasis is placed on practice after attainment of satori;

---

35. The six stages are: original oneness with true reality (*risoku*), knowing this through words (*myōjisoku*), contemplation and practice (*kangyōsoku*), sweeping away dichotomous thinking and nearing enlightenment (*sojisoku*), elimination of the roots of illusion and partially realizing truth (*bunshinsoku*), and ultimate attainment (*kukyōsoku*). In Huáyuán thought, the "first awakening of the mind of enlightenment" is present at the very beginning of the causal element in the scheme of the six *soku*, however, there is even a stage of those who have yet to awaken the mind of enlightenment.

36. Zhànrán 湛然 (711–782) in *Zhǐguān dàyì* 止観大意 T46, 459c.

The Mahāyāna Structure of Shinran's Thought

this is because attaining buddha-hood is conceived of in terms of the structure outlined above.

The concept of birth in the Pure Land tradition from India up through Hōnen meant ending life in this world and reaching the other world, where practice for attaining non-retrogression was possible. In Shinran, birth has two meanings, for it has come to signify becoming a buddha. That birth means both attainment of non-retrogression in the present and supreme enlightenment in the Pure Land implies the abandonment of the traditional Pure Land focus on the point of death (*rinjū*) in favor of a standpoint in normal life (*heizei*). Through this change, Shinran incorporates into the concept of birth one of the fundamental conditions of Mahāyāna Buddhist thought, the structure of simultaneous identity and transformation that we have considered in Part I.

The Place of Realization: Ordinary Life Versus Moment of Death

In *Inscriptions*, Shinran explains a passage from Shàndǎo, "The practiser who aspires to be born is grasped by the power of the Vow and brought to attainment of birth when his life ends." For Shàndǎo, a practicer is grasped by Amida at the moment of death and at that time brought to birth in the Pure Land. This understanding was prevalent before Shinran, and led to an emphasis on sustaining religious practice throughout one's life and on achieving a settled state of mind particularly at the moment of death. Shinran rejects such an interpretation, however:

> This [passage] refers to the person who has already realized *shinjin* in ordinary times, not to one who becomes definitely settled in *shinjin* and who is blessed with Amida's compassionate grasp for the first time at the point of death. Since the person who has realized the diamond-like heart has been grasped and protected by the light of Amida's heart from ordinary times, he dwells in the stage of the truly settled. The moment of death is not the crucial matter; from ordinary times he has been constantly grasped and protected, never to be abandoned, and so is said to be *grasped [by the power of the Vow] and brought to attainment of birth*. (*Inscriptions*, 53–54)

Here, Shinran clearly conceives of birth as a matter of ordinary life and denies the centrality of the moment of death. It may appear that "being grasped by the power of the Vow" refers to reaching the stage of the truly settled and belongs to the present life, while "attainment of birth" refers to realization of nirvana, for which one must wait until death. Shinran, however, presents such an interpretation with implied criticism:

> On the other hand, there may be people lacking true *shinjin* in ordinary times who, by the merit of having long engaged in saying the Name, first encounter the guidance of a true teacher and realize *shinjin* at the

> very end of their lives; at that moment, being grasped by the power of the Vow, they attain birth. But those who await Amida's coming at the end of life have yet to realize *shinjin* and so are filled with anxiety, anticipating the moment of death. (*Inscriptions*, 54)

For "those who await" the moment of death, the experience of being "grasped and brought to attainment of birth" can occur only at the very end of life. By contrast, for one who stands in the position of ordinary life, Shàndǎo's words mean that "the moment of death is not the crucial matter; from ordinary times one has been constantly grasped and protected, never to be abandoned." Having been grasped by the power of the Vow, already one will never be abandoned, and becoming one who will never be abandoned is attaining birth.

To speak of reaching the stage of non-retrogression as attainment of birth is to take a stance rooted in ordinary life. From this position, the moment of death has already lost its basic significance with regard to birth. For a person who has already been grasped by Amida's light in ordinary life, Amida's coming at the moment of death is unnecessary. This fundamentally distinguishes Shinran's thought from the traditional concept of birth attained at the moment of death. But this is not all. Shinran's position further treats the religious significance that the moment of death held formerly, the problem of transcending *saṃsāra*, as an issue of normal, ongoing life to be solved in ordinary times.

To confront the question of afterlife is to take up the problem of transcending life, of what pervades and connects both life and death. The solution lies in completely severing attachments to life and parting from *saṃsāra* while one still has one's physical existence. The *Tannishō* states: "That both oneself and others part from birth-and-death is the fundamental intent of all the Buddhas." In Shinran, the religious significance that the future world held—transcending *saṃsāra* and seeking and attaining the eternal—is to be found in the present. The true moment of death is not the death of the physical body, but the moment when *shinjin* becomes settled in a person. According to Shinran, this is the meaning of the phrase, "In the preceding thought-moment life ends" (see Part I, 74). Asahara Saichi states:

> The final moment (*rinjū*) is the final moment in which I die,
> The final moment in which I become *Namu-amida-butsu*.

It may be argued that the significance of physical death remains crucial, for it marks the boundary between the stage of the truly settled and nirvana, between this world and the other world, and as long as the physical body is alive, one is in the stage of the truly settled and cannot attain nirvana. This assertion raises two important problems, which are ultimately one. The first is the question of where time and timelessness touch and fuse. The second is whether death can form the boundary between form and formlessness.

Time and Timelessness

For Shinran, nirvana is synonymous with the uncreated, oneness, *dharmakāya*, and suchness; it is the realm in which there is no arising and perishing. In contrast to the world of *saṃsāra*, which is created through causal conditions (*saṃskṛta*), nirvana is the world of the uncreated (*a-saṃskṛta*). To be created through causal conditions means to exist in time. Shinran states that the person who dwells in the stage of the truly settled attains nirvana simultaneously with death in this world: "On the eve of the instant of death one realizes great nirvana." At the end of life, one enters the timeless realm of the uncreated. It is easy to assume that entering nirvana after death means that nirvana lies in the future, but this is not the case. The future, the present, and the past make up the Buddhist concept of the "three times," and these "three times" together comprise *saṃsāra*. Since nirvana transcends birth-and-death, it transcends time itself. It does not lie in the future. Of course, neither does it lie in the present or the past. Where, then, is it? Shinran states:

> The realm of nirvana refers to the place where one overturns the delusion of ignorance and realizes the supreme enlightenment.... Nirvana is called extinction of passions, the uncreated, peaceful happiness, eternal bliss, true reality, *dharmakāya*, dharma-nature, suchness, oneness, and Buddha-nature. Buddha-nature is none other than Tathāgata. This Tathāgata pervades the countless worlds; it fills the hearts and minds of the ocean of all beings. Thus, plants, trees, and land all attain Buddhahood. (*Essentials,* 42)

The realm of nirvana exists precisely in the world of *saṃsāra* where sentient beings live. It fills the hearts and minds of all beings. In temporal terms, nirvana (timelessness) fills the immediate present of time that spans the past, present, and future. Hence, it is not appropriate to say merely that nirvana transcends time; nirvana (the uncreated) fills the karmically created world of birth-and-death, so that the eternal is one with the world of impermanence. These two realms are not, of course, simply identical; they stand in a relationship of mutual exclusion and opposition. This mutual exclusion is, from another perspective, the mutually contradictory relationship of the realm of supreme enlightenment where "one overturns the delusion of ignorance," and *saṃsāra*, the realm of ignorance. Further, it is the relationship between the world of eternal bliss and the world of suffering. It is also the mutual contradiction between the true and real versus the provisional and the false and empty. At the same time that they stand in these relationships of mutual contradiction, nirvana fills *saṃsāra*.

Human beings dwell in *saṃsāra* because they are unable to awaken to nirvana that is one with *saṃsāra*. For the person of *saṃsāra*, nirvana or suchness "has neither colour nor form; thus, the mind cannot grasp it nor words describe it." (*Essentials,* 43). It cannot be seen, heard, or even conceived. Nirvana, however, is not inactive, but is itself great wisdom. This wisdom is non-discriminative; in it, seer and seen, buddha and sentient being are non-dual. It is supreme truth, beyond verbal expression, and Buddha as *dharmakāya*. Such wisdom, while maintaining its non-discriminative character, naturally gives rise to discrimination, and when it does so, it is worldly truth, and wisdom and object are distinct. At that time, the fulfilled and accommodated buddha-bodies are manifest, and great compassion works to preach the dharma and grasp beings. The non-duality of sentient beings and buddha established in *dharmakāya* (suchness)[37] is the foundation upon which great compassion functions. Therefore, following Tánluán, Shinran calls nirvana *dharmakāya* suchness, in relation with which he discusses the *dharmakāya* as compassion (lit. skilful means):

> From this oneness (*dharmakāya* as suchness) form was manifested; this form is *dharmakāya* as compassionate means. Taking this form, the Buddha proclaimed his name as Bhikṣu Dharmākara and established the forty-eight great Vows that surpass conceptual understanding. Among these Vows are the Primal Vow of immeasurable light and the Universal Vow of immeasurable life, and to the form manifesting these two Vows Bodhisattva Vasubandhu gave the title, "Tathāgata of unhindered light filling the ten quarters." This Tathāgata has fulfilled the Vows, which are the cause of his Buddha- hood, and thus is called "Tathāgata of the fulfilled body." This is none other than Amida Tathāgata. "Fulfilled" means that the cause for enlightenment has been fulfilled. From the fulfilled body innumerable personified and accommodated bodies are manifested, radiating the unhindered light of wisdom throughout the countless worlds. Thus appearing in the form of light called "Tathāgata of unhindered light filling the ten quarters," it is without colour and without form, that is, identical with the *dharmakāya* as suchness, dispelling the darkness of ignorance and unobstructed by karmic evil. For this reason it is called "unhindered light." "Unhindered" means that it is not obstructed by the karmic evil and blind passion of beings. Know, therefore, that Amida Buddha is light, and that light is the form taken by wisdom. (*Essentials,* 43–44)

To summarize, human beings in *saṃsāra* have no means whatever of knowing the nirvana that fills *saṃsāra*. Thus the *dharmakāya* as compassion, Amida Buddha, emerged from oneness or nirvana and manifested

---

37. Ed. The author glosses *dharmakāya* as "suchness", but the term literally refers to the dharma body of the Buddha, and is here presented as synonymous with suchness.

form in the temporal world of *saṃsāra*. " 'Compassionate means' refers to manifesting form, revealing a name (*Namu-amida-butsu*) and making itself known to sentient beings" (*Once-calling*, 46). Although form is manifested, this is "the form of light" which is "without colour and without form"; in this respect it is "identical with the *dharmakāya* as suchness." The "form of light" is "the form taken by wisdom"; it has no colour or shape. This wisdom, however, radiates "the unhindered light of wisdom throughout the countless worlds," "dispelling the darkness of ignorance" of sentient beings and bringing them to realization of supreme enlightenment. Sentient beings are possessed of karmic evil and blind passions, but the light of wisdom is unobstructed; it sweeps away their ignorance, and "for this reason it is called 'unhindered light.'" Speaking from the perspective of sentient beings, Shinran states, continuing from the passage on the realm of nirvana quoted above:

> Since it is with this heart and mind of all sentient beings (i.e., the mind filled by Tathāgata) that they entrust themselves to the Vow of the *dharmakāya* as compassion, this *shinjin* is none other than Buddha-nature. This Buddha-nature is dharma-nature. Dharma-nature is the *dharmakāya*. For this reason there are two kinds of *dharmakāya* in regard to the Buddha. The first is called *dharmakāya* as suchness and the second, *dharmakāya* as compassion. *Dharmakāya* as suchness has neither colour nor form; thus, the mind cannot grasp it nor words describe it. (*Essentials*, 42–43)

The sentient being in *saṃsāra* is brought by unhindered light to entrust himself to the Vow of *dharmakāya* as compassion. Since it is with the mind pervaded by Tathāgata that a person entrusts to the Vow, that entrusting mind or *shinjin* signifies the awakening or wisdom born when "one overturns the delusion of ignorance." Although not yet supreme enlightenment, it is what arises when the sentient being, who had been completely immersed in *saṃsāra* and incapable of knowing nirvana or suchness, has his ignorance swept away by unhindered light. It is wisdom "received from the Tathāgata," and signifies having awakened, in the form of entrusting to the Vow, to the nirvana or the uncreated that fills one. In other words, it signifies having reached the dimension where mutually opposing elements—*saṃsāra* and nirvana, time and timelessness, falsity and truth—fuse and mutually interpenetrate. This is for the sentient being, who up to then has lived solely in the realm of time, to awaken to that which transcends time. Shinran states:

> After long waiting, we have been able to encounter the moment
> When *shinjin*, firm and diamond-like, becomes settled:
> Amida's compassionate light has grasped and protects us,
> So that we have parted forever from birth-and-death.[38]

---

38. *Kongō kengo no shinjin no / sadamaru toki o machi-ete zo / Mida no shinkō shōgo shite /*

To have parted forever from birth-and-death means to have entered the timeless. Since the timeless fills the hearts and minds of all beings, one does not leave the world of *saṃsāra*—the ocean of all beings—and go to a place where there are no beings of *saṃsāra*. Rather, precisely within the realm of time (*saṃsāra*) one enters the timeless (the ocean of the Primal Vow, which transcends *saṃsāra*). While living in this world, one encounters "the moment when *shinjin*, firm and diamond-like, becomes settled," parts completely and forever from *saṃsāra*, and immediately attains birth. One does not part from one's physical existence, which must undergo death, or the passions it entails; hence, one is still in the world of impermanence. While in time one experiences that which transcends time (that which pervades both life and death); herein lies the special characteristic of Mahāyāna Buddhist experience. In Shinran's thought, that which transcends time is experienced as the Primal Vow and the Name of *dharmakāya* as compassion. The *dharmakāya* as compassion enters the world of time and space, but the fundamental nature of the uncreated is not lost. In *Kyōgyōshinshō*, Shinran quotes the following passage from Tánluán explaining the relationship between *dharmakāya* as compassion and *dharmakāya* as suchness:

> Among Buddhas and bodhisattvas there are two aspects of *dharmakāya*: *dharmakāya* as suchness and *dharmakāya* as compassion. *Dharmakāya* as compassion arises out of *dharmakāya* as suchness, and *dharmakāya* as suchness emerges into human consciousness by means of *dharmakāya* as compassion. These two aspects of *dharmakāya* differ but are not separate; they are one but not identical.[39]

The two aspects of *dharmakāya* cannot be wholly identical, for *dharmakāya* as suchness completely transcends time, and the unenlightened are incapable of knowing it, while *dharmakāya* as compassion has entered into time as that which can be known by human beings. In their relationship, there is difference together with their being one and "inseparable."

The *dharmakāya* as compassion that has entered time has not become simply temporal. If it did, its significance as *dharmakāya* would be lost and it would only be a part of *saṃsāra*. It can be called "*dharmakāya* as compassion" because while remaining as it is, transcendent of time, it has entered time:

> Since Amida's attainment of Buddha-hood
> Ten *kalpa*s now have passed, it is taught;

---

nagaku shoji o hedatekeru (*Kōsōwasan* 77).

39. From Tánluán (562–645), *Commentary on the Treatise on the Pure Land* (by Vasubandhu), *Jìngtǔlùn zhù* 浄土論註, T40, 841b.

> But he seems a Buddha more long-lived
> Than *kalpa*s countless as particles.⁴⁰

The ocean of Amida's Vow transcends time, for Amida is "one" with and "inseparable" from timeless *dharmakāya* as suchness. Thus, a person living within time naturally and spontaneously enters that which transcends time through entering the ocean of the Vow. In this way, to realize *shinjin* is none other than to enter the realm of nirvana. This takes place in the immediate present, not at the moment of death. In the realization of *shinjin*, timelessness and time mutually inter-penetrate and fuse. This is the "one thought-moment of [the realization of] *shinjin*" (*shin no ichinen*), which Shinran explains as "time at its ultimate limit" (*Once-calling*, 32). One need not reach the end of present time (ongoing life) in death for time to become one with the realm of nirvana that transcends time:

> When the waters of blind passion turn and enter
> The ocean water of the great compassionate Vow
> Of unhindered light filling the ten quarters,
> They become one taste with the ocean water of wisdom.⁴¹

The heart-waters of blind passions—the entire working of our minds and bodies—become one with the ocean water of wisdom, the ocean of the Primal Vow, in which the flow of birth-and-death is "one" with and "inseparable" from the timeless. This "oneness" is termed "the oneness of the mind of Buddha and the mind of the foolish being" (*busshin to bonshin no ittai*).

It is often held that entrance into nirvana takes place at death, and that as long as the physical body is alive, the world we exist in is a defiled world and not the Pure Land; in that case, it would seem that entrance from time into timelessness in fact occurs at physical death. Though the hymn quoted on page 40 states that when one encounters the moment of realizing *shinjin* one parts forever from *saṃsāra*, it is impossible to deny that as long as the physical body lives, one exists in *saṃsāra*. The *Tannishō* 15, after quoting this hymn, states:

> At the moment *shinjin* becomes settled, a person is immediately
> grasped, never to be abandoned, and therefore he will not transmigrate
> further in the six paths; thus, "We have parted forever from birth-and-
> death." Should realizing this be confusedly labeled "enlightenment"?
> Such misunderstanding is indeed pitiful. The late master said, "Accord-
> ing to the true essence of the Pure Land way, one entrusts oneself to

---

40. *Mida jōbutsu no konokata wa / ima ni jikkō to tokitaredo / jinden kuon go yori mo / hisashiki butsu to mietamō* (*Jōdowasan* 3).
41. *Jinjippō muge kō no / daihi daigan no kaishii ni / bonnō no shuryu kishinureba / chie no ushio ni ichimi nari* (*Kōsōwasan* 42).

the Primal Vow in this life and realizes enlightenment in the Pure Land; this is the teaching I received."

Although one "has parted forever from birth-and-death," as long as one has one's physical existence and continues one's present life, one cannot be said to have attained enlightenment. As Shinran states, "Our desires are countless, and anger, wrath, jealousy, and envy are overwhelming, arising without pause; to the very last moment of life they do not cease, or disappear, or exhaust themselves" (*Once-calling*, 48). Clearly one is not a person dwelling in the Pure Land. Notwithstanding a full realization of this, however, the hymn states: "We have been able to encounter the moment when *shinjin*...becomes settled...so that we have parted forever from birth-and-death."

In the present, one still has one's existence as a human being. But because one has realized *shinjin* and entered the ocean of the Vow, one's life has fundamentally parted from the world of birth-and-death. Since a person still possesses bodily existence full of blind passions, he lives in the causal stage facing outward from birth-and-death. At the same time, however, he has reached the point of non-difference with the result; he has cast off birth-and-death forever and immediately attained birth. Moreover, he experiences such life not as fraught with contradiction, but as harmonious and complete: "When one has boarded the ship of the Vow of great compassion and sailed out on the vast ocean of light, the winds of perfect virtue blow softly and the waves of evil are transformed" (*Kyōgyōshinshō*). When a person has entered the world of the Primal Vow, the waves of evil, which up to then had raged furiously in him, turn calm, becoming one with the winds of virtue.

From Form to Formlessness

In his "Letter on Jinen hōni," Shinran states:[42]

> [Amida's] Vow is the Vow to make us all attain the supreme Buddhahood. The supreme Buddha is formless, and being formless, is called *jinen*. When this Buddha is shown as having form, it is not called the supreme nirvana (Buddha). In order to make us realize that the true Buddha is formless, it is expressly called Amida Buddha; so I have been taught. Amida Buddha is the medium through which we are made to realize *jinen*. (*Letters*, 29–30)

---

42. *Jinen hōni* 自然法爾. Shinran defines *jinen*: *Ji* means "of itself" (*onozukara*)—it is not through the practiser's calculation; one is made to become so. *Nen* means "one is made to become so" (*shikarashimu*)—it is not through the practiser's calculation; it is through the working of the Vow of Tathāgata (*Letters*, 29). Shinran uses *jinen* to express both suchness or true reality and the working of *dharmakāya* as compassion to save each being.

Amida's Vow is intended "to make us all attain the supreme Buddhahood," which is synonymous with nirvana, *dharmakāya* as suchness, or oneness. As we have seen, "From this oneness was manifested form, called *dharmakāya* as compassion (Amida)" (*Essentials,* 43); hence, Amida Buddha "is the medium through which we are made to realize *jinen.*" *Jinen* here signifies true reality or formlessness, and thus is a synonym for supreme Buddha. To entrust oneself to the Primal Vow of the *dharmakāya* as compassion is itself to become formless *jinen* or supreme Buddha with one's entire existence. Through that which has form one is made to attain that which is beyond form. This is Amida's Vow. The progress from foolish being (*bonbu*)[43] to supreme Buddha, from form to formlessness, has two levels. First, one enters the ocean of Amida's Vow. Amida is form manifested from the oneness without form. This *dharmakāya* as compassion, however, "is the form of light; it is without colour, without form; it is the same as *dharmakāya* as suchness." The form of the *dharmakāya* as compassion is not the form and colour that can be perceived by foolish beings. Hence, to take refuge in Amida's Vow is the first level in going from the world of forms to the world of formlessness. Compared with *dharmakāya* as suchness, however, the Vow is still possessed of form. One can know the significance behind *Namu-amida-butsu* and sense the compassion of the Vow. The light of wisdom cannot be seen with the eyes, but it is possible to "receive the wisdom of Amida" (*Tannishō*). This takes place when the Buddha's mind and the mind of the foolish being become one in the realization of *shinjin*. At the second level, then, through entering the world of the forms of *dharmakāya* as compassion, which can be felt and thought, one enters the dimension of *dharmakāya* as suchness. We cannot know or perceive the formless *dharmakāya* as suchness; nevertheless, Shinran teaches that *dharmakāya* as compassion and *dharmakāya* as suchness "are one but not identical, different but not separable," and that therefore to become one with *dharmakāya* as compassion is to become one with *dharmakāya* as suchness.

On the path extending from present life toward the formless supreme Buddha, the final overcoming of form comes at the moment of death. Nevertheless, the movement from *dharmakāya* as compassion (ocean of the Vow) to *dharmakāya* as suchness (nirvana) occurs not through the effort and calculation of the foolish being, but through the inconceivable working of the Buddha's wisdom. We cannot know how or when the movement from the ocean of the Vow to the formless supreme Buddha takes place. It is impossible to determine a boundary line, such as the moment of death, to that which is formless. For Shinran, who had truly and profoundly entered the ocean of the Vow, the world of *dharmakāya* as suchness was known and experienced. From "Letter on *Jinen hōni*," a

---

43. Ed. The original has *bombu*.

record of Shinran's words made when he was eighty-six, it is apparent that his religious awakening had matured so fully that it reached the *dharmakāya* as suchness. Through the experience he called realization of *shinjin*, Shinran came to know *jinen*. Hence he states, "*Shinjin* is Buddha-nature; Buddha-nature is *dharmakāya* (suchness)." Further: "Great *shinjin*...is the ocean of *shinjin* that is suchness or true reality."

What Shinran calls *shinjin* transcends even the "forms" of Amida Buddha, Primal Vow, and Name, and reaches the supreme Buddha that is without form in any sense. Therefore Shinran is able to assert that Amida "is the medium through which we are made to realize *jinen*." Through entering the ocean of the Primal Vow, he went beyond the Primal Vow (form), and through deepening his experience of "hearing the Name" (realizing *shinjin*), he transcended the "form" of *Namu-amida-butsu* and attained the true and real existence (*jinen*) that works without forms. While saying the nembutsu, he transcended its "forms" (the voice audible to the ears, the meaning or concept of *Namu-amida-butsu* grasped by the mind) and came to carry on his life within true and real existence itself. For this reason, although Shinran was still in this sad world—in the stage of the truly settled—and had not yet attained nirvana, he states that "necessarily to attain nirvana is eternal bliss," in this way asserting with conviction the non-difference of *shinjin* and suchness.

Realization of shinjin

Identity and Transformation of Blind Passions and Enlightenment

The realm of time and form called *saṃsāra* and the timelessness and formlessness called nirvana fuse and become one; thus, *saṃsāra* is transformed. This "becoming one," however, signifies a mutual interpenetration rather than complete fusion. By time entering timelessness, their identity is formed, while simultaneously they retain their mutually contradictory character. The first point at which this transformation occurs is the moment a person realizes *shinjin* and enters the ocean of the Vow. This takes place when he is awakened to the utter futility of self-power. By entrusting himself to Other Power, he is grasped by and becomes one with it. This point marks the attainment of the stage of non-retrogression. While this initial attainment is central, transformation is not completed immediately but undergoes further development. The entire process from the attainment of the stage of non-retrogression to the moment of death, when one realizes nirvana, possesses the character of "transformation" (*tenzu*), the structure of which may be seen as a dynamic opposition and interaction between *saṃsāra* and nirvana simultaneous with their identity. This is expressed in terms of the relationship of karmic evil and virtues, or blind passions and great compassion:

> Through the benefit bestowed by unhindered light,
> One realizes the *shinjin* of vast transcendent virtues:
> Unfailingly the ice of blind passions melts
> And immediately becomes the water of enlightenment.⁴⁴

Here it is stated that with realization of *shinjin*, karmic evil becomes the water of enlightenment. At the same time, however:

> Obstructing evils have become the substance of virtues;
> It is like the relation of ice and water:
> The more ice, the more water;
> The more hindrances, the more virtues.⁴⁵

According to the first hymn, blind passions disappear, becoming the waters of enlightenment.⁴⁶ The second hymn appears to contradict this, for in it not only virtues are abundant, but also hindrances. In other words evil, while having been turned into good, remains as it is. As one's blind passions melt and become the same as the Buddha's virtue or wisdom, the karmic evil that had been hidden because of ignorance is brought to light; hence, one's evils are said to increase. Moreover, as obstructing evils increase, one naturally repents, and at the same time is filled with gratitude for Amida's compassion. In this way, karmic evil continues to be transformed into virtue. Thus, all our acts—the roots of our existence itself—come to be seen as characterized by karmic evil, so that all possibility of living as a person free of evil vanishes, and at the same time, this evil is transformed into good. As the identity of karmic evil and virtue broadens and deepens, so does the opposition (the sense of distance). The Buddha, who is wisdom-compassion, becomes one with the karmic evil and blind passions of beings in order to awaken them to self-knowing, that is, to bring them to buddha-hood. This oneness of Buddha and sentient being, of virtue and karmic evil, is the fundamental nature of Amida Buddha, manifested as Amida's "grasping, never to abandon" the evil person. Since Amida's virtue is not simple goodness but holds evil within itself, not only does a person's karmic evil not disappear, but it is illuminated and protected by the Buddha's wisdom and compassion, and thus it comes to perform the function of virtue. The person of *shinjin*, the essence of whose existence is karmic evil, is nevertheless filled with the Buddha's virtues, for his karmic evil is the

---

44. *Mugekō no riyaku yori / itoku kōdai no shin o ete / kanarazu bonnō no kōri toke / sunawachi bodai no mizu to naru* (*Kōsōwasan* 39).

45. *Zaishō kudoku no tai to naru / kōri to mizu no gotoku nite / kōri ōki ni mizu ōshi / sawari ōki ni toku ōshi* (*Kōsōwasan* 40).

46. "When, into the vast ocean of Amida's Vow of wisdom, / The waters of the foolish beings' minds, both good and evil, / Have entered, then immediately / They are transformed into the mind of great compassion" (*Shōzōmatsuwasan* 40).

substance of those virtues.

Here it is possible to investigate the nature of *shinjin* in the light of the structure of *prajñā* or non-discriminative wisdom in general Mahāyāna thought. The first hymn expresses the mind of the foolish being becoming the mind of the Buddha, while the second states that the mind of the foolish person remains as it is. The experience of realizing *shinjin* possesses this logically self-contradictory structure in which virtues and karmic hindrances, truth and falsity, good and evil are identical while remaining distinct. This structure corresponds precisely to the *soku-hi* structure of *prajñā*, expressed in "*saṃsāra* is itself nirvana," in which *saṃsāra* is negated (broken through and made empty) and simultaneously affirmed by the nirvana of no abiding place. Two elements that are mutually exclusive (*hi*) are identical (*soku*), and even while having become identical (*soku*) always remain two (*hi*).

Further, as we have seen in Part I of this article, the early Yogācāra analyses of non-discriminative wisdom illuminate this structure by articulating the relationship between the seer and the seen that occurs in "seeing only" (*vijñaptimātratā*), and also by clarifying the relationship of non-duality between such wisdom and the defiled discrimination arising from karma and blind passions.

"Seeing only" is the true subjectivity that knows without the imposition of any objectification or subject-object dichotomization. It is the seeing of no-seeing expounded in the Prajñāpāramitā *sūtras*, and since there is nothing seen apart from the seer, it is true self-knowledge, or the subject knowing itself as subject. The situation of the subject knowing completely without object, however, harbours an impossibility, like the finger pointing to itself. "Seeing only" also means, therefore, that the subject appears as object (the various things of the world).

In the first meaning of "seeing only," there is only the subject and no object; that is, the subject exists as that which arises through causes and conditions, but there is no object of any discriminative thinking. In the second sense, the subject appears as object—it becomes the seen. Apart from the object there is no subject, and the object, while it is object, holds the subject within. In this way, the subject perceives the object by wholly becoming it. Thus, the subjectivity is also non-subjectivity. Without the subjectivity becoming things and in that way being known, subjectivity is impossible, and at the same time, this means that what arises through causes and conditions (subjectivity) has its own negation or non-existence as its nature. This concept that what arises through causes and conditions is itself nothingness follows Nāgārjuna's thought. The subjectivity that knows through becoming all things is not simply existent, but exists through its non-existence, by dissolving into and fusing with emptiness. In the subject passing into complete negation and at the same time becoming objects, all things are known as they are, from within themselves, and this is for the subject to know itself just as it is.

In terms of the three natures, on the one hand, the conceptualized objects (discriminated nature) of false discrimination have been eradicated through practice. That there is no object grasped means, at the same time, that the subjectivity that perceives (other-dependent nature) has been eliminated. This non-existence of the discriminated object and the discriminating subject is consummated nature (non-discriminative wisdom and suchness together). On the other hand, while being identical with consummated nature, other-dependent nature (seer) is also said to exist, for it comes into being through causes and conditions. This seeing that is one with emptiness is "seeing only."

Thus, that there is no seeing and that there is only seeing are established simultaneously. In "seeing only," seer and seen are both existent and nonexistent: there is only the subject without any objectification, and this is true self-knowing in which the subject has wholly become the object. This is the discriminative seeing of non-discriminative wisdom. It is self-realization as the interpenetration of *saṃsāra* and nirvana, form and emptiness. Thus, the nothingness that is consummated nature is not a relative non-existence that stands in opposition to existence, but absolute nothing-ness in which sentient being and buddha, existence and non-existence, and *saṃsāra* and nirvana, without ceasing to be distinct, are completely non-different. *Dharmakāya* that is the foundation of the three bodies of Tathāgata is none other than this consummated nature; therefore it is stated that *dharmakāya* "has as its characteristic (*lakṣaṇa*) the non-duality of karma-created and uncreated" (*Mahāyānasaṃgraha*). The karma-created is all dharmas or discriminative mind (other-dependent nature); the un-created is emptiness (consummated nature). Their mutual interpenetration underlies the early Yogācāra analysis of non-discriminative wisdom.

Further, in order to clarify the realization of such wisdom, Asaṅga developed the theory of the three natures in a new direction. The structure of awakening involves the identity of *saṃsāra* and nirvana based on their non-discrimination. This identity, however, is achieved only through the transformation of *saṃsāra* into nirvana or emptiness through absolute negation. Thus, realization of nirvana includes both the identity of mutual opposing elements and a dynamic transformation in which *saṃsāra* disappears and becomes nirvana.

Shinjin, as the Buddha-mind of wisdom-compassion that pervades the false, temporary mind of blind passions, may be seen to parallel in structure the analyses of early Yogācāra. The first hymn above ("ice of blind passions melts and becomes the water of enlightenment") corresponds to the movement from *saṃsāra* to nirvana, from discriminative thinking to Prajñāpāramitā. This is the transformation first clearly articulated by Asaṅga. The second hymn corresponds to *saṃsāra* and nirvana having been brought, through negation, into the identity of opposites expressed by *soku* and analyzed as the mutual interpenetration, while remaining distinct, of other-dependent nature (existence) and consummated nature (absolute nothingness). Thus, karmic evil is negated and at the same time affirmed: "The more hindrances, the more virtues."

To attain Buddha-hood is to awaken to one's true self. In other forms of Mahāyāna Buddhism, this is accomplished through the practice of the three learnings, by which one's discriminative thinking and blind passions are eradicated and non-discriminative widsom is realized. In Shinran's Buddhism, one's mind is transformed by the Buddha's power, so that one acquires the Buddha's wisdom. This realization of *shinjin* is not a union of our minds and the Buddha's mind brought about through a gradual deepening of human trust or acceptance—perhaps this is a fundamental distinction between *shinjin* and our ordinary conceptions of faith. Rather, it comes about through an utter negation in which all our efforts and designs fall away into meaninglessness, being found both powerless and tainted by egocentric attachments. In this negation our minds of blind passions are transformed into wisdom-compassion, and at the same time they remain precisely as they are—or rather, their fundamental nature becomes radically clear for the first time. With the wisdom that we realize as *shinjin*, we are enabled to see ourselves as we are—the foolish being whose every act is conditioned by eons of karmic evil and dominated by passions, thoroughly devoid of truth and reality—and also to know, and to be filled with gratitude for, the working of the Primal Vow.

The Process: Negation of Human Calculation

This realization is established when our usual perspective is turned upside down and acts we normally consider good or virtuous are seen to be evil. The foundations of our judgments—law, morality, religious precepts—themselves break down and in their entirety become evil, for they are based on human consciousness and intellect and cannot escape the ego-centricity of our blind passions. Thus, there is no possibility of accomplishing good left to one, and a nihilistic void opens up. This nihilistic void is grasped as empty of truth and reality not from a moral viewpoint, for such a viewpoint has lost its validity; it is seen so only from the perspective of the Primal Vow, whose fundamental nature is wisdom-compassion. Viewed from this wisdom, both good and evil as commonly understood are karmic evil.

The process leading from our ordinary judgments to the position of karmic evil in Shinran's sense is not linear and direct; it involves a transformation by which the latter is established and affirmed through the complete disintegration of the former. That our ordinary distinctions of good and evil crumble away means that their essential nature becomes manifest. Shinran states:

> I know nothing of what is good or evil. For if I could know thoroughly, as is known in the mind of Amida, that an act was good, then I would know the meaning of "good." If I could know thoroughly, as Amida knows, that an act was evil, then I would know "evil." But with a foolish being full of blind passions, in this fleeting world—this burning house— all matters without exception are lies and gibberish, totally without truth and sincerity. (*Tannishō*, Postscript)

This nihilistic void (non-existence) turning into evil is itself salvation, for such a transformation comes about only through the falling away of the self that judges good and evil according to its own reflection and intellect, and that chooses between good and evil according to its own will—the self characterized by egocentric intent and self-attachment. In other words, it occurs only within the realm of the Primal Vow (the Buddha's mind), which transcends morality:

> It is when one simply leaves both good and evil acts to karmic recompense and entrusts wholeheartedly to the Primal Vow that one is [in accord with] Other Power."(*Tannishō* 13)

Here we find two different directions expressed: that of the person who lives committing good and evil acts solely in accord with karmic recompense, and that of the person who wholly entrusts to the Primal Vow. In both of these, however, we see the absence of ego-self and freedom from self-will, and this very negation of self is Other Power. Karmic evil maintains its independence from Other Power, for it exists and functions according to its own laws. Its action cannot be altered by Other Power. Nevertheless, the foolish being is grasped just as he is, living out the consequences of his acts. His freedom from calculation and his entrusting to the Vow are united as the activity of Other Power, which is both compassion that grasps karmic evil and karmic evil grasped by compassion, and form a unified human personality.[47]

The Dynamic: The Working of *Jinen*

Since our blind passions persist until death, the melting of the ice of blind passions to become the waters of *bodhi* is not restricted to the moment of realizing *shinjin*; it occurs afterwards also, continuing to the end of life. This is the Buddha's working, which Shinran calls *jinen*:

> *Jinen* means "to be made to become so." "To be made to become so" means that without the practiser's calculating in any way whatsoever,

---

47. See Ueda Yoshifumi, "Muga to shutaisei," in *Daijō bukkyō no shisō*, 195–216.

> all his past, present, and future evil karma is transformed into good. To be transformed means that evil karma, without being nullified or eradicated, is made into good, just as all waters, upon entering the great ocean, immediately become ocean water. We are made to acquire the Tathāgata's virtues through entrusting ourselves to his Vow-power; hence the expression, "made to become so." Since there is no contriving in any way to gain such virtues, it is called *jinen*. (*Essentials*, 32–33)

Through entrusting oneself to the power of Amida's Vow, one is spontaneously brought to receive Amida's virtues. All one's karmic evil, past, present, and future, is transformed into good, but without the karmic evil "being nullified or eradicated"; thus, that virtues increase means at the same time that karmic evil (awareness of it) deepens. It is precisely in the awakening in which one's entire existence becomes karmic evil that absolute compassion and buddha wisdom are manifest.

As we have seen, the term *jinen* indicates the formless supreme Buddha and is synonymous with nirvana or suchness. In addition, Shinran uses *jinen* to signify the activity of the Vow of Amida, the *dharmakāya* as compassion, "to have each person entrust himself in *Namu-amida-butsu* and be received into the Pure Land." In this activity, four other meanings of *jinen* may be distinguished. 1) *Jinen* is said to "bring sentient beings to awaken *shinjin*," which also signifies attainment of non-retrogression. 2) *Jinen* transforms the karmic evil of the person who has attained the stage of non-retrogression. 3) Shinran states: "Drawn with the Primal Vow as the karmic cause, one attains birth in the Pure Land naturally, by *jinen*" (*Inscriptions*, 37). Thus, *jinen* brings the person in the stage of non-retrogression to birth in the Pure Land and to attainment of supreme Buddha-hood . 4) "*Jinen* is itself the fulfilled land" (*Kōsōwasan* 82). The interrelationships between fundamental concepts of Shinran's Buddhism—Amida Buddha, Primal Vow, realization of *shinjin*, attainment of the stage of non-retrogression, Pure Land—and the places they occupy in his teaching are clearly revealed in his usage of this single term *jinen*.

Formless suchness or *dharmakāya*—the true Buddha—manifests itself in the world of sentient beings and grasps each being, bringing each to "the city of dharma-nature" (supreme Buddha-hood). Thereupon, "with great love and great compassion immediately reaching their fullness in [the being], he returns to the ocean of birth-and-death to save all sentient beings" (*Essentials*, 34). Thus attainment of buddha-hood is none other than return to the world of *saṃsāra*. The first stage of this attainment is non-retrogression, for at the roots of the existence of the person of *shinjin* is supreme Buddha, which transcends all such distinctions as buddha and sentient being, nature and man, self and other.

The Temporal Structure of Realization

As we have seen above, "Time at its ultimate limit" means that all past, present, and future time condenses into the moment of the realization of *shinjin*. There time reaches its fullness or limit; time as we conceive it ends. To have realized *shinjin* means that one has already arrived at the point where samsaric time has ceased flowing. This is also seen in the passage on the transformation of karmic evil quoted above, which states that "all one's past, present, *and future* evils are transformed into good." Although one has realized *shinjin*, as long as one is alive, one exists within *saṃsāra*. Nevertheless, through having realized *shinjin*, one has entered the timeless realm of the Vow. The moment one realizes *shinjin*, one's bonds to samsaric life are severed in their entirety; samsaric cause and result both vanish. Hence, "the darkness of ignorance has already cleared and the long night of birth-and-death has already dawned" (*Inscriptions*, 72). Since one leaves *saṃsāra* at this point, "The heart of the person of *shinjin* is always in the Pure Land" (*Letters*, 27). This is the meaning of "immediately attaining birth and dwelling in the stage of non-retrogression." While standing beyond birth-and-death, the person of *shinjin* lives out his samsaric existence within it. As long as he is in *saṃsāra*, for him the Pure Land lies in the future. Nevertheless, through having realized *shinjin* and entered the ocean of the Vow, he has already entered the pure, undefiled land that transcends *saṃsāra*; for him, the Pure Land lies also in the present.

This double-faceted temporal structure of the Pure Land is also seen in the Primal Vow, in terms of past and present. Dharmākara fulfilled his Primal Vow to save all beings ten *kalpa*s in the past and became Amida. At that time, the salvation of all beings was fulfilled as *Namu-amida-butsu* and the Pure Land was established. That Primal Vow, however, is truly fulfilled for the first time at the moment one realizes *shinjin* in the present. The fulfillment of the Primal Vow has a dual structure whereby it occurred ten *kalpa*s in the past and it also occurs with the realization of *shinjin* in the present. The Pure Land was established ten *kalpa*s ago when the Primal Vow was fulfilled; for sentient beings in *saṃsāra*, however, that Pure Land lies in the future. When a person in *saṃsāra* realizes *shinjin*, that future Pure Land, while remaining in the future, becomes the present.

Amida's Primal Vow grasping beings and their salvation has this dual structure because the thought-moment when *shinjin* becomes settled is the point in which the flow of time and timelessness are fused. While it is one point within the flow of time from past to present to future, simultaneously it holds the timeless (Primal Vow, Pure Land, wisdom-compassion) that transcends the onward flow of time. In other words, while a person lives within *saṃsāra*, he has also reached the Pure Land,

and while he is evil, he is also the equal of *tathāgatas*. This is the self-contradictory structure of "becoming a buddha" that pervades Mahāyāna Buddhism all the way from the Prajñāpāramitā *sūtras* to Shinran, and that is expressed in Shinran as the simultaneous establishment of the two meanings of birth. The person possessed of blind passion, "without anything of truth or sincerity," and the world of impermanence, a "burning house," while remaining devoid of truth and reality, are pervaded by that which is true, real, and sincere."[48]

(Translated by Dennis Hirota)

---

48. The concept of birth which Shinran had brought to such a high level of development seems to have re-acquired a focus on the moment of death by the time of his descendant Zonkaku (1290–1373). Zonkaku states concerning "immediately attain birth" in the *Larger Sūtra*: "*Attain birth* means that it is settled that one will be born" (*Jōdoshin'yōshō*). Here, birth is interpreted as having only one meaning (birth in the Pure Land at death). As we have seen, in Shinran two meanings of birth are established simultaneously, but it appears that the self-contradictory character of this concept (see above) has prevented its implications from being well understood. Most commentators after Zonkaku follow his interpretation, and it remains the dominant understanding among Shin scholars even today.

Shinran and Contemporary Thought

Takeuchi Yoshinori

The Secularization Problem

I once had the privilege of hearing Arnold Toynbee (1889–1975) lecture on the problem of dealing with population concentration in the cities. I had never met the famous historian and I remember that I attended with the intention of getting a look at him. As it happened, his remarks provided me with a number of valuable and helpful insights. He spoke about the effect which massive concentrations of people have on the spirit of man. The pollution problem had not yet achieved the wide recognition it has today, and he focused mainly on how the human spirit could be warped by this phenomenon of urban population concentration. Today, the pollution of the world's cities has turned our attention away from this even graver threat to our humanity. No clue to the solution of the questions Toynbee raised has yet been found. The problem is in fact assuming even more serious proportions.

In the case of earthquakes, the closest attention is paid to slight changes in the earth's crust. Formidable efforts are marshaled to foretell an approaching calamity. But when it comes to cracks and depressions of the spirit, it is as if everybody has determined to take no notice of the danger until the catastrophe is upon us. And it could well be that the most culpable pollution problem is that we have steered the issue away from the spiritual level, indicated by Toynbee, to the realm of the merely material.

Some might dismiss Toynbee's remarks as the fanciful musings of a historian. But the impression I came away with was that I had come into contact with a true historian in the line of Albert Schweitzer (1875–1965), a man who, through the historical study of the past, had managed to extend several-fold his range of vision into the future. There was one more reason for my receptivity to Toynbee's ideas that day: I had just returned from a stay in America, where the urban population problem was already acute.

At about that same time, *The Secular City* (1965), a book by Harvey Cox, a professor of theology at Harvard University, had aroused wide interest even beyond the confines of the theological world. It soon became the center of a big controversy, which was later recorded in a book, *The Secular City Debate* (1966). The problem of the secular city became a *cause célèbre*. I shall have to come back to this later, but the problem in broad outline is as follows. The concentration of populations in big cities, especially in America, has led to a situation whereby groups of cities along, for example, the Eastern seaboard of the United States—cities from Boston, through New Haven, New York, Philadelphia, and all the way to Washington—show signs of fusing in the future into a long chain which will turn the cities into a megalopolis and their society into one of a specifically urban nature. The question is, what becomes of religion in such a situation? The fact that in such a society religion becomes secularized has been set forth as the most fundamental problem. With the secularization of culture as a whole, the social structure itself becomes secularized. As a result, religious phenomena take on a different meaning. For example, while the distinction and opposition between the sacred and profane, long considered to be the most basic of religious categories, are eroded, those things like religious ceremonies, once held in some sense sacred in that society, lose all their meaning.

In such a secularized society, religion cannot maintain the old forms, no matter how hard it tries. The flood of secularization is too strong and rapid. As a result, the meanings of the church buildings, the holy days, and the like undergo a brusque transformation. How can cities survive, and, on the other hand, how can religion—especially in Western society, Christianity—survive in the midst of such secularization? That is the problem.

A few years earlier, John Robinson's *Honest to God* (1963) had already tackled the problem from a similar point of view. He used the expression "honest to God" in its literal sense of "man sincere in his relationship with God."[1] What standpoint should contemporary man take, he asked, if he wants to have such a relationship? This work had a big impact, and has gone on to become the best-selling theological work of the century. Another book entitled *Honest to God Debate* (1963), containing the reactions of various scholars to Robinson's work, has also appeared.

At present, shifts in theological fashion are rapid: changes occur overnight, almost like the fashions in hemline or hairstyle. Nevertheless the significance of the problem broached by Bishop Robinson remains. One

---

1. Ed. More specifically, Robinson's usage reflects colloquial English of the time in which the phrase "honest to God" signified "I really mean it" or "telling it straight." The "honesty" lay in the abandonment of literalistic notions of "God" or of the mythological elements of religion.

could even compare his book to a flower blooming before its season; once one flower blooms, many others will follow. It is not so much depth of thought we find, as a reflection of change in the spiritual climate.

Among the articles collected in the *Honest to God Debate* is one by Rudolf Bultmann (1884–1976). He published a separate appraisal of Robinson's ideas, *Der Gottesgedanke und der moderne Mensch* (The Idea of God and Modern Man), which appeared originally in 1963 in a theological journal. Although written in response to Robinson's book, it is, on the level of ideas, more important than the work it comments on. It is worth noting, then, how Bultmann evaluates the problem introduced by Robinson.

Right from the beginning Robinson addresses himself to the great change the idea of God has undergone in the mind of modern man. Traditionally, God had been thought of as dwelling "in Heaven," somewhere "up there." But ever since modern man came to see the earth as a round globe rotating on its own axis and revolving through space, the up-down distinction lost its absolute meaning. The idea of God thus changed, and God's existence came to be placed, not "up there" any more but "out there," outside, in a direction away from the earth. God's transcendence thus changed its direction from above, in the heavens, to outside the world. Since Ptolemy's geocentric world view gave way to Copernicus's heliocentric system, the "out there" or "beyond" idea became central, and the symbolism of God "up there" lost its potency.

When we reflect carefully on the representations we have today of the Transcendent (no matter how vague these are) and on the concepts which common sense relates to it, we cannot help conceding that there is something in them, even though we may not feel inclined to swallow them whole. Robinson contends, however, that the Transcendent, as it exists in the contemporary way of thinking—supposing we can still really conceive of it today—has turned into something that can no longer be adequately expressed by the traditional world "transcendence." For, he argues, the Transcendent in the metaphysical sense (at least in the philosophy of modern times) is regarded as something that goes beyond the present sensual world, as one pole in the opposition of the Yonder Shore (the intellectual, the rational) and the This Shore (the sensual, the material). For us today, though, beyond-ness of this sort is rapidly losing its meaning.

As a matter of fact, Robinson is not alone in this view. He has been strongly influenced by Paul Tillich (1886–1965), to the extent that he has even been criticized as being too Tillichean. On many points, his idea of God can, indeed, be traced back to Tillich's systematic theology. The real reason, then, that Robinson's ideas caused such a stir lies in the fact that he was making his outspoken and provoking statements as a bishop of an important [episcopal] See in London.[2] When we look more care-

---

2. Ed. J.A.T. Robinson was at that time the Bishop of Woolwich, London.

fully, we find that his thought is not really so new: it has been greatly influenced, not only by Bultmann and Tillich, but also by Bonhoeffer, a theologian to whom we shall refer later on.

A religious editor of the New York Times met Tillich (shortly before his death) in order to hear his opinions on these questions; then he went to Germany to interview the elder but still hale giants, Karl Barth (1886-1973) and Bultmann; finally, he crossed over to England to meet Robinson and several other religious figures. With a reporter's skill and engaging style, he wrote down his findings in a highly interesting book, *The New Theologian* (1965) which became a general introduction to the subject. As he mentioned in his book, these problematics gave rise in America to the idea of the "Death of God," which initiated a new trend in theology. The "Death of God" Theology has also been introduced to Japan. It involves many problems which must be studied in their own right. One of these, to which I will refer in passing later on, is the question of how this theology differs from European atheism or nihilism, and in which points it shows American characteristics. In Harvey Cox's *The Secular City,* the problem of atheism is deliberately left untouched in order to think out from an entirely new angle the problem of religion's meaning in the modern secularized world. In his later works, however, Cox approaches the atheism of Germany's Ernst Bloch (1885-1977), whose philosophy, especially as expressed in *Das Prinzip Hoffnung* (The Hope Principle), he then uses as an underpinning for his own ideas. But we cannot go into these questions here.

The World and the Beyond: The Hither Shore and the Yonder Shore

Bultmann's advocacy of "demythologization" (*Entmythologisierung*) as a method for the interpretation of Scripture, which dates from the end of the Second World War, is quite well known. He uses the worldview of the New Testament as a prime example. In the Bible, the world is presented as consisting of three layers: the celestial, the underworld, and the world of man. (Robinson calls this the three-storied or three-decker universe.) The New Testament posits such a universe on the belief that, within this whole, the world of man is frequently visited by supra-human powers coming from the celestial or underworld layers. To cite only one example, it is believed that man's illnesses are the work of evil spirits from the underworld. According to Bultmann, a worldview based on that diagram is presented by the New Testament as self-evident, but that does not mean it belongs to the contents of faith in the sense of being something upon which modern man should base his life.[3]

---

3. Bultmann's demythologizing process aims at: (a) eradicating this kind of mythological worldview and view of life, which has lost its relevance in present times, and thereby removing from the scriptural content these elements that constitute

A similar way of thinking is at work in the ideas of Robinson. But Robinson is not satisfied, like Bultmann, with simply removing the mythological constructions of an old worldview. He stresses the point that, in each age, the philosophico-scientific worldview and the concepts of God (or the Transcendent) must positively correspond to each other. In the article quoted above, Bultmann expresses his agreement with Robinson's ideas, and goes on to develop, from his own standpoint and in connection with the atheism of Nietzsche and Heidegger, his idea of how modern man's concept of God has changed.

I am convinced that all this applies, *mutatis mutandis*, to the doctrines of today's Shin sect, where we face the question of how to conceive of the beyond-ness of the "Pure Land Paradise in the West." Also, with regard to this tenet as expressed in the doctrine of *shihō rissō* 司法立相 (literally, indicating direction and setting up form), the question of what this Pure Land Paradise and its transcendence can mean for modern man from the standpoint of Shin faith must be reexamined in a novel and contemporary way.

Robinson honestly confesses that he himself, as a modern man, cannot take seriously the idea that God is "up there." Thence, he tries to rethink what it could mean that God is in heaven or again that God is transcendent. And, especially under the influence of Tillich, he concludes that God, as a transcendent being, transcends as it were in the direction of the depths of the human spirit, rather than transcending to the outside. In this way he tries, with Tillich, to think of God as the ground of being.

For Tillich, in his existential-ontological way of thinking, God is, on the one hand, the dark but creative "deeper layer" within man's self-awareness, which embraces the realm of the unconscious—including, for example, the Jungian collective unconscious—and, on the other hand, the ground of being, the transcendent ground of all existence, lying still deeper at the bottom of that inwardness. By adopting that way of thinking, Robinson tries to locate the question of transcendence at the depths of his own inwardness. When we compare Robinson's ideas with those of Tillich, we miss in Robinson that kind of depth, that insight into the dynamic structure of the deepest level of existence that we find in Tillich. For Tillich, the problem of the ground of being—or, for man, the foundation of life—always implies a sort of ambiguity or mystery. Tillich is always conceptually joining two conflicting aspects: on the one hand, the

---

for modern man an unwarranted obstacle to the acceptance of the faith; (b) reinterpreting the myth by means of existential philosophy, in these cases where the myth expresses something which religious existence experienced on a transcendent level; (c) bringing out in fuller relief, by means of these processes, the full shape of the specific "scandal" of Christianity. The last point in particular is seen by Bultmann as the central task of his Bible exegesis.

problem of his own ground having something terrifying for man, something that makes him shrink back when he catches sight of it; on the other, the aspect of this ground being that in which man has his source, and the seeing of which makes him a true man (*Existenz*). Robinson does not delve into this so deeply. In his thinking of the transcendence at the depths of man, he is in a sense much nearer to Bultmann, and it could be said that his is an attempt to rationalize Tillich. Be that as it may, we can certainly say that God and man unite in a new way when God is considered to be acting as the ground of man. The traditional representation of heaven could in this sense even be interpreted in such a way as to become a symbolic expression of the harmony in the foundational unity of God and man. But can we be satisfied with this? Buddhists will have to ponder that selfsame problem, though from their own distinctive viewpoint.

The question raised above may show us the relevance of these problematics for Buddhism: Is it allowable, in Pure Land doctrine, to think in such a way about the transcendence of the Pure Land Paradise in the West? Personally I approach this problem in a rather different way. I am of the opinion that, in relation to man, God (or the Transcendent) is indeed "up there," a reality dwelling above, or at least implying something which makes it unavoidable to symbolize it in that way. For it seems to me that as long as man's being is determined by his bodily existence, man cannot help thinking of God as being "up there," even in the face of contemporary physics—that is, even as man's view of nature acclimatizes itself to the relativity theory and atomic physics, the Copernican revolution long past.

Also, when it comes to the "world beyond," the "yonder shore," or, for me as a Pure Land believer of extremely conservative markings, the Pure Land Paradise, I cannot help attaching extreme importance to the meaning of transcendence implied in the idea of *shohō rissō*, that all things are forms of ultimate truth. For that which is also transcendent (or "yonder shore") to the world, cannot be a transcendent reality in the sense simply of God over against man, that is, envisaged exclusively from the viewpoint of the man-God relationship. It has to be understood equally in its relationship to the world—as a world over against a world as well as a Thou over against an I. True transcendence necessarily comprises the meaning of transcendence over the world. For me, transcendence must always have a "Thou" aspect, transcendent with regard to religious *Existenz* ("I"), and, at the same time, an aspect of a yonder shore, transcendent in regard to the world.

In his early period, the period of *Being and Time* (1926) and *The Essence of Ground* (1929), Heidegger saw world-transcendence as human existence ecstatically going out of and beyond itself into the world, and the world correspondingly opening up in its non-designative truth-totality and becoming world, i.e. "worlding."⁴ In that way, through *Existenz* as being-in-the-world, the emergence of the historical world is made possible. In the early Heidegger, the problem of transcendence is thus considered solely from the standpoint of such a self-transcendence. In his later period, Heidegger's thinking is markedly inspired by Greek art, which becomes for him the model of reality. He conceives of a halo behind all works of art, something like the aureoles or background of light depicted behind the Buddha statues. He sees this as the world. Such a world is, of course, a place where man can really dwell (*wohnen*). There man is given from time to time a wink from the gods above and, while he dwells on earth as man (that is, a being that must die) there is in man's earthliness something that makes it plausible to see a chthonic pulling force at work in him. Bultmann, however, as we shall see later, does not accept the interpretation of the world as such a *Geviert*, a quadrate or fourfold harmony of heaven and earth, gods and men. It is enough, therefore, to consider here, as premises of his existential theology, the transcendence of *Existenz* as being-in-the-world, and the historicity which this entails.

Originally, however, the idea of "world-transcendence" implies the idea of a world beyond this world, the viewpoint of a world-to-world relationship. The Transcendent, like the Yonder Shore, must contain the aspect of being a world beyond, and standing over against this world. Transcendence implies a "from-to" element, which must involve not only a transcendence from this shore to the yonder shore, but equally a transcendent working, "advening"⁵ to this shore from the yonder shore. Transcendence is then bound to be the encounter of these two processes. This is how a world-to-world relationship is truly realized.

In brief, the idea of transcendence contains three elements: the Transcendent, *Existenz*, and the world; and the meaning of a transcendent world cannot be omitted from the idea of transcendence. If Jaspers is right in viewing the Transcendent and *Existenz* as a pair, then it must also be said that the Transcendent and the world form a pair. Indeed, within this world-to-world relationship it becomes possible to conceive of a truly concrete existential "dis-tance."⁶ Like a single bridge connect-

---

4. Note by translator (Jan van Bragt): "Non-designative" here stands for Heidegger's *unbedeutsam* (insignificant): transcending the realm of particular signification— "worlding" refers to "welten," which implies the notion of rotation. *Ed.* It should be recognized that *welten* is an artificial verb invented by Heidegger, which is intended to refer to the metaphysical emergence of "world" as an event, hence the equally artificial term "worlding."
5. Note by Translator: "Advene" stands for the Japanese *shōrai suru* 将来する, wherein the Heideggerian meaning of *Zu-kunft* is taken up: the future as coming towards, the letting-itself-come-towards-itself.
6. Heidegger's *Ent-fernung*. Heidegger interprets existential distance as an over-coming of separation. The Japanese philosopher Kuki Shūzō 九鬼周造 followed him in this.

ing two shores of a river, a bridge of transcendence links the hither shore and the yonder shore. That is encounter in the religious sense; from the standpoint of Shinran as a religious seeker, it was his encounter with the *yoki hito* (the "good man" or "master who carries grace for me"), Hōnen. Amida's Sacred Name was thrown as a bridge from the yonder shore to this shore; in the dual form of *ōsō* (going to the Pure Land) and *gensō* (coming back to the samsaric world for the benefit of all living beings).

In speaking of transcendence or beyondness as a world-to-world matter, I do not wish to inject surreptitiously a premise of one universe as a spatial entity—like Robinson's "out there"—in which the two worlds would relate like mutually relative celestial spheres. I shall explain later, in *saṃsāra*, the realm of animals and the realm of heavenly beings are seen, from the viewpoint of the human realm, as events of that realm; seen from the realm of animals, men belong to the animal world. Still, between those various realms, every one of which is a totality encompassing all the others, there is an encounter, within which takes place a "from-to" movement working in world-to-world transcendence.

Let us take the example of encountering a friend in the street. Even here we cannot conceive of the encounter by envisaging A and B as two points on a straight line, and the distance between A and B shortening *ad infinitum*. From my vantage point, everything, my friend included, lies within my range of vision, and from his point of view I fall within his vision. The scene in which my friend and I greet one another has many possible scenarios. He may be aware of me long before I am aware of him; or he may come into my range of vision first and see me only after sensing my eye on him; or we may catch sight of one another at the same time. And a meeting is a meeting only insofar as it allows of different attitudes: I can, for example, avoid his gaze or I can welcome it. If my seeing took in images as purely as the eye of a camera, and if the meeting of persons were like two objects bumping into each other in physical space, there could be no question of transcendence or encounter in the religious sense. Therefore, I have come—as I shall explain later on—to regard the meaning of transcendence as a meeting between a world of a lower order and a world of a higher order, whereby one part of that lower world becomes nonetheless the place of the encounter of both worlds.

I can perhaps summarize my way of thinking in this way: transcendence must include the idea of a world over against the world, a Yonder Shore over against This Shore. At the basis of this conception of world transcendence, in connection with which the problem of the finitude of man and his world is considered, lies the idea of a "Paradise in the West." For me (and it can be argued that I myself am hereby demythologizing the meaning of the Pure Land in the West), this means that we must consider fully what is signified by the symbol of such a Pure Land,

and by this symbol alone, namely, at the same time transcendence as world-transcendence, the transcendence of the world by finite beings and the corresponding advening movement of a transcendent world and Transcendent Other. This also reflects on the meaning of God or Buddha: as long as man is what he is and lives in the world, every world transcendence must, in some sense, imply the meaning of a "Paradise in the West."

In his *Being and Having*, Gabriel Marcel (1889–1973) writes that the human body must be considered in line with the Christian concept of Divine Incarnation. That way of thinking strikes me as very deep and extremely enlightening. Referring this to our present problem, it could mean that, in the very fact of man's existing as such a corporeal being, as such a "being-in-the-world," lies the necessity for God to be, with respect to man, in some sense *up there*. That God is "above" is for me a bodily revelation. As long as the place of the world-to-world encounter is my body—as long as man walks the earth in an upright position and looks up at the heavens—God must reveal himself as fundamentally "above."[7] He cannot reveal himself in any other way.

Similarly, as long as man lives in the world and relates to it as a being opened to the world through bodily existence, a Transcendent that is truly transcendent to the world must be thought of as "advening" from the future into the present in the form of an advent of a transcendent reality. In other words, world transcendence is something that, while transcending, "advenes": becoming present in the present from the future in the form of a coming from the transcendent yonder shore world into the present world. I am convinced that true transcendence is that which emerges into the present as something advening in a real transcendence towards us. For me, therefore, the symbol of the Pure Land in the West is extremely meaningful; it carries a weight of meaning that cannot be shaken or replaced by any other symbol.

The New Form of Religious Awareness

In spite of all this, it remains true that in a world of especially vehement secularization—in the present world which, with science in the vanguard, is busily secularizing us all—some policy must be devised in order to reach a new understanding of the meaning of traditional religious symbols. Among scholars of the Jōdo Shin sect of the last one hundred years, Soga Ryōjin (1875–1971) was undoubtedly possessed of the strongest speculative powers. In April 1961, in a colloquium held on Mount Hiei to commemorate the 700th anniversary of sect founder Shinran Shōnin's death, Soga declared that "the 'body' does not change;

---

7. In Japanese, the words for "god" 神 and "above" 上 have the same pronunciation: *kami*.

only the 'manifestation' does."[8]

I for one have difficulty with this formulation. Let us consider the problem in concrete terms through the example provided by Bishop Robinson himself. Robinson writes that as a priest in the contemporary world, holding an important position in the Church, he finds that he cannot really pray any more. This extremely honest and frank admission strikes us as the authentic voice from the depths of a man's soul, and arouses our sympathy. It is like a Shin believer being unable to invoke Amida's Name (*nembutsu*) any longer because of the manner of life in the modern secularized world. The *nembutsu*, however, should be something that "does not choose between moving or standing still, sitting or lying down. It should be amenable to any time, place, or occasion." This means that its recitation does not require that one brings one's heart to transparency first in a solitary and quiet place. Over against the idea that a specially consecrated time and place—prerequisites of all traditional religious rites—are the only locus for the realization of the Holy, the spirit of the *nembutsu* in both Hōnen and Shinran is precisely such a realization of the Holy in the midst of the secular, within the everyday behaviour of "moving or standing still, sitting or lying down."

Still, reciting the *nembutsu* in a streetcar, or saying "*Namu Amida Butsu*" in a coffee shop at the moment when the waitress brings you your coffee, is after all a bit awkward. On the other hand, it does not sound strange at all to see an old lady saying "*Namu Amida Bu*" while being served green tea in a tea house. Why is it awkward to do exactly the same in a coffee house? Something, somewhere, must be out of joint.

Soga Ryōjin says that the "body," the *nembutsu* as substance, does not change; but in this technological age of ours it rather looks as if the "body" itself undergoes change and is being progressively corroded. From the standpoint of the "body," no contradiction should be felt over saying *Namu Amida Butsu* in a coffee house. On the contrary, the spirit of the *nembutsu* demands just such a locale. It is still possible to maintain that this kind of awkwardness is due to the change in "manifestation." But when the problem presents itself in the acute form of prayer becoming impossible in the midst of secularized life, we cannot help concluding that this change in "manifestation" implies also a change in "body." To borrow one of Robinson's expressions, the God of modern man has become "a Grandfather in heaven, a kindly Old Man who could be pushed into one corner while they got on with the business of life."[9] This certainly indicates a change in God's "body" in a prayer-less world.

That the image of such a "Daddy-God" is a blasphemy was pointed out

---

8. Note by Translator: Soga uses the categories *tai* 体 (body, *quidditas*) and *gi* 義 (manifestation, *modus*).

9. John A. T. Robinson, *Honest to God* (London, 1963), 41.

with great perspicacity by Søren Kierkegaard (1813–1855). Writing about the faith of his fiancée, Regine Olsen, he remarked that Regine's God was like a doting uncle who at Christmas time is good for a few presents. The picture is, then, that of a softhearted man, a kind uncle somewhere in another town whom it is nice to have because from time to time he gives us the things we desire. But God has then ceased to be an immediate reality, a serious matter that has to do with our every daily act (our "moving and standing still, sitting and lying down"). No longer is he someone who in my prayer enters into earnest dialogue and negotiation with me. He has become a remote being that comes like a breeze for only an occasional visit. But what man has to establish, and establish in the midst of this secular age, is not such a spineless relation with a grandfather God, but a true relationship with a true God. How can and must man as a man truly pray to God? That is the object of Robinson's quest.

Robinson was led to questioning of this kind mainly by the influence of Dietrich Bonhoeffer (1906–1945). As he was killed in a Nazi prison at the age of thirty-nine, it is often said that Bonhoeffer's thinking did not have sufficient time to mature, that his assertions are full of contradictions, and a good deal of what he says is even incomprehensible. Robinson believes, however, that his thought represents a profound testimony of our age, and that we will need many more years to really understand its message. He voices a particular approval of Bonhoeffer's idea of a "beyond within," a "beyond in the midst of our life." In Pure Land doctrine this corresponds to *heizei gōjō* 平生業成, the accomplishing or attaining of faith in daily life.[10] In both the Transcendent is found in the midst of present reality, and what is not found among the things of actual reality is not the true Transcendent. It is also Bonhoeffer's contention that for man to live with Jesus Christ as such a Transcendent is the truth of Christianity. It naturally follows that he does not admit of any relationship with the Transcendent apart from that just described. That is why Bonhoeffer attempts to go beyond all traditional interpretations (those of his master Karl Barth included) which accept as a premise Christianity as a Church-centered religion.

Karl Barth, too, asserts that Christianity is not a religion. But for him the term "religion" means the belief that man can attain and grasp God or the Holy self-centeredly and by his own power, and consists in the attempt to do exactly that. This, as he sees it, pertains to all religions except Christianity. For him, the task of theology is to elucidate, in the name of the Church and according to the needs of every age, the truth of

---

10. This is the idea that the authenticity of the believer's faith is not first attested to at the hour of death, by entering the Pure Land with feelings of gratitude and an un-troubled heart, but that true faith must realize and prove itself every day, in the midst of daily life.

the Gospel entrusted to the Church. Consequently, Church-centeredness becomes the first premise for the whole of theology, the totality of its content. Bonhoeffer, on the other hand, maintains that Christianity was not a religion in the beginning, when it appeared in the ancient world in its primitive form. From the standpoint of the Hellenistic world and the concept of religion current in the Greco-Roman mind, the original doctrines of Christianity were viewed as extremely secular, profane, even shameless.

What thus appeared to non-Christians as a "scandal" beyond the common-sense bounds of religion—from whatever viewpoint: the ritual, the moral, or the philosophical—was accepted by the Christians in all simplicity as their God. On the other hand, in the present secularized world, Christianity, no matter how hard it tries, cannot sustain the Church. What, then, is to be done? It is Bonhoeffer's conviction that we have to conceive means to communicate the new contents of Christian faith in a secular language, a totally new form with new words—a language that might sound almost immoral to the pious ears of those contemporaries wedded closely to the traditional ways of thinking.

Robinson makes that conviction his own, and his thought is further influenced by Tillich's theology and Bultmann's theory of demythologization. It could be said that his combining of these three, especially around Bultmann's idea of the proclamation of the Gospel (*kerygma*), represents a personal reflection on his own religious faith. The ideas of Bultmann which influence Robinson so much gave rise, especially in Germany and America, to a new theological trend which has come to be called the post-Bultmann school, which Ebeling and Fuchs represent very actively. Ebeling, especially, gives a theological presentation of the essence of Protestant Christianity by means of a new hermeneutics that are a further development of Bultmann's methods. While Ebeling was deeply influenced by his master Bultmann, we see from the outstanding treatise on Bonhoeffer in his book *Wort and Glaube* (Word and Faith, 1960) that he was also influenced by Bonhoeffer. In his other works, *Das Wesen des Christlichen Glaubens* (The Essence of the Christian Faith, 1959), for example, Ebeling sets forth his own standpoint with the utmost clarity and leads us to think that there is a marked difference between his way of thinking and that of Bultmann. But I cannot go into these matters here. Comparing Bultmann and his disciples, it appears after all that the master stands head and shoulders above them all, and everything indicates that in the foreseeable future the problems he raised and the theses he defended will continue to influence the theological world.

For Bultmann, *kerygma* is the central idea. When he considers the problems of history in general, he always focuses on the world as the scene of the salvific event and, especially, on the historical *Existenz* in the world.

Even in his most universal speculations, he never strays an inch from the existential standpoint. For him, the historical world by itself is forever relative and the meanings which we can grasp there irretrievably fragmentary and relative, so that nothing absolute can appear anywhere in it. Consequently, the history that we are aware of (and investigate in the science of history) cannot obtain any ultimate meaning as a whole. If a total meaning can be found in history, it is, in his opinion, only through the history of the individual as a person and the self-understanding involved therein. Put more concretely, history seems to obtain its structure or plot through the person of Jesus Christ. But for the present, it is enough to emphasize that a person is invariably required as a core, and that around that core history crystallizes and comes to posses a total structure as history. Only through the mediation of a historical existence does a total meaning and direction become apparent in history.

And this kind of historical existence, and likewise the world as the "seat" of this existence, realizes itself only on the basis of an encounter with the *kerygma*. For through the mediation of the decision of the religious existence, this encounter brings the subject to its fulfilment as historical existence, brings the world therein to unity, and, finally, brings out the ultimate significance of history.

History and Nature

In 1961, during my stay at Marburg, I had the good fortune of meeting with Bultmann frequently. He was then seventy-seven years old, but he was still gifted with very lively speculative powers. On one of these occasions, Bultmann took down from his bookshelves a commentary on the Zen "Oxherding Pictures,"[11] in a German translation by Tsujimura Kōichi, a professor of philosophy at Kyoto University, and said:

> This is an admirable book. What is explained here is the same as is taught in Christianity. In my understanding, the ox stands for the human heart. Chasing this ox must mean the quest for the true self. Pursuing the true self means forgetting the self; the self becomes the true self only when it is forgotten. In the Ox-herding Pictures, this is presented in an extraordinarily clever way, but the content does not

---

11. This booklet tells the story—in ten pictures, to which explanatory poems by Master Kùo'ān Sīyǔan (Kakuan Shi-en) and others are added—of an oxherd looking for a stray cow, up to the moment that he brings it back home. It shows, in the form of a parable, the process of the quest for the true mind of the self. Towards the end, the cow has become completely docile, so that the oxherd returns home sitting on the back of the cow and playing a flute, without even bothering anymore about the tether. From that point on, all concern for the cow is forgotten. The German translation alluded to is *Der Ochs and sein Hirte*, translated by Kōichi Tsujimura and Hartmut Buchner (Pfullingen, 1958).

differ practically from Christian truth. The only difference is that history does not appear in it. I do not find the idea, so strong in Christianity, that truth is realized in history.

I replied with a remark that certainly betrays the influence of Nishitani Keiji on my thinking: "Indeed, history may not be present in this work, but is it not equally true that, in Christian, especially Protestant, doctrine, Nature is absent?"

Bultmann then asked me what I understood by "Nature." I answered that I meant existential Nature, the Nature that must be present when existence becomes true existence and not nature that comes under the spatialized categories of abstract time and space—what existential philosophers would call "the vulgar world concept." I then asked again if it was not true that this existential Nature did not appear clearly enough in Christian doctrine. After a moment's reflection, Bultmann answered in the affirmative. He then inquired how I interpreted existential Nature. At that moment, I recalled his interpretation of the bodily resurrection of Jesus Christ. According to Saint Paul, resurrection is meaningless if it is not bodily resurrection; he goes so far as to say that if Christ did not rise up (in the flesh), his own faith would be in vain. While treating Paul's theology in his *Theology of the New Testament, I*,[12] Bultmann explains these passages by making a distinction between the Greek word *sarx*, meaning the "flesh," or body of sin, and *soma*, meaning the body of resurrection. In the English translation, this distinction is rendered by two words, "flesh" and "body." The "resurrection in the flesh" (in ordinary parlance) then means resurrection in the *soma* and not in the *sarx*. *Soma*, according to Bultmann, is the locus where the real truth manifests itself. With these recollections in mind, I replied:

If you want an example of the existential meaning of Nature, would not the way you conceive of the corporality of the risen Christ, the *soma* as the place of the resurrection, be a good example of that existential Nature?

This time, Bultmann was lost in thought for quite a time, and then, referring to Heidegger's conception of the *Geviert* (the quadrate or fourfold),[13] inquired whether my conception of Nature resembled this "*Geviert*"—which Heidegger had started using at just about that time as a symbol of the world.

Since I had been strongly influenced by these Heideggerian ideas, I had to say that my thought on the subject came near to that of Heidegger.

---

12. Translated by Kedrick Grobel (London, 1952). The original work, *Theologie des Neuen Testaments*, was published in 1948.
13. I alluded to this earlier. In brief, it is the idea that sky and earth, gods and mortals are bound together into oneness, and all four mirror each other. This is then symbolized by the quadrate, the square, or the fourfold.

Bultmann declared that he was against that way of thinking. He explained his objection by saying that although this *Geviert* is a world wherein truth is disclosed, there is no place in it for a true encounter with a Thou. At the moment it struck me that this critique of Heidegger was altogether typical of Bultmann. His remarks have stayed with me to this day. Not to be satisfied with the idea of the Fourfold or "world-openness" through which the later Heidegger deepened his awareness of the world, but to struggle earnestly for a congenial conception of the necessity of the encounter with a Thou, and to proceed from this encounter to conceive of history in its full sense—this, in my opinion, is an inevitable outcome, given Bultmann's standpoint.

If I may be allowed a personal word of interpretation on Bultmann's view, I would say that his "decision in faith," with the world as its mediation and the place of its conversion, wants to exchange the traditional idea of a historical transmission of the revelation (God's Word) in the past for that of a here-and-now encounter with the Gospel *kerygma* that advenes from the future. With the world as its mediation, history can thus spread into world history from the individual history of the *Existenz*, and the being-in-the-world of the existence can become the religious existence that makes its decision in the historical world. Consequently, the full meaning of history can strictly speaking only be conceived of through the meaning of religious existence as a being in the historical world. And it is the "*welten*" (with its implication of rotation) of this world that constitutes the encounter for our religious existence, by giving the existence of Jesus Christ in the past a cyclic turn and making us meet the Christ event as something advening into the present from the future. In other words, through the mediation of the world, the past-to-present direction is switched to a future-to-present one, and therein the encounter with the Word of God may come about.

In the case of the Buddha's Name as well, the two movements come into being together. I encounter, here and now, Amida's Name advening as eternity from the Pure Land. This occurs in the form of an I-Thou encounter in the actual present, with the Name (as the Thou) advening from the future. And on the other hand, at the moment of this encounter, by the religious act of *Namu Amida Butsu* as a decision which brings evocation and response into unison, the symbolic world (in which all Buddhas are praising the Name of Amida Buddha and guaranteeing the truth of that Name and birth in the Pure Land through its invocation) is discovered directly underfoot.

In even more concrete form, this symbolic world, the background for man's encounter with the Name, also signifies the opening up of the world in which the *nembutsu* is historically transmitted. This means, in turn, just as in Heidegger's *Geviert*, the realization of the world of all Buddhas praising and guaranteeing Amida's Name—a world wherein everything mirrors everything else. And precisely in this world, just as in Bultmann's historical world, the encounter with the Thou, the meeting with the Name, obtains. In that sense, we find here, in a concrete form, a synthesis of the standpoints of these two thinkers.

In the second chapter of the *Kyōgyōshinshō*, entitled "True Living," Shinran Shōnin calls the Seventeenth Vow (or Prayer) "the Vow of the praise of all Buddhas, the Vow of the utterance in praise of the Name by all Buddhas." This means that all Buddhas praise Amida Buddha and exalt his Name; that is, by pronouncing his Name, all Buddhas praise Amida. Understandably, this is generally interpreted as referring not to our recitation of Amida's Name, but to an event belonging to the absolute world in which *Namu Amida Butsu* occurs on the side of the Dharma (*hottai myōgō* 法体名号)—something taking place among the Buddhas in their Buddha-worlds transcendent to the world of man. In other words, it is a matter of all Buddhas praising one another and exalting the Name of Amida.

If that were the whole truth, however, it would be difficult to see how this praise by the Buddhas relates to our own religious practice of the *nenbutsu*. Right at the beginning of the same "True Living" chapter, Shinran says clearly: "The Great Living is to pronounce the Name of the Tathāgata of Unimpeded Light." I would like to interpret this term "Great Living" as religious or symbolic activity, in which the practice whereby all Buddhas praise Amida's Name is mirrored in the practice whereby we, on our side, "pronounce the Name of the Tathāgata of Unimpeded Light." Here, we are aware that our recital of the Name is praise and exaltation of the Name. And our recital of the Name is, in turn, mirrored in the praise of all the Buddhas. This makes it clear that the "Vow of the praise of all Buddhas" is the "Prayer in which All Buddhas pronounce the Name."[14]

---

14. The exact wording at the beginning of chapter two of the *Kyōgyōshinshō* is: "*As I reverently reflect on the outgoing ekō, I find therein the great living and the great faith.*" [The adjective great has been added to living (practice) and faith with the intent of exalting them. *Ekō*, or merit-transference, has two directions: the "outgoing phase" (*ōsō*) is the direction from us to the Buddha; the "coming phase" (*gensō*) is the direction from the Buddha to all living beings (insofar as it is thought of relatively, over against *ōsō*). Merit-transference is the working of Amida Buddha's Compassion in the form of the Name; the working of an absolute love, whereby the Buddha's substantiality and totality are, as such, handed down to our side. In this working there is an "outgoing phase" and a "coming phase." Living (practice) and faith are both discussed from the viewpoint of the "outgoing phase."

The *Kyōgyōshinshō* text reads further:

"*The great living is to pronounce the Name of the Nyorai of Unimpeded Light. In this living are embraced all good things and all the roots of merit. They are instantly perfected (as soon as the Name is pronounced).* [In other words, the ultimate desire of man

In other words, the Pure Land and this world, all Buddhas and all living beings, the cosmic chorus sounding the Name throughout the Ten Quarters and the career of the historical *nembutsu* on earth, form, in this symbolic action, a locus of *Geviert*. At this point occurs the encounter of Amida and me. Symbolic action of this sort can be called, with Jaspers, absolute action, wherein all opposition of subject and object melts away and concrete reality appears in its purity on the standpoint of action. It is precisely there that the encounter and mutual evocation of I and Thou are realized.

This standpoint of action must certainly be explored further in connection with Nishida Kitarō's view of Action-Intuition and Tanabe Hajime's elucidation of action from the viewpoint of Practice-Faith, but it seems to me equally relevant to the difference in viewpoint just mentioned between Heidegger and Bultmann. In any case, in my opinion, the *Namu Amida Butsu* which comes forth at the point where the opposition of subject and object is overcome, in the "Great Living" characteristic of religious action shows an extraordinary depth. And its significance for the present day may become much clearer when explored in the light of the contemporary problematics of philosophy of religion and theology.

Translated by Rev. Prof. Jan van Bragt

---

is promptly fulfilled therein.] *The Name is the treasure-ocean of the merits accruing from the absolute reality of Suchness.* [The Name is the absolute truth as Suchness; it is the ocean of merit wherein this truth is realized as it is, in a unique and unduplicatable way.] *Therefore, it is called the great living."*

"*So it is that this great living issues out of the Prayer (or Vow) of Absolute Compassion, for which reason the Prayer is known as that which is praised by all Buddhas, or that in which all Buddhas pronounce the Name, or as that which is heartily applauded by all Buddhas."*

[The "True Living" chapter, indeed, explains the text of the Seventeenth Vow (or Prayer) further as a Prayer that the Name shall be uttered in praise by all Buddhas.]

"In The *Larger Sutra of Eternal Life* (vol. I), we find:

'*If, upon my attaining Buddhahood, all the innumerable Buddhas in the ten quarters were not approvingly to pronounce my Name, may I not attain the Supreme Enlightenment.'"*(D. T. Suzuki *trans.*)

Part V

A Dialogue of Shin Buddhism and Zen Buddhism

Shinran's World: A Dialogue of Shin Buddhism and Zen Buddhism[1]

Nishitani Keiji (moderator) with Suzuki Daisetsu, Kaneko Daiei and Soga Ryōjin

Introduction by Kurube Shin'yū[2]

On April 17, 1961, four of the most eminent Japanese Buddhist thinkers of this century gathered on Mount Hiei for a three-day dialogue on Shin Buddhism. This event was one of several commemorating the 700th anniversary of the death of Shinran Shōnin (1173–1262), the founder of the Jōdo Shin-shū or True Pure Land sect, otherwise known as Shin Buddhism. Two of the participants were leading figures from within Shin Buddhism, Soga Ryōjin (1881–1976) and Kaneko Daiei (1875–1971). Suzuki Daisetsu[3] (1870–1966), well known for his work in Zen, also had a deep interest and knowledge of Shin. In fact, at the time of the discussion, he was engaged in the task of translating Shinran's major work, the *Kyōgyōshinshō*. The discussion was chaired by the philosopher Nishitani Keiji (1900–) who, like Dr. Suzuki, has trained in Zen but is also deeply knowledgeable about Shin Buddhist thought. The dialogue was later published as a book entitled *Shinran no sekai* (Shinran's World). Though it was recorded nearly a quarter of a century ago, the issues discussed are just as relevant today. At times highly philosophical and at other times thoroughly down to earth, their views manifest a profound religious awareness. In this first installment, they go deeply into the problems of expression and meaning involved in the art of translating.

---

1. Ed. This dialogue was first published in *The Eastern Buddhist* in Three parts as: "Shinran's World (Suzuki Daisetz, Kaneko Daiei, Soga Ryōjin and Nishitani Keiji (moderator))." The first installment was originally published in *Shinran no sekai* (Kyōto: Higashi Honganji, 1964), 3–23, and translated by Mark Unno. Except where otherwise indicated, footnotes are as originally published in *The Eastern Buddhist*.
2. Ed. Kurube Shin'yū 訓覇信雄 (1906–1998).
3. Ed. Occasionally written Daisetz, as in the original edition of this presentation.

Nishitani Keiji with Suzuki Daisetsu, Kaneko Daiei and Soga Ryōjin

Nishitani Keiji   Suzuki Daisetsu

Kaneko Daiei   Soga Ryōjin

Part I

Buddhist works: Language and Spirituality

Translating Religious Writings

NISHITANI: Dr. Suzuki, could you relate some of your thoughts regarding the translation of Shinran's *Kyōgyōshinshō*?

SUZUKI: Well, rather than thoughts I had specifically concerning the *Kyōgyōshinshō*, these would be my general impressions concerning the expression of Eastern thought or Eastern ways of thinking in European languages.

Two types of literature might be distinguished here. On the one hand, there are erudite works like the *Kyōgyōshinshō* which are not simply expressions of faith but contain quite a bit of theory, and on the other hand there are works intended more for the public at large.

The Chinese way of thinking differs significantly from that of the Europeans. It is unlike that of the Indians as well; the Chinese, in many ways representative of the East as a whole, tend to think in more concrete terms. They must have had great difficulty in translating Sanskrit, and many of the concepts they came across were no doubt completely alien. I always use *nyo* 如 as an example. The Buddhist concept *tathatā* or "suchness" represented by this Chinese character is rather abstract, and I doubt the Chinese originally had anything like it in their own vocabulary. Thus I find the choice of this character to be quite ingenious.

And there is the character *hō* 法 or "law" for the Sanskrit Dharma. This, too, was a skillful adaptation, but Dharma is quite troublesome; it is sometimes aptly characterized by *hō*, but at other times might be better represented by *dō* 道 "path," "the Way." With the advancement of Buddhist scholarship, such matters as the relationship between *ki* 機 and *hō* had to be taken into account, making the usage of the individual characters more complex.[4] Then there are such two-character words as *chie* 智慧, the Chinese translation of the Sanskrit *prajñā*. This is another term

---

4. Elsewhere, D. T. Suzuki writes: "*Ki*, originally meaning 'hinge', means in Shin especially the devotee who approaches Amida in the attitude of dependence. As long as his self-power is involved, he stands against Amida. *Hō* is "Dharma," "Reality," "Amida," and "the other-power." This opposition [between *ki* and *hō*] appears to our intellect as contradiction and to our will as a situation implying anxiety, fear, and insecurity. When *ki* and *hō* are united in the *myōgō* as '*Namu-amida-butsu*', the Shin devotee attains *anjin*, 'peace of mind'." From *Mysticism: Christian and Buddhist* (New York: Macmillan Company, 1969), 116.

which presents a big problem for today's translators, just as it did for the ancient Chinese. They combined two characters of similar meaning, *chi* and *e*, apparently feeling that neither was sufficient in itself. When even this proved inadequate, they resorted to *hannya no chie* 般若の智慧 in which the first two characters transliterate the original Sanskrit *prajñā*, and the last two represent an attempt at translation.[5]

This term, *hannya*, or *chie*, is one of the most difficult to translate into the languages of the West. "Intuition" is not very suitable. "Transcendental wisdom" has also been tried, but I have misgivings about both "transcendental" and "wisdom." "Insight" has also been used, but it doesn't really fit either. The difficulty lies in the fact that *prajñā* is not discriminating knowledge, but non-discriminating knowledge. There are even problems with calling it non-discriminating knowledge because the word "knowledge" implicitly signifies discrimination; the Indians certainly showed their ingenuity in applying the term *prajñā*.

There are even more problems with the term *bodhi* or "enlightenment." In one sense it is interchangeable with *prajñā*. The Chinese either transliterated this term as *bodai* 菩提, or translated it as *dō*. Is there a suitable equivalent in the West, perhaps used in philosophy or theology?

NISHITANI: I'm not sure...

SUZUKI: I haven't found any, either. How was it that the Chinese were able to interpret this term so successfully? My feeling is that if one is able to understand *bodhi*, then one has grasped the essence of Buddhism.

If I might bring in my own philosophy, I would like to say that the truly concrete is the truly abstract; the abstract is none other than the concrete, the concrete is none other than the abstract. Even though the Chinese tend to see things in concrete terms, I feel that they were able to understand such matters as *prajñā* and *bodhi* through this correspondence of the concrete and the abstract.

In ordinary usage, concrete and abstract terms are regarded as quite different. Abstract nouns did not originally exist in Chinese. In order to translate abstract Buddhist concepts, the Chinese added the character *shō* 性 to a concrete noun. *Busshō* 仏性 "buddha-nature" and *hosshō* 法性 "dharma-nature" are examples of this. In Sanskrit the suffixes -*tā* or -*tvā* are added, producing words like *buddhatā* and *dharmatā*. In European languages as well, abstraction is expressed through the use of suffixes, as with -*ness*, -*ship*, and -*hood* in English. The suffix construction does not

---

5. Ed. The third of the five characters shown here is not Chinese, but the Japanese particle *no* indicating a genitive relation. Although many of the terms below are referred to as Chinese the pronunciations are given in Japanese, and this approach has been maintained in correspondence with the original publication.

exist in Chinese, so when *shō* 性 was added to *butsu* 仏, readers must have found the resultant combination difficult to comprehend. They would have asked what was meant by *butsu* and *shō* as individual characters. Such difficulties as these hindered the Chinese for centuries in their attempts to understand Indian thought; in fact it was not until the Sui and Tang dynasties that they really began to grasp the meaning of these terms.

The Passage of Words

SUZUKI: The same kinds of problems arise in translating the *Kyōgyōshinshō* into English. As I said, when the Chinese could not convey the meaning of the original Sanskrit in a single character, they often used a compound of two characters. *Chie* is one such example, and whoever conceived it had a specific significance in mind for each of the characters, *chi* 智 and *e* 慧. In this way various interpretations became associated with the compounds depending on the understanding of the individual translators, and this inherent complexity of meaning makes it impossible to find suitable equivalents in English.

Even more difficult than *chie* is *hōben* 方便 or "skillful means." Just what is meant by *hō* and *ben* individually is very difficult to determine. Other terms such as *gyakutoku* 獲得 or "realization," it seems to me, could have just as well been translated into Chinese by either character alone. Perhaps they just wanted to reinforce the meaning. There were probably various factors involved, and they make the translation of these terms into English very difficult.

Hongan 本願, which is the Chinese translation of the Sanskrit *pūrvapraṇidhāna*, is another case in point. *Hon* corresponds to *pūrva* and *gan* to *praṇidhāna*, and the latter we translate into Japanese as *negai*.[6] *Negai* expresses the feeling that one wishes to acquire something because it is lacking in oneself, or aspires to fulfill a wish not presently realized. In modern Japanese it is something like *kibō* 希望 "hope." It is often translated into English as "desire" or "wish," but these are not adequate, and "will" overemphasizes intent.

The *gan* 願 of *hongan* is unlike any of these preceding terms. If Christian terminology were adopted, "prayer" would be the closest, but this word is so heavily laden with traditional Christian thought that it would take hundreds of years before it became properly Buddhist, that is, until it came to reflect the meaning of *gan* in its usage. The standard trans-

---

6. *Hongan* refers to Amida Buddha's forty-eight Original Vows, which were made when Amida commenced his training as Bodhisattva Dharmākara incalculable aeons in the past. These vows, made to help all beings attain Buddhahood, are also known as *seigan*. *Sei* is read as *chikai* in Japanese and means something like "vow." *Gan* is read as *negai* and is in some sense akin to "prayer."

lation today seems to be "vow." I cannot recall whether it was Nanjō Bun'yū or Takakusu Junjirō who first used "vow"; the Sanskrit scholars of the West tend to use "prayer." This latter term is very awkward, while "vow" is really closer to *chikai* 誓い. I even have doubts as to whether the Chinese grasped the meaning of *gan* when they first began using it. After hundreds of years, actually more than a thousand years now, this term has become imbued with the meaning it was originally intended to convey.

SOGA: Since my knowledge of English is rather limited, I don't have much of a feel for the term "prayer." I have the impression that it refers to supplication. If that is indeed the case, the meaning of *seigan* 誓願 [7] needs some clarification to see how it contrasts with "prayer."

The forty-eight Vows of Amida Buddha are all statements of the conditions for attaining enlightenment as well as expressions of the vow to fulfill them. In Shin Buddhism the Eighteenth Vow is particularly important: "If...the beings in all quarters of the universe...desire to be born in my land and say my Name even ten times with true and entrusting mind, but should still fail to be born there, then may I not attain supreme enlightenment."[8] The first part of this and all the other Vows, in which the conditions are laid down, is a concrete expression of *gan* or *negai*. The second part represents the standpoint of *sei* or *chikai* and means, "If I can't fulfill my own conditions, then I will not become thoroughly enlightened, a real Buddha." However, the first part already includes the second insofar as it embodies the aspiration to fulfill the given conditions. The second part includes the first insofar as there is already an awareness of what the conditions are. Thus *negai* and *chikai* are fundamentally one. All forty-eight Vows are expressive of this unity.

SUZUKI: Exactly. It must have taken a long time for the Chinese to sense this unity.

The Transmission of the Living Essence

SOGA: The Chinese probably did their first translations without too much reflection. But as the number of translations increased, the readership did as well; where there were ambiguities, later scholars researched the matter until the fine points were clarified.

SUZUKI: It was in just this way that the meaning of *gan* has become fairly well-defined. This took the Chinese hundreds of years of experience and

---

7. See previous note.
8. For a list of all forty-eight Vows and a discussion of their significance, see D.T. Suzuki, "The Shin Teaching of Buddhism," in *Collected Works on Shin Buddhism* (Kyoto: Shinshū Ōtani-ha, 1973), 36–77.

reflection. Thus, rendering *gan* into English is not simply a matter of translating it as "vow" or "prayer."

SOGA: Doesn't this term prayer have similarities to *chikai*?

SUZUKI: I feel that it is closer to *negai*. A prayer is an earnest desire directed towards God.

SOGA: An earnest desire directed towards God?

SUZUKI: This actually has a twofold meaning. A prayer made to God with the expectation of the fulfillment of one's desires, a prayer which demands a positive response from God, is not authentic. There must be no expectations. It's not a true prayer if one has some idea such as: "If I plea to God, he will surely hear me." There are some theologians who say that in real prayer, there is no God who hears and the devotee has no means of even pleading.

NISHITANI: Though not necessarily all of them...

SUZUKI: Yes.

NISHITANI: Such an interpretation exists, but there isn't any common agreement yet in theological circles...

SUZUKI: Common agreement? There must be significant differences even among Buddhist scholars on the interpretation of *chikai* or *seigan*. I have my own ideas about the meaning of *seigan*. I don't know how others have interpreted it, but my approach is to return to its philosophical origins.

In the beginning there was emptiness. I do not mean the beginning of time, but the beginning in the logical sense. Emptiness began to move within emptiness. No one knows why it started to move, and there's no need to ask. Emptiness began to move, and this movement is what is referred to as *gan*.

NISHITANI: Of course there are various problems implied in that.

SUZUKI: This is indeed where things get rather complicated. I would like to translate *gan* tentatively as "vow" and then see if anything needs to be added to qualify it.

NISHITANI: Yes.

SUZUKI: God was said to have decreed in the beginning, Let there be light. What made him say that was his *gan*, his vow. You might not say this if you weren't a Christian, but such matters are irrelevant for Buddhists. At any rate, in terms of Christian thought, God's first words, *Let there be light*, constitute God's vow. In Buddhism there is the statement, "In salvation there is no one to be saved" (Tánluán, *Commentary on the*

Treatise on the Pure Land). Even though it is said that all sentient beings are to be saved, there are no sentient beings to be saved, and hence no Buddha who saves. It is in this way that the activity of salvation functions. "Vow" and "prayer" could be receptacles for this kind of understanding, but the matter of giving it a name comes after the fact and involves the long process of imbuing a word with the flavour of the reality it represents. So it is difficult to say now whether "vow" is really the best translation. But for the translation of the *Kyōgyōshinshō* I have to make a choice, however tentative. I am deliberating between "original vow" and "original prayer," and have even considered "will." This is not the merely psychological will to which we usually refer when using the term, but rather its source, or the fundamental will. This use of the word "will," though, is based too much on my own interpretation, so I am thinking of using "original vow."[9]

Chie presents similar problems. *Hannya no chie*, "*prajñā*-wisdom," refers to the knowledge of no knowledge. Everything is known; knowing everything, nothing is known. This is my explanation. In Christianity there is the term "omniscience." This does not refer to the knowledge of each thing individually: a bowl as a bowl, a dish as a dish, an orange as an orange. It is knowledge of reality as a whole, though in speaking of "the whole" we are already limiting ourselves; it is knowledge which knows and yet does not know. When asked what makes it possible to say such a thing, all answers are futile. This knowledge is present before one even thinks of speaking. Shin Buddhism also recognizes this. Here is where we return to fundamentals, and again where matters become rather involved.

Form Is Emptiness, Emptiness Is Form

SOGA: What you've been saying isn't explicitly stated in the writings of Shinran Shōnin himself, but can be found in Tánluán's *Commentary on the Treatise on the Pure Land*.

SUZUKI: Yes.

SOGA: In that work it is stated, "One ought truly to know the three attainments in which the adornments are attained by the vow-mind... because it is stated that these are in essence the entrance into the one Dharma." This means that the three attainments constitute the entrance into reality as it is, that they are therefore the adornments of the vow-mind. It is further stated, "The One Dharma is called the Pure, the Pure is called the true and real wisdom, and is therefore the uncreated Dharma-body." These quotations from Tánluán's *Commentary* appear in

---

9. Actually, Dr. Suzuki finally opted for "original prayer" in his translation of the *Kyōgyōshinshō*.

the fourth fascicle of the *Kyōgyōshinshō*, "Chapter on Realization." Shinran has thoroughly grasped the meaning of Tán-luán's words, and that's why he quotes him.

SUZUKI: That's right. He quotes him and goes on with his own explanation. Then—I'm afraid our discussion is wandering a bit—we must clarify the standpoint of Shin Buddhism in terms of the greater context of Mahāyāna Buddhism.

NISHITANI: Many important problems seem to be emerging at this point in the discussion, and I'm sure many other things need to be said, but we appear to have lost our focus. I wonder if it might not be a good idea to take up the issues one by one, as we did with *chie* and *hongan*.

SOGA: This goes back to what has already been discussed, but the One Dharma, the Pure, and the true and real Wisdom, or the uncreated Dharma-body, are called "the three expressions." Tánluán's *Commentary* states, "These three expressions mutually interpenetrate one another. As to the principle upon which this is based, it is called Dharma." This Dharma is the same as the One Dharma. For a clue to the reason why it is called Dharma, we can turn to the phrase, "because it is the Pure." Dharma is the Pure because it is untouched by human discrimination. It is originally pure. Next, "As to why it is called the Pure, this is due to its being true and real Wisdom, the uncreated Dharma-body." This is the manner in which these expressions mutually interpenetrate.

Further he states:

> As for true and real wisdom, this is the wisdom of reality. Because reality is formless, true knowledge is no knowledge. The uncreated Dharma-body is the body of Dharma-nature. Because Dharma-nature is tranquil, the Dharma-body is formless. But because it is formless, it cannot be without form. Thus the Dharma-body possesses the major and minor characteristics of an Enlightened One. Because it is no knowledge, it cannot be devoid of knowing. Thus omniscience is true and real Wisdom. To describe wisdom as being true and real elucidates the fact that wisdom neither functions nor does not function. To signify the Dharma-body as being uncreated elucidates the fact that the Dharma-body is neither form nor not-form. Since it is not negation, the negation of negation is affirmation!

SUZUKI: It is so. One cannot say it's this way or it's not this way. It is divorced from such discrimination.

SOGA: Tánluán goes on to say, "Where there is no negation, this is called affirmation. It is affirmation by itself; again, affirmation does not wait for negation." Affirmation does not wait to be negated.

SUZUKI: Just so. "It is not affirmation, it is not negation. It stands beyond negation."[10] *Shōjō* 清浄, "the Pure," really means "the Absolute." It's not that there is an affirmation and a negation which stand in relative opposition to each other. It is the affirmation wherein there is neither negation nor affirmation. I use this kind of logic as the basis of interpretation when translating. This is especially pertinent in the case of *shōjō*. Its meaning is clearer if translated as "the Absolute" rather than as "the Pure."

SOGA: *Shōjō* refers to purity.

SUZUKI: However, when *shōjō* is translated into ordinary terms, it's most easily understood as "the Absolute."

NISHITANI: But what about using "purity" in context, as in the case of translating a work of some length. A given passage could be translated so as to cause "purity" to be understood in the sense of "the Absolute."

SUZUKI: That's the way I would like it to be. The term *shinjitsu* 真実, "true and real," presents similar problems. In my own words, this refers to things as they exist *sono mama*, "just as they are"; *shinjitsu* is the aspect of things *sono mama*. Reality in itself, things as they are—this is what is meant by *shinjitsu*. But it won't do to translate this into English as "reality." So *shin* was interpreted as "true," *jitsu* as "real," and the result was "that which is true and real," an awkward translation at best. According to my understanding, however, this becomes "things as they are," or "as-it-is-ness." The significance of *shinjitsu* does not reveal itself without the use of such peculiar expressions.

As one more example, let us examine the phrase, *Hosshin wa jakumetsu nari* 法身は寂滅なり. *Hosshin* is Dharma-body. *Jakumetsu* ordinarily means something like "quiet," "tranquility," or "stillness." These do not point to its real meaning, which again refers to things *sono mama* "just as they are." Going a step further, this is emptiness. There is the phrase, *Hosshin musō* 法身無相, which means, "The Dharma-body is formless"; because it is formless, it is not without form. My interpretation of this is that the body of emptiness is emptiness itself; furthermore, it reveals itself as both body and function. It contains infinite possibility which functions without functioning. Individual particulars emerge, yet these particulars are not individual things. This is called "emptiness."

It should be clear then, that the formulation, "Form is none other than emptiness," must be accompanied by "Emptiness is none other than form." Form is emptiness, emptiness is form. People usually stop at the stage of "Form is none other than emptiness," but in truth, as form is emptiness, so emptiness is form. Again, zero is infinity, and infinity is

---

10. A quotation from Tánluán's *Commentary*.

zero; becoming is being, being is becoming. However things may appear from the standpoint of philosophy, the matter is clear when thus stated. This manner of expression follows the style of classical Chinese. In terms of the formulation, "Emptiness is none other than form," Shin Buddhism emphasizes the aspect of form rather than resting in emptiness. This is the basis from which I proceed in explaining Shin Buddhism.

Between East and West

NISHITANI: Interpretation seems to occur inevitably when translating such works as the *Kyōgyōshinshō* and the sutras into European languages.

SUZUKI: That's right.

NISHITANI: Here's an opportunity to interpret these ancient works not only for contemporary Westerners but also for the Japanese, who have become highly Westernized. Furthermore, these works are not only interpreted for the contemporary reader, but are also interpreted from the standpoint of the contemporary world. We assume this stand-point naturally, whether we are conscious of it or not. New interpretations emerge. Do you agree?

SUZUKI: Yes, that's why this is not really translation. It's not that a Western interpretation emerges either; that which lies at the foundation of Eastern thought is interpreted in terms of the languages of the West. These languages are in turn interpreted on the basis of Eastern ways of thinking.

What does this mean? Well, these days students and scholars often say that the East has no philosophy, no aesthetic principles. This may be true in a sense, but that does not indicate a lack of development in the East. The East has eschewed frivolous philosophizing, and has instead pursued matters existentially. As an example from the arts, we can look at landscaping. Japanese gardens are fashioned so as to bring peace to one's soul after the day's work. The garden does not exist apart from the frame of mind of the one for whom it is intended. This is the kind of aesthetics at work in the East. It is likewise with philosophizing, playing the *biwa*, or playing the *shamisen*; these become vehicles for spiritual cultivation. This is the Eastern way of life, and it would be a great mistake to label this as good or bad. It's just that such things exist in the East, and are what set it apart from the West.

I recently heard that a famous Indian musician was approached by an American recording company. I don't remember whether he was the composer or performer, but he apparently said he did not create his music for such purposes as they had in mind and refused their offer. His music was something borne forth from his innermost heart, and not created to be "music" per se. This is the spiritual basis of the East. That's why I want today's young people to pause before they conclude that the East is inferior.

NISHITANI: Today's youth are finding it increasingly easier to understand English than classical Japanese. This may provide them with an opportunity to examine and understand what lies in the East through the translations now emerging.

SUZUKI: That's what I've really wanted in my own writings.

SOGA: However, there are points of both difference and similarity between the West and the East. If they were totally different...

SUZUKI: That's right.

SOGA: When we speak of differences, a commonality must be presupposed. It's after all the latter from which differences emerge. Commonality is in fact more basic; it is equality.

NISHITANI: Which means that there is something here which Westerners can grasp as well.

SOGA: If there were an essential difference between the East and the West, then there would be no basis for mutual understanding. In any case, it's a single foundation out of which diverse histories and traditions arose over a long period of time and in various lands. It's this basic unity which is important, since it is this which makes it possible for Westerners to come to an understanding of our thought.

SUZUKI: Yes, that's it. This is the approach necessary for making Shin Buddhism understood.

SOGA: The basis is one.

SUZUKI: It must be made known that in the East such a thing as Shin exists, a tradition different from Christianity. Though the two may seem similar at first glance, they are in fact not at all alike. I don't think a mutual understanding between East and West is possible unless this is made clear.

NISHITANI: That's true not only for people of the West. If Westerners come to understand, then today's Japanese will as well.

SOGA: It's true with anything. It must be taken once to the West and then brought back again. Even something as Japanese as Shin Buddhism cannot be understood by the Japanese simply as it stands.

NISHITANI: To borrow an expression from Shin Buddhism, this could be called *gensō ekō* 還相回向, "the transference of merit in the returning phase." [*Laughter*]

SOGA: It is through the interpretation of Westerners that we will really come to understand ourselves. That's the way the Japanese have been throughout their history, isn't it? Right now the other side is seen as being on top, and so we are struggling to catch up. The other side looks down on the East a bit as well. But not so far in the future, they may come to appreciate the greatness of the East. Though they have had a sense of superiority until now, by virtue of "the transference of merit in the returning phase" this feeling will dissipate and then things will be all right, will be healed. I think such a time will come.

NISHITANI: We must work in that direction.

SOGA: It's no good to criticize and disparage each other. Each must properly see the other's standpoint and give it due respect. If we can understand each other in this way, then neither is better or worse. Everything is all right if we are equal. There's no need to be superior.

In Understandable Terms

NISHITANI: This may bring us farther and farther into the future, but actually, it can be dealt with as a present concern as well. I was wondering about those like myself, the general public which isn't knowledgeable about traditional religious studies or Buddhist thought. Is there some interpretation to which we might have recourse, something which might give us a real feeling for the teachings? There is a genuine need for this.

SOGA: The *Kyōgyōshinshō* might not meet such a need, but wouldn't a work like the *Tannishō* be readily accessible even to the Westerner.[11]

NISHITANI: It is easily understandable to contemporary Japanese. It is very widely read.

SOGA: It's quite accessible to both the Japanese and Westerner alike, I should think.

NISHITANI: Yes, the readership of the *Tannishō* is not limited to Shin believers.

SOGA: It should be quite accessible to the Westerner as well.

NISHITANI: Yes, the readership of the *Tannishō* is not limited to Shin believers. And then there is the Christian Bible, quite a curious phenomenon, but it is universally read.

SOGA: It's something on the order of a national scripture.

---

11. The *Kyōgyōshinshō* is Shinran's most important philosophical work. The *Tannishō* contains statements made by Shinran which were compiled by his disciple Yuien.

NISHITANI: It's not just Christians who read it; the average Japanese reads it as well. This certainly hasn't made them believers, but it seems people do find various passages in the Bible highly appealing. I imagine that for the most part their reading of it is rather deficient, but it has a certain universal applicability. Whether the *Kyōgyōshinshō* can be read in such a manner…

SOGA: All the passages Shinran quoted in the *Kyōgyōshinshō* are accepted as the words of Shinran himself, but his own words exist in the work apart from the quotations. So I think that we can clearly distinguish between the two.

NISHITANI: This is a question of personal interest for myself, and concerns the quoted passages within the *Kyōgyōshinshō*.

SOGA: They are properly called *monrui* 文類 "scriptural passages," rather than quoted passages.

NISHITANI: I wonder if we can assume Shinran accepted the contents of all the *monrui* as true.

SOGA: He accepted them all. These *monrui*, which are not simply quoted passages, are all taken from the scriptures. For this reason we can assume that he accepted them all. He wouldn't have arbitrarily accepted some passages while rejecting others.

Part II[12]

The Original Vow

From Sino-Japanese to Native Japanese

KANEKO: I wonder if the Japanese understand such terms as *hongan* 本願 "Original Vow" and *seigan* 誓願 "vow" in quite the same way as the ancient Chinese did. I think it's reasonable to say that the *Kyōgyōshinshō*, though written in classical Chinese, is basically a native Japanese work. If so, it must be understood in terms of the Japanese language. For example, we have the words *negai* 願い "wish" and *chikai* 誓い "vow" in Japanese. I don't know if *negai* conveys exactly the same meaning as the Sino-Japanese *hongan* or if *chikai* corresponds precisely to *seigan*, but I can't help feeling that such native Japanese words, used in their everyday sense, provide the best approach to understanding the true meaning of the *Kyōgyōshinshō*.

---

12. The second part of this dialogue, which begins here, is a translation of *Shinran no sekai* (Kyōto: Higashi Honganji, 1964), 23–48, which was prepared by Mark Unno and Thomas L. Kirchner for *The Eastern Buddhist*.

Even the title itself, *Kyōgyōshinshō*, would be better understood if rendered into Japanese. The Sino-Japanese *kyō* 教 or "teaching" would be read as the native *oshie*, *gyō* 行 or "practice" as *okonai* and so on. Shin Buddhism has traditionally interpreted this text in quite an abstruse way, but I wonder if we haven't gone too far in that direction. I would prefer to bring it closer to everyday Japanese. There are many colloquial Japanese expressions, for instance, which convey the same message as passages from the classical Chinese texts, like this one which came up in conversation the other day: "When you've truly grasped something, you're free to express it in any way you like."

NISHITANI: "When you've truly grasped something...

KANEKO: ...you're free to express it any way you like."

SUZUKI: What does it mean?

KANEKO: This means that if one really understands the essence of a concept one can express it any way one likes.

SUZUKI: I see.

KANEKO: I think this Japanese expression means the same as the following line from a Chinese Buddhist work by Jízàng: "Utterly unrestricted even by the fourfold propositions of logic and the dialectic of the one hundred negations." Both carry the same sense of free, unobstructed action. This is what I am seeking—easily understandable Japanese expressions which convey the sense of the original.

NISHITANI: I find Professor Kaneko's approach to reading the *Kyōgyōshinshō* very appealing. First, the Chinese laboured to translate Sanskrit. The Japanese then read the Chinese texts in accordance with the rules of Japanese grammar; instead of reading the Chinese characters in their original order, they rearranged them to fit the Japanese syntax through the use of *kaeriten*, or "return-marks." Though a given work may originally have been Chinese, it became half-Japanese by virtue of its adaptation to the linguistic structure of the latter; even though most of the characters have retained their Chinese readings, the Japanese student most likely thinks of these characters in terms of their meanings in his own native language. Thus people generally understand the Chinese character *kyō*, "teaching," in terms of its Japanese reading, *oshie*.

However, we cannot simply change all Sino-Japanese readings into native Japanese readings, as the two readings often have differing connotations. This is what makes a work like the *Kyōgyōshinshō* so complex. For example, the Sino-Japanese readings, *kyō* and *gyō*, carry nuances which are quite different from those conveyed by *oshie* and *okonai*, the native Japanese readings of the same characters. These words have been adopted into the Japanese language, but still retain some of their original Chinese connotations.

KANEKO: I still think that the essential meaning is conveyed by the Japanese reading.

NISHITANI: Then the work becomes completely Japanese.

KANEKO: Yes, and I'm wondering if there isn't a similar method of transmitting these texts to the West. For example, rather than translating *hongan* literally as "Original Vow," wouldn't it be better to look for a term in ordinary English which conveys the same concept, much as *negai* does in Japanese?

NISHITANI: That, finally, is what has to happen. Each word, after all, must be expressed in the language it's being translated into, whether it be English, French, or something else. But let's go back to the problem of the different readings in Japanese. The Sino-Japanese *kyō* does possess the meaning conveyed by the Japanese reading *oshie*, but it also carries a unique nuance when read in its Sino-Japanese form. This is also true of the Sino-Japanese *gyō*, "practice" or "training," which contains nuances not present in the Japanese *okonai*, "the actions of daily life." Each character contains two levels of meaning. It's fascinating, really—the ways of thinking of two peoples have been superimposed in the Chinese ideograms as they are now used in Japan. They are the product of a joint effort.

SUZUKI: The term *shinjitsu* 真実 which literally means "true and real," is another interesting word. Both *shin* and *jitsu* have the same reading in Japanese, *makoto*. Here is a case where the indigenous Japanese word encompasses the meaning of more than one Chinese character.

KANEKO: Earlier in the discussion, someone quoted the passage which reads, "*Shinjitsu* is reality." This may adequately define the term as it is used in its original Chinese or Indian context, but is insufficient for conveying the meaning of the Japanese reading, *makoto*. In the third fascicle of the *Kyōgyōshinshō*, "Chapter on Faith," there is a passage in which *makoto* is applied to three characters: *Shinnari jitsunari seinari*, "True, real, sincere." They express various aspects of *makoto*, and yet point to the same fundamental reality. The first two characters are *shin* and *jitsu* which we have already seen in *shinjitsu*. The third character, the Chinese *sei* 誠, reflects the sense of fidelity or sincerity of heart implied in the statement, "He is a sincere person." This doesn't just mean he isn't a liar. There's a positive quality implied.

NISHITANI: I think it's akin to another Japanese word, *magokoro*, which means something like sincerity of heart or earnest devotion.

KANEKO: The concept of *magokoro* is contained in the word *shinjitsu*, "truth as reality." In discussions of philosophy or religion these days, people often speak of *shinri* 真理 "ultimate truth" or "fundamental principle," but frankly speaking I don't really like this word. *Shinjitsu* is much better.

Freely Expressing Oneself

SUZUKI: While I was reflecting on Professor Kaneko's expression, "When you've truly grasped something, you're free to express it any way you like," I recalled an ink drawing by the Zen priest Sengai 仙厓 (1750–1837). The inscription accompanying the drawing reads,

> When I see [Reality's] shadow
> Thrown into the emptiness of space,
> How boldly defined
> The moon
> Of the autumnal night![13]

Sengai describes the moon here as "boldly defined." "Boldly" is a translation of the Japanese *omoikittaru*, which can be rendered more literally as "thoughts cut off." One acts boldly when no longer hindered by extraneous thoughts. Thus one sees the moon boldly, that is, in its full reality, when thoughts are cut off and nothing remains. There is only the brightly shining moon. I feel that this is akin to Professor Kaneko's expression.

Scholars often base their opinions on the words of others, saying, "The Buddha teaches," "Socrates says," "Hegel states," and so forth. I don't agree with this way of thinking. Instead, scholars should express themselves more freely, saying, "My view is as follows, and the Buddha is in agreement with me." This may sound arrogant, but it's not. Even if you are a student of the teachings of Hegel, Kant, or the Buddha, you must still be able to say, "I feel this way," and if you can do that, there is no longer any need for Buddha or Christ. This is the significance of the words Buddha uttered at the time of his birth: "In heaven above and earth below, I alone am the honoured one." How about doing things this way? What do you think? [*Laughter*]

NISHITANI: Yes, it's just as you say. But let us remember that it is only after we have grasped something thoroughly, be it the philosophy of Kant or Hegel, that we can express it with complete freedom. There are many quotations from various scriptures in the *Kyōgyōshinshō*. Shinran grasped the meaning of these passages, systematized them over time, and then expressed them anew in the form of the *Kyōgyōshinshō*. Would

---

13. From Daisetz T. Suzuki, *Sengai the Zen Master*, London (Faber and Faber 1971), 107.

you say this is Shinran's way of freely expressing himself?

SUZUKI: Yes, I think so. Otherwise the *Kyōgyōshinshō* would be meaningless.

KANEKO: I agree. Its meaning lies in the way Shinran uses quotations. He is expressing himself through the words of others.

NISHITANI: So he has to make them his own first. Then, having grasped their meaning, he could use them to represent his own understanding. The sense of "freely expressing oneself" is quite apparent here.

KANEKO: There is yet another aspect to "freely expressing oneself." At times one wishes that someone else would say what one seeks to express oneself. For instance, one can't very well congratulate or praise oneself. It's only if someone else does these things for you that they have any meaning.

This is why Shinran quotes from scriptures. Though his standpoint is no different from that of Shàndǎo and Genshin, he continues to express himself through their words because of their deep effect on him. He finds freedom of expression through the words of others. Instead of saying, "My opinion is...," he quotes others, saying, " Shàndǎo says." We must keep in mind that it is really Shinran himself who is speaking, however—he uses quotations to express his own realization. The error occurs when, paying too much attention to what Shàndǎo and Genshin say, we become entangled in the words of their works and lose sight of the *Kyōgyōshinshō* itself.

The Bestowal of the Buddha's Vow

NISHITANI: Let us return to the discussion of *hongan*, Original Vow. Dr. Suzuki traced it to its origins in Emptiness which has just started to move. This was followed by a discussion of *prajñā*-wisdom, and then of Tánluán's *Commentary on the Treatise on the Pure Land*. Is there anything we should add to the understanding of the Original Vow which emerged in the context of this discussion?

KANEKO: My understanding of the Original Vow begins with the view that humanity is the recipient of the Buddha's earnest and active desire to save all beings. This desire, this ardent movement of will, is what is called "vow." Just as everyone wants a sick person to get well again, and all children are the recipients of their parents' hopes, it is in the nature of human existence to be bestowed with a vow. That which bestows this vow or prayer upon us is what we call the Buddha. But the important thing is to awaken to this vow; what the Buddha is will then become clear of itself.

NISHITANI: In the previous discussion of Tánluán's *Commentary*, there was a reference made to the phrase quoted by Shinran in the *Kyōgyōshinshō*: "Wisdom is the Pure." It seems to me that this phrase raises the problem of the origin of this prayer or vow which is bestowed upon us.

KANEKO: In his use of words like *shinjitsu* and Original Vow, Tánluán seeks to clarify the source of the fundamental truth underlying the vow.

SOGA: The two main branches of Indian Mahāyāna thought are the Mādhyamika school founded by Nāgārjuna, and the Yogācāra schools founded by Asaṅga and Vasubandhu. The *Treatise on the Pure Land* was authored by Vasubandhu and thus belongs to the latter school. We must keep in mind, however, that Tánluán's *Commentary* on this work is based on Nāgārjuna's Mādhyamika school. There are significant differences between the respective systems of thought of these two schools. In the *Zàn āmítuófó jì* [Verses in praise of Amida Buddha], Tánluán refers to Nāgārjuna as one of his "true teachers," but not Vasubandhu. For Tánluán Nāgārjuna represents the orthodox lineage of Mahāyāna Buddhism, and Vasubandhu an offshoot. This is why he interprets Vasubandhu's work on Pure Land Buddhism in terms of Nāgārjuna's thought; for him the former is unintelligible without the latter. In order to really understand Vasubandhu, one must study Nāgārjuna. This is the basis of Tánluán's *Commentary*; I feel that his notion of Amida's Other-power is rooted in Nāgārjuna as well.

The Inner Mirror is Serene

NISHITANI: What is Shinran's standpoint?

SOGA: I think he felt the same, though he did not say so explicitly. For example, in his *Kōsōwasan*, Shinran addresses Nāgārjuna, Tánluán, Dàochuò, Genshin, and Hōnen as "my true teachers." Vasubandhu and Shàndǎo are not referred to in this way. The same holds true for Shinran's *Shōshinge*. There must be some reason for this, though I'm not sure what it is. In any case it is safe to say that the philosophy of Asaṅga and Vasubandhu constitute something of a departure from the mainstream of the Mahāyāna. The *prajñāpāramitā* philosophy to which Dr. Suzuki often refers belongs to the line of Nāgārjuna's thought.

SUZUKI: Yes.

SOGA: I think one can say that the orthodox lineage of the Mahāyāna is basically that of Nāgārjuna's Mādhyamika. This isn't so much Shinran's personal view, but the basic trend throughout the history of Mahāyāna Buddhism. As I just mentioned, Tánluán refers to Nāgārjuna as his "true teacher" in his *Zàn āmítuófó jì*. However, the differences between Nāgārjuna and Vasubandhu should not be exaggerated. Though their standpoints seem to be in conflict, these two great figures are fundamentally of one mind. The Tiāntái master Zhìyǐ commented upon the relationship between them by stating, "The inner mirror is serene."

NISHITANI: Did Shinran feel the same way about the basic unity between the two?

SOGA: Certainly. This was the standard view in Buddhism since long before Shinran's time. Even Tánluán's eulogy of Nāgārjuna presupposes this unity. When he distinguishes between the two, calling Nāgārjuna "my true teacher" but not Vasubandhu, it isn't because he didn't respect the latter. Nāgārjuna has always occupied a more central position in Chinese Mahāyāna Buddhism. For example, both the seven and ten-fascicle Chinese translations of the *Laṅkāvatāra-sūtra* predict the appearance of the Bodhisattva Nāgārjuna. Shinran refers to this prediction in his *Kōsōwasan*: "There is to come to Southern India a *bhikṣu* by the name of Nāgārjuna." This prediction was accepted as historically genuine by all Buddhists, including of course Tánluán and Shinran. Vasubandhu is accorded much less attention in Shinran's *gāthā*s and hymns. The only mention made of him is that he authored the *Treatise on the Pure Land*. But the basic unity of Nāgārjuna and Vasubandhu was never in doubt. It was just that, long before even Shinran, Nāgārjuna's Mādhyamika was recognized as the orthodox teaching.

The Place to Which the Vow Returns

NISHITANI: Earlier on Dr. Suzuki explained Original Vow in terms of emptiness.

SOGA: We can refer once again to Tánluán's *Commentary*. In the section of the Treatise dealing with the "adornments," or special characteristics of the Pure Land, Vasubandhu states,

> In contemplating the power of the Buddha's Original Vow, those who encounter it but once do not pass their lives in vain, for they are swiftly filled with the great treasure-ocean of virtue.

This is the most important of the Pure Land's "adornments." Commenting on this line, Tánluán expresses the implicit relationship between the Vow and its power:

> What gives the Pure land its continual unfailing activity is the establishment of the Forty-eight Vows by Dharmākāra Bodhisattva in the past and the freely-working divine power of Amida Buddha in the

present. The Power is manifest by virtue of the Vows; the Vows are fulfilled by virtue of the Power.

The Vows generate the Power, and the Power fulfills the Vows.

The Vows are never idle; the Power is always at work. Power and Vow are mutually fulfilling; ultimately there is no difference between them. The actualization of this fact is called the fulfillment of the Vow.

This, according to Tánluán, is the meaning of the fulfillment of the Original Vow, and this interpretation is in accord with the views of Nāgārjuna. Tánluán's exposition is spirited and full of joy. In contrast, I find the works of the Yogācāra school rather sad and depressing. When I read them, I start feeling gloomy myself. [*Laughter*]

SUZUKI: What do you mean?

SOGA: Well, I find myself getting depressed when I read Yogācāra works like the *Chéngwéishí lùn* or the Mahāyānasaṃgraha.

SUZUKI: I know how you feel.

SOGA: Nāgārjuna, on the other hand, makes me cheerful.

SUZUKI: Yes, I agree.

KANEKO: I feel that Dr. Suzuki's explanation of Original Vow in terms of emptiness is in accordance with orthodox Mahāyāna thought. However, I would like to examine Original Vow in relation to suchness (Skt. *tathatā*) as well. In the *Ānlè jí*, Dàochuò states, "According to the Mahāyāna, the fundamental source of reality and suchness is none other than emptiness. The truth of this is something we have never grasped." We can talk about such concepts as "suchness" or "reality," but these things are beyond the reach of ordinary beings like us. We must first contemplate Amida Buddha's Original Vow, for it is in the thorough realization of the Vow that we will eventually reach the realm of suchness. My feeling is that the destination lies at the source.

SOGA: The Vow originally arose out of suchness, since Amida Buddha is a Tathāgata, "the one who came from suchness." In any case, suchness is the ultimate source.

KANEKO: I think that's basically correct, but I prefer to think of the process as moving in the opposite direction.

NISHITANI: You feel that the realm of suchness lies in the future?

KANEKO: Yes, and that means that eventually we will reach this realm. The place we are going or returning to is nothing but the ground of our existence. Though we talk about returning to it, however, we should realize that this is only possible because it is the place from which we originally came. What Dr. Suzuki was saying about Vow and emptiness is no doubt true, but I can't help feeling that we ordinary beings lack the ability to attain a direct experience of this truth.

NISHITANI: I see. Then what's important is the destination.

KANEKO: Yes, various problems with interpretation remain, but I think that's true regarding the place to which the Vow returns.

NISHITANI: The place to which the Vow returns? Do you mean the place it returns to or the place from which it comes?

KANEKO: We are talking here about the world of *kie* 帰依, where the place to which we return (*ki*) is the same as the place from which our existence originally came (*e*). I think everyone would agree with this understanding of "return."

SOGA: From the standpoint of ordinary beings, I prefer to see it as the place to which we return. For the Buddha, it is the place from which he emerged. For those of us who have become lost and deluded and are unable to find our way home, it is the place we seek to return to.

KANEKO: That expresses the character of Shin Buddhism very well.

There is Something Interesting about Being Deluded

SUZUKI: About this matter of being deluded…

SOGA: If there were no suchness, there would be no delusion.

SUZUKI: Don't you think that there is something interesting about being deluded?

SOGA: You can say that delusion is interesting because you're enlightened, Dr. Suzuki, but to those who are actually deluded, there's nothing interesting about it. [*Laughter*]

SUZUKI: Let's look at it this way. Say something happens, an accident or something similar. Objectively speaking, the facts can't be changed: those who live, live, and those who die, die. But suppose, for example, there's a person who has cancer, and the doctors give him no chance of survival. Still, from my standpoint, I hope something will happen that will enable him to live. This is my earnest hope. Even if it's clear that the patient is going to die, I want him to get better. Again, with the number of people traveling these days, it is inevitable that wrecks and collisions will occur, but my earnest desire is that all travelers reach their destination safely and return home without any of these misfortunes happening. This desire just wells up from within. From the standpoint of reason, this is a kind of delusion, because whatever happens, happens. Even so, this deluded thought wells up ceaselessly within my mind. This is what I find interesting, though perhaps the word "interesting" sounds a bit irreverent. What I am trying to say is that in the midst of the grief and suffering of human passion, there's something very warm and embracing as well. This is where delusion becomes interesting.

SOGA: Then it's not simply pain and suffering, but enjoyment in the midst of suffering as well?

SUZUKI: No, it mustn't be called enjoyment. It's all suffering. It's all very painful, but...

SOGA: Unless there's warmth there can't be suffering.

SUZUKI: That's right. Professor Kaneko would say that there's something to be thankful for in that.

KANEKO: Yes.

SUZUKI: That can only be said in light of Amida's teaching. For me it's something interesting rather than something to be thankful for.

SOGA: It's both, I feel.

SUZUKI: Looking at the world around us, I guess we'd have to say that. [*Laughter*]

SOGA: What would we do if nothing interesting ever happened?

The Vow of Dharmākara Bodhisattva

NISHITANI: Dr. Suzuki, you once expressed some very interesting views during a talk you gave on the vows of Dharmākara Bodhisattva, and I was wondering if you would be willing to repeat what you said for our benefit.

SUZUKI: Certainly. I'd be grateful if you would comment on my views. Well, actually, it doesn't really matter whether you do or not. [*Laughter*] At any rate, here is the way I view the matter.

The *Larger Sūtra of Eternal Life* has its start in the vow formulated by Dharmākara. This vow was not something he contemplated for just a year or two, but over *kalpa*s, aeons. Why did he make his vow? What made him do so? I think it must have been a feeling like the one I described concerning the cancer patient: "Nothing can be done; still I can't help but hope for recovery." There's no question that such a thought stirred in the mind of Dharmākara Bodhisattva. As to what gave rise to that thought, I think it was something at the very source of Dharmākara's existence. The vow was not something originated by Dharmākara, but rather, the Bodhisattva originated from the Vow. This is why it is called the Original Vow: it is that from which Dharmākara originated. He is the "voice" of the Vow, the conveyer of its message, as it were. So it doesn't matter whether he spent five *kalpa*s or ten *kalpa*s in his religious quest, or what vows he made or which places or teachers he visited. There is no need to limit the Vows to forty-eight, either.

SOGA: At the beginning of the *Larger Sūtra of Eternal Life*, Dharmākara Bodhisattva utters "The *Gātha*s in Praise of Buddha." He then addresses the Tathāgata Lokeśvararāja: "I vow to attain unexcelled supreme enlightenment and earnestly seek to fulfill this vow. To this end, O Buddha, I solicit thee for thine instruction." Whereupon Lokeśvararāja replies, "You must know for yourself the contents of the vow you seek to fulfill." In other words, he's saying, "You've awakened the *bodhi*-mind, the vow to attain supreme enlightenment. But that vow is rather undefined, and you aren't really clear about what it entails, are you? You don't need to ask me. It's your vow, so you ought to understand what it is." But that is the nature of a true vow; one doesn't understand it oneself. It transcends Dharmākara Bodhisattva.

Dharmākara presses Lokeśvararāja further, saying, "Its significance is vast and profound; it is beyond my limits." "Significance" refers to Dharmākara's vow, a vow which transcends Dharmākara's limits as an individual. It is in fact the Tathāgata's vow at the source of Dharmākara's existence. That's why he says,

> This vow is beyond my limits—I don't want to fulfill a vow which is restricted by my capacities as an individual. I wish to go beyond myself, attain to the Vow of the Tathāgata, and fulfill it with this very body. Although I myself am not the Tathāgata, I wish to know and fulfill the vow of the Tathāgata, that which transcends myself. Thus, O Tathāgata, I earnestly desire that you expound the teachings to me.

This is the meaning of his statement, "Its significance is vast and profound; it is beyond my limits." Lokeśvararāja ponders this plea for instruction, then explains the specific causes of the twenty-one billion Pure Lands of the various Buddhas and describes in detail the strengths and weaknesses of the various inhabitants of these lands, both human and divine. He tells Dharmākara of the various Original Vows underlying the numberless Buddha realms. He then manifests these lands before Dharmākara and shows him in detail what they are like. Dharmākara reflects for five *kalpa*s on all he has seen and heard, and then condenses the numberless vows of the Buddhas into forty-eight of his own. Infinity is a concept one can't really talk about, so he expresses the essence of the numberless vows in the form of these forty-eight. It's not as though he drew up a specific list of forty-eight from the start.

SUZUKI: In that case, one must see innumerable vows in the forty-eight, and the forty-eight vows in the innumerable. The forty-eight are again divisible into the innumerable.

SOGA: One could put it that way.

Amida's Realization of Buddhahood

SUZUKI: One of Amida's vows was that he would defer the realization of Buddhahood until all sentient beings had attained enlightenment.

SOGA: Well, we don't really know about the original existence of Amida Buddha.

SUZUKI: And whether he existed is not really important.

SOGA: In any case, Dharmākara Bodhisattva pledges to make *Namu Amida Butsu* his Name upon his fulfillment of the Tathāgata's vow, the salvation of all sentient beings.[14] He chooses *Namu Amida Butsu* as his Name in this way in the Seventeenth Vow: "If the Buddhas in all quarters of the universe do not praise my Name [by saying *Namu Amida Butsu*], then I will not attain unexcelled enlightenment." "To praise my Name" means "to praise the Buddha's virtue."

SUZUKI: I see. But don't some people give the following interpretation: When Amida attained enlightenment, that meant everyone else did, too, so there's no need to recite the nembutsu (*Namu Amida Butsu*) or to do anything else.

SOGA: That might be the Zen interpretation.

SUZUKI: No, Zen doesn't look at things this way. It's a view held by certain Pure Land believers who say that Amida's enlightenment means there's no need for religious practice or for *Namu Amida Butsu*. This mistaken view is called "presuming upon the Original Vow."

SOGA: Such followers are obviously in error.

SUZUKI: I think so too. It doesn't follow that just because Amida Buddha is enlightened, I am as well. When one realizes that one has attained enlightenment, at that moment Amida also attains enlightenment. Just because Amida attained enlightenment ahead of us does not mean that we too are now enlightened and no longer have to do anything. The moment of my enlightenment is the moment in which Amida is enlight-

---

14. When Dharmākara Bodhisattva fulfills his Vows, he becomes Amida Buddha. His ultimate concern in becoming Amida Buddha, however, is to make possible the salvation of all beings through the recitation of *Namu Amida Butsu*. Thus *Namu Amida Butsu* is Amida Buddha's true Name, that which enables the salvation of all sentient beings.

ened, and not only Amida but everything else as well—the mountains, streams, grasses, trees. So when Shinran, upon his attainment of faith, stated that "It was for me, Shinran alone, that Amida went through his aeons of training," at that moment it was not only Shinran but all sentient beings who attained Buddhahood.

KANEKO: I don't know if I would go that far.

SUZUKI: Well, perhaps I could have expressed the idea a little bit better. [*Laughter*]

SOGA: You're an optimist.

SUZUKI: No, I don't think I'm being overly optimistic.

KANEKO: Both the Tathāgata's enlightenment in the past and our enlightenment in the future meet in the present moment—in Shin terminology this experience is called "the assurance of non-retrogression," the assurance of obtaining birth in the Pure Land during this life. Hence the issue at hand is always the present.

SUZUKI: Professor Kaneko, earlier you described our existence as that which has had the Buddha's vow bestowed upon it. Since our present life unfolds into our future one, all we have to do is to recognize our own present existence as the locus for fulfilling the vow.

KANEKO: Yes.

SUZUKI: We cannot accept ourselves as having been bestowed with the Buddha's vow unless this vow is in some way our own as well. If it belongs completely to someone else, then it has nothing to do with us. We can receive the vow only if we recognize it as something already present in ourselves.

KANEKO: One can think of it in those terms, but I prefer to see it from the opposite standpoint. My feeling is that I who possess nothing am bestowed with the great Vow. That's what moves me.

SUZUKI: I suppose one can look at it in those terms.

SOGA: We have forgotten the vow, though it is there within us. We are in possession of this vow from the beginning, but we have forgotten it.

SUZUKI: You can say we have forgotten it, but the words really don't matter.

SOGA: The teachings are essential. It is through them that we remember the vow.

SUZUKI: Exactly. One can say that the vow is drawn forth from within us by means of the teachings.

Human Idealism and the Tathāgata's Vows

KANEKO: I would like to return to the issue of the specific number of Amida's Original Vows. It was previously mentioned that the numberless vows of the Buddha were condensed into forty-eight. In the *Kyōgyōshinshō*, however, Shinran Shōnin speaks of the Five True Vows. My feeling is that, of the forty-eight vows given in the *Larger Sūtra of Eternal Life*, only these five are to be regarded as the pure Vows of the Tathāgata Amida; all the others are alloyed with human idealism. Human idealism of course resembles the vows of the Tathāgata in that they are an expression of hope and desire. Still, I think it's important to consider whether human idealism is the same as the Tathāgata's vow.

The First Vow has attracted much attention from sociologists and others for its utopian aspirations: "If in my land, upon my attainment of Buddhahood, there should be a realm of hellish existence, hungry spirits, or beastly existence, then may I not attain supreme enlightenment." I feel that such vows are concerned with society and humanistic ideals, and may not be the same as the authentic vows of the Tathāgata. This matter requires clarification.

SUZUKI: Do you mean that the nature of the Tathāgata's vows needs to be clarified?

NISHITANI: I think Professor Kaneko wishes to separate human idealism from the pure Vows of the Tathāgata.

SUZUKI: That's what he's just done, isn't it?

NISHITANI: What Professor Kaneko is saying is that only the Forty-eight Vows of Amida are pure, and the rest are merely expressions of human idealism.

KANEKO: Actually, what I said was that human idealism appears even among the Forty-eight Vows.

NISHITANI: Even among the Forty-eight?

KANEKO: Yes. When Shinran compiled the *Kyōgyōshinshō*, he selected only the pure Vows of the Tathāgata, eliminating those which were tainted with human idealism.

SUZUKI: Do you mean to say that human ideals and those of the Tathāgata are different?

KANEKO: I think one can properly conceive of a difference.

SUZUKI: That's certainly possible, as long as you view human beings and the Tathāgata as separate. However, one must clearly see the unity which precedes this separation.

KANEKO: I suppose one can say that human idealism is included within the Original Vows of the Tathāgata, but my feeling is that unless we distinguish them, the teaching of Shin Buddhism loses its clarity of purpose.

SUZUKI: What I'm trying to say is that they should be seen as separate yet not separate. For the time being, we can't help separating them, but this is only due to the limitations implicit in the human way of thinking.

SOGA: The first of the Five True Vows begins with the Eleventh, since it includes the essence of the first ten. These ten all have their source in the Eleventh Vow. From the First Vow, that there be no realms of suffering in Amida's Pure Land, through the successive Vows that all beings attain the six supernatural powers as an aid to the attainment of enlightenment, their essence is expressed in the Eleventh, that all beings are unfailingly assured of attaining Nirvana. Hence, even though the first ten Vows appear to express human ideals, they are fundamentally based upon the Eleventh Vow of the Tathāgata.

KANEKO: That's right.

SOGA: The Vows really begin with the Eleventh, and the Twelfth and Thirteenth form a backdrop for this.[15]

SUZUKI: I just can't help disliking this business of forty-eight. It shouldn't matter whether it's forty-eight, a hundred, or two hundred.

SOGA: Well, it could be two hundred or three hundred, but the Great Vows of the Tathāgata are totally contained in these forty-eight. We can go one step further and say that five or eight of the Vows are enough.

SUZUKI: Yes.

KANEKO: Precisely.

SOGA: Shinran himself said that forty-eight is excessive, and suggested that the number be reduced to eight.

SUZUKI: I think one is enough. Having more is too much of a bother.

SOGA: Having one vow, in fact, is the traditional Pure Land standpoint.

SUZUKI: Really? [*Laughter*]

---

15. The Twelfth Vow states: "If, upon my attainment of Buddhahood, the light which issues therefrom should prove to be limited and thus fail to illuminate the ten trillion *nayutas* of lands of the various Buddhas, then may I not attain supreme enlightenment." The Thirteenth Vow states: "If, upon my attainment of Buddhahood, the life which extends therefrom should prove to be limited and thus fail to last the ten trillion *nayuta kalpas* [necessary for liberating all sentient beings], then may I not attain supreme enlightenment."

SOGA: Hōnen Shōnin stated that the Eighteenth Vow[16] alone is sufficient, and in this he stood within the tradition of the Seven Patriarchs of Pure Land Buddhism. He regarded all the other vows as skillful means of liberation. For Shinran, however, this was not enough to clarify the relationship between *ki* and *hō*,[17] a concept not thoroughly understood even by such great disciples of Hōnen as Seizan and Chinzei. Shinran sought to clarify this by choosing seven other vows from among the forty-eight, and adding them to the Eighteenth to form the eight essential vows. He then used these as the philosophical basis for the *Kyōgyōshinshō*. In any case, forty-eight is far too many.

PART III

The Locus of the Original Vow

Shin Buddhism and the Demands of the Age

NISHITANI: Dr. Kaneko, the Forty-eight Vows of Bodhisattva Dharmākara are given in the form of conditions for enlightenment: "If (the chosen conditions are not satisfied), then may I not attain supreme enlightenment." Is it possible to say that the prayers of sentient beings are included in these conditions?

KANEKO: Yes, as Shinran says, "All of the vows and practices of sentient beings are already fulfilled (by means of the power of the Original Vow)."

NISHITANI: In these Forty-eight Vows the prayers of sentient beings are described in considerable detail, but among them we do not find all the prayers of people today. For example, one major concern is the elimination of nuclear weapons and the achievement of peace for all humanity. Another which has gained a great deal of attention recently is the desire for a society free of class conflict and oppression. There may be others, but these are today's prayers. Can they be added to those given in the *Sukhāvatīvyūha-sūtra* (*Larger Sūtra of Eternal Life*)?

KANEKO: I feel they can.

NISHITANI: Then we can see today's prayers and vows as extensions of

---

16. The Eighteenth Vow states: "If, upon my attainment of Buddhahood, the sentient beings in all quarters of the universe desire to be born in my Land, utter the nembutsu even ten times with the mind of true entrusting, and should still fail to attain birth, [in my Pure Land], then may I not attain supreme enlightenment."

17. For a detailed discussion of the concept of *ki* and *hō*, see the earlier part of this dialogue.

the Forty-eight. Conversely, the various contemporary concerns such as world peace are ultimately included in the Forty-eight. Each new age will give rise to its own prayers expressing its own ideals. In this infinite succession we can see, as Dr. Suzuki says, that the number of Vows may be regarded as innumerable.

KANEKO: That may be so, but let me give the traditional Shin Buddhist interpretation of "Vow," or *negai* which is the indigenous Japanese rendering. Etymologically *negai* is said to come from the noun *"ne"* which means "sound" or "voice"; the original meaning of *negai* is "to summon with one's voice," or more simply "call."

Who is being called? "The sentient beings in all quarters of the universe." This phrase only appears in the Three Vows, namely, the Eighteenth, Nineteenth, and Twentieth. All the other Vows express a desire for some ideal realm or for sentient beings to be possessed of certain abilities or qualities. But the Three Vows differ in that they are Amida Buddha's direct call to all sentient beings. Actually, Amida's call is to himself in the second person. In these three Vows, Amida calls to each and every sentient being as his second self.

On the other hand *chikai* means "promise," just as it's given in the *Tannishō*. It means that Amida will always be with us. It originates with Amida's Vow: "If there is anyone who does not attain rebirth into my Pure Land, then I will not attain supreme enlightenment." In order to help sentient beings realize Buddhahood, Amida tries all kinds of prayers, but in reality we are hopelessly lost. The only way we can be saved is through the fundamental vow that Amida will refuse enlightenment if there remains even a single being who does not attain birth in his Land. My feeling is that the promise of the Pure Land teaching is ultimately realized in the Eighteenth Vow On the other hand *chikai* means "promise," just as it's given in the *Tannishō*. It means that Amida will always be with us. It originates with Amida's Vow: "If there is anyone who does not attain rebirth into my Pure Land, then I will not attain supreme enlightenment." In order to help sentient beings realize Buddhahood, Amida tries all kinds of prayers, but in reality we are hopelessly lost. The only way we can be saved is through the fundamental vow that Amida will refuse enlightenment if there remains even a single being who does not attain birth in his Land. My feeling is that the promise of the Pure Land teaching is ultimately realized.

NISHITANI: That's fine. So...

KANEKO: I would like to hear what each of you thinks about human ideals in light of this basic vow. The path I have followed is best exemplified by a passage from the *Tannishō*:

> There is a difference in compassion between the Path of Sages and the Path of Pure Land. Compassion in the Path of Sages is expressed through pity, sympathy, and care for all beings, but truly rare is it that one can help another as completely as one desires. (*Tannishō*, Section IV, trans, by Taitetsu Unno)

This phrase, "as one desires," reveals that one somehow wishes to do something for others. In contrast to this one is struck by the profundity of the statement, "Truly rare is it that one can help another." This expresses the realization that all contrived efforts are useless. The direction that Shin Buddhist thought will take in the future remains to be seen. But as to whether the Pure Land teaching should be confined to this standpoint or go beyond to embrace the prayers of all generations, my view is that there must be the awareness of finitude. Rather than thinking that I can respond to the various demands of the age, I wish to listen for the real voices of the people and ask if the Shin teachings might not be helpful. There's nothing that can be done if they are judged to be useless. I often hear of the need to respond, but Shin Buddhism takes the opposite approach of appealing to the conscience or religious heart of the people of each age. This seems to be particularly characteristic of Shin Buddhism.

NISHITANI: Yes, that may well be.

KANEKO: I will leave whatever else can be done to others. There's no need to oppose them. I'm quite willing to say that what they are doing is fine, but there's no need for me to try to do everything.

Resignation

NISHITANI: Would you say that the most basic element is enlightenment?

KANEKO: Yes, the Pure Land teaching does not hold any hope in the merely human way of life. I don't like the word despair; perhaps it is a kind of radical resignation. The Nembutsu teaching emerged through resignation. This can be seen in the *Tannishō*.

NISHITANI: That's true of the *Tannishō*.

SUZUKI: Dr. Kaneko, what is the "*ne*" of "*negai*"!

KANEKO: What did you ask?

SUZUKI: This "*ne*" What is it?

KANEKO: According to the scholars of Classical Japanese, "*negai*" means summoning oneself in the second person. This means to impart one's innermost feelings to another, from "I" to "Thou." This is Amida's call to all sentient beings, "I will always be with thee." "I" is Amida Buddha. "Thee" is the practicer. Pure Land Buddhism is characterized by an awareness of oneself in the second person; one discovers oneself as "thou." The one who directs this call to us is named Amida Buddha. Our age seems to want to attain transcendence directly in this world. The Shin Buddhism we learned teaches resignation. We can talk about the Pure Land teachings only after this resignation.

NISHITANI: This is not peculiar to the Pure Land tradition, but characterizes Buddhism as a whole. The religious character of Buddhism does not become apparent unless one passes through resignation. Then what emerges out of the resignation?

KANEKO: I don't know. In any case, I don't wish to go too easily beyond resignation.

The Vow Which Transcends This World

NISHITANI: No, I don't know either, but... Dr. Soga, you were saying that Bodhisattva Dharmākara went to the Tathāgata Lokeśvararāja.

SOGA: Bodhisattva Dharmākara called his vow the Original Vow because he realized that his vow to save all beings was not merely a personal affair. This is why he said, "I don't know what the vow is because it is beyond my world."

Although the Tathāgata Lokeśvararāja said, "You ought to know what your own vow is," it transcended Dharmākara. This is why he needed someone to teach him.

NISHITANI: Does this mean that the Original Vow was that of the Tathāgata Lokeśvararāja?

SOGA: The Tathāgata existed within the mind of Bodhisattava Dharmākara. The latter was a human being. Hence the Tathāgata who transcends the human existed within the mind of the human being. The desire to realize the Original Vow of the Tathāgata in his own being was Bodhisattva Dharmākara's Vow which transcends this world.

NISHITANI: In that case, is it all right to understand this term for Buddha, "Tathāgata," as "*tathā-āgata*" "the one who has come from suchness"?

SOGA: Yes, one can explain it in those terms.

NISHITANI: I see. The Original Vow of the Tathāgata was within Bodhisattva Dharmākara and somehow...

SOGA: It is within, and it must be resolved by oneself, but it transcends one. That's why one cannot understand it through one's efforts alone; here is the reason for the appearance of Tathāgata Lokeśvararāja. Dharmākara sought someone who could teach him the Vow. Upon meeting him Dharmākara thought, "I'll be able to understand my Vow if I ask this sage; I can't understand it by myself."

Dharmākara had a Vow which transcended him, went beyond his capacities. He didn't know what the Vow was, so he asked Lokeśvararāja to teach him. The latter said, "The nature of the twenty-one billion Buddha Lands, the strengths and weaknesses of the humans and gods inhabiting those lands, and all the details of these lands are..."

He went on to describe the various Buddha-Lands where beings are reborn and the good and evil characteristics of the inhabitants. There were innumerable Buddhas and their Vows, and having heard Lokeśvararāja's descriptions, Dharmākara made his selections. These were the Vows that transcended him. He selected forty-eight of his own conditions after examining the innumerable Great Vows of the Tathāgatas, and then declared his Forty-eight Original Vows.

Selection

NISHITANI: Is it correct to say that Dharmākara selected his Vows from among the innumerable... ?

SOGA: ...among the Vows of the Buddhas of the twenty-one billion Pure Lands.

NISHITANI: What I want to ask is if they were already in existence.

SOGA: Yes, they were already there in a sense.

NISHITANI: And he chose from among them.

SOGA: Yes, he chose them.

NISHITANI: But didn't Dharmākara contemplate the Vows for a long time and then establish his own which did not previously exist?

SOGA: They did not exist among all the other Buddhas.

NISHITANI: He set forth vows which did not exist before?

SOGA: Yes.

NISHITANI: What is the relation between selection and the new vows which he set forth?

SOGA: Hōnen has explained this in his *Senchakuhongannenbutsushū* (The Collection of Passages Concerning the Nembutsu of the Selected Original Vow), beginning with Dharmākara's very first Vow.[18] The existence of the Vow, the Vow of the Pure Land without the Three Evil Realms, implies the existence of the Pure Lands with the Three Evil Realms. That is, among the Pure Lands of the various other Buddhas, there are some which contain the Three Evil Realms. Dharmākara wished to establish a Pure Land to compensate for this, so he declared the Vow of the Pure Land without the Three Evil Realms. In this manner Hōnen relates the nature of each Vow.

Now we come to the Eighteenth Vow of Amida Buddha. Birth in the Pure Land of one of the other Buddhas is attained by performing the meritorious act of giving. There are other Pure Lands in which one attains birth through other acts, such as practicing forbearance and exerting oneself on the path of the Buddha. Dharmākara examined each of these. There were also Pure Lands that one attained birth in through *shōmyō* 称名, calling the Name of the Buddha. This does not refer to *Namu Amida Butsu*.[19] There were other Names besides *Namu Amida Butsu*, the Name of Amida Buddha, and the other Buddhas promised to welcome the practicer into their Pure Lands if he intoned their names. The Buddhas of each of the Pure Lands had his own Name, and the intoning of the Name of some of these was the proper cause to be reborn there. There were numerous other causes for rebirth in the Pure Lands of the other Buddhas, each established as the result of fulfilling different vows.

In his Eighteenth Vow, Dharmākara promises to save all those who intone his Name. In the Seventeenth Vow, Dharmākara selects the characteristics of this Name: "If, when I attain Buddhahood, the innumerable Buddhas in all the quarters of the universe do not intone my Name in praise of my virtue, then may I not attain supreme enlightenment." It is Shinran Shōnin who teaches us that "my Name" is "*Namu Amida Butsu*." He says that all the Buddhas of all quarters exalted the intoning of *Namu Amida Butsu* and authenticated the nobility of the Name. This is at the basis of Shinran's notion of "The Vow of the Ocean of the One Vehicle" (*seigan ichijōkai* 誓願一乗海). This was originally Master Shàndǎo's term,

---

18. The First Vow reads, "If, when I attain Buddhahood, there should be a realm of hellish existence, of hungry ghosts, or brutish creatures, then may I not attain supreme enlightenment." These realms are called the Three Evil Realms.

19. Amida Buddha is the name of the Buddha of the Pure Land in the West, but when those wishing to be born in his land call to him, they use the Name, *Namu Amida Butsu*, which means, "I take refuge in Amida Buddha." This is his true name, because Amida Buddha's very being is embodied in the voice of the practicer who single-mindedly entrusts himself to the Buddha of Infinite Light and Eternal Life by intoning, "*Namu Amida Butsu*."

but Shinran gives his interpretation in the *Kyōgyōshinshō* in the chapter on "Act" (*gyō* 行). He quotes passages from all of the Seven Patriarchs of Pure Land Buddhism and the spiritual successors of Shàndǎo; he even quotes the masters of other sects. Then he gives his own interpretation of Other-Power (*tariki* 他力) and the Ocean of the One Vehicle.

NISHITANI: The Vow of Bodhisattva Dharmākara which you just mentioned is one's own vow, but at the same time transcends oneself and is the Original Vow of the Tathāgata.

SOGA: That's right. It's not a personal prayer, but that of all the Buddhas. It is the vow at the source of the vows of all the Buddhas; it transcends them. This spirit of the Seventeenth Vow is called the Ocean of the Vow of the One Vehicle. This is *Namu Amida Butsu*. In the *Shōshinge* (*Gāthās* on True Faith) Shinran states,

> If a single thought of joyful devotion is awakened in one's heart, then Nirvana is attained without severing the passions. When fools, sages, sinners, and abusers of the Dharma all alike turn and enter the ocean of Amida Buddha's Vow, then it is like water from many different streams entering the ocean of one taste.

This is also the Ocean of the Vow of the One Vehicle.

NISHITANI: In one sense this Vow is new and did not exist among the vows of the other Buddhas.

SOGA: Yes, a new vow which all the other Buddhas join in praise and agreement. It is as if they said, "We didn't realize it before, but now that we have heard this Vow, we can clearly see that it is our true Vow." The Buddhas came to know this Vow for the first time in this way. It is a manifestation of "The Buddhas' mindfulness of each other." This is its origin.

The Ocean of the Wisdom-Vow

NISHITANI: The "Tathāgata" in the "Original Vow of the Tathāgata cannot be exhaustively described by referring to those Buddhas who made their appearance prior to Amida because this Tathāgata transcends the others.

SOGA: There are numerous Tathāgatas, each with his own vows; having fulfilled their vows, each has his own Pure Land. But if it stops here, there is a lack of universality. The Vow of the One Buddha Vehicle (*seigan ichibutsujō* 誓願一仏乗) saves all beings equally since it has one cause and one result. There is a clear result and a clear cause. "Fools, sages, sinners, and abusers of the Dharma all alike turning and entering the ocean of Amida's Vow" is this one cause. "It is like water from many different streams entering the ocean of one taste." This is the single result. Both the cause and result belong to the One Vehicle. Amida Buddha had vowed that there would be a single cause and a single result (*in'itsu kaitsu* 因一果一). Birth in the Pure Land of the other Buddhas has various results. If one views Amida Buddha's Pure Land with the same eye with which one sees the other Pure Lands, it appears as simply one among many. But Shinran Shōnin says this is mistaken: "Since the pure Original Vow of the Tathāgata leads to the birth of no-birth, there are no diffences between the nine classes of beings who attain birth" (*Kōsōwasan*),[20] In the *Jōdoronchū* (*Commentary on the Treatise on the Pure Land*), Tánluán gives his interpretation: "(Amida Buddha) made his Vow and said, 'My Land which has the one taste of the Mahāyāna shall have the one taste of equality.'"[21] The Pure Land of Amida Buddha belongs to the world of the One Vehicle because it was established through the fulfillment of the One Vehicle Vow.

NISHITANI: Bodhisattva Dharmākara vowed to fulfill the Original Vow of the Tathāgata. The Vow being spoken of here is not that of the various Buddha-Tathāgatas, but more fundamental…

SOGA: The Buddhas whom Dharmākara heard about from the Tathāgata Lokeśvararāja were already in existence. They lacked unity because each had his own particular character. The real Tathāgata who Dharmākara had in mind is the one who unites.

NISHITANI: Dr. Suzuki previously spoke about the origin of the Vow of Bodhisattva Dharmākara, and now we can perhaps say that it emerges from the Tathāgata who fundamentally unifies…

SOGA: The various Buddhas established many different Pure Lands according to their various vows. These Buddhas had manifold realizations, but their vows lacked universality. They had different practices which led to different results. In contrast Dharmākara brings all beings to the realization of the one taste of equality. This is the Ocean of the One Vehicle. Shinran also refers to this as the Water of the Ocean of the Wisdom-Vow: "When the water of the entrusting of Other-power enters the Water of the Ocean of Amida's Wisdom-Vow, blind passions and enlightenment come to have the same taste in the True Land of Recompense."

One returns and enters (*kinyū* 帰入) the Ocean of Amida's Wisdom-Vow. This expression appears in the chapter on "Act" in *Kyōgyōshinshō*. The term *kimyō* 帰命 "to take refuge," may be more familiar, but here

---

20. Donran section, 26.
21. At 巻上, 総説分観察門.

we have *kinyū*. To return and enter is the cause. When one returns and enters the Ocean of the Original Vow, one obtains the result which is equal for everyone; this is the Pure Land. The attainment of the result which is equal for all sentient beings is itself the Pure Land; the equal cause for attaining this equal result is the Ocean of the Tathāgata's Wisdom-Vow.

First There Is Act

NISHITANI: There is the expression, "the Ocean of the Wisdom-Vow." Earlier on Dr. Suzuki gave his interpretation of *gan* as emptiness which begins working. I wonder how these two...

SOGA: Emptiness is act; it is not simply *prajñā*-wisdom. Emptiness may be regarded as a philosophical principle, but true emptiness must be the act of emptiness.

SUZUKI: What do you mean?

SOGA: Emptiness is act, right?

SUZUKI: Emptiness is act?

SOGA: Yes, act.

SUZUKI: Ah, yes.

SOGA: I don't know about Zen, but in Tiāntái Buddhism emptiness is regarded as a principle.

SUZUKI: Principle?

SOGA: The principle of emptiness. But in Shin Buddhism we speak of the act of emptiness. Emptiness is universal.

SUZUKI: That's correct.

SOGA: An act equal for everyone, since everything is equal in emptiness.

SUZUKI: Yes.

SOGA: The call of Amida's Buddha's name, "*Namu Amida Butsu*," is the act of emptiness.

SUZUKI: Yes, yes.

SOGA: This is the way it must be; your thinking returns to this point as well. This is why Shinran entitled his work *Kyōgyōshinshō*. In general the Buddhist path may be characterized by the phrase *kyōrigyōka* 教理行果, the sequence of teachings, principle, act, and realization. The term, *ri*, principle, does not appear in the title *Kyōgyōshinshō*.

SUZUKI: No.

SOGA: What do you think, Dr. Suzuki?

SUZUKI: That's right.

NISHITANI: In the *Kyōgyōshinshō* Shinran himself states that *Namu Amida Butsu* is this act.

SOGA: "That which is called Amida Buddha is none other than this act." (in the section on *gyō*, quoting Shàndǎo's *Commentary on the Meditation Sūtra / Guānjīngshù*).

NISHITANI: Dr. Soga, please elaborate on the meaning of *gyō*, act.

SOGA: *Namu Amida Butsu* is the act:

The Great Act is the call of the Name of the Tathāgata of Unhindered Light. This single act contains all the good teachings and the root of all virtues; complete and perfect, it is the actualization of suchness, the great treasure-ocean of virtues. These are the reasons why it is called the Great Act. (section on *gyō*)

That's why the title, *Kyōgyōshinshō*, begins with *Kyōgyō* 教行, "teaching and act." There is no principle; there is act in conformity with the teachings. Then there is *shin* 信, true entrusting, and *shō* 証, realization, both corresponding to *ri* 理, principle. The act comes first, and then the principle becomes clear. This is what is meant by "Hearing this Name [*Namu Amida Butsu*] one attains the joy of faith-awakening." Tiāntái Buddhism also recognizes the failure of principle without act: "The three thousand dharmas understood as principle is ignorance. Once they are realized as the fruit of enlightenment, they are called 'constant joy.'" (attributed to the Tiāntái master Zhànrán 湛然). Once the fruit ripens, all dharmas bring eternal joy. "Dharmas" refer to all existence, even that of a hungry spirit or hellish realm. There is joy even if one goes to hell. Our founder Shinran Shōnin states, "I have nothing to regret, even if I should have been deceived by my teacher, (Hōnen Shōnin), and saying the Nembutsu, thus fall into hell...hell is my only home." (*Tannishō* II.) There is no fear of hell. In any case, principle without act is nothing more than an illusion. That's why act comes first, not principle. This is the meaning of the title *Kyōgyōshinshō*.

Where Are All the Buddhas?

NISHITANI: Dr. Soga, your notion of "emptiness as act" seems to be in accord with Dr. Suzuki's explanation of Vow as dynamic emptiness.

SOGA: I think so.

SUZUKI: Dr. Soga's notion of act is really interesting.

SOGA: You are referring to the act of emptiness?

SUZUKI: The act of emptiness.

SOGA: Act refers to the enlightenment of the Buddha. First of all, the enlightenment of the Buddha is manifested in the form of "act." There is not enlightenment without act. Right faith (*shōshin* 正信) is based upon act. True enlightenment is attained only when there is right faith.

SUZUKI: That's right.

SOGA: That's why the act is so important.

SUZUKI: I agree, but have had one lingering doubt all along. Earlier on you mentioned the Vows of the various Buddhas and their praise of Amida Buddha. Then there was a reference to sentient beings. What is the relationship between the Buddhas and sentient beings?

SOGA: The Buddhas and sentient beings are not separate. They are two and yet not two. In your terms, Dr. Suzuki, this is the logic of *sokuhi* 即非, wherein A is A precisely because it is not-A.

SUZUKI: Let's leave that aside for now. In the Pure Land *sūtras* the various Buddhas appear quite often. Are the Buddhas over there and sentient beings over here? Is it correct to say that, from the standpoint of all the Buddhas, all sentient beings are none other than Buddhas, and from the standpoint of the sentient beings that all the Buddhas enter the realm of the former?

NISHITANI: From the standpoint of the Original Vow of the Tathāgata, it seems to me that Amida has broken through to a more fundamental reality than the various other Buddhas.

SUZUKI: That's right.

NISHITANI: In other words the other Buddhas are varied and limited. It might be a poor choice of words to say that Amida transcends the other Buddhas, but I would like to say that the true form of the Tathāgata must be free of multiplicity, of the characterization "various."

SUZUKI: That's it.

NISHITANI: We can say that the Tathāgata's Original Vow transcends the various other Buddhas. That's why the other Buddhas praise him and exalt his Name.

SUZUKI: At this point don't the sentient beings also appear and praise Amida Buddha in agreement with all the Buddhas?

NISHITANI: From what we've just heard concerning the various Buddhas' praise of Amida Buddha, is it correct to conclude that the Original Vow of the Tathāgata Amida transcends them?

SUZUKI: I feel that transcending the various Buddhas at the same time implies a descent.

Nishitani Keiji with Suzuki Daisetsu, Kaneko Daiei and Soga Ryōjin

NISHITANI: Transcendence of the various Buddhas simultaneously implies that the Vow enters them, but this doesn't account for the sentient beings. The Original Vow of the Tathāgata enters the Buddhas from a standpoint which transcends them, but must also enter sentient beings. Can we say that they are united through the Vow of the Tathāgata which transcends both?

SUZUKI: That may be the case, but I would like to know where all these Buddhas are.

SOGA: In the *Commentary on the Treatise on the Pure Land*, Tánluán states:

The various Buddhas and Bodhisattvas have two types of *dharmakāya* (Body of Truth), the *dharmakāya* as Dharma-in-itself and the *dharmakāya* in its manifested form. While the two types of *dharmakāya* are different, they are inseparable; while they are one, they are not identical.

SUZUKI: Where are all these Buddhas and Bodhisattvas? Where are they?

SOGA: What?

SUZUKI: I don't care about scriptural passages; where are they?

SOGA: The various Buddhas are right here.

SUZUKI: Where?

SOGA: Here, right here.

SUZUKI: Where's that? They're right here, aren't they?

SOGA: Yes, right here. "Here" refers to this room. In the *Vimalakīrtinirdeśa-sūtra* all the Buddhas are said to be in the Dharma Hall of the layman Vimalakīrti.

SUZUKI: Everyone enters this room including you and I.

SOGA: Yes, and all sentient beings and Buddhas also enter the Dharma Hall of Vimalakīrti. That's the way it is.

SUZUKI: But in the *Larger Sūtra of Eternal Life* there are innumerable Buddha-lands, and the various Buddhas and bodhisattvas do this and that, all of which is very difficult to understand. I wonder if we can't just...

SOGA: It is incomprehensible to humans. It is the Ocean of the Tathāgata's Wisdom-Vow...

SUZUKI: Isn't it a human being who is saying that it's incomprehensible to humans?

SOGA: It is a human being, but one who is seeking to grasp something beyond his comprehension.

SUZUKI: No, that's not it. One understands when one sees that which cannot be understood as incomprehensible.

SOGA: One isn't satisfied with understanding (laughter). It is human nature to seek understanding of that which is beyond understanding.

SUZUKI: Certainly.

SOGA: So one can't say, "Don't make incomprehensible statements." Human wisdom will come to a halt if we cease to utter the incomprehensible.

SUZUKI: That's right, but... (laughter)

SOGA: Human wisdom becomes limitless through seeking to know the unknown.

The Form and Content of Wisdom

NISHITANI: I don't understand this very well, but it seems to me that the Tathāgata is that which is present.

SOGA: In Huáyán Buddhism, it is said that each of the Three Periods (past, present, and future) contains the Three Periods. The past contains all three, and the present and future as well. These are referred to as the Nine Periods. The nine together constitute the Great Present. Counted separately, the Nine periods and the Great Present are called the Ten Periods.

NISHITANI: Perhaps this Great Present is what I'm talking about.

SOGA: All nine together constitute the present.

NISHITANI: Yes.

SOGA: The one who realizes the present as the synthesis of the nine is called the Buddha.

SUZUKI: That's right.

SOGA: The Buddha. We humans cannot understand this.

SUZUKI: It's useless to say that we can't understand, since we have this understanding, don't we? (laughter)

SOGA: No, we actually don't understand, but we remain unfulfilled as long as we don't.

NISHITANI: Dr. Suzuki asked where the various Buddhas and bodhisattvas were. This "where" also refers to the Great Present...

SOGA: The Absolute Present.

SUZUKI: Yes, the Absolute Present. What is our conclusion, then? Do we understand or not? We already understand, don't we?

SOGA: I know you would like to conclude that we do understand (laughter), but this desire to understand has been grasped only schematically. We've only seen the scheme. We haven't seen the contents, just the form.[22]

SUZUKI: We've grasped its form, but not the contents…

SOGA: Not the contents. Only the Buddha grasps the contents.

NISHITANI: I suppose that's true.

SOGA: Humans think they understand when they see merely the form, but this does not constitute true understanding. This is acquired for the first time when the entire contents are grasped. This failure to understand the contents is described in the scriptures: "(To grasp) the three thousand dharmas in terms of principle is ignorance." This is the realm of *avidyā*, ignorance (laughter). Humans feel that they understand when they see the form, but this is just ignorance.

NISHITANI: But the form must somehow be related to the contents. Unless the contents are included in some way…

SOGA: One may say that the form must already include the contents, but these are just words, and the contents are not really contained in mere understanding.

NISHITANI: That's what happens if we are only concerned with humans.

SOGA: The Buddha contains everything, (laughter). "Act" is established for the first time when the contents are included. When the content has been grasped, it is realized as act. Not principle, but act.

SUZUKI: This is *Namu Amida Butsu*, right Dr. Soga?

SOGA: Yes.

SUZUKI: Does each utterance of the Nembutsu constitute this act, or are they really just form?

SOGA: The Nembutsu is act.

SUZUKI: Act, but one by one, correct?

SOGA: It is simply act. In the "Chapter on Act" in the *Kyōgyōshinshō* it is described as "Great Act."

SUZUKI: Act.

SOGA: Great Act.

---

22. Ed. We should recall that in the original Japanese there would be no distinction between singular and plural for an abstract noun like "content/s," and so the meaning of the exchange might come out more clearly if "content" were used in the singular instead of the plural. This becomes clear in Soga's concluding comments below.

SUZUKI: Great Act, right?

SOGA: It embraces all acts.

SUZUKI: All acts... In that case, everything is grasped by *Namu Amida Butsu*.

SOGA: What do you mean?

SUZUKI: Everything is understood by one utterance of *Namu Amida Butsu*. All the Buddhas exalt it, don't they?

SOGA: That's right. Everything is grasped, but only in principle.

SUZUKI: Not just in principle. You already understand, don't you? When this is done (Dr. Suzuki places his palms together in *gasshō*), all the Buddhas are already singing in praise.

SOGA: That's true, but faith is the essence. Actually it is faith-knowledge (*shinchi* 信知). One knows in faith.

SUZUKI: Yes.

SOGA: One doesn't simply believe, but knows in faith. It is knowledge.

SUZUKI: Yes, faith-knowledge.

SOGA: Deep knowledge in faith, not simply belief. There must be the knowing in faith.

SUZUKI: Faith-knowledge... Our viewpoints seem to differ somewhat, but they are really the same. What I find...

SOGA: In the end what we are really saying amounts to the same thing, because we are human. I have to say, however, that whoever created this term "faith-knowledge" was rather advanced.

SUZUKI: Yes.

SOGA: There's no question that those such as Shàndǎo were a step ahead of where we stand. I came across this term for the first time in reading his writings and would never have come upon it otherwise. In Buddhism faith is faith-knowledge, knowledge of everything in faith.

SUZUKI: Indeed.

SOGA: To know everything. We can say that to know the Tathāgata is to know everything. It is all-embracing wisdom.

SUZUKI: That's right.

SOGA: To know the Buddha is all-embracing wisdom.

NISHITANI: I wonder if it's all right to say, instead of "knowing," that one lives in the Ocean of the Tathāgata's Wisdom, the Ocean of the Great Wisdom (*daichikai* 大智海), or the Ocean of the Wisdom-Vow which was mentioned earlier.

SUZUKI: The Ocean of Wisdom.

SOGA: One returns and enters (*kinyū*) the Ocean of Wisdom. The "*ki*" of "*kinyū*" is the same as the "*ki*" of "*kimyō*" "to take refuge."

SUZUKI: Yes, the "*ki*" of "*kimyō*" And "*nyū*" means "to enter."

NISHITANI: It was said that to know actually means that one does not know, but this leads to the conclusion that we are ignorant.

SOGA: That's not true...

NISHITANI: However, if *Namu Amida Butsu* is the return and entrance into the Ocean of Wisdom...

SOGA: The act, *Namu Amida Butsu*, is the act of returning to and entering the Ocean of Wisdom. This Ocean is ultimately the Pure Land. The Pure Land is the result of the Ocean of Wisdom.

NISHITANI: Since one returns to and enters this Ocean, the Ocean of Wisdom must know...

SUZUKI: That's correct.

SOGA: Yes, it is the Ocean of Wisdom which knows. *Namu Amida Butsu* is itself this Ocean. The Ocean of Wisdom creates the Pure Land as *Namu Amida Butsu*. The Pure Land is borne forth. It is born, created.

(Translated by Mark Unno and Satō Taira)

Synoptic List of Text Titles

This list shows Buddhist texts which are directly referred to by the writers in this book and a few others which may be relevant for the reader.[1] These include texts from the Buddhist Canon, whether in Pāli, Sanskrit or Chinese, and also texts by later Indian, Chinese and Japanese Buddhist commentators, thinkers and teachers. As far as Japanese Buddhists are concerned the normative texts are those of the Chinese Buddhist Canon. This includes not only material which corresponds indirectly to the Theravāda Canon, as well as the major texts of Mahāyāna Buddhism, but much else besides, originating both from India and from China. At the same time, later writings by Japanese exponents such as Hōnen and Shinran took on an authoritative aura of their own.

In the early twentieth century the manner of referring to all such texts varied considerably. As far as the older ones are concerned, Japanese writers were usually thinking of them as known to them in a Chinese form, which may not be exactly the same as a corresponding Sanskrit or Pāli text, if indeed there is one. On the other hand modern scholarship had by then set in train a tendency to use Sanskrit titles as a kind of *lingua franca*, even to the extent of reconstituting or in effect inventing such titles retrospectively. A classic case, mentioned in the Conventions on Names, Titles and Scripts, is *The Awakening of Faith in the Mahāyāna* (大乘起信論 *Dàshèng qǐxìn lùn*, Japanese: *Daijōkishin-ron*) which was provided with a Sanskrit title on the grounds of a pious ascription to Aśvaghoṣa, even though modern scholarship agrees that it has only ever existed in Chinese. Our Japanese authors also took different decisions about how to refer to other texts which lie behind many of their thoughts. The titles are sometimes translated, sometimes provided with the original characters, and so on.

Out of respect to the authors, the policy adopted in this volume is to leave the references in the various articles basically as they were. Where confusion might arise about which text is meant, an indication is given in square brackets or an editorial footnote has been added. One important reform has been carried out however: the Pāli and Sanskrit transliterations have been standardized in accordance with modern practice.

Since non-standard or abbreviated titles may still leave some difficulties, an integrated list of texts has been devised for cross-checking.

---

1. The list is therefore similar to, but not identical with that published in the first volume of this series. A consolidated list is planned for a later occasion.

Synoptic List of Text Titles

In most cases a title is first correlated with its Japanese name (i.e. the Japanese pronunciation for its name in Chinese characters). This leads to a main entry in larger print, showing the main variants in the relevant languages.[2] Not all variants in the small print are repeated in the main entries, since they are often just alternative attempts at translation made in those early days. In the case of a number of texts, especially those in Pāli, it would be misleading to add gratuitous references in Chinese or Japanese. In such cases there is no main Japanese entry and other languages appear as main entries, by default. The cross-references only arise when related texts are in fact referred to, e.g. Āgama > Agon. When no Chinese pronunciation is given, the implication is that (although a suitably educated Chinese person could read it, and would probably imagine a Chinese pronunciation for the title) the text is a Japanese one.

The listing of a Sanskrit title in a main entry indicates that there is a corresponding Sanskrit text, but it should be remembered that such titles are generic, referring to various manuscripts of varying length, and do not definitively identify an original text for any particular Chinese version. In cases where an identification is particularly imprecise, or was even simply invented retrospectively, a Sanskrit form may be given in brackets. Where Pāli texts are listed without a further cross-reference, the symbol (P) is added. Pāli texts do not usually occur in the main entries except with a "cf." because they did not form the basis of Chinese versions.

In this index, Japanese titles are not separated out into component parts. Endings such as -ron (treatise), -kyō (*sūtra*), -ge (verses) or -san (hymn) are normally thought of as being an integral part of the title. The transcription of Chinese titles on the other hand does provide subdivisions, and this may be helpful for the understanding of the relevant Japanese readings as well. Sanskrit and Pāli endings such as –*nikāya*, -*śāstra*, -*sūtra* and -*sutta* are hyphenated, following widespread usage.

In sum, the pattern for the main entries is as follows:
Romanized Japanese title / title in characters / romanized Chinese for Chinese texts (In *sūtra* names 経 also stands for Chinese 經)
Correct Sanskrit form of title if any
[non-standard, presumed or invented Sanskrit; or comment thereon]
Title in English (by ..*author's name*..)
[non-standard or abbreviated form, or other comment]

---

2. This corresponds to the method for multilingual lists devised by the present editor and first presented in Christoph Kleine, Li Xuetao and Michael Pye (eds.), *A Multilingual Dictionary of Chinese Buddhism. Mehrsprachiges Wörterbuch des chinesischen Buddhismus* (with Appendix and Corrections), iudicium-Verlag (for: Haus der japanischen Kultur (EKŌ), Düsseldorf), 1999. The difference is that there the "home language" is Chinese, and here it is Japanese, but the principle is the same.

Synoptic List of Text Titles

Abhidhammattha-sangaha (P)

Abidatsumadaijōkyō 阿毘達磨大乗経 Āpídámódàshèng jīng
   [Abhidharma Sūtra]
   [known only from citations in the *Shōdaijōron* 摂大乗論]

Abidatsumashutara 阿毘達磨修多羅 Āpídámóxiūduōluó
   [no known sutra of this name: = Abidatsumadaijōkyō]
   [Abhidharma Sūtra]
   [known only from citations in the *Shōdaijōron* 摂大乗論]

Āgama > Agon

Agon 阿含 Āhán
   Āgama
   [general term for Chinese equivalents to the Āgamas, cf. Zōagon, Zōitsuagon]

Aṅguttara-nikāya (P)
   The Gradual Sayings
   [see also Zōitsuagonkyō]

Amidakyō 阿弥陀経 Āmítuó jīng
   Sukhāvatīvyūha-sūtra
   [N.B. In Sanskrit this sūtra bears the same name as the "larger" one]
   Amida Sūtra
   [Smaller Sukhāvatīvyūha-sūtra]
   [Amitāyus Sūtra]

Amitāyurdhyāna-sūtra > Kanmuryōjukyō

Amitāyus Sūtra > Amidakyō

Ānlè jí > Anrakushū

Anrakushū 安楽集 (安樂集) Ānlè jí
   Collection on Peaceful Ease (by Dàochuò)

Avataṃsaka-sūtra > Kegonkyō

Awakening of Faith in the Mahāyāna > Daijōkishinron

Bonmōkyō 梵網経 Fànwǎn jīng
   Brahmā's Net Sūtra
   [Brahmajāla Sūtra]

Brahmā's Net Sūtra > Bonmōkyō

Bosatsukaikyō 菩薩戒經 Púsàjiè jīng
   The Sūtra of Bodhisattva Precepts
   [T1484 =10th chapter of Bonmōkyō/Fànwǎnjīng]

Brahmaparipṛcchā-sūtra

Bṛhadāraṇyaka Upaniṣad

Chāndogya Upaniṣad

Chéngwéishí lùn > Jōyuishikiron

Synoptic List of Text Titles

Chinese Āgama > Zōagon

Chūron 中論 Zhōng lùn
    Middle Treatise
    [i.e. a commentary on the "Middle Stanzas," verses by Nāgārjuna, referred to in Sanskrit as Madhyamakakārikā or on the basis of Tibetan sources as Mūlamadhyamakakārikā, the latter being rendered Konponchūronge in Japanese]
    [Madhyamika-śāstra: may refer to Chūron (not in Sanskrit) or to Prasannapadā, a similar, later commentary by Candrakīrti]

Commentary on the Treatise on the Pure Land > Ōjōronchū

Commentary on [Vasubandhu's] Treatise on the Pure Land > Ōjōronchū

Dàshèng qǐxìn lùn > Daijōkishinron

Daiamidakyō 大阿弥陀経 Dàāmítuó jīng
    Larger Sūtra on Amitābha

Daichidoron 大智度論 Dàzhìdù lùn
    Treatise on the Perfection of Great Insight
    [Great Treatise on the Perfection of Wisdom]
    [Great Treatise]
    [Mahāprajñāpāramitā-śāstra, no known Sanskrit text]

Daijōkishinron 大乗起信論 Dàshèng qǐxìn lùn (or Dàchéng qǐxìn lùn)
    Awakening of Faith in the Mahāyāna

Daikyō > Daimuryōjukyō

Daimuryōjukyō 大無量寿経 Dàwúliàngshòu jīng
    Sukhāvatīvyūha-sūtra
    [The Sanskrit title has the divergent meaning of "Sūtra on the Adornment of the Land of Bliss." For a different sūtra with the same Sanskrit name, see Amidakyō.]
    Larger Sūtra on Unlimited Life
    [I.e. on the Buddha of Unlimited Life-span, Amitāyus. Also Larger Amitāyus, Larger Sūtra of Infinite Life, Larger Sūtra on the Buddha of Eternal Life, The Larger Sūtra, etc.. English titles for this sūtra are often imprecise and vary when drawn from Chinese or Sanskrit respectively.]

Daśabhūmika > Jūjūbibasharon

Daśabhūmikavibhāṣā-śāstra > Jūjūbibasharon

Daśabhūmivibhāṣā-śāstra > Jūjūbibasharon

Dàshèng qǐxìn lùn > Daijōkishinron

Dhammapada (P)

Diamond Sūtra > Kongōkyō
    Discourse on the Pure Land > Jōdoron

Dìzàng [púsà] běnyuàn jīng > Jizō[bosatsu]hongankyō

Doctrine, Practice, Faith, and Attainment > Kyōgyōshinshō

Doctrine-Work-Faith-Attainment > Kyōgyōshinshō
Essentials > Yuishinshōmon'i
Essentials of Faith Alone > Yuishinshōmon'i
Fànwǎnjīng > Bonmōkyō
Flower Garland Sūtra > Kegonkyō
Gobunshō 御文章
    Letters of Rennyo (by Rennyo)
    [Gobunshō is the preferred title in the Hongwanji-ha; see also Ofumi]
Godenshō > Honganjishōninden'e
Goichidaikikikigaki > Rennyo Shōnin Goichidaikikikigaki
Hōjisan 法事讃 Fǎshì zàn
    Hymns on the Religious Rite (by Shàndǎo / Zendō)
Hokekyō > Myōhōrengekyō
Honganjishōninden'e 本願寺聖人伝絵
The Honganji Illustrated Scroll of the Shōnin's Life (by Kakunyo)
    [Godenshō 御伝鈔 is an abbreviated title]
Húayán jīng > Kegonkyō
Hymns on the Last Age > Shōzōmatsuwasan
Hymns on the Three Dharma-Ages > Shōzōmatsuwasan
Ichimaikishōmon 一枚起請文
    One-Sheet Document (by Hōnen)
Ichinentanenmon'i 一念多念文意
    The Meaning of Once-Calling and Many-Calling (by Shinran)
Ichinentanenshōmon 一念多念証文
    Notes on Once-Calling and Many-Calling (by Shinran)
Inscriptions > Songō shinzō meimon
Jīngāng jīng > Kongōkyō
Jizō[bosatsu]hongankyō 地蔵[菩薩]本願経 Dìzàng [Púsà] běnyuàn jīng
    Kṣitigarbhapraṇidhāna-sūtra
    Sūtra on the Original Vows of Jizō [Bosatsu]
    Sūtra on the Original Vows of Kṣitigarbha
Jōdoron 浄土論 Jìngtǔ lùn
    Treatise on the Pure Land (by Vasubandhu)
    [Discourse on the Pure Land]
Jōdoronchū 浄土論註 Jìngtǔlùn zhù
    Commentary on the Treatise on the Pure Land (by Tánluán)
    [The treatise is by Vasubandhu. Also called Ōjōronchū 往生論註.
    Full name: Muryōjukyōubadaisharonganshōgechū 無量寿経優婆提舎願生
    偈註 Wúliàngshòu jīng yōpótíshè yuànshēng jìzhù]
Jōdoshinyōshō 浄土真要鈔

Synoptic List of Text Titles

    Comment on the Essentials of the Pure Land (by Zonkaku)
Jōdowasan 浄土和讃
    Songs on the Pure Land (by Shinran)
Jōyuishikiron 成唯識論 Chéngwéishí lùn
    [Vijñānamātrasiddhi-śāstra, no known Sanskrit text]
    Treatise on the Attainment of Consciousness Only
Jūjūbibasharon 十住毘婆沙論 Shízhù pípóshā lùn
    [Daśabhūmi(ka)vibhāṣā-śāstra, no known Sanskrit text]
    Treatise on the Explanation of the Ten Stages
Kangyōsho > Kanmuryōjukyōsho
Guānjīngshù > Guānwúliàngshòu jīng shù
Kanmuryōjukyō 観無量寿経 Guānwúliàngshòu jīng
    [Amitāyurdhyāna-sūtra N.B. no known Sanskrit text]
    The Meditation Sūtra
    The Sūtra of Meditation on Amida
    The Sūtra on Visualising the Buddha of Unlimited Life-span
Kanmuryōjukyōsho 観無量寿経疏 Guānwúliàngshòu jīngshù
    Commentary on the Meditation Sūtra (by Shàndǎo / Zendō)
    [Abbreviation: Kangyōsho 観経疏 Guānjīngshù]
Kegonkyō 華厳経 (華嚴經) Húayán jīng
    Avataṃsaka-sūtra
    Flower Garland Sūtra
Kegongokyōshō 華厳五教章 Húayán wǔjiàozhāng
    Chapters on the five teachings of Kegon (Húayán) (by Fǎzàng)
    [Full name Húayán yíshèng jiàoyì fēnqí zhāng 華嚴一乘教義分齊章]
Kegongokyōshōtsūroki 華厳五教章通路記
    Sketch of the chapters on the five teachings of Kegon (by Gyōnen)
    [abbreviated title: Tsūroki]
Kenjōdoshinjitsukyōgyōshōmonrui 顕浄土真実教行証文類
    Collection of Passages Revealing the True teaching, Practice and Enlightenment of the Pure Land (by Shinran)
    [Full title of Kyōgyōshinshō]
Kishinron > Daijōkishinron
Kongōkyō 金剛経 Jīngāng jīng
    The Diamond Sūtra
    Vajracchedikā-sūtra
Konkōmyōkyō 金光明経 Jīnguāngmíng jīng
    Suvarṇaprabhāsottama-sūtra
    Suvarṇaprabhāsa-sūtra
Kōsōwasan 高僧和讃 Hymns on the Patriarchs (by Shinran)
Kṣitigarbhapraṇidhāna-sūtra > Jizō[bosatsu]hongankyō

Kyōgyōshinshō 教行信証
    Teaching, Practice, Faith and Enlightenment (by Shinran)
    [Doctrine, Practice, Faith, and Attainment]
    [Doctrine-Work-Faith-Attainment]
    [For full title > Kenjōdoshinjitsukyōgyōshōmonrui]

Larger Amitāyus > Daimuryōjukyō

Larger Sukhāvatīvyūha-sūtra > Daimuryōjukyō

Larger Sūtra > Daimuryōjukyō

Larger Sūtra on Amitābha > Daimuryōjukyō

Larger Sūtra of Infinite Life > Daimuryōjukyō

Larger Sūtra of Eternal Life > Daimuryōjukyō

Letters of Rennyo > Ofumi

Lotus Sūtra > Myōhōrengekyō

Madhyamakakārikā > Chūron

Madhyamika-śāstra > Chūron

Madhyāntavibhāgakārikā

Madhyāntavibhāga

Mūlamadhyamakakārikā > Chūron

Mahāprajñāpāramitāśāstra > Daichidoron

Mahāyānasaṃgraha > Shōdaijōron

Mahāyānasūtrālaṃkāra

Maitreya Upaniṣad

Miàofǎ liánhuā jīng > Myōhōrengekyō

Mūlamadhyamakakārikā > Chūron

Myōhōrengekyō 妙法蓮華経 Miàofǎ liánhuá jīng
    Saddharmapuṇḍarīka-sūtra
    Lotus Sūtra
    [Hokekyō 法華経: widely used shorter name for the Lotus Sūtra]

Nankaikikinaihōden 南海寄帰内法伝 Nánhǎi jìguī nèifǎ zhuàn
    Record of the Journey across the Southern Sea to seek the Dharma (by Yìjìng)

Notes Lamenting Differences > Tannishō

Ofumi 御文
    Letters of Rennyo (by Rennyo)
    [Ofumi is the preferred title in the Ōtani-ha, see also Gobunshō]

Ōjōjōdoron 往生浄土論
    [=Jōdoron]

Ōjōraisan 往生礼讃 Wǎngshēng lǐzàn
    Hymns in Adoration of Rebirth (by Shàndǎo / Zendō)

Synoptic List of Text Titles

Ōjōraisange 往生礼讃偈 Wǎngshēng lǐzàn jì
    Hymns in Adoration of Rebirth (by Shàndǎo / Zendō)
    [=Ōjōraisan]

Ōjōronchū 往生論註 Wǎngshēnglùn zhù
    Commentary on the Treatise on Rebirth (by Tánluán)
    [The treatise is by Vasubandhu. Also called Jōdoronchū 浄土論註.
    Full name: Muryōjukyōubadaisharonganshōgechū 無量寿経優婆提舎願生偈註 Wúliàngshòu jīng yōpótíshè yuànshēng jìzhù]

Ōjōyōshū 往生要集
    Teachings Essential for Rebirth (by Genshin)
    [A Collection of Essentials on Rebirth in the Pure Land]

Once Calling > Ichinentanenmon'i

Once-calling and Many-calling > Ichinentanenmon'i

One Sheet Document > Ichimaikishōmon

Prajñāpāramitā-śāstra > Daichidoron

Rennyo Shōnin Goichidaikikikigaki 蓮如上人御一代記聞書
    Sayings and Doings of the Great Life of Rennyo Shōnin (author unknown)

Saddharmapuṇḍarīka-sūtra > Myōhōrengekyō

Saṁyutta-nikāya (P)

San'amidabutsuge 讃阿彌陀佛偈 Zàn āmítuófó jì
    Verses in praise of Amida Buddha (by Tánluán)

Senjakuhongannenbutsushū 選択本願念仏集
Selected Passages on the Nenbutsu of the Original Vow (by Hōnen)
    [short form: Senjakushū, pronounced Senchakushū in Jōdo Shin-shū contexts]

Senjakushū > Senjakuhongannenbutsushū

Shikantaii 止観大意 (止觀大意) Zhǐguān dàyì
    The Essential Meaning of Meditation (by Zhànrán)

Shōdaijōron 摂大乗論 Shèdàshèng lùn
    Mahāyānasaṃgraha (by Asaṅga)
    Treatise on the Essentials of the Great Vehicle

Shōdaijōronshaku 摂大乗論釈 Shèdàshènglùn shì
    Commentary on the Treatise on the Essentials of the Great Vehicle (by Vasubandhu)

Shōzōmatsuwasan 正像末和讃
    Hymns on the Ages of Dharma (by Shinran)

Shōshinge 正信偈
    Verses on True Faith (by Shinran)
    [widely used abbreviation for Shōshinnenbutsuge]

Shōshinnembutsuge > Shōshinnenbutsuge

Shōshinnenbutsuge 正信念仏偈
    Verses on True Faith in the Nenbutsu (by Shinran)
    [see also Shōshinge]

Shōzōmatsuwasan 正像末和讚
    Hymns on the Three Dharma-Ages (by Shinran)
    [Hymns on the Last Age]

Songōmeimon 尊号銘文
    Inscriptions for the Revered Name (by Shinran)
    [abbreviation for Songōshinzōmeimon]

Songōshinzōmeimon 尊号真像銘文
    Inscriptions for the Revered Name and the Portraits (by Shinran)
    [Notes on the Inscriptions on Sacred Scrolls]
    [Inscriptions]

Sukhāvatīvyūha-sūtra > Daimuryōjukyō

Sūtra of Bodhisattva Precepts > Bosatsukaikyō

Sūtra of Meditation on Amida > Kanmuryōjukyō

Sūtra on Meditation on the Buddha of Eternal Life > Kanmuryōjukyō

Sūtra on the Meditation on Amitāyus > Kanmuryōjukyō

Sūtra of Eternal Life > Daimuryōjukyō

Sūtra of Meditation on Amida > Kanmuryōjukyō

Sūtra on the Great Infinite One > Daimuryōjukyō

Sūtra on the Land of Bliss > Daimuryōjukyō

Suvarṇaprabhāsa-sūtra > Konkōmyōkyō

Tannishō 歎異抄
    Notes Lamenting Differences [recording sayings of Shinran] (by Yuienbō)
    [Tract on Deploring Heterodoxies]

Tract on Deploring Heterodoxies > Tannishō

Treatise on Being Born in the Pure Land > Jōdoron

Treatise on the Pure Land > Jōdoron

Treatise on the Explanation of the Ten Stages > Jūjūbibasharon

Triṃsikā > Yuishikisanjūron

Tsūroki > Kegongokyōshōtsūroki

Vajracchedikā-sūtra > Kongōkyō

Vimalakīrti-nirdeśa > Yuimagyō

Vimalakīrti-sūtra > Yuimagyō

Vinaya-piṭaka (P)

Wasan 和讚
    Songs in Japanese
    [Sometimes short for Jōdowasan, but at the same time a generic term for

the genre which also includes Kōsōwasan and Shōzōmatsuwasan by Shin-
ran]
[Psalms]

Yuimagyō 維摩経 Wéimó jīng
Vimalakīrtī-nirdeśa
The Vimalakīrti Sūtra
[Short for : Yuimakitsushosetsukyō]

Yuimakitsushosetsukyō 維摩詰所説経 Wéimójié sǔoshūo jīng
Vimalakīrtīnirdeśa-sūtra
The Sūtra of the Teaching of Vimalakīrti

Yuishikinijūron 唯識二十論 Wéishí èrshí lùn
Viṃśatikā Vijñaptimātratāsiddhi
[Vijñānamātra]
Treatise on Twenty Verses on Consciousness Only
[Concise Treatise on the Theory of Vijñaptimātratā]

Yuishikisanjūron 唯識三十論 Wéishí sānshí lùn
Triṃsikā Vijñaptimātratāsiddhi
[Vijñānamātra]
Thirty Verses on Consciousness Only
[Concise Treatise on the Theory of Vijñaptimātratā]

Yuishinshōmon'i 唯信鈔文意
Explanations of the Yuishinshō (by Shinran)
Explanations of the Texts of the Commentary on Faith Only
[Essentials of Faith Alone]
[Essentials]

Zàn āmítuófó jì > San'amidabutsuge

Zhǐguān dàyì > Shikantaii

Zōagon(kyō) 雑阿含 (経) Zá āhán (jīng)
[approximate equivalent to Pāli Saṁyutta-nikāya]

Zōitsuagon(kyō) 増一阿含 (経) Zēngyī āhán (jīng)
[approximate equivalent to Pāli Anguttara-nikāya]

Character List for Historical Persons

This list includes characters for the names of historical persons who occur in the main text and a few others of general relevance for the subject matter. A similar list was published in Volume 1 of this series, and a consolidated version is planned for Volume 3.

Indian names follow the pattern: Indian / Chinese / characters / Japanese
    e.g. Aśvaghoṣa Mǎmíng 馬鳴 Memyō

Chinese names follow the pattern: Chinese / characters / Japanese
    e.g. Shàndǎo 善導 Zendō

Korean names are treated similarly with "(Korean)" added.

Japanese names are recognized by having no alternatives
    e.g. Genshin 源信 (942-1071)

Characters shown in brackets are alternative forms for the same character.

Cross references are shown from the derivatives back to the original:

    Chinese to Indian, e.g. Mǎmíng = Aśvaghoṣa
    Japanese to Indian, e.g. Memyō = Aśvaghoṣa
    Japanese to Chinese, eg. Zendō = Shàndǎo 善導

Cross references to alternative Japanese names for the same person are also shown with the symbol = e.g. Dengyō Daishi 伝教大師 = Saichō.

A number of titles are in widespread use for leading figures:

    Kokushi 国師 i.e. "national teacher," as in Kanchi Kokushi 鑑智国師
    Daishi 大師 i.e. "great teacher," as in Dengyō Daishi 伝教大師
    Shōnin 上人 i.e. "saint" or "elevated person", as in Kakunyo Shōnin 覚如上人
    more rarely, Shōnin 聖人 i.e. "saint" or "holy person" as in Shinran Shōnin 親鸞聖人.

Asahara Saiichi 浅原才市 (1851–1933)

Asaṅga (fourth–fifth century CE) Wúzhù 無著 Mujaku

Aśvaghoṣa (first century CE) Mǎmíng 馬鳴 Memyō

Candrakīrti (seventh century) Yùechēng 月称 Gesshō

Chigi = Zhìyǐ

Character List for Historical Persons

Chéngguān 澄観 Chōkan (737-787)
Chōkan = Chéngguān

Dàochuò 道綽 Dōshaku (562-645)
Dengyō Daishi 伝教大師 = Saichō
Donran = Tánluán
Dōshaku = Dàochuò
Ennin 圓仁 (円仁) = Jikaku Daishi

Fǎzàng 法蔵 (法藏) Hōzō (643-712)

Genju = Xiánshǒu (= Fǎzàng)
Genkū 源空 = Hōnen Shōnin
Genshin 源信 (942-1071)
Gesshō = Candrakīrti
Gyōnen 凝念 (1240-1321)

Hōnen Shōnin 法然上人 (1133-1212)
Hōzō = Fǎzàng
Hyakujō = Hyakujō Ekai
Hyakujō Ekai 百丈懐海 (749-814)

Ippen Shōnin 一遍上人 (1239-1289)

Jízàng 吉蔵 Kichizō (549-623)

Kakunyo Shōnin 覚如上人 (1270-1351)
Kanchi Kokushi 鑑智国師 = Shōkū
Kichizō = Jízàng
Kōbō Daishi 弘法大師 (774-835)
Kūkai 空海 = Kōbō Daishi
Kūya Shōnin 空也上人 (903-972)

Línjì 臨濟 (臨済) Rinzai (d. 867)
Lóngshù = Nāgārjuna

Mǎmíng = Aśvaghoṣa
Memyō = Aśvaghoṣa
Mujaku = Asaṅga

Nāgārjuna (second–third century CE) Lóngshù 龍樹（竜樹）Ryūju
Nichiren 日蓮 (also Nichiren Shōnin 日蓮聖人) (1222–1282)

Rennyo Shōnin 蓮如上人 (1415–1499)
Rinzai = Línjì
Ryūju = Nāgārjuna

Saichō 最澄 (767–822)
Seishimaru 勢至丸 = Hōnen Shōnin (as a child)
Seshin = Vasubandhu
Shàndǎo 善導 Zendō (613–681)
Shinran Shōnin 親鸞聖人 (1173–1262)
Shíchānántúo = Śikṣānanda
Shìqīn = Vasubandhu
Shōkū 証空 (1177–1247)
Śikṣānanda Shíchānántúo 實叉難陀 (J. Jisshananda 実叉難陀)

Tánluán 曇鸞 Donran (476–542)
Tannen = Zhànrán
Tendai Daishi = Zhìyǐ

Vasubandhu (fourth–fifth century CE) Shìqīn 世親 Seshin

Wúzhù = Asaṅga

Xiánshǒu 賢首 Genju (643–712) = Fǎzàng

Yìjìng 義淨 Gijō 義浄 (635–713)

Zendō = Shàndǎo
Zhànrán 湛然 (711–782) Tannen
Zhìyǐ 智顗 Chigi (538–597)
Zonkaku 存覚 (1290–1373)

Full Details of Original Publication

If the title of the article has been edited for the present volume, the original title is given immediately above the other publication details

Bloom, Alfred: Shinran's Way in the Modern World
 (also shown as "Shinran's Way in Modern Society")
 The Eastern Buddhist 1978 New Series Vol. XI 1, 85–97 (under Views and Reviews)

Buri, Fritz: The Concept of Grace in Paul, Shinran and Luther
 The Eastern Buddhist 1976 New Series Vol. IX 1–2, 21–42

Editors of *The Eastern Buddhist*: Editorial
 The Eastern Buddhist 1934 Vol. VI 3, 317–319

Editors of *The Eastern Buddhist*: Editorial
 The Eastern Buddhist 1949 Vol. VIII 1, 1–4

Nishitani, Keiji (moderator) A Dialogue of Shin Buddhism and Zen Buddhism
 (with Suzuki Daisetsu, Kaneko Daiei and Soga Ryōjin)
 Original title: Shinran's World (Suzuki Daisetz, Kaneko Daiei, Soga Ryōjin and Nishitani Keiji (moderator)) (Part I, Part II, Part III)
 1: *The Eastern Buddhist* 1985 New Series Vol. XVIII 1, 105–119
 2: *The Eastern Buddhist* 1986 New Series Vol. XIX 1, 101–117
   (Translated by Mark Unno and Thomas L. Kirchner)
 3. *The Eastern Buddhist* 1986 New Series Vol. XXI 2, 78–94
   (Translated by Mark Unno and Satō Taira)

Kanamatsu, Kenryō: Goodness and Naturalness
 The Eastern Buddhist 1951 Vol. VIII 2, 43–57

Kaneko, Daiei: The Buddhist Doctrine of Vicarious Suffering
 The Eastern Buddhist 1927 Vol. IV 2, 145–161

Kaneko, Daiei: Shin Religion as I Believe it
 The Eastern Buddhist 1951 Vol. VIII 2, 22–42

Kaneko, Daiei: The Meaning of Salvation in the Doctrine of Pure Land Buddhism
 The Eastern Buddhist 1965 New Series Vol. I 1, pp.48–63

Full Details of Original Publication

Pallis, Marco: Nembutsu as Remembrance
The Eastern Buddhist 1977 New Series Vol. X 2, 31–48

Rhys Davids, C.A.F.: The Idea and the Man (a response to Yamabe Shūgaku)
Original title: The Idea and the Man
The Eastern Buddhist 1932 Vol. VI 1, 94–98 (under Correspondence)

Takeuchi, Yoshinori: Shinran and Contemporary Thought
The Eastern Buddhist 1980 New Series Vol. XIII 2, 26–45
(Translated by Jan van Bragt)

Ueda, Yoshifumi: The Mahāyāna Structure of Shinran's Thought (1 and 2)
1: *The Eastern Buddhist* 1984 New Series Vol. XVII 1, 57–78
2: *The Eastern Buddhist* 1984 New Series Vol. XVII 2, 50–54

Ueda, Yoshifumi: Freedom and Necessity in Shinran's Concept of Karma
The Eastern Buddhist 1986 New Series Vol. XIX 1, 76–100
(Translated by Dennis Hirota)

Yamabe, Shūgaku: Mahāyāna Buddhism and Japanese Culture
The Eastern Buddhist 1931 Vol. V 4, 318–323

Yamabe, Shūgaku: A rejoinder to Mrs. Rhys Davids' Comment
The Eastern Buddhist 1932 Vol. VI 1, 99–102 (under Correspondence)

Yamaguchi, Susumu: The Concept of the Pure Land in the Teaching of Nāgārjuna
Original title: The Concept of the Pure Land in Nāgārjuna's Doctrine
The Eastern Buddhist 1966 New Series Vol. I 2, 34–47

A Note on *The Eastern Buddhist*

In 1921 a group of leading Buddhists in Kyōto founded The Eastern Buddhist Society in order to propagate the spirit of Buddhism in the modern world. The leaders of this group were Suzuki Daisetsu (D.T. Suzuki), Sasaki Gesshō, Akanuma Chizen and Yamabe Shūgaku. Suzuki's wife Beatrice Lane Suzuki also played a significant role. These writers were variously interested in Zen Buddhism and Shin Buddhism, and in the relations between these two and earlier forms of Buddhism. They were also concerned with the question of how best to express Buddhist teaching in a world which was becoming increasingly internationalized. The well-known journal *The Eastern Buddhist* was also founded in 1921, being edited in the first instance by Suzuki Daisetsu and Beatrice Lane Suzuki. In the Foreword to the first issue of the journal, Suzuki wrote as follows: "The Society has for its objects the study of Buddhism, the publication of the result of such study, and the propagation of the true spirit of Buddhism." These objectives have found ample expression in the pages of the journal over some ninety years so far. In their fulfilment, the journal carries articles on all aspects of Buddhism as well as English translations of classical texts and writings by modern Buddhist thinkers.

While the society became most widely known for *The Eastern Buddhist* it has also encouraged many other projects such as the translation of Buddhist texts and the arrangement of seminars and lectures. Its main office is housed in Ōtani University, Kyōto, and its researchers benefit from the fine library holdings which are easily accessible there. There is also a close connection with the Higashi Honganji and the leading branch of Shin Buddhism (Ōtani-ha) which is based there. At the same time the approaches of both the society and of the journal have always been open to, and widely appreciative of various aspects of the Buddhist tradition. It is well known that Suzuki Daisetsu himself was devoted to the Zen tradition, while the traditions and texts of other branches of Mahāyāna Buddhism have frequently been presented as well.

The publication of the journal was interrupted by World War II. It was picked up again in 1949, under the editorship of Suzuki Daisetsu and Sugihira Shizutoshi, but the difficulties of the times led to irregularity of appearance and a new pause in 1958. In 1966 Suzuki Daisetsu passed away, aged 96. *The Eastern Buddhist* was relaunched as a "New Series" in

1967, the first issue constituting a memorial to Suzuki. Thereafter the general editorship passed through various hands, notably Nishitani Keiji (1900–1990), Abe Masao (1915–2006) and and Nagao Gajin (1907–2005). Indeed, quite apart from the editorship, writings by some of the best known names in modern Japanese Buddhist thought may be found in its pages. Increasingly, non-Japanese advisors with excellent reputations in Indian, Japanese and Buddhist studies played supporting roles.

While there has often been a strong interest in Zen, matching the expectations of an international public at particular periods, the presentation of Shin Buddhism has also been actively pursued in the journal. Moreover, Japanese contributors have increasingly been joined by foreigners who have offered translations of texts as well as matters for discussion. If we consider the overall trajectory over many years, it may be said that the balance has shifted from the straightforward presentation of substance in the early years to an emphasis on interaction and dialogue later on. This movement is reflected and celebrated in volumes 1 to 3 of the present series of collected papers. At the same time, the original objectives of the Eastern Buddhist Society have by no means been forgotten, and the overall approach, integrating Buddhist scholarship and thought, is continued by the present editors under the leadership of Yasutomi Shin'ya.

The Eastern Buddhist now looks back on a history of nearly a century and with some interruptions has flourished in an excellent manner. The publication of selections in *Eastern Buddhist Voices* is a collaborative project designed to celebrate the 90th anniversary of the foundation of The Eastern Buddhist Society. Congratulations!

Index

Abhidhammattha-sangaha 34
Abhidharma 181
Abhidharma-sūtra 181–2
Abidarumadaijōkyō 181
abstract/concrete 236
acitta 180
act 269
Action-Intuition 229
Acts (of Apostles) 91–2, 97
Addison, Prof. 41
agada 126
Āgama/s 28–9, 33
ālayavijñāna 139
alienation 132–3
America 6, 213
Amida 47–52, 57–8, 67–72, 76–81,
　　87, 93–6, 98–101, 103–4, 140,
　　149–150, 152–3, 186, 196, 202–3,
　　205, 210–1, 235, 237
　Buddha 6, 75, 88, 90, 127, 175, 198,
　　204–5, 252–3
　Buddhism 95, 105
　Tathāgata 67, 70, 73, 198
　See also Amitābha
Amidaization 95–6
Amidism 98
amitābha 67, 75
Amitābha (Buddha) 6, 47, 67, 111, 113,
　　117–8
　See also Amida
amitāyus 67, 75
Amitāyus 67
anātman 167
anātmatā 139
Aṅguttara-nikāya 33
Anglo-German school 3
anjin 235
Ānlè jí 253
Anna 91

antinomianism 72
anupalambha 180
apocalyptic/ism 88
apratiṣṭhita-nirvana 174
apriori-self 24
Āryadeva 183
Asahara Saichi 175, 196
asaṃskṛta 139
Asaṅga 139, 179, 181–3, 251
Aśoka 114
āśrayaparāvṛtti 182
Aśvaghoṣa xv
ātman 33
attainment 132
attan 33–4
authenticity xv, 152–5
Avalokiteśvara 23, 84, 91, 110
Avataṃsaka-sūtra 15–8, 20, 25
　See also Kegonkyō
avidyā 62
awakening 193
Awakening of Faith in the Mahāyāna xv,
　　193
　See also Daijōkishinron
āyatana/s 164

Bandō Shōjun 7
Barth, Karl 95, 216, 223
bhakti 114
Bible 88, 217, 245
Biblical 100, 102
bīja 179
birth 185–8, 212
　See also *ōjō*; rebirth
birth-and-death 202
bishop 6, 215
Bloch, Ernst 216
Bloom, Alfred 9–10
bodai 236

Index

bodhi 24
Bo tree 163
bodhi 176–7
Bodhi Tree 163
bodhisattva/s xiii, 272
Bodhisattva 15–25, 107–9, 111–2
Bodhisattva-ship/hood 16, 110
bonbu 175, 203
bonshin 201
Bonhoeffer, Dietrich 12, 223–4
bonnō-joku 49
Brahmā 161–2, 168
Brahman 127
Brahmaparipṛcchā-sūtra 181–3
Bṛhadāraṇyaka Upaniṣad 34
Buddha xiii, 107–8, 121, 140–1, 148–52, 154, 159, 173
  Buddhas/buddhas xiii, 126, 171, 228, 271–2
  land/s 48–50, 265
  mind 201
  of Infinite Light 110
  World-honoured one 182
buddha-anusmṛti (buddhānusmṛti) 77
Buddhahood 110–1, 142–3
Buddhaization 103
Buddha-nature 38
buddhatā 38, 236
Buddhism 124–7, 130
Buddhist:
  concept 144
  perspective 144
Buddhist-Christian relations 12, 87–105
Bultmann, Rudolf 12, 216–8, 224–7
Buri, Fritz 8–10
Burma 35
busshin 201
busshō 236
Butschkus, H. 87
byōdo 48

calculation 155, 208–9
California 6
calling 50–2, 262
Candrakīrti 163

Catholic (Church) 12, 87, 89, 90, 95
causality 143, 145–7, 159
causation 8, 140, 142
Central Asia 9
cessation 48, 50, 55
Ceylon 35
Chāndogya Upaniṣad 33
Chan Wingsit 126
Chéngguān 16
Chenrezig 110–3
chie 235–7
chikai 237–9, 246, 262
Chikushi Jogakuen 11
China 4, 38, 40, 43
  Chǔ 124
Chinese xv
  characters 235
  way of thinking 236–8, 243
  Zen 125
Chōkan 16–7, 19–21, 25
Christ 87, 89, 92–6, 98, 100, 103, 105
Christian thought 237–9
Christianity 87, 92–3, 102–5, 117
Christianization 95, 103
Chǔ 124
church 6
Chūron 163
citta 34
class conflict 261
Commentary on the Treatise on the Pure Land 272
Commentary on Vasubandhu's Treatise on the Pure Land 65
Commentary on the Meditation Sūtra 64, 68
comparative hermeneutics 4, 9
comparative religion 10
comparison 10
compassion 63, 71, 110, 158
confessing faith 163
Confucianism/ists 8, 128
consciousness 118
contemplation 161–2
conversion 158
Coomaraswamy, Ananda 10
Corinthians I (Epistle to) 92

Corinthians II (Epistle to) 91–2
Cox, Harvey 12, 214, 216

Dàchéng qǐxìn lùn xv
Daichidoron 179
daichikai 275
Daijōkishinron xv
Daimuryōjukyō 67
  See also Larger Sukhāvatīvyūha (Sūtra)
Dalai Lama 112, 114
dāna 108
Dàochuò 253
Daśabhūmikavibhāṣā-śāstra 163
daśabhūmi 163
dead 40
death of God theology 216
defilement 49
degeneration 40
delusion 62
demythologization 117, 216
Dessì, Ugo 1
devil 91
Dhamma/dhamma xiii, 34
Dhammapada 145
Dharma xiii, 38, 59, 63–5, 240–1
dharma/s 270, 274
Dharma body 241–2
  See also dharmakāya
  See also hosshin
Dharmākara (Bodhisattva) 108–9, 111, 115, 117–10, 153, 170, 237, 252, 255–7, 264–8
Dharmākara-bhikṣu 25
dharmakāya 38, 139–40, 180, 184, 189–90, 198–201, 203, 207, 272
  See also Dharma body
  See also hosshin
dharmatā 29, 236
dhātus 164
dhikr 108
dhyāna 108
Diamond Sūtra 178
disciples 133–4
discipline 130–1

discrimination:
  mental 179–182, 236, 241
  social 1
dō 235–6
Doctrine, Practice, Faith, and Attainment 75
  See also Kyōgyōshinshō
Dōgen 174, 194
dokkaku 162
Donran 64
  See also Tánluán

Eastern Buddhist Society 42, 44, 87
East/West 243–4
Ebeling, Gerhard 224
Echigo (province) 131
Eckhart, Meister 118
editorial 4
education 4
ego 123, 127
eighteenth promise 98
eighteenth vow 261, 266
eighteen dhātus 164
eightfold path/way 35, 43, 116, 120
ekō 228
emptiness 35, 139, 164, 166–9, 177–8, 242–3, 269–70
encounter 229
enlightenment 15, 17, 43, 108, 158, 162–3, 193, 257
  Tree of 163
Episcopal Theological School 41
equality 48
eschatology 105
Eshinni 132
Essentials of Faith Alone 173, 186, 198–9, 210
Eternal Life 47
ethics 1, 101, 128
evil:
  acts/deeds 21–2, 141, 145–7
  karma/-ic 25, 140, 141, 145–151, 155, 158
existentialist 135
  philosophy 217

Index

Existenz 218–9, 224

Fabre 62
faith 126
faith-knowledge 275
Father 84
Fǎzàng 16, 192
final moment 196
  See also *rinjū*
First World War 5
five:
  aggregates 139, 164
  skandha/s 164
  True Vows 259–260
flesh 226
form/emptiness 240, 242
formless/ness 202–4
forty-eight vows 48, 23, 252, 256–7,
    259–62, 265
Fourfold, see *Geviert*
Fourfold Noble Truth 43
Franco-Belgian school 4
Frankl, Victor 130
free will 145–7
fruits 71
Fuchs, Ernst 224

Galatians (Epistle to) 91, 97
gan 237–8
  See also vow
ganriki jinen 148
gasshō 275
gāthā 163
Gautama (Buddha) 125
  See also Buddha (the Buddha);
    Gotama
gedatsu 81
Genju 16–7, 20–1, 25
Genkū 134
  See also Hōnen
Genshin 250
gensō (*gensō-ekō*) 56–7, 128, 228, 244
Germany 40
Gesshō 163
geta 175

Geviert 219, 226, 229
Gobunshō 150
God 42, 88–9, 92, 97, 100, 103, 105,
    214–5, 218, 223
  Kingdom of 89, 94, 104
  God's vow 239
gōdōjinen 148
Goichidaikikikigaki 150
goodness 76, 84
good deeds 78
Goshōsokushū 156
Gospel 10, 224
Gotama 33, 35, 37–8
  See also Gautama (Buddha); Buddha
    (the Buddha)
grace 9, 10, 87–8, 90–2, 96, 99, 101–5
grace-monism 96, 98
gratitude 191
great awakening 108
Guénon, René 10
gyakutoku 237
gyō 247, 267
Gyōnen 193

hakarai 156–8
hannya 236, 240
Heart Sūtra 118
Hebrews (Epistle to) 97
Hegel, Friedrich 249
Heidegger, Martin 217–9
hell/s 111, 270
Hellenistic 89
Hepburn system xiv
hermeneutics 224
Hiei (Mount) 130, 221
Higashi (Eastern) Honganji
  See Cover and Frontispiece
Hīnayāna (Buddhism) 27, 29, 33, 36,
    90, 105, 143, 174
Hīnayānism 36
Hinduism 127, 129
Hirota, Dennis 140, 159, 212
hō 235
hōben 237
Hokekyō

See Saddharmapuṇḍarīka-sūtra
Holy, the 223
Hōnen (Shōnin) 11, 65, 69, 78, 90, 109, 120, 131, 174–5, 189, 265, 270
honest to God 214–5
hongan 237, 246, 250
  See also Original Vow
Honganji/Hongwanji 9
  See also Higashi (Eastern) Honganji; Nishi (Western) Honganji (Hongwanji)
hope 237
hope principle 216
hosshin 242
hosshō 236
hour of death
  See *rinjū*
Huáyán 183, 192, 194, 273

Ichimaikishōmon 69, 77
Ichinentanenmon'i 148
  See also Once-calling and Many-calling
iconoclasm 125
idealism 259
ignorance 62
Inagaki, Hisao 119
India 114
  politics 124
individualism 129
inga 8, 148
Inscriptions 173, 195–6,
interdependent origination 161, 165, 170
  See also pratītyasamutpāda
invocation 113
Ireland 124
I/Thou 193, 218, 227, 264
Ich-Will 148

jakumetsu 48
Japan 38, 40, 43
Jaspers, Karl 148, 229
Jātaka tales 16, 25, 107,
Jesus (Christ) 223, 225
jewel 112

Jewish 88–9, 92
  Jewish Christianity 87, 93
  See also Judaism
jinen 7, 79, 148, 202–4, 209–10
jinen hōni 129, 202–3
jinshin 149
jiri 56
jiri funi 194
jiriki 77, 83, 95
  See also self-power
Jízàng 183, 194, 247
jñāna 66, 167
jōdo 49, 78
Jōdoronchū 268
Jōdo Shin (–shū or sect) 9, 119, 121
  See also Shin Buddhism
Jōdowasan 81
  See also Wasan
Judaism 87, 89
  See also Jewish
Jūjūbibasharon 163, 169

Kamakura era 130
kana xiv
Kanamatsu Kenryō 6–8, 10
Kaneko, Daiei 3, 5–6, 12
Kangyōsho 64
kanji xiv
Kanmuryōjukyō xv
  See also Sūtra on the Meditation on Amitāyus
Kanmuryōjukyōsho 64
Kannon 84, 110
Kant, Immanuel 249
Kantō 131
karma 15, 21, 25, 53, 58, 64, 117, 139–149, 153, 155
  law of 121
karman 164
karmic evil 153–9, 205, 208–10
karuṇā 63, 94, 167
kata sarka 96
kartṛ 164
Kegonkyō (*Kegon sūtra*) 15
kendō 185

Index

ken-joku 49
kerygma 224–5
kie 254
Kierkegaard, Søren 223
ki/hō 235, 261
killing 157
kimyō 268, 276
kinyū 268–9, 276
Kiyozawa, Manshi 69, 70
kleśa 62 170
Kōbō (Daishi) 40
komu 81
Kōsōwasan 81, 141, 150–1, 251, 268
Kōya (Mount, Kōyasan) 40
kṣānti 108
kṣatriya 33
Kṣitigarbha 23
Kumārajīva 166
kumāra/s 33
Kwannon 111
   See also Kannon
kyō 247
Kyōgyōshinshō xiv, 47, 65, 70, 75, 81,
   87, 93, 97–8, 10, 126, 132, 13, 176,
   228, 235, 240–1, 246, 248, 251, 259
kyōrigyōka 269
Kyōto 10, 12, 132
Kyōto School 12
kyūsai 61

laity 173
lay and monk 173–5
lakṣaṇa 182, 207
Lancaster 87
Larger Sukhāvatīvyūha (Sūtra) 47–8, 78
   See also *Daimuryōjukyō*
Larger Sūtra 67
   See also *Daimuryōjukyō*
   Larger Sūtra on Amitābha 75
   Larger Sūtra of Eternal Life 167, 170,
      229, 255–6, 259, 261, 272
laukikavyavahāra 165
law 97
leap of faith 156
Letters (of Shinran) 148, 173, 186, 202

   See also *Mattōshō*
lineage 251
Línjì 125
Lokeśvararāja (Buddha) 256, 264–5
lotus 112
Lotus Sūtra
   See *Saddharmapuṇḍarīka-sūtra*
lung 112
Luther, Martin 87–91, 95–105

Mādhyamakakārikā 179
Mādhyamika 162
Madhyāntivibhāga/kārikā 180
Magadha 28
magga 35
magic 127
mahākaruṇā 167
mahāsattva 192–3
Mahāyāna (Buddhism) 3, 9, 11–12,
   27–31, 36–9, 90, 105, 107–8, 110,
   140, 154–5, 161–2, 173–7, 186,
   191–2, 200, 208, 21, 251–3
Mahāyānism/ist 36, 171
Mahāyānasaṃgraha 20, 181
Maitreya (Bodhisattva) 185–6, 193
   See also Miroku
Maitreya (Buddhist thinker) 17, 139,
   179, 189–90, 192
Maitreya Upaniṣad 33
magokoro 248
makoto 248
makoto no kokoro 140, 150
Man 35–6
manas 34
mani 112–4
   walls 114
   wheels 113
mantra 34, 113
Māra 116–7
Marburg 225
Marcel, Gabriel 12, 221
marriage 132
Mattōshō 128, 148
medicine 126
Meiji Restoration 40

Index

Mensching, G. 87
mercy 47–8
merit transfer 244
metanoia 121
metsudo 55
Mikawa (province) 158
Milarepa 108
mind 34, 37
Miroku (Bosatsu) 13
   See also Maitreya (Bodhisattva)
modernity 11
moment of death 195–7
   See also *rinjū*
monastery/monastic 130
monrui 246
morality 22, 49, 53, 76
moral values 36
Mosaic Law 97
Moses 97
Mother 84
Mūlamadhyamakakārikā 162–4
mūlapraṇidhāna 168
music 243
myōkōnin 175
mystery religion 89
mysticism 9
mythology/ical 93, 107, 161, 217

Nāgārjuna (Ryūju) 11, 161–171, 179–81, 183–4, 192, 206, 251–2
Nagoya University 11
name 95
   Name/s (Amida) 75, 228
Namo/Namu 77, 153
Namu Amida Butsu (and variants) 51, 69, 90, 153, 196, 199, 203, 210–11, 222, 227, 229, 235, 257, 266, 269, 274, 276
Nanjō, Bun'yu 238
Nankaikikinaihōden 162
Nanrei Sōhaku Kobori 2
nationalism 5, 8
naturalness 6–8, 79, 83, 129
Nature 226
negai 246, 262–3

negation 242
Nembutsu, *see* nenbutsu
nenbutsu (Nembutsu) xiii, 9, 47, 50–9, 69–73, 77–8, 116, 121, 222, 227–9, 274
never abandon 205
New Testament 93, 216
Nichiren (Shōnin) 119
Nietzsche, Friedrich 217
nihilism 166, 208, 216
Nirvana/nirvana/*nirvāṇa* xiii, 55, 59, 83, 103, 109, 174–7, 201
   of no abiding place 174
Nirvāṇa Sūtra 81, 134
nirvikalpa-jñāna 177
Nishida, Kitarō 229
Nishitani, Keiji 12, 152
Nishi (Western) Honganji (Hongwanji) 9, 11
niṣyanda 168
non-duality 139
no-hindrance 72
no-karma 147–8
non-duality 191–2, 194
non-retrogression 186, 196, 258
northern Buddhism 3
Notes Lamenting Differences: see *Tannishō*
Notes on Once-calling and Many-calling 173
   See also Once-calling
Notes on the Inscriptions on Sacred Scrolls 173
   See also *Inscriptions*
nuclear weapons 261
nyo 235
nyorai (Nyorai) 75, 81, 162, 228

Obendiek, H. 91
ocean 266–9, 275
ocean of (great) wisdom 275–6
ōjō 78, 185, 187, 191
okonai 247–8
Oldenberg (H) 33
Olsen, Regine 223
Om mani padme hum 110, 112

Index

Once-calling and Many-calling 148, 152–3, 173, 186–8
  See also *Ichinentanenmon'i*
Once-calling: see Once-calling and Many-calling
One Sheet Document (*Ichimaikishōmon*) 69, 77
One Vehicle 267
one vow 260
onozukara 202
opposites 178
Orient 38, 42
original prayer 240
Original Self 17
Original Vow (*hongan*) 47–8, 50–3, 55–8, 66–9, 80, 126, 170, 237, 250, 252, 264, 267, 271–2
oshie 247–8
Ōtani University 2
Other Power 120–1, 135, 209, 267
others-profiting 56
own power 120
  See also *jiriki*
Ox-Herding Pictures 225

pacifism 5
Palestine 124
Pāli:
  Canon 107
  piṭaka 37
  scriptures 3, 27, 33–4
  [Text] Society 36
  Tipiṭaka 33
  Vinaya-piṭaka 37
Pallis, Marco 9
paramārtha-satya 192
pāramitā/s 108
paratantra-svabhāva 179, 181
parikalpita-svabhāva 179, 181
pariṇāma 15
pariṇāmana 15
pariniṣpanna-svabhāva 180–1
passions 20–1, 49, 142, 150–1, 204
  intentional retention 20–1
patriarchs 126

Path of Sages 263
Paul 87–105
peace 73, 261
pecca fortiter 99
perennial philosophy 9
phala 35
Philippines 124
pīnyīn xiv
Piṭaka 34
Plato 35
Platonic 38
Platonists 35
Practice-Faith 229
pradakṣiṇa 113
prajñā 66, 108, 206, 235–6
prajñāpāramitā 139, 177–9, 184, 193, 251
Prajñāpāramitā sūtras 28, 183
praṇidhāna/s 17, 23, 78, 237
prapañca 164–171
pratītyasamutpāda 140, 161, 164–6
Pratt, J.B. 40–1
pratyātmāryajñāna 175
pratyekabuddha 162, 166
Pratyutpannasamādhi-sūtra 134
prayer/s 237–40, 261–2
prayer-wheel 113
preaching 162–3, 168, 171
present 152–5
Primal Vow 152–6, 204, 208–9, 211
promise 262
  See also vow
Ptolemy 215
Pure Land/s 48, 50, 56, 66–9, 87, 90, 98, 104, 111, 119, 131, 154–5, 157, 161, 169–71, 195, 227, 256, 258, 266, 268, 276
  Buddhism xv, 71, 73, 108, 176
  doctrine/teaching 127–8, 189, 195, 218, 260, 263
  Paradise 218
  Seizan branch 187
purity 242
puruṣa 33
pūrvapraṇidhāna 168, 237
  See also Original Vow

302

quarters (ten) 229

realization 194–5, 211, 237, 257
rebirth 48, 83
  See also birth; ōjō
Reformation 123
reformers 87–8, 97
refuge/s 268
Refutations of Heterodoxies 47
Régamey, Constantin 4
religion 223
Renaissance 123
Rennyo (Shōnin) 150, 190
renunciation 173–4
repentance 1
resignation 264
resurrection 92–3, 226
revealer 7
revival 40–1
Rhys Davids, C.A.F. (Mrs.) 3–4, 37–39
Rhys Davids, T.W. 3
rinjū 195–6
Rinzai 125
Rising Sun 36
rita 56
Robinson, John 12, 214–5, 217–8
rōhatsu sesshin 163
Romans (Epistle to) 92, 97, 100, 103
Russian school 4
sacraments 89–90
sacrifice 16, 92
Saddharmapuṇḍarīka-sūtra 21, 28
Saichi 175, 196
Sakamoto, Hiroshi 73, 171
Śākya 36
  See also Śākyamuni (Buddha)
Śākyamuni (Buddha) 8 15–6, 35, 37, 59, 140, 161–4, 166, 170–1, 173, 175, 177
  See also Shakyamuni
salvation 6, 18, 21, 57, 61, 71, 88, 120
  by grace 9, 88, 98
samādhi 161, 170
Samantabhadra 25–6, 192–3
Saṃgha xiii
saṃkleśa 170

saṃsāra 21, 109, 117–8, 121, 139, 173–4, 176–85, 197–201, 204, 207, 211
  saṃsāra and nirvana 178–183
saṃskṛta 139
saṃvṛti-satya 192
Saṃyutta-nikāya 34
Sangha xiii
Sānlùn School 183, 194
Sanskrit 235
Sanskrit titles xiii
sarx 226
saviour 7, 20, 93, 95
Scheel, Otto 91
Scheinfreiheit 148
Schleiermacher, F. 70
Schuon, Frithjof 10, 111
Schweitzer, Albert 87, 213
Second World War 1, 42–3
sectarianism 124
secular 174
secularism 104
secularization 105, 124, 214
seeing only 206–7
seigan 237–9, 246
Seizan branch 187
self 33–5
self-power 77
  See also jiriki
self-profiting 56
self-reflection 24
self-sacrifice 23
Senchakushū 65, 265
Sengai 249
Senjakushū 65
sentient beings 17, 21, 24, 48, 52, 185, 262, 271–2
services for dead 40
sesshin 163
settled mind: see *anjin*
Seventeenth Vow 228, 266–7
Shakyamuni 7
  See also Śākyamuni
Shàndǎo 195, 250, 266–7, 275
Shichisaburō 158–9
Shin (Buddhism) 1–3, 6, 8–12, 47, 49–50,

303

Index

59, 244, 254, 264, 269
thought 263
shinjin 82, 140, 147, 150–2, 154–5, 157, 159, 185–91, 195–6, 199–211
shinjin no chie 82
shinjitsu 242, 248–9, 251
Shinran (Shinran Shōnin) 10,11, 47, 65, 68, 72, 75–8, 82–3, 87–8, 90–105, 109, 123, 127–8, 130–5, 140–43, 144–9, 152–9, 175–6, 185–93, 195–7, 199–204, 208–10, 212, 249–52, 258–9, 261, 268
Shin
  Buddhists 88
  followers 49, 58
shinri 249
Shin Sect: *see* Jōdo Shinshū; Shin Buddhism
Shin-shū 133
  See also Jōdo Shinshū; Shin Buddhism
Shintō 1, 4–5
  Shintoism 42
  Shrine Shinto 42
shō (realization) 190
Shōdaijōron 182
Shōdaijōronshaku 177
Shōkū 187
shōmyō 77, 266
Shōshinge 251, 267
Shōtoku, Prince 27, 84
Shōzōmatsuwasan 149, 158
shu (practice) 185
shudō (path of practice) 185
shukugō 140–1
Shunchō 21
Siam 35
Śikṣānandha 15–6
sinfulness 64–5
six:
  non-dualities 194
  soku 194
  syllables 110, 113–4
skandha/s 164
skilful means, skillful means 21, 237
smṛti 109

Socrates 249
soku 178, 187, 194, 206
sokuben ōjō 187
soku-hi 178, 206
sokutoku 187
Soga, Ryōjin 12, 221–2
sola fide 95
sola gratia 95
soldier/s 6, 79
soma 226
sono mama 7, 242
soul 42
Spencer, Herbert 41
spirituality 235
substitution 25
suchness 7, 30, 35, 139, 178, 189–90, 253
suffering 15–26, 48, 61–3, 255
Sufi/s 109
Sui 237
Sukhāvatīvyūha-sūtra 25, 28, 241
  See also *Daimuryōjukyō*; *Larger Sukhāvatīvyūha (Sūtra)*
sukui 61
Sunday schools 40
śūnya/tā 11, 28–30, 62, 164, 166–171, 177, 180, 192–4
śūnyatā-artha 168
śūnyatāyām prayojanam 166–7
supreme good 81–2
superstition 42
sūtra/s xiii, 28, 96
Sūtra of Bodhisattva Precepts 134
Sūtra of Eternal Life 97–8, 128
Sūtra of Meditation on Amida 63
  See also *Kanmuryōjukyō*
Sūtra on the Meditation on Amitāyus xv
  See also *Kanmuryōjukyō*
Suzuki, Beatrice Lane (Mrs.) 2
Suzuki, Daisetsu (D.T.) 2–5, 11–12, 87, 91, 93, 96, 100–2, 148, 175, 178, 180
synergism 95

Taishō edition 39
Takakusu, Junjirō 39, 238
Takeuchi, Yoshinori 11

Tanabe, Hajime 229
Tang 237
Tánluán 64, 186, 200, 239–242, 250–3, 272
Tannishō 47, 53, 72, 76–80, 82–3, 94, 98, 119, 131, 140, 142–3, 146, 151, 153, 156–8, 209, 245
Tāntric initiations 112
tariki 79, 81, 83, 95
tathāgata/Tathāgata 35, 38, 75, 126, 162, 170, 184, 189, 198, 202, 228, 256–60, 264
 See also Amitābha (Amida) Tathāgata
tathāgatagarbha 189
tathatā 7, 29–30, 38, 62, 166, 168, 178, 235, 253
tattva 178
Taoism 129
Teaching of Vimalakīrti xiii
Teaching, Practice, Faith and Enlightenment, 75
 See also: Kyōgyōshinshō
teleology 105
temporality 143–5
ten quarters 229
tensha 169–70
tenzu 155, 185, 204
theologia crucis 97, 103
Theologische Zeitschrift 87
theology 223
Theravāda 3, 107,
three thousand dharmas 274
three vows 262
three:
 evil realms 266
 periods 273
Tiāntái 183, 192, 194–25, 270
Tibet 9, 108, 110
Tibetan/s 112
Tillich, Paul 12, 215–7
time 143–5, 197–202
Tipiṭaka (Pāli, Hīnayāna) 33, 38
tōgaku 192–3
Tokyo University 11

tōtoku ōjō 187
Toynbee, Arnold 12, 213
Tract on Deploring the Heteredoxies 76
 See also: Tannishō
transcendence 215, 218–21
translation/s 235–8, 243–4
transformation 181–5, 204
transmigration 49
Treatise on the Pure Land 251
Tripiṭaka (Chinese) 37, 39
Tripiṭaka (Hīnayāna) 38
 See also Tipiṭaka
tri-svabhāva 179
tṛṣṇā 62
True Light 47
True Pure Land Buddhism: see Shin Buddhism
tsumi 140
Twelve:
 āyatana/s 164
 links of causation 43

Ueda, Yoshifumi 10, 173–4, 178, 181, 209
United States 214
Universal 7
universality 52
Unno, Taitetsu 263
unobstructedness 140
unhindered light 199
unimpeded light 228
Upaniṣad/s 33–4
upāya 21, 109, 120–1
urban population 213

van Bragt, Jan 12, 229
Vasubandhu (Seshin) 139, 179, 183, 251–2
vicarious suffering 3, 15–26
vijñāna 34
vijñaptimātratā 206
vikalpa 177–9
Vimalakīrtī 63, 174
Vimalakīrtīnirdeśa (Yuimagyō) 63, 162, 272
Vimalakīrtī-sūtra (Yuimagyō) 28, 174
Vinaya Piṭaka 33

Index

vīrya 108
voidness 125
vow/s 17–9, 21, 23–4, 26, 78, 115, 228, 232, 238–240, 250, 254–78, 266–7
 eighteenth 261, 266
 forty-eight 48, 23, 252, 256–7, 259–62, 265
 of Amida 210
 seventeenth 228, 266–7
 of the One Buddha Vehicle 267
 See also Original Vow, Primal Vow

Wǎngshēnglùn zhù 65
war 1–2, 4–8, 42–3
Wasan 81
 See also *Jōdowasan, Kōsōwasan, Shōzōmatsuwasan*
Watanabe, K. 39
western mind 10
Western culture 42
White Path Society 6
wisdom 47, 50–1, 56, 110–1, 207
wisdom-compassion 207–8
world religion/s 42–3
world views 87

Xavier, Francis 94–5
Yamabe, Shūgaku 3–4, 33–6, 70
Yamaguchi, Susumu 10–11
Yìjìng 162
Yogācāra 162, 179–80, 206–7
Yokogawa, Kenshō 2
young men (thirty-seven) 37
Yuien-bō 72, 132–3
Yuishinshōmon'i 173
 See also *Essentials of Faith Alone*
Y.M.B.A. 40
Y.W.B.A. 40

zaigō 140
Zànāmítuófó jì 251–2
Zen (Zen Buddhism) 10, 12, 87, 109, 148, 163, 175, 249
Zendō 64
 See also Shàndǎo
Zenpuku (Prince) 16
Zenran 133
Zhànrán 194, 270
Zhìyǐ 252
Zonkaku 212

www.ingramcontent.com/pod-product-compliance
Lightning Source LLC
Chambersburg PA
CBHW070015010526
44117CB00011B/1584